TAMIL FOLK MUSIC
AS DALIT LIBERATION THEOLOGY

Ethnomusicology Multimedia

Ethnomusicology Multimedia (EM) is an innovative, entrepreneurial, and cooperative effort to expand opportunities for emerging scholars in ethnomusicology by publishing first books accompanied by supplemental audiovisual materials online. Developed with funding from the Andrew W. Mellon Foundation, EM is a collaboration of the presses at Indiana and Temple universities. These presses gratefully acknowledge the help of Indiana University's Institute for Digital Arts and Humanities, Digital Library Program, and Archives of Traditional Music for their contributions to EM's web-based components and archiving features.

For more information and to view EM materials,
please visit www.ethnomultimedia.org.

ETHNOMUSICOLOGY MULTIMEDIA SERIES PREFACE

GUIDE TO ONLINE MEDIA EXAMPLES

Each of the audio, video, or still image media examples listed below is associated with specific passages in this book, and each example has been assigned a unique Persistent Uniform Resource Locator, or PURL. The PURL identifies a specific audio, video, or still image media example on the Ethnomusicology Multimedia website, www.ethnomultimedia.org. Within the text of the book, a "PURL number" in parentheses functions like a citation and immediately follows the text to which it refers, e.g. (PURL 3.1). The numbers following the word "PURL" relate to the chapter in which the media example is found, and the number of PURLs contained in that chapter. For example, PURL 3.1 refers to the first media example found in chapter 3; PURL 3.2 refers to the second media example found in chapter 3, and so on.

To access all media associated with this book, readers must first create a free account by going to the Ethnomusicology Multimedia Project website www.ethnomultimedia.org and clicking the "Sign In" link. Readers will be required to read and electronically sign an End Users License Agreement (EULA) the first time they access a media example on the website. After logging in to the site there are two ways to access and play back audio, video, or still image media examples. In the "Search" field enter the name of the author to be taken to a webpage with information about the book and the author as well as a playlist of all media examples associated with the book. To access a specific media example, in the "Search" field enter the six digit PURL identifier of the example (the six digits located at the end of the full PURL address below). The reader will be taken to the web page containing that media example as well as a playlist of all the other media examples related to the book. Readers of the electronic edition of this book will simply click on the PURL address for each media example; once they have logged in to www.ethnomultimedia.org, this live link will take them directly to the media example on the Ethnomusicology Multimedia website.

TAMIL FOLK MUSIC
AS
DALIT LIBERATION THEOLOGY

ZOE C. SHERINIAN

Indiana University Press

This book is a publication of

Indiana University Press
Office of Scholarly Publishing
Herman B Wells Library 350
1320 East 10th Street
Bloomington, Indiana 47405 USA

iupress.org

First paperback edition 2020

The paper used in this publication meets the minimum requirements of the American National Standard for Information Sciences—Permanence of Paper for Printed Library Materials, ANSI Z39.48-1992.

Manufactured in the United States of America

The Library of Congress has cataloged the 2014 edition as follows:

Sherinian, Zoe C.
Tamil folk music as Dalit liberation theology / Zoe C. Sherinian.
pages ; cm. — (Ethnomusicology multimedia)
Includes bibliographical references and index.
ISBN 978-0-253-00233-4 (cl : alk. paper) — ISBN 978-0-253-00585-4 (ebook) 1. Church music—India—Tamil Nadu. 2. Folk music—India—Tamil Nadu—History and criticism. 3. Folk music—Religious aspects—Christianity. 4. Dalits—India—Tamil Nadu—Religious life. 5. Dalits—India—Tamil Nadu—Music—History and criticism. 6. Appavoo, James Theophilus. I. Title.
ML3151.I4S44 2012
781.71'7940095482—dc23

2012018988

ISBN 978-0-253-05677-1 (pbk)

To Paraṭṭai
and Elyssa

Yār vēṇālum, eppaḍi vēṇālum

(Whoever wants to, can use [sing] it however they want)

Rev. J. T. Appavoo (Paraṭṭai)

Contents

Preface xi
Acknowledgments xxiii
List of PURL Audio and Video Files xxix

Introduction: Context and Concepts:
Singing The Lord's Prayer as Freedom in a Tamil Land 1

1 How Can The Subaltern Speak? Musical Style, Value, and the Historical Process of (Re)indigenization of Tamil Christian Music 34

2 Sharing the Meal: A Dalit Family's Dialogue with the History of Tamil Christian Music, 1850–1994 62

3 Paraṭṭai's Theology: Greeting God in the Cēri 119

4 Ethnography as Transformative Musical Dialogue 167

5 Reception and Transformation from Seminary to Village 202

6 Performing Global Dalit Consciousness 254

Appendixes

Appendix 1: Song Transcriptions
Transcription 1: "Iyēsusāmi Kantuttanda Sebam" (The Lord's Prayer) 270
Transcription 2: "Kuttam Uṇaruṟadu" (Repentance of Sin) 272
Transcription 3: "Virundu Parimāṟuṟadu" (Meal Sharing Song) 273
Transcription 4a–4d: "Sāmiya Vaṇaṅguṟadu"
(Greetings and Praise of God) 274

Appendix 2: Song Lyrics by Rev. J. Theophilus Appavoo (Paraṭṭai)
"Ammāḍi Kuṭṭi Poṇṇē" (My Little Girl) 285
"Inikkāda Tēnumilla" (Without Sweetness There Is No Honey) 286
"Allēlūyā Allēlūyā" (Alleluia) 286
"Pudiya Pudiya Talaimuṟaikku, Pudiya Pudiya Siluva"
(For Every New Generation There Is A New Cross) 287

"Bumiyil Vāṟuṟa" (Living on Earth) 287
"Āṇḍavanē Eṅga Āṭṭiḍaiyan" (The Lord Is Our Shepherd) 288
"Āṇḍavanē Nī Eṅga Koṭṭai" (Lord, You Are Our Fortress) 288
"Aṇṇaṭa Aṇṇaṭa" (Elder Brother) 289
"Āṇṇē Tambi Māppiḷḷē" (Elder and Younger Brother, Son-in-law) 290
"Otta Saḍa, Reṭṭai Saḍa" (One Braid, Two Braids) 291

Notes 293
References 319
Index 331

Preface

This book is an ethnomusicological ethnography of the creation, transmission, and recreation of Tamil folk music as Dalit liberation theology in India and beyond. The focus of its narrative is a heterogeneous community of poor Tamil Christian villagers, lay workers, seminary students, activists, theologians, and artists, inspired by the personality and music of a theologian/composer they call Paraṭṭai Annan ("big brother with messy hair"). This is an apt description and pen name for the Rev. Dr. James Theophilus Appavoo (1940–2005),[1] the central trickster figure in this story. Paraṭṭai and a network of other Dalit or anti-caste actors are essential nodes in the transmission process that make up the contemporary reform movement for liturgical and theological change within the mainline Protestant Church of South India (CSI) in the state of Tamil Nadu. This movement is a grass-roots manifestation of cultural and theological agency by Dalits (or former untouchables, those oppressed by caste hierarchy from birth). While it borrows ideas from Latin American liberation theology, this movement's indigenous roots lay in the Indian social gospel missions of the nineteenth century and the secular/social equality Dravidian language movement of the early twentieth century (Bate 2009, 44). Further, this Christian cultural movement takes a strong dose of intellectual inspiration from the leader of the modern Dalit movement, Dr. Bhimrao Ramjee Ambedkar, the foundational thinker who has influenced the contemporary Tamil Dalit Liberation Movement of the late twentieth century (Larbeer 2003).

This is a story about so called "untouchable outcastes," those who are most socially, politically, culturally, and religiously marginalized in India through the hierarchy of caste in society and through its continued practice in the Tamil Christian churches over the last 500 years. In the last two centuries a significant number of lower- and outcastes were motivated to convert to Christianity as a means to escape at least the philosophical discourse of caste. Yet, it has only been in the last three decades that Christian outcastes, through the transformative power of Tamil folk music are changing the liturgical and political culture of the Tamil mainline churches and in the process transforming their identities to become Dalit.[2] The term "Dalit" comes from "dal," in Marathi meaning to oppress or crush. It is a self-chosen term of political and cultural opposition used to unite those formerly called outcastes, harijans, untouchables, or in the modern period, scheduled castes. In this study I adopt Appavoo's praxis-oriented definition of Dalit as "an identity of the oppressed people fighting for liberation."[3] This definition represents the practice of unity in resistance to oppression of all kinds including gender and class, but particularly the violent and all-pervasive system of caste hierarchy in India.

Two issues are particularly notable in Paraṭṭai's music and at the center of this Dalit musico-theology movement: 1) The indigenization of Christianity through musical style, theology, and language to direct the purpose of religious discourse back to the social emancipation of the poor and oppressed in this world and in this time period; 2) the process of social identity reformation for Dalit Christians through the transformative and recreative power of music in the performance context. Appavoo developed a theory that Dalit theology should be embodied in a medium accessible to poor Dalit villagers who need it the most. While many theologians at Indian Christian seminaries experimented with creating progressive theology in musical form, or making theology "singable," as Rev. Thomas Thangaraj has written (1990), it was Appavoo who transformed this idea into an accessible Dalit theology—one that is easily transmittable, usable, and thus liberating to the poor, Dalits, and women of Tamil Nadu through the alternative, recreative media of folk music and folklore (Appavoo 1986). My primary interest in studying Paraṭṭai's music and its transmission is to understand through ethnographic observation and experience the efficacy of Tamil folk music to transmit a liberating theology. My intent is to understand the meaning of its use by Tamil Christians and in turn, the social dynamics in the process of creation, transmission, and re-creation of this music that Appavoo argues can result in a cultural and personal transformation from untouchable to Dalit, or liberated, through attaining an anti-caste consciousness and an active stance against caste identity.

For scholars and students of religious music and social resistance this raises the common question: Can Christian music be liberating for the oppressed? In my process of participation, observation, and analysis within the Protestant Tamil Dalit community, Paraṭṭai Annan helped me reformulate the question (and thus the relationship between Christian indigenization and agency) as: How have Dalits made Indian Christianity liberating, through re-creating it in musical practice? How have Dalit cultural forms and values helped facilitate this process of liberation? These are more precise ethnomusicological questions that recognize the agency of the people and the cultural processes of Christian indigenization, and that posits music as the source of the creation and transmission of theology. One indigenous answer to these questions can be found in the lyrical reference to folk drumming in Paraṭṭai's song "Nalla Seydi" or "Good News" (fully analyzed in chapter 6):

> Fear not! Fear not! Oh, Dalit people!
> Only *you* have the war drum to drive your fear away.
> If you play the uṟumai, uḍukai, paṟai, pampai, tavil, tappu, tarai, and tappaṭṭai drums[4] with one heart, hallelujah will resound in Galilee.
> Fear Not! Fear Not!
> All people come together in Christ to bury the corpse of caste.

With these lyrics accompanied by the rhythmic energy and emotive tunes and rhythms of Tamil folk music, Paraṭṭai asks the oppressed to re-examine the empowering potential of their own village cultural products, like their paṟai drum, that were devalued and considered polluting by upper castes and deemed inappropriate for Christian ritual by many missionaries as well as Indian theologians. Indeed, Paraṭṭai proclaimed to me, "we are drumming our theology." Paraṭṭai's vision entails cultural reclamation and reversal of values to transform internalized casteism, sexism, and classism in order to unify the oppressed community "as one heart." His intent was to change the values within the church that bound it to dominant caste cultural forms of media, and to instead redirect the church to embrace alternative media of the village poor that support their struggle for social justice. As in other liberation theology movements such as those in Latin America, the goal is "the transformation of passive, voiceless, dominated communities into active shapers of their own destiny" (Rodriguez 2003, 4). But, how can religious folk music have such transformative political power?

As a communications scholar and faculty member for twenty-six years at the Tamil Nadu Theological Seminary (TTS) in the city of Madurai, in central Tamil Nadu, Theophilus Appavoo studied Tamil folklore to understand its potential as "an alternative media system" that allows for participation by those with the least access to hegemonic power (Appavoo 1986, 3 and 8). Through conducting a three-year fieldwork project in Tamil folklore, which culminated in the book *Folk Lore for Change* (1986), Appavoo studied how Tamil villagers, in particular, have used folk music as an "everyday form of resistance" (James Scott 1985, xvi). Appavoo understood that inherent in villagers' engagement with Tamil folk music as orally transmitted and unauthored media was the attitude that it can be recreated in performance to address their specific ritual and political needs or to simply make the music more accessible and participatory, thereby unifying the community as the primary function of music making. The process by which Appavoo's students and in turn their village congregants have effected a personal or community transformation through the practice and recreation of his Tamil Christian folk music is the focus of this study. In particular, I try to answer the question, What sorts of social networks, relationships, and contexts support successful empowerment and motivation toward action and in turn identity reformation through music for Dalit Christians?

Paraṭṭai adopted a neo-Marxist cultural analysis as the foundation of his theology. His method was to deconstruct the techniques and effects of cultural oppression in India and their impact on communication systems with the goal of creating meaningful social change in all areas of life (politics, religion, gender, ecology, etc.). He tried to accomplish this through raising the consciousness of poor Dalits and their allies (while often "pricking" the consciousness of the middle class, as he would put it) to understand the continued internalization of hegemonic cultural values by outcastes and their structural embeddedness within Indian Christian culture. Ideologically this hegemonic culture took the form of Sanskritization or the valuing of upper caste culture, especially encoded in the song genre of Christian *kīrttaṉai*. Appavoo also challenged the secular values of capitalism, other aspects of Westernization in music, caste discrimination, patriarchy, elitism, and fundamentalist (Evangelical) Christianity. His intention was to reverse these values through a theologically driven counter cultural movement drawn from Tamil folklore that could provide the oppressed at least a ritual experience of liberation through the agency and re-creative power of folk music.

This movement transmits its message through Humanly Produced and Transmitted Media (HPTM), Appavoo's designation for purposeful alternative folk media such as street theater, puppetry, and drama serving not only as a medium of the message, but as a source for alternative discourse and subject formation through participatory re-creation and trans-physical spiritual catharsis possible in performance. This book examines ways in which this Dalit musico-theology has been and potentially could be a means to social change that, as James Scott argues, is "most significant and most effective over the long run" as an everyday practice of resistance, even more than direct political action (Scott 1985: xvi–xvii).

ENGAGED ETHNOMUSICOLOGY: TRANSFORMED ETHNOMUSICOLOGIST

In the process of the 1993–94 fieldwork for this study, I wanted to know if and how this music indeed liberates or socially transforms people—what this means for villagers. What were the dynamics of transmission, reception, and recreation on the ground with the people for whom this Dalit theology is meant to serve? What I did not realize at the time was the transformative experience I would have through this engagement. Much recent literature in ethnomusicology (and anthropology) supports the idea that fieldwork is inherently transformative for the fieldworker, as they become active participants in the transmission of the music they research (Shelemay 1997). Jeff Titon describes the particular process of self-reflexivity and transformation for ethnomusicologists as located in the shared experience of playing music together in cross-cultural relationships (Titon 1997, Sherinian 2005, 1). My engagement in hearing, studying, and performing Tamil Christian folk music, my participation in the daily rituals of shared eating and in a dialogue of shared values with the community members who most supported this music at the Tamil Nadu Theological Seminary, is the place from which I intend to locate my participation and self-transformation in this study.

With an understanding of the active involvement of contemporary ethnomusicologists as actors in the field, a number of my ethnomusicology colleagues began to ask probing questions about my personal Christian religious beliefs after hearing my conference papers on Appavoo's theology. With a sense of liberal skepticism toward anything Christian, which in their minds read as right-wing-socially-conservative and as Evangelical cultural imposition in a third-world postcolonial context, they wanted to know what sort of Christian I had become. How was I transformed in belief or religious identity in the process of this fieldwork? Ironically, these questions of belief and religious identity were not ones about which I ever worried, because the primary identity with which I felt an affinity in relation to the members of this community of Dalit Christians was their Dalitness, their oppositional stance against social cultural oppression. As a feminist and as a lesbian (as well as an Armenian whose family survived the genocide in Turkey with the help of American Congregational missionaries), I felt the greatest affinity with the social justice and resistance ideology within these songs and the Dalit Christian community. Furthermore, as a leftist activist who had been involved in cooperative food movements, I appreciated the nurturing Dalit community in which this music was created and transmitted, that maintained at its core the value of sharing the means to subsistence.

The best way I can contextualize my understanding of the politics of Tamil Christian folk music is to argue that it has a similar, complex socio-religious role within the Dalit Liberation Movement in India as did the Christian hymn "We Shall Overcome" for the 1940s U.S. labor movement and 1960s Civil Rights movement, or the Negro spirituals for the nineteenth-century Abolition movement. Charismatic leaders like Paraṭṭai played similar inspirational and activist roles as did Bishop Desmond Tutu in the South African Apartheid movement, or as Leonard Crow Dog did through bringing indigenous Native American Christian practices like using peyote and reviving the ghost dance to the American Indian Movement.[5] I would argue that this Dalit theology movement has nothing to do with Evangelical Christianity. Indeed Appavoo strongly critiques the rhetoric of Evangelical preachers believing they dupe poor people into contributing the little money that they have for the Evangelists to pray for their salvation in heaven after they die. Dalit theology is not about conversion to Christianity (especially in the sense of salvation). It is about the reformation of Indian Christianity to the identity of the Dalit: the transformation of the Indian heart and Indian values to the needs of those oppressed by social injustice, poverty, caste and gender discrimination at this time, in this world.[6]

Further, and not to be underemphasized, as a percussionist brought up on the 1970s polyrhythmic grooves of African American funk and jazz, I was physically responsive to the rhythmic style and percussive timbres of this folk music. Through the quality or grain of the music's voice, my body resonated with the form of sociality between the sound, its power, and its community of production (Downey 2002, 501).[7] My ideological beliefs are invested in music as resistance, a source of consciousness that sparks action, musicking as the practice of everyday politics and performative resistance that has potentially more impact than direct political action (Small 1998). Through engaged practice of Paraṭṭai's music as living theology, I gained an accepting community that continues to sustain me intellectually and spiritually, that models the possibility of positive identity reformation for the oppressed, and continues to exemplify resilience in the face of adversity.

This ethnography attempts to tell a story of the process of creating relationships between Appavoo, his music, his students, and me (by extension) that supported the transformation for many from untouchable to Dalit. In order to set the stage, I begin with the story of how my own transformation to and through Paraṭṭai's music began: an anecdote of the praxis of liberation through shared musical relationships.

FINDING PARAṬṬAI'S ACTIVIST ETHNOMUSICOLOGICAL PATH

I first heard of Theophilus Appavoo as Paraṭṭai (his folk pen name given to him by villagers with whom he worked in a rural theological education program in the 1980s) during an exploratory field trip to the city of Madurai, Tamil Nadu in the summer of 1991. I had noted his name in my field notebook in connection with music production at the Tamil Nadu Theological Seminary (TTS). However, I was unable to follow up on the lead by meeting him (in fact he was in Edinburgh, Scotland at the time pursuing his Masters in Theology). Instead, I met other professors at TTS, such as Rev. Satiya Satchi, who were involved with Christian music composed in the classical karnatak indigenous style called *kīrttaṉai*. I thus began to develop my project around the indigenization of this elite genre with its theological and cultural values grounded in Brahminical Christian philosophical concepts.

I decided to pursue an ethnography of the indigenization of the music of the Tamil Christian community in Madurai, as it was a community with whom I had previously established ties during two years as a cultural exchange representative (1985–87) from Oberlin College to Lady Doak College.[8] Lady Doak is a Christian women's college with ties to the Church of South India and roots in nineteenth- and early twentieth-century Congregational American missions with which Oberlin had strong historical ties. During my two-year Oberlin Shansi Memorial Fellowship at Lady Doak, I privately studied classical (Hindu) karnatak drumming (the *mrdangam* barrel drum) and vocal music while serving the college as conductor of their Western style choir. My Indian faculty colleague Dr. Sheila Premorthy conducted the Tamil choir, which sat on the floor singing Christian *kīrttaṉai* in highly Sanskritized Tamil using raga musical modes and tapping out the *tala* rhythmic cycle patterns with hand gestures on their legs. As I flung my arms around trying to conduct pieces by Bach, I was much more attracted to the karnatak Christian "lyrics" or hymns in the style that I was learning in my karnatak music studies. Yet I was intrigued to discover that while the poetry of these *kīrttaṉai* was Christian, it borrowed Hindu metaphors and images. Further, famous Tamil Christian poets such as Vedanayakam Sastriar had composed these songs more than two hundred years earlier. No ethnomusicological research had been conducted on this music, and theoretical questions of indigenization seemed just the approach needed to understand this phenomenon and the minority Indian community that produced it.

When I returned to Madurai to conduct fieldwork on the indigenization of Tamil Christian music in 1993, I moved into the campus of the Tamil Nadu Theological Seminary and began to create musical relationships with members of the community. On the day I arrived in August 1993, Rev. Honest Chinniah, one of the best-known teachers of karnatak Christian music in Tamil Nadu, serendipitously was visiting campus. Although it was his last day to conduct a special karnatak music course for seminary students at TTS, he invited me to observe him teach and then agreed to an interview. He was generous and honest, sharing with me his vast knowledge. In the end he recommended that I work with his student Rev. Theophilus Appavoo, who taught communications, and was a musical theologian at TTS. Little did I know then that Chinniah, a revered Christian karnatak music guru and one of the innovators of organ accompaniment for the modal based Christian *kīrttaṉai,* had sent me to his prize student who would soon direct me away from classical genres and their association with elite Christian culture toward studying Tamil folk music as Dalit liberation theology. My personal musical transformation in this project began through the common South Asian ethnomusicological phenomenon of discipular ethnography or entering a musical lineage (a *gharānā* of sorts). Further, my own preconceptions of what was culturally valuable (classical music) within the community was inverted and transformed by Rev. Chinniah, a middle caste (Nadar) who had spent his entire life engaged in the practice of destroying caste prejudice within the Protestant Christian community through arranging mixed caste marriages, while he also experimented with musical innovations. Both of these qualities played a key role in Theophilus Appavoo's musico-theological education, the development of his own theology, and its radically inclusive method of musical transmission.

James Theophilus Appavoo was born a middle-class urban Christian Paṟaiyar (one of three primary Tamil outcaste groups) who inherited from his father and his music guru a dedication to classical karnatak music used in Christian composition and liturgy. Yet in the 1980s Theophilus Appavoo was transformed through theological engagement with villagers and his own ethnographic study of Tamil folk music to become "Paraṭṭai Annan," or the Tamil Dalit trickster—the opposite of the middle-class, upright seminary professor—whose primary tools to create social justice and destroy caste oppression were Tamil folk music and folklore. This book is also the story of Appavoo's relationship with his students at the Tamil Nadu Theological Seminary and with his co-creators in the Rural Theological Education for Christian Commitment and Action (TECCA) network. It is a story about relationships that nurture, empower, and transform untouchables into Dalit activists who create cultural change through performance and re-composition. That is, it is a story of how subaltern agency expressed through folk music is constructed, enacted, transmitted, and received in a continuous musical feedback system.

Theophilus Appavoo was my teacher, friend, colleague, and a father figure for over twelve years. As I conducted ethnographic research on Tamil Christian music at TTS, I became his student. He helped me understand (and completely re-evaluate) the liberating potential of Christianity through the possibilities of its indigenization to the values of Dalit identity politics, vernacular Tamil language, Tamil village cultural metaphors, polyrhythms, rhymes, and tunes of folk music. He showed me how theology can be drummed by bringing the paṟai frame drum into the sacred space of the church building and to the center of liturgy. A drum played primarily by untouchables at funerals (which are polluting and thus considered unclean by upper castes), the paṟai symbolizes the general degradation and untouchability of folk music in Tamil culture. Appavoo signaled the kind of transformation Dalits seek by bringing the paṟai, and by extension Tamil folk music's worth as an empowering tool for Dalit Christian identity formation, to the center of ritual. He also played a significant role in labeling my personal development as an activist anthropologist. Toward the end of my fourteen-month stay he told me that he approved of how I had conducted my research, that my research process was creating action in its subjects. He felt that my analysis of performance at the seminary had helped various professors and musicians become aware of areas, particularly in the practice of music, in which they were contradicting their own feminist values (Sherinian 2005). As he said to me in July 1994,

> I think real research should create some action. So if I do some research that should create something, some change in what we call the subjects of research. As you have been doing. You are doing that, because you always remind us about the women, . . . you know the women's perspective . . . So this should be research of a person who is committed to humanity in general. All my articles and everything are connected with that kind of thing. It's not just research for the sake of getting a degree.[9]

Years later he named me *Paraṭṭai Kural,* or Paraṭṭai's musical voice, blessing me with the responsibility to spread his songs and their message, particularly through writing. As a dialogical ethnography, this book reflects the trans-cultural relationship between Appavoo and me as partners in an ethnomusicological duet of interpretation, political debate, shared values and an active attempt to create liberating change through music.

I entered the field intellectually valuing karnatak music particularly for its rhythmic complexity. I entered the field with an activist past, ready to closet my personal identities that might get in the way of the field project and thus my career. I entered the field with a religious background as a "smells and bells" (high church) Episcopalian who had never been moved to action by a sermon, who had never read the entire Bible or understood how it might have resonance with ideologies of feminism and social justice that I held dear. A year later I returned to the U.S. transformed musically to the polyrhythmic grooves of Tamil folk music, as an activist anthropologist supported by an accepting community that I was confident would always be with me (and would never allow me to fully leave the field), and with a task to transmit a story with an important message of how the oppressed in India accomplish social justice for themselves through musical processes. Indeed my enduring spiritual beliefs lie with this community.

Appavoo died from congestive heart failure in Oklahoma City, Oklahoma on November 3, 2005 while visiting the U.S. on a lecture tour sponsored by the University of Oklahoma. Through this tour, which was to include giving workshops at the Episcopal Divinity School, Yale Divinity School, and General Theological Seminary we had both hoped to further internationalize his musical theology and bring awareness to the plight of Dalits. It was the saddest day of my life. Yet, in the last several weeks of his life spent with him in the hospital along with his wife and son-in-law, I learned and lived Appavoo's lesson of sharing. As we tried to manage this crisis, many people reached out to my partner and me from our Oklahoma neighborhood, St. Anthony Hospital, and the local Indian community. I learned to allow others to share with me, accepting with an open heart, in a time of great vulnerability, their love and generosity. I hope in some way through this book that I am able to return this gift and keep Paraṭṭai's spirit and vision alive and growing. Yet I also bring the spirit of critical academic dialogue to the limitations and shortcomings of his ideas with the hope that it will only lead to improved re-creations of them.

In her eulogy for Rev. Appavoo at the Episcopal Cathedral in Oklahoma City, Rev. Cannon Carol Hampton, a scholar of Native American Christian theology and a member of the Caddo tribe, compared Rev. Appavoo's work to Jesus' mission outlined in the fourth chapter of the Gospel of Luke, the same chapter Paraṭṭai had referenced in his final lecture at the University of Oklahoma on creating Christian music:

> James Theophilus Appavoo was such a person who took the Good News of God in Christ and proclaimed it to those who had neither seen nor heard that news, to those who had been oppressed both by others and by their own acceptance of oppression. Theophilus accepted his appointment by God to bring Good News to the poor. He was a liberator of his own Dalit people. Through his efforts the church has tried to become incarnate in the interest of the poor. Along with theologians from South America he taught, "what humans reject, God chooses as his very own."[10]

Appavoo's journey from a middle-class, educated, urban Dalit toward becoming "a liberator of his own Dalit people," especially poor village Dalits, involved a process of transformation of not only a caste consciousness, but also his class and gender consciousness. This was perpetuated by action and reflection with villagers, which Latin American philosopher and educator Paulo Freire argues requires conversion to the people or a profound rebirth (Freire 1984, 119). Freire, whose work has been read by many Dalit theologians, further describes this transformative process saying, "Only through comradeship with the oppressed can the converts [to the problems and needs of the oppressed] understand their [own] characteristic ways of living and behaving which in diverse moments reflect the structure of domination" (1984, 47). Understanding the social value that music carries was the key to facilitating Appavoo's conversion to Tamil folk music. The impact of his transformation and transformative music was signified by the presence of hundreds of people, many of them non-Christian social activists, at his funeral in Chengalpattu, Tamil Nadu. While singing one after another of his songs at the funeral, several of his students realized that through his powerful music, he was present among them and would live on.[11]

Acknowledgments

This book is the culmination of contributions and inspiration of many who shared in the music and presence of Paraṭṭai (aka Rev. James Theophilus Appavoo). This includes the extensive community of Paraṭṭai's colleagues, students, friends, comrades, family members, and distant admirers. We miss him and continue to hold his spirit through the inspiration of his music. I offer my most heartfelt thanks to this community for sharing their music, knowledge, theological interpretations, experience, and love with me. You have sustained this work for many years and I hope that, through this book, I am able to return even a morsel of the food of social justice, Dalit liberation, and love that you have given me.

I am deeply grateful to the Tamil Nadu Theological Seminary (TTS) community and the greater Christian community of Madurai, which supported and facilitated this research.

I especially thank my field assistants Dr. Arun Raja Selvan and T. Adri Paul for their professionalism and commitment. Theophilus Appavoo's daughters, T. Adri Paul and T. Neena, and his wife, Mrs. Dorathy Appavoo, assisted me as translators and interpreters at several points, but more significantly took me in as their sister and daughter, as a member of their family. I thank them and their husbands for sharing their father, their home, and their knowledge with me. While we all struggle with the loss of our dear Paraṭṭai, our relationship will always remain through our dedication to his message. My cook Kamala Mary not only nurtured me with the love and support of a friend and sister, but shared with me her knowledge of village style *kīrttaṉai* and was one of my best Tamil teachers.

I am deeply indebted to the faculty, staff, and alumni of TTS, notably Principals Kambar Manickam, Dhyanchand Carr, Mohan Larbeer, and M. Gnanavaram, and; the many seminary students who taught me and shared their learning environment and lives. Those in Tamil Nadu who were my teachers or generously shared their knowledge include, V. P. K. Sundaram, Thomas Thangaraj, Israel Selvanayagam, M. Gnanavaram, Sathiya Satchi, Margaret Kalaiselvi, Gabriele Dietrich, Bas Wielenga, M. J. Ravi, S. Manickam and Alice Manickam, Samuel Timothy, Honest Chinniah, Mrs. Kamala Ramamurthy and Dr. Ramamurthy, N. Ramanathan,. B. M. Sundaram, Sathiyanathan Clarke, Paladam Ravi, and Kavi Nassen. I am eternally grateful for the blessings and vision of Bishop M. Azariah. Special thanks for the continued support of John Jayaharan. Rajasekaran and Vidya of the University of Wisconsin in India and Chella Minakshi have given me friendship and field support for almost three decades. I thank Ilango Samuel Peter for his wonderful photographs.

There are several students of Paraṭṭai's who contributed substantially to this study through sharing their lives and the theology and practice of Paraṭṭai's songs with me over the last 18 eighteen years. Rev. Jacqulin Jothi, Rev. Enose Magimai Doss, and their daughter Eucharista have continually opened their home, family, and hearts to sustain this work and my on-going relationship with the Church of South India community. I am so grateful that there is always a place at their table for me, while it is the depth of our relationship that has blessed the hundreds of meals we have shared. I have learned more about the application of Dalit theology from Jacqulin's work with women's groups, tsunami survivors, and union members than from any other source. I have seen how the transmission of Paraṭṭttai's songs is possible among both poor rural and middle class urban congregations through the dedicated work of Rev. Enose. I am grateful to Rev. Jaquelin and Rev. Enose and their extended family for being my family in India.

Other students of Paraṭṭai's and of TTS who contributed tremendously to this research include Benjamin Inbaraj and his extended family, Ebenezer Kirubakaran, M. Rajamanikam, Francis Devadoss, Cruz, Anandan Selvaraj, T. Charles Danaraj, Johnson Jebakumar, Adlin Ragina Bai, and the late Kavi Nassen.

The subject of this research was sparked through my experience as an Oberlin Shansi Memorial Association Representative to Lady Doak College in Madurai from 1985-87. The LDC and American College Christian community introduced me to Tamil Christian music and its rich history. Members of this community also provided a greater understanding of the historical links between the American Madura Mission and my own family roots on both the Sherinian (American Board of Commissioners for Foreign Missions mission in Turkey) and the Chamberlain sides (Vellore and the Reform Church of America in Vellore) sides. I am grateful to the LDC faculty and administration as well as to Carl Jacobson and Deborah Cocco of Oberlin Shansi for their on going support of my career. In particular I acknowledge Dr. Rani George, Miss Manuel,

Dr. Gandhi Mary, Mr. and Mrs. Stanley Jayasingh and their daughter Anu, Dr. Beulah J.M. Rajkumar, and Principal Nirmala Jayraj. I also thank American College faculty members Immanuel Jebarajan and Christopher Sherwood for their keen understanding of music and Christian community dynamics.

The original research for this project was generously funded by the Fulbright Foundation and the American Institute of Indian Studies. In addition, the University of Oklahoma provided me two Junior Faculty Research Fellowship as well as a Presidential International Travel Fellowship to support the village reception study and writing of this manuscript. Franklin and Marshall College also provided a timely travel grant.

I was a visiting fellow with the South Asian Council at Yale University in 2003-2004 where I had the opportunity to share my work with many inspiring colleagues in South Asian studies and music. I am particularly grateful to Barney Bate for including me in his graduate seminar on caste, for his on-going support of this publication, and for sharing this journey of the love of Tamil culture. My year at Yale with my partner Elyssa Faison, who was a post-doctoral fellow with the Yale Council on East Asian Studies, brought us into the intellectual orbit of one of the greatest thinkers in South Asian studies, Dilip Menon. This book and my life have been so enriched through the intellectual guidance of Dilip and his wife, Lara Jacob, along with his two sisters, Dr. Nivedita Menon and activist Pramada Menon, and their parents. I am also thankful to Judith Casselberry, Mridu Rai, and Serene Jones for an amazing year at Yale. Other South Asian Studies colleagues and friends who have supported my work from its very early stages include Eliza Kent, Corinne Dempsey, Indira Peterson, Davesh Soneji, Dennis Hudson, Eleanor Zelliot, and Martha Selby.

I gratefully acknowledge my teachers, friends, and colleagues in Ethnomusicology who created an environment of intellectual rigor and disciplined practice that nurtured my studies. At Wesleyan, T. Viswanathan, Mark Slobin, Kay Shelemay, Vijay Pinch, and Gage Averill provided an education with theoretical breadth that I hope I have been able to apply here. I thank my mrdangam guru, the late Sri Ramnad Raghavan, my teaching mentors, Bill Lowe and Linda Saarnijoki, and my extended Wesleyan University community: Aaron Page, David Nelson, Tomie Hahn, Sriram Parasuram, Frank Gunderson, Matthew Allen, Amanda Minks, and Miranda Arana. Other important teachers include Rod Knight and Carol Babiracki.

I am constantly inspired by my network of feminist theory and music friends, especially Deborah Wong, Ellen Koskoff, Susan Thomas, Sarah Morelli, Tomie Hahn, Eileen Hayes, and Liz Tolbert. For their on-going support of my research and professional life I also thank Ann Morrison, Tim Cooley, Greg

Barz, Ingrid Monson, Ernie Brown, Susan Asai, Richard Wolf, Portia Maultsby, Maria Mendoncia, Jayson Beaster-Jones, Regula Qureshi, Amie Maciszewski, Katherine Butler Schofield, Nila Bhattacharjya, Anna Schultz, T. M. Scruggs, Claudia Macdonald and my student Jason Busniewski. Shubha Choudhury and the staff of the Archives and Research Center for Ethnomusicology in Delhi were generous with their time and material. I thank Dr. Nazir Jairazbhoy and Dr. Amy Catlin who who provided access to the Bake collection. For the care and commitment of colleagues and friends who have read all or parts of the manuscript I thank Peter Manuel, Sean Williams, Eileen Hayes, Amanda Weidman, and Richard Wolf.

At the University of Oklahoma I am sustained by a wonderful community of scholars and friends including Amanda Minks, Clemencia Rodriguez, Jill Irvine, Marvin Lamb, Josh and Manar Landis, Sarah Reichardt, Sarah Tracy, Peter Cahn, Leslie Rankin-Hill, Aparna Mitra, Mark Frazier, Misha Klein, and Jacqueline Cook.

I want to thank Jyoti Sahi for use of the powerful woodcut design image of the *Dancing Drummer,* (1989), as the book cover. I offer my appreciation to Rebecca Tolen and Nancy Lightfoot along with their editorial and production staff at the University of Indiana Press for their continued belief in this project and their patience, especially at the end. I am so pleased that Clara Henderson and the Andrew W. Mellon Foundation facilitated the inclusion of the on-line material for this book in the Ethnomusicology Multimedia (EM) project.

My family has been a constant source of support especially my parents who have both inspired this work through their interests in Christian art and culture as well as their own social justice work. From an early age, they nurtured within me a keen appreciation for disciplined study and intellectual curiosity. As this project comes to a close I find myself in the mystery of life's transitions. To my dear partner, Elyssa Faison, who supported me intellectually, emotionally, and through her companionship, generosity, and love over the past twelve years, I hope the wonders of life's journey that nurtured our family (Bijay and Sushi) and our life together always remain in our hearts as home, wherever we may find ourselves on the adventurous path of life.

I offer special recognition of the spiritual inspiration in my life to two departed souls Randy Giles and Merrie Lea Fielder. You are always with me.

Finally, it is with all my love and respect that I dedicate this book to Rev. J. T. Appavoo, Paraṭṭai and all who sing his songs. I only hope that as "a voice of Paraṭṭai" (*Paraṭṭai Kural*), through this writing I have done justice to his musical theology and contributed in even a small way to liberating the Dalits of India and the oppressed of the world.

Portions of chapter 2 were previously published as "Musical Style and the Changing Social Identity of Tamil Christians," *Ethnomusicology*, vol. 51, no. 2, Spring/Summer 2007: 238–280. Portions of chapter 1 were previously published as "The Indigenization of Tamil Christian Music: Musical Style and Liberation Theology," *The World of Music*, edited by Max Peter Baumann, guest edited by T. M. Scruggs. Berlin, Germany. Vol. 47 no. 1. 2005: 125–165.

PURL Audio and Video Files

INTRODUCTION

PURL 0.1 | "Iyēsusāmi Kantuttanda Sebam" (The Lord's Prayer) from *Girāmiya Isai Va̤ripāḍu (Village Music Liturgy)*
http://purl.dlib.indiana.edu/iudl/em/Sherinian/910069

PURL 0.2 | "Sāmi Aṟaikkiṟadu" (Invocation) from *Girāmiya Isai Va̤ripāḍu (Village Music Liturgy)* Sung by Rev. J. T. Appavoo
http://purl.dlib.indiana.edu/iudl/em/Sherinian/910078

PURL 0.3 | "Bumiyil Vāṟuṟa" (All the People Living on Earth) by Rev. J. T. Appavoo
http://purl.dlib.indiana.edu/iudl/em/Sherinian/910065

PURL 0.4 | "Otta Saḍa, Reṭṭai Saḍa" (One Braid, Two Braids) from Orathapalayam Village
http://purl.dlib.indiana.edu/iudl/em/Sherinian/910089

CHAPTER 1

PURL 1.1 | *Girāmiya Isai Va̤ripāḍu (Village Music Liturgy)* by Rev. J. T. Appavoo
http://purl.dlib.indiana.edu/iudl/em/Sherinian/910063

PURL 1.2 | Sharing Poṇgal at the End of the 1994 Poṇgal Festival at TTS.
http://purl.dlib.indiana.edu/iudl/em/Sherinian/910093

PURL 1.3 | "Kuttam Uṇaruṟadu" (Repentance of Sin) from Rev. J. T. Appavoo's *Girāmiya Isai Va̤ripāḍu (Village Music Liturgy)*
http://purl.dlib.indiana.edu/iudl/em/Sherinian/910068

PURL 1.4 | Paṟai Drummers in Munaivendri Village Bring on Possession by the Hindu Deity
http://purl.dlib.indiana.edu/iudl/em/Sherinian/910214

CHAPTER 2

PURL 2.1 | "Virundu Parimāṟuṟadu" (Meal Sharing Song) from Rev. J. T. Appavoo's *Girāmiya Isai Vaṟipāḍu (Village Music Liturgy)*
http://purl.dlib.indiana.edu/iudl/em/Sherinian/910070

PURL 2.2 | Photo of Funeral Carriage at the Central Church in Vellore, Tamil
http://purl.dlib.indiana.edu/iudl/em/Sherinian/910178

PURL 2.3 | Rev. J. T. Appavoo's Karnatak-Style Song "Pudiya Ulaham Vēṇḍum" (I Want a New World)
http://purl.dlib.indiana.edu/iudl/em/Sherinian/910161

PURL 2.4 | "Pudiya Siluva" (A New Cross)
http://purl.dlib.indiana.edu/iudl/em/Sherinian/910032

CHAPTER 3

PURL 3.1 | "Sāmiya Vaṇaṅguṟadu" (Greetings and Praise of God) Rev. J. T. Appavoo's *Girāmiya Isai Vaṟipāḍu (Village Music Liturgy)*
http://purl.dlib.indiana.edu/iudl/em/Sherinian/910067

CHAPTER 4

PURL 4.1 | TTS Carol Service: Community Lanterns
http://purl.dlib.indiana.edu/iudl/em/Sherinian/910088

PURL 4.2 | TTS Carol Service: Opening Gītam
http://purl.dlib.indiana.edu/iudl/em/Sherinian/910084

PURL 4.3 | TTS Carol Service: Dramatic Vignettes on the Theme "Let's Make Peace"
http://purl.dlib.indiana.edu/iudl/em/Sherinian/910085

PURL 4.4 | TTS Carol Service: "Maṉasamātta" (Change of Heart) by Rev. J. T. Appavoo
http://purl.dlib.indiana.edu/iudl/em/Sherinian/910086

PURL 4.5 | Reception of the TTS Carol Service and Song "Maṉasamātta" (Change of Heart)
http://purl.dlib.indiana.edu/iudl/em/Sherinian/910087

PURL 4.6 | Palm Sunday Procession from TTS Chapel
http://purl.dlib.indiana.edu/iudl/em/Sherinian/910062

PURL 4.7 | "Ammāḍi Kuṭṭi Poṇṇē" (My Little Girl) by Rev. J. T. Appavoo
http://purl.dlib.indiana.edu/iudl/em/Sherinian/910208

PURL 4.8 | Poṅgal Festival: Kuppai (Garbage) Gathering Procession in TTS
http://purl.dlib.indiana.edu/iudl/em/Sherinian/910071
PURL 4.9 | Poṅgal Eve: Prayers and Singing
http://purl.dlib.indiana.edu/iudl/em/Sherinian/910072
PURL 4.10 | Collecting Poṅgal Pānai (Pots) from Around TTS Campus on Poṅgal Morning
http://purl.dlib.indiana.edu/iudl/em/Sherinian/910073
PURL 4.11 | Poṅgal Procession Arrives at Festival Ground
http://purl.dlib.indiana.edu/iudl/em/Sherinian/910074
PURL 4.12 | Singing Appavoo's Songs While Poṅgal Cooks
http://purl.dlib.indiana.edu/iudl/em/Sherinian/910075
PURL 4.13 | Poṅgal Community Entertainment
http://purl.dlib.indiana.edu/iudl/em/Sherinian/910076
PURL 4.14 | Poṅgal Pots Boil Over
http://purl.dlib.indiana.edu/iudl/em/Sherinian/910077
PURL 4.15 | Sharing Poṅgal, Sugar Cane, and Dancing
http://purl.dlib.indiana.edu/iudl/em/Sherinian/910079
PURL 4.16 | Poṅgal Celebration at the Rural Theological Institute (RTI)
http://purl.dlib.indiana.edu/iudl/em/Sherinian/910080
PURL 4.17 | Poṅgal Puja Worship and Singing "Tāyi Tagappanārē" (Oh, Mother and Farther) by Rev. J. T. Appavoo at RTI
http://purl.dlib.indiana.edu/iudl/em/Sherinian/910081
PURL 4.18 | Singing of "Tāyi Tagappanārē" (Oh, Mother and Farther) at RTI, part 2
http://purl.dlib.indiana.edu/iudl/em/Sherinian/910082

CHAPTER 5

PURL 5.1 | Jacqulin Jothi in the TTS Christmas Carol Service Drama
http://purl.dlib.indiana.edu/iudl/em/Sherinian/910083
PURL 5.2 | Enose Magimaidoss and Paraṭṭai during Poṅgal Procession
http://purl.dlib.indiana.edu/iudl/em/Sherinian/910162
PURL 5.3 | Magimaidoss, Father of Enose, Sings Christian Karnatak Music
http://purl.dlib.indiana.edu/iudl/em/Sherinian/910092
PURL 5.4 | Rev. Jacqulin Jothi Giving Christmas Sermon at Vedal Village
http://purl.dlib.indiana.edu/iudl/em/Sherinian/910060
PURL 5.5 | *Girāmiya Isai Vaṟipāḍu* by Rev. J. T. Appavoo at Vedal (Lord's Prayer Section)
http://purl.dlib.indiana.edu/iudl/em/Sherinian/910039

PURL 4.7 | "Ammāḍi Kuṭṭi Poṇṇē" (My Little Girl) by Rev. J. T. Appavoo
http://purl.dlib.indiana.edu/iudl/em/Sherinian/910208

PURL 5.6 | "Āṇḍavanē Eṅga Aṭṭidayan" (The Lord Is Our Shepherd) by Rev. J. T. Appavoo
http://purl.dlib.indiana.edu/iudl/em/Sherinian/910209

PURL 5.7 | "Āṇḍavanē Nī Eṅga Koṭṭai" (You Are Our Fortress) by Rev. J. T. Appavoo
http://purl.dlib.indiana.edu/iudl/em/Sherinian/910210

PURL 5.8 | "Āṇṇē Tambi Māppiḷḷē" (Big Brother, Little Brother, Brother-in-Law) by Rev. J. T. Appavoo
http://purl.dlib.indiana.edu/iudl/em/Sherinian/910211

PURL 5.9 | Dialogic Sermon Led by Rev. Francis Devadoss in Devanthavakkam Village
http://purl.dlib.indiana.edu/iudl/em/Sherinian/910052

PURL 5.10 | "Sagalajaṉaṅgaḷe" by Rev. J. T. Appavoo
http://purl.dlib.indiana.edu/iudl/em/Sherinian/910215

PURL 5.11 | Rev. Francis Devadoss Teaching "Bumiyil Vāṟuṟa"
http://purl.dlib.indiana.edu/iudl/em/Sherinian/910049

PURL 5.12 | Rev. J. T. Appavoo Teaching "Tāyi Tagappanārē" (Oh, Mother and Father)
http://purl.dlib.indiana.edu/iudl/em/Sherinian/910037

PURL 5.13 | Mandapasalai Villagers: "Inikkāda Tēnumilla" (Without Sweetness There Is No Honey)
http://purl.dlib.indiana.edu/iudl/em/Sherinian/910030

PURL 5.14 | "Tāyi Tagappanārē" (Oh, Mother and Father) by Rev. J. T. Appavoo, Sung by Boys in the Kanchipuram, Church of South India (CSI) Boarding School
http://purl.dlib.indiana.edu/iudl/em/Sherinian/910044

PURL 5.15 | Orathapalyam Christian Villagers Share Music and Dance
http://purl.dlib.indiana.edu/iudl/em/Sherinian/910090

CHAPTER 6

PURL 6.1 | "Nalla Seydi" (Good News) by Rev. J. T. Appavoo
http://purl.dlib.indiana.edu/iudl/em/Sherinian/910207

PURL 6.2 | Sakthi Kalai Kural in the Chennai Sangamam Festival Final Procession
http://purl.dlib.indiana.edu/iudl/em/Sherinian/910216

TAMIL FOLK MUSIC
AS DALIT LIBERATION THEOLOGY

INTRODUCTION

Context and Concepts: Singing The Lord's Prayer as Freedom in a Tamil Land

Iyēsusāmi Kantuttanda Sebam **(The Lord's Prayer)**
From *Girāmiya Isai Vaṟipāḍu* (*Village Music Liturgy*)
Words and music composed by Rev. James Theophilus Appavoo
English translation by James Theophilus Appavoo and Zoe Sherinian

1. *Vānatilla vāṟuhiṟa pettavarē sāmi—om*
The divine one, our parent living in heaven,
Pēr veḷaṅga vēnṇuñcāmi viḍutalai varavēṇum
Let the meaning of your name be understood as, "Let there be freedom!"

2. *Kēṇappaya āṭci vēṇām pettavarē sāmi—on*
We do not want the rule of wicked fools, O divine parent.
Nērmaiyuḷḷa āṭci vēṇum uttamarē sāmi
But we want your just rule, O perfect divine one.

3. *Vānatilla oṉadu sittam koḍiparappadu pōla—eṅga*
As the flag of your will flies high in heaven
Olahattilūm naḍakka vēṇum petavarē sāmi
So let it also be in this world, O perfect one.

4. *Ottumayā oru olaiyil sēndu tiṉṉum sōṟu*
Give us daily the *oru olai* food that is shared
Nittanittam keḍaikkaṇumē pettavarē sāmi
in unity, O divine parent.

In the opening stanza of "The Lord's Prayer" from his *Girāmiya Isai Vaṟipāḍu* or *Village Music Liturgy*, Theophilus Appavoo (also known by the pen name Paraṭṭai Annan or "big brother with messy hair") (re)composes the name of the Christian God using the secularist Tamil vernacular call to action *viḍutalai varavēnum*. In so doing, Paraṭṭai the trickster intentionally draws on the root *viḍu*, which contains the concept of resistance as well as sprouting or creative potential (see Fig. 1; PURL 0.1). Thus *viḍutalai* as used here means release from societal bondage as well as liberation from forces such as colonialism through creative action.[1] Further, revealing the concept of prayer as a ritualized dialogic request for action, Appavoo emphasizes that God's state of being and the supplication for action among people are also *viḍutalai;* God is understood as a liberator who responds to people's unified action (Brown 2000, 597). He uses the liturgical centrality of the Lord's Prayer as a call to those people especially oppressed by caste, gender, and class (the broad meaning of Dalit) to reclaim Christianity as a socially liberating religion emphasizing an essential practice of sharing food in a daily Eucharistic lifestyle of communal living. As he indigenizes theology to the cultural identity of poor village outcastes (at least sixty percent of Tamil Christians), he facilitates the ritual action of singing in the vernacular language of spoken Tamil, the use of folk music style, and metaphors of rural life that reflect the personal experiences and beliefs of village and oppressed people in India. Moreover by choosing to present his message musically and lyrically in *girāmiya isai* (folk music), rather than sanskritized or elite forms, Appavoo facilitates a process of ongoing daily resistance through music (see Appendix 1, Transcription 1).

Appavoo argues that the means to social and psychological transformation are embedded in the transmission system of Tamil folk music. The flexible nature of folk music as orally transmitted and ostensibly unauthored permits villagers to freely reinterpret or adapt both a song's lyrics and musical elements in order to make the music accessible, to facilitate the communication of the ritual, theological, and political needs of the moment, and to represent the identity of the people who use and (re)produce it. Thus the meaning of Appavoo's Lord's Prayer lies not only in the theological content of the text, but in the music's sound and the liberating action of recomposition in the ritual moment as an alternative form of communication (Appavoo 1986: 16).

Ethnomusicologists study music as human expression and meaning (Campbell 2004, 27). This study is an ethnography of music *as* theology or the human experience of and relationship to the divine through the lens of music. Reflecting on Theophilus Appavoo's version of the Lord's Prayer, Dr. Rev. M. Gnanavaram, Principal of the Tamil Nadu Theological Seminary, declared, "To glorify God's name is to sing his liberative actions. It is not simply words.

Singing is action."[2] Gnanavaram, like other scholars of religion, regards the Lord's Prayer as a defining expression of the Christian's relationship with God. Further, as a liberation theologian, he specifically emphasizes that theological constructions of God and God's relationship with people stem from an everyday local experience of, and action within, the present situation; he does not promote a universalist understanding of God (Gnanavaram 2001, 61). From this perspective then, all theology, like all politics *and* all musical meaning, is local. As theology, sound becomes a means to action for social justice.

Appavoo's Lord's Prayer is a liturgical expression of his philosophy that both Christian theology and the process of its creation should be socially liberating; that is dialogical, critical, and contextualized to be emblematic of the identity and culture of the oppressed. Appavoo intended the practice of Tamil folk music as Dalit liberation theology to support a process of self-transformation for the outcaste. The practice would transform the outcaste's internalized self-understanding from polluted untouchable—less than human and barely worthy of treatment as a village dog—to empowered person, an anti-caste Dalit, fighting for social justice through everyday acts of resistance. In the Tamil cultural context where elites often think of village culture as degraded, Appavoo facilitates this transformation by (re)locating the resistive power of folk music at the center of Christian liturgy.

This ethnomusicological study elucidates the agency of those who use and freely recompose Christian folk songs as everyday acts of resistance to the inhuman systems of caste, gender, and class oppression in India. More specifically, I focus on the cultural historical phenomenon of Rev. Dr. James Theophilus Appavoo, his music and his Dalit community. Appavoo was one of the most influential Tamil Dalit composer/theologians, creating over one hundred songs, a sung liturgy in Tamil folk music, plays, stories, a handful of significant academic articles, and a book on the transformative power of folklore. However, none of this was produced in a vacuum, but in a cyclical dialogue of hermeneutic inspiration, composition, transmission, reception and re-creation of music as theology, or what I call dialogical (re)creative praxis. At each node of the (re)creative cycle of this network of transmission, we see the activity of shared music-making in the relationships between these cultural actors (including the ethnographer). That is, "participatory engagement in social dialogue" (Bakhtin [1934/35] 1981) through music.

The narrative of this story and the process of production, transmission, and reception that organizes the chapters of this book begin with an understanding that Dalit theologians such as Appavoo and a handful of others first created Tamil Christian folk music in the late twentieth century by listening to the biblical hermeneutics and observing the cooperative lifestyles of villagers. In turn, the villagers who have received Christian folk songs from these theologians and their students have re-created them, changing the lyrics and musical elements to articulate political and cultural critiques in worship, as well as political action. This includes an understanding of the Christian deity as both father and mother. In the Latin American liberation theology context, Gutierrez argues that "we shall not have a quantum theological leap until the oppressed themselves theologize" (Gutierrez 1983, 65). Through Appavoo's re-creative transmission process, Christian folk songs and his fully sung liturgy in folk music style, vernacular Tamil language, and Dalit theology have transformed the nature of worship in the mainline Protestant Churches of South India to redirect its theology toward Dalit people and village culture: a significant step to contribute to their social emancipation.

To understand the impact, potential, and limitation of Appavoo's production of folk music as Dalit liberation theology this ethnography examines the ways Tamil subalterns have dialogically produced, transmitted, and re-created their forms of religious expression through folk music. I argue that the most transformative process and realization of the music's effect have occurred in the context of dialogical relationships informed by a commitment to emancipation from caste, gender, and class oppression through cultural empowerment, social action, and a theological conviction of equality and sharing. In the spirit of an interactive pedagogy of the oppressed which involves active listening to the biblical interpretation and social needs of villagers, Appavoo positioned himself as a Dalit leader or culture broker who was not "thinking without the people, nor for the people, but only with the people" (Freire 1970 [1984], 126). More specifically, I demonstrate how people create a context for liberation through shared musical relationships. Music is a means to dialogically generate the sources of empowerment and the motivation toward action. Furthermore, as the subaltern use folk music to create Dalit theology, they in turn indigenize Indian Christianity to make it continually locally relevant and reflective of their religious as well as social experience.

Below I continue to introduce Theophilus Appavoo, the sound of his music, and the community setting for its production and performance as well as that of my fieldwork. This elaboration is followed by a discussion of the three forms of discrimination—caste, class, and gender—as well as the importance that language plays in the construction of value and identity in Appavoo's Dalit liberation theology. Finally I introduce Appavoo's neo-Marxist strategy of social analysis, arguing that it brings these multiple factors of identity together in the process of ideological production in his songs to unify the oppressed community to which the message is aimed.

THE TAMIL NADU THEOLOGICAL SEMINARY (TTS)

What kind of institution—and what kind of community—produces religious music in India with the intent of social liberation? What does this music sound like, who is (re)creating it, and how does the community nurture the dialogical process of its creation? These may be the questions that enter the reader's mind, but they were not the questions with which I entered the idyllic campus of the Tamil Nadu Theological Seminary (TTS) located in Madurai, Tamil Nadu, in the late summer of 1993. I was intent on conducting ethnographic research on the indigenization of Tamil Christian music in the mainline Protestant institution best known for indigenized musical and theological production in South India. When I left fourteen months later, I had a solid understanding of Tamil Christian music's use and history. Further, I had a clear vision of the Appavoo's compositional process and the dialogical re-creation possible in his folk music's transmission within a highly politicized community conscious of caste, class, and gender oppression in society. Yet I had little first-hand observation of the music's transformative potential for village people (for whom it was primarily intended) or the possibility of its use and impact in the wider Dalit liberation (civil rights) movement (or, as Appavoo described such visionary change, the possibility of space flight in the minds of the Wright Brothers while building the first airplane). In other words, I had not been able to do research to know what substantial long-term psychological and material impact the music could have on the Dalit or outcaste villagers for whom it was intended. After completing my dissertation, with these questions still burning, I came back to Tamil Nadu in 2002 to conduct a village reception study following several students of the seminary, with whom I had worked closely in 1993–94 and who were now stationed in Tamil villages as Church of South India priests implementing Paraṭṭai's vision through practicing his musico-theology. Thus I was able to complete the cycle from production, to transmission, and back to re-creation. It is this cycle of dialogical (re)creative praxis that I analyze in these pages.

TRANSFORMATION TO PARAṬṬAI'S MUSIC

The TTS campus was an ideal place to conduct my fieldwork. It is located in the provincial town of Madurai in central Tamil Nadu. The Minakshi Amman (mother goddess with fish eyes) Brahminical Hindu temple sits at the center of the city, its four ornately carved *gopuram* towers marking the cardinal directions from great distances. Downtown streets that encircle the temple are fashioned like a classical Hindu mandala (Dutt and Nobel 2003, 264). For the modern consumer, the streets are dotted with specialty shops selling everything from gold jewelry, to paper, electronics, Bollywood cassettes, and freshly roasted coffee. Four former American Congregational mission churches, South Gate, West Gate, East Gate, and North Gate, were built as modern correspondents to the South, West, East, and North gates of the temple and Madurai's medieval Hindu city planning. Several main thoroughfares extend diagonally from this city center. Old Dindigul Road crosses over the train station by the large Lutheran church, past the Railway Colony with its Catholic Anglo-Indian church that marks the edge of the modern neighborhood known as S. S. Colony. Just off of Dindigul Road, the Tamil Nadu Theological Seminary campus sits behind a large stone wall almost a quarter of a mile long in an area called Arasaradi.

As one enters the seminary's main gates from the road, on the left a dirt cricket and football field used by local school children creates a buffer between the campus and life outside. Passing the inner gates and the watchman's booth, one enters the palm tree–lined paths of the seminary campus. Off to the right, the path is dotted with faculty houses and graduate student cottages, one of which I rented. This area also includes a children's playground and daycare center, basketball court, and the college's own dairy and poultry cooperatives as well as a fully equipped recording studio and an indoor auditorium: all the facilities needed for a self-sustaining community.

The straight path from the main gate runs past staff quarters, women's and men's dormitories, the principal's bungalow, the college outdoor gathering ground/stage called the *mānadōppu*, the library, printing press, book store, administrative buildings, classroom buildings, and a beautiful open air chapel. With its marble floors, a simple wooden alter and cross, the chapel offers a serene setting for worship. Its indigenous-style tower shaped like the Hindu temple *gopuram* is strikingly syncretic in this city known since the 1830s as the American Congregational "Madura Mission Station" where New England style church architecture attempts to dominate the style and height of the medieval Hindu Minakshi temple.

In August of 1993, after settling into my two-room cottage on the TTS campus, I conducted my first interview with Rev. Honest Chinniah who was visiting the campus for a few weeks. When I explained to him my interest in documenting a variety of styles of music used by Tamil Christians, he suggested that I seek out his former student Rev. Theophilus Appavoo as an advisor and primary source for my research. Little did I realize the transformative path this suggestion revealed.

It was the early morning of October 14. The cold fall monsoon threatened. I could barely get myself out of bed for the morning service and crawled into the chapel right at 6:45 AM as the last bell rang. With no time to organize and bring my recording equipment, I carried only my field notebook in which I wrote observations of the services and noted which pieces were performed. Yet I would not forget that morning's chapel experience, as "Theophy Annan" brought into practice a radically transformative approach to liturgy.

As I entered the chapel, students were instructed to sit in a big circle, with men and women sitting together, which I had never seen before. The usual sex-segregated chapel configuration had men sitting on the ground on the left side of chapel with women on the right, an aisle between them assuring their separation. Older faculty members sat on benches at the back. Instruments were typically played at the front left side of the chapel, on the men's side, essentially prohibiting any significant degree of involvement by women as musicians. Such sex segregation is a norm in many Church of South India (CSI) congregations. Despite its progressive curriculum, which included feminist theology and women's studies, TTS continued the physical segregation of men and women in formal and ritual spaces primarily to protect the reputations and thus potential marriagability of their female students. Needless to say, I was surprised and intrigued by Appavoo's unusual configuration of the space.

Appavoo opened the service with the invocation from his *Village Music Liturgy* that he had just begun to compose: an *a cappella* solo chant in spoken Tamil based on the village practice of invoking or calling God to come as the people had settled their disputes and gathered for the annual festival/worship (PURL 0.2).

SĀMI AṞAIKKIṞADU (INVOCATION OR GOD CALLING)

1) LEAD:
Saṉamellām vandiricci saṇḍai sattam ētumilla
All the people have come. There is no quarreling noise.
Sāmiyē nīyum vanduviḍu vanduviḍu
You too, come, O god come!
RESPONSE:
Vanduviḍu vanduviḍu
Come, O come!
2) LEAD:
Paṅgāḷi moṟaiyellām pāṅguḍanē vandiricci
All sisters, brothers, and in-laws come elegantly!

Pārulagai pettavarē parivuḍanē vanduviḍu
You, who gave birth to the universe, come graciously.
RESPONSE:
Vanduviḍu vanduviḍu
Come, O come!
3) LEAD:
Taṇṇi pōṭṭā mayakkam varum
If one drinks, dizziness comes.
Taṟudalaikkō tuṉbam varum
So to the wicked misery comes.
Saṇḍai pōṭṭā pagai vaḷarum
Quarrels nurture [grow] enmity.
Sāmi oṅga kōvam varum
God, your anger will come.
RESPONSE:
Kōvam varum kōvam varum
Anger will come. Anger will come.
4) LEAD:
Oṇṇupaṭṭā nī varuvē ottāsai paṇṇiḍuvē
If we are one, you will come and help us.
Koṇṇupōṭṭōm vēttumayē kōlamuḍaṉ vanduviḍu
We have killed our differences (or distinctions),
So come in splendor.
RESPONSE:
Vanduviḍu vanduviḍu
Come, O come.

Drawing on the folk chant-like style called *tohera,* the tune of the invocation was comprised of four motifs, made up of four notes each, that wove up and down the scale with minimal distance between the notes. The words described the community gathering and unifying, having settled any disagreements, while its mood was one of pleading for God's presence with the people. Appavoo followed this opening line with a jump up the scale punctuated by an emphatic cry of "*sāmiyē,*" the generic and gender-neutral Tamil village name for deity. The tune then moved back down the scale on the words "you also" and repeated the earlier four-note motif on the words "Come, O come!" (*vanduviḍu*). Appavoo further encouraged participation in the invocation through having the congregation repeat this refrain at the end of each line.

The invocation was followed by the entire community singing Appavoo's well known song "Bumiyil Vāṟuṟa" (All the People Living On Earth). First published in the seminary songbook *Puttuyir Pāḍalhaḷ* or *Songs of New Life* (1985), it is one of his most popular Christian folk songs. Its tune is based on the folk style genre and women's circle dance called *kummi.* Its rhythm is the common Tamil folk pattern that consists of a lively up-tempo polyrhythmic duple against triple meter. This song was also appropriate for calling the people to worship because it uses the rural colloquial term *kumbiḍalām* (let's worship) to describe people coming together in unity to enthusiastically worship God through song. God is named using the Tamil political term *talaivaru*, or leader of the community. At the end of this performance the tempo sped up and participants began to clap, which I had also never seen before in the TTS chapel. (PURL 0.3).

Bumiyil Vāṟuṟa **(All the People Living On Earth)**

CHORUS
Bumiyil vāṟuṟa makkaḷē ellārum
Everyone on the earth come
Kūḍiyē vāruṅga kumbiḍalām
together to worship
Āravārattōḍa ānandamā pāḍa
Sing with enthusiasm and happiness
Āṇaḍavan saṉṉidi sērndiḍalām
Let's join God's presence.
VERSE
1. Kaḍavuḷḷ oruvarē namakku deyvaṅga, avara
God is our only Deity
Viḍḍālulakil tuṇaivar yārumilliṅga ēṉṟeṉṟum avaru, eṅgal talaivaru
He is our community leader
Eṉṟē sattam pōḍḍu kempīramā pāḍa

Appavoo's sermon was similarly participatory. Indeed he engaged in a Socratic dialogue with students over social issues encouraging women in particular to share their opinions, which they did freely. The service ended with the introduction of a new song, one that would become the song of the academic year, "Tāyi Tagappanārē" (Oh, Mother and Father) and contained many of the elements of his theology: God as parent, Mother and Father; reclaiming folk culture through using vernacular Tamil; and recognition that the greatest gift of the poor (or their most powerful action) is unity.

Tāyi Tagappanārē **(Oh, Mother and Father)**
By J. T. Appavoo
CHORUS
Tāyi tagappanārē sagalattaiyum pettavarē—eṅga
Oh, Mother and Father,[3] parent who created everything,
Sāmi uṉṉaïvaṇaṅgi sentamiṟil pāṭṭu paḍiccōm
Our *sāmi*, we will worship you singing songs in pure Tamil.
Kāsilla meṟugutiri Koṇḍu varala

> We have no money so have not brought candles.
> *Yeṅga ottumaya ottumaya Kāṇikkaiyā paḍaiccōm*
> Our unity, our unity we offer to you.

During this first hearing, I recognized that this song named God as both mother, *tāyi,* and father, *tagappanārē.* It also emphasized the use of spoken Tamil, which is very unusual for Christian hymns, in which formal written Tamil is the norm. However, it was the lively folk tune based on the kummi circle dance genre accompanied on the tabla drum by the typical duple-against-triple polyrhythmic drum pattern that moved me to want to dance (see chapter 5 for a full analysis). The students seemed to be equally excited as they joyfully joined in the call and response exchange of the catchy tunes and clapped to the syncopated rhythms: a rare occurrence in the mainline Christian contexts I had observed.

I was delightfully moved by this service and intrigued by the eccentric aura of this round fellow wearing a *jiba* (long shirt), beard, and long hair, befitting of his village pen name Paraṭṭai Annan. While I only understood basic aspects of the theology in his lyrics and sermon at this point in my fieldwork, his music and participatory style of engagement were so attractive that it only took one session for the focus of my project to be transformed by this experience. I knew I wanted to include his folk style Christian music in my research. After the service I approached Theophy Annan to tell him briefly about my project on the indigenization of Christian music and to ask if I could interview him. He kindly, though without overwhelming enthusiasm, invited me to his house the following Saturday.

FIRST INTERVIEW: A SEAT AT THE TABLE WITH THE TEACHER

With anticipation I arrived for an interview at Appavoo's cottage at TTS that Saturday afternoon. In Dalit fashion of reversal of middle-class values, our relationship as teacher and student began by sharing *sukukkapi* (a poor man's hot tea of ginger pepper, coriander, turmeric, fenugreek and other spices) instead of middle-class Brookbond milk tea. This gesture in many ways symbolized Appavoo's own intellectual and social transformation. He was a middle-class urban Paṟaiyar raised in an Anglican Christian community in the east-coast town of Cuddalore. His father was a manager in a sugar factory and a semi-professional karnatak musician, and his mother was a teacher. Appavoo eventually became a teacher himself earning a B.A. in History and Geography and an M.A. in Religion and Philosophy before he completed his Bachelor of Divinity at TTS and was ordained. Yet it was almost a decade of immersion in Tamil folk culture and theological dialogue with poor village outcastes that transformed him into a Dalit theologian and composer of folk music.

I sat with Appavoo and his youngest daughter, seventeen-year-old Neena, who freely involved herself in the conversation and sang examples of his feminist songs. It was in this initial interview that he offered me an extensive overview of his Dalit theology and his theory of the use of folk music as a means to the transmission and re-creation of liberating Christian theology by Dalits. He also shared with me the first kernels of his liturgy in Tamil folk music that he had begun to write (he had written the invocation we had sung at the chapel service for a seminar in Geneva a few months earlier in April of 1993). He would finish the thirteen-part, fully sung liturgy in vernacular Tamil six months later and we would spend much of the summer of 1994 translating it and conducting a theological analysis of the lyrics and music.

Theophy Annan was very open to me. However, at this early point I did not fully understand the meaning of everything he told me. Ideas and possibilities entered my mind, but did not penetrate deeply. While my consciousness of the power of Tamil folk music at TTS, the center for the production of Dalit liberation theology, had been emotionally sparked, I had not made the complete intellectual shift away from my intended focus on classical Indian karnatak Christian music.

Near the end of the interview, after we had talked about his understanding of Christian indigenization, I asked his opinion of the potential focus of my fieldwork. He suggested I pursue the music of Dalit Christian women. He had my ticket. That was an exciting option, however I felt at the time to focus on Dalits instead of surveying musical use by the variety of Christian castes would require spending a great deal of time in the villages, which was not part of my fieldwork plan. However, I was to discover that there were many Dalit women (some middle class as well as those with village roots) in the seminary with a variety of opinions about the meaning and use of music styles by Tamil Christians. Further, it was these women, his female students, who would soon bring me into their daily practice of Paraṭṭai's theology of sharing food in community and in turn, through sharing their emotional and intellectual friendship, would facilitate my social transformation through participation in a united community.

My musical transformation began the first time I heard Appavoo's music. My social transformation was an ongoing process of relationship building with Appavoo, his family, and students: a process of earning a seat at the table through showing my commitment to Dalit liberation. Both musical and social transformations eventually led to an intellectual transformation of musical and Christian theological understanding in dialogue with this community. The foundation of my education in Dalit theology involved understanding the triple axis of oppressed identities of caste, class, and gender that village Christians faced. Furthermore, understanding the devaluation of spoken Tamil and folk music were essential. After defining these below, we will see how Appavoo's system of neo-Marxist social analysis provides a way to understand the relationship between these identity and aesthetic elements.

THE PERVASIVENESS OF CASTE AND UNTOUCHABLITY

Since the earliest conversions by Catholic missionaries in the 1500s, Christian communities in South India have retained caste hierarchy or practiced caste distinctions within their communities. An understanding of caste within the greater society as well as how it continues to be practiced among Christians can illuminate the dynamics of the contemporary Dalit Christian struggle over caste. In the widest sense, caste in India is a hierarchical system of religious and social distinction based on descent. The indigenous term *jāti* or *cāti* in Tamil (meaning species, kind, or type) references the thousands of distinct caste subdivisions often categorized under the four-fold Vedic *varna* division of Hindu society. Religiously, geographically, and historically diverse communities throughout South Asia share some common constructions of caste, which are legitimized by Sanskrit religious texts as well as social and economic practices. According to the Lutheran World Federation at the United Nations Commission on Human Rights in 2002, among these are:[4]

> 1) The concept of "purity-pollution," with certain social groups being regarded as "dirty," and contact with them as being ritually or actually polluting.
> 2) An inherited occupational role, typically the most menial and hazardous roles within the society (given to outcastes).
> 3) Socially enforced endogamy.
> 4) Segregation of living areas, as well as access to and use of public places.[5]

The category of "untouchable" is a social distinction or social ranking at the bottom, indeed outside (*avarna*) of the caste hierarchy; hence the term "outcaste." It is a state of complete impurity and pollution associated with one's birth ranking, one's ritual ranking, and one's occupation. In many locations untouchables are separated from the caste communities physically and socially. They are required to live in a village ghetto, or areas of wasteland called the *cēri*. They are regularly segregated from the main village, and in Tamil Nadu forced to live on its western edge, downwind from the middle and upper-caste neighborhoods so they can ritually absorb the "bad" air thus purifying the upper castes.[6]

Untouchables are subject to daily humiliations that mark their degraded status. In the recent past and in many places today, they are not permitted to wear sandals when they walk through the main village, even if they could afford them; men are not permitted to wear the *tuṇḍu*, or towel on their shoulder as a marker of status. Until the twentieth century untouchables had to move fully off the path and even hide themselves from view when an upper-caste person walked by. They were not allowed on main roads and could not come to certain public gathering places in the late afternoon when their shadow was longest (Kent 2004: 3). It was believed that if even the shadow of an untouchable fell upon an upper-caste person it would pollute them.

The fear of pollution from shared saliva prevents castes from eating together or having *paṟakkam* or social intimacy. The idea of sharing the Christian Eucharist, especially drinking wine from the same cup, is thus a radical infringement of caste practices in India. Traditionally, upper castes will only receive raw food (uncooked grain) from a lower-caste person, whereas they can give cooked food to those of lower rank. For similar fears of ingesting something polluted, untouchables cannot take water from the same well as upper castes and thus outcaste women often have to walk for miles to acquire clean water.

The traditional occupational hierarchy associated with the *varna* system starts with Brahmins at the top, who are teachers and priests or those who control knowledge, followed by kings, landowners, merchants, artisans, and servants. Outcastes are those who clean the night soil or wastes of all the others. Yet they are also the primary agricultural laborers producing raw food on which others depend, and in contemporary contexts make up the primary pool of unskilled workers who construct buildings and houses. Specific outcaste communities also hold hereditary musical occupations. Instruments that require engagement with polluting substances such as saliva (wind instruments like flutes or the double reed *nāgasvaram*) or animal skin (such as drums) continue to be performed primarily by lower castes or outcastes. The paṟai frame drum is performed to announce social and ritual occasions as a *kaḍamai*, or polluting caste duty, by the Paṟaiyar outcaste community of Tamil Nadu. In the last few decades the paṟai drummer has become the icon of the Tamil Dalit liberation movement and in turn the drum has been reclaimed by Dalit theologians through being played in church and referenced in song lyrics.

"Dalit" is a self-selected term of oppositional politics derived from a Marathi and Hindi word meaning "broken down" or "oppressed." Dr. Bhimrao Ramjee Ambedkar, the leader of the modern movement for emancipation of untouchables and the architect of the Indian constitution, introduced the term in 1928.[7] The socio-political organization called the Dalit Panthers (who took their name from the Black Panthers) and writers from the Maharashtran Dalit movements brought renewed attention to the term in the 1970s, while the Dalit theology movement among Christians in Tamil Nadu began in the 1980s.[8] Today "Dalit" is used by activists to erase subcaste distinctions between those formerly called by caste or *jāti* names such as the Tamil Pallars, Chakkiliyars (also called Arundhatiyar), and Paṟaiyars (from which comes the English word "pariah" or outcast), or between those called by the general term "outcaste" (*avarna*), by the term "untouchable," by the governmental designation of "scheduled castes," and by Mahatma Gandhi's term *harijan*.[9] Many Christian Dalit activists reject the term *harijan* saying it is paternalistic because it means "children of God," a term used to describe dancing girls (*devadasis*) who were "married" to God, yet in the early twentieth century were looked down upon as prostitutes by the Victorian middle class, including Christians. Gandhi also strongly opposed the conversion of outcastes to Christianity (Thumma 2000: 79). Thus each of these terms carries with it specific political and historical associations, and those who may be included or excluded in each category shifts historically and locally.[10]

Untouchability was abolished in Article 17 of the Indian Constitution, ratified in January of 1950. Yet the practice of oppressing those at the bottom of the caste hierarchy, who make up seventeen percent of the total Indian population, persists. Indeed South Asian historian Dilip Menon asserts that "caste violence—the daily humiliation and killing of dalit men and women—is the central fault line of contemporary Indian society" (Menon 2006, 1). In his book *The Blindness of Insight*, Menon explains Gandhi's realization that "violence was constitutive of Indian society, particularly in the maintenance of a hierarchical Hindu order. Incidents of religious or caste violence were not exceptions, nor were they precipitated only by colonial strategies of rule" (Menon 2006, vii). Earlier modernist discourses attempted to relegate caste, religion, and the vernacular to the domestic sphere, while the public, modern, postcolonial subject was secular and English speaking. In a new configuration of this dichotomy, Menon contends instead that the public spaces of modern India are inflected by violence against lower castes, while its domestic spaces remain structured by strict prohibitions against caste miscegenation.

Arjun Appadurai (1986, 745) has critiqued the focus on caste by Western scholars as an essentialized category of analysis that fetishizes hierarchy and inequality (Dumont 1970, Moffat 1979). He supports scholarship that "deconstruct[s] caste as the central problematic of Indian society, and of hierarchy as its most compelling trope" and instead wants to see more emphasis on the postcolonial process of subjectivity and culture construction (ibid.). He ultimately concludes that Indian society is hierarchical, but that caste has been incorrectly conceived, particularly by Western structuralists, as a systematic whole, "insulated from whatever else is outside it" (1986, 751). It is clear that colonial policy and Western anthropological writing reified caste, and I take seriously the necessity of studying caste as a historically fluid and shifting construction. Yet I fear that the scholarly authority behind Appadurai's statement could potentially contribute to Western *and* Indian scholars of Indian music continuing to ignore the relationship between social identities and music. I believe his critique, if un-nuanced by the voice of those Indians particularly affected by the violent cruelties of the caste hierarchy, deters a full investigation of how caste hierarchy and inequality affect music and other cultural forms, let alone daily lives. In particular, I am interested in the continuum of Indian music valued as either otherworldly (classical) or degraded (folk). Since Appadurai published his critique in the mid-1980s it has been hard to ignore the voluminous production of literature on the Dalit movement published by Indians (mostly Dalits) in India. Most of these critique the dominant local views of untouchables and provide evidence for which Appadurai advocates of Dalits improving their everyday lives (1986, 751). Yet, in his critique, Appadurai fails to provide a recognition or analysis of the daily violence that is perpetuated by dominant hegemonic forces in India, beginning with the state.

Reports like "Broken People: Caste Violence against India's 'Untouchables'," produced by Human Rights Watch reflect the struggle of Indian Dalits to have caste recognized internationally as a legitimate category of descent-based discrimination at the United Nations Conference on Racism in Durban, 2001. Indeed this was a campaign that met its greatest objection from the Indian government, which did not want these "domestic issues" debated in an international forum (see chapter 6).

Dalit civil rights activists in India continue to work to eradicate discrimination based on the Hindu caste distinctions of purity and pollution, as well as to protest the limitation of economic opportunities that relegates untouchables to occupations such as agricultural workers or urban toilet and street cleaners. Menon argues that it is largely accepted in Indian society "that Hinduism—as religion, social system or way of life—is a hierarchical, inegalitarian structure" (2006, 1). Stressing the universal presence of this hierarchy throughout South Asia, he explains further that this system of fundamental inequality has "leaked" into the other religious practices on the subcontinent including Christianity, Sikhism, Buddhism, and Islam. However, Menon believes that the theological foundation and aspirations of the South Asian practitioners of these other faiths remain egalitarian (Menon 2006, 1). A close examination of the discrepancy between egalitarian religious ideal and practice within Indian Christianity reveals that the hierarchy of Brahmanical Hinduism has been replicated within the social structure of the Tamil churches and has had significant influence on Indian Christian theology. Furthermore, while much scholarship has been produced on Dalit movements in general and within Christianity, very little of it has analyzed the challenge to these hierarchies by contemporary Dalit Christians through liturgical practice, theology, and social action.

Through hundreds of hours of interviews and analysis of musical data, I found caste to be one of the most salient socio-cultural categories of identity that Tamil Christians, particularly the middle and upper castes, use to differentiate among themselves.[11] This study shows the complexity, malleability, and changing contextual nature of caste within the Protestant Christian community, thereby supporting Appadurai's criticism that caste is not coherent, complete, stable and systematic (1986, 758). Indeed historical and contemporary evidence show that there has been both economic and cultural movement (shifts in meaning and function), particularly by Tamil Christian Nadars (middle caste) and Dalits, to subvert or escape the hierarchical weight of caste. With such clear evidence, there is little place to deny that caste identity and violence matters for Dalit Christians.[12]

Thus despite the ostensibly egalitarian underpinnings of Christianity, many Tamil Christians identify themselves by a specific caste or *jāti* (subcaste) group. Although most of the Protestant mission societies stationed in India beginning in the nineteenth century worked hard to eliminate hierarchical distinctions and prejudicial treatment among converts, maintaining caste identity was often a point of negotiation in conversion, especially for upper-caste converts.[13] Throughout the first half of the twentieth century, upper-caste Christians maintained their power in the Protestant churches through holding important clerical and lay positions eventually gaining complete control of the church hierarchy after most of the missionaries left by 1947. Dependence on the church for employment and social power further reinforced the maintenance of caste identity among upper- and middle-caste Protestants.

TAMIL CHRISTIAN CASTES

Tamil Protestant Christians recognize three major caste groups and several minor groups among them. Vellalars, Nadars, and Paṟaiyars make up the numerical majorities and have the greatest power and influence in particular congregations and dioceses.[14] The forward or upper-caste Vellalars makeup approximately ten percent of Tamil Protestants. As Hindus, they were considered Śaiva Vellalars (ritually pure and vegetarian) and thus second only in rank to Brahmins. They come from both the Tanjavur and Tirunelveli areas and were prominent landowners as well as the first Tamil Christian priests, poets, and composers in the eighteenth and nineteenth century. Until about thirty years ago they held the key positions of power in the Protestant churches, particularly in the Lutheran church.

The Nadar caste community makes up about twenty percent of Protestants, with a larger percentage in urban areas and the Southern districts of Tirunelveli and Kanyakumari from which they originally migrated. Until the nineteenth century they were considered ritually impure low-Śudra caste toddy tappers (those who create alcohol from coconut sap), although some were landowners in the Nagarcoil area cultivating palmyra trees (Hardgrave 1970:21–22 and 24). Many Shanars were converted by British missionaries in the nineteenth century, lived in segregated Christian towns or colonies, and with the assistance of caste-based community development organizations became merchants, school teachers, educational administrators, and police officers. They also changed their caste name and designation in the *varna* system from Śudra-level Shanar to Kshatriya-level Nadar (Hardgrave 1970: 71). Many migrated from the southern districts to all of the major cities in Tamil Nadu and South India. Although Nadars make up a significant population of the urban CSI churches, they also maintain distinct Anglican congregations.

The Paṟaiyars are one of three primary untouchable groups in Tamil Nadu. They make up the majority of Tamil Protestant outcastes and from sixty to seventy percent of the entire Protestant community. They have actively converted to Christianity since the earliest Catholic missions in the 1500s and the Protestant missions in the 1700s. While they are found throughout the state, Paṟaiyars are concentrated in the Northern districts (Chingelput and Arcot) where they make up at least ninety percent of village congregations.

It is very difficult to determine the exact population of particular Christian castes today since presently neither the government nor the churches maintain caste census records, and some intermarriage has occurred, particularly between upper-caste converts who converted as individuals (not as a family group) and lower castes. However, I found it a commonly held belief that approximately eighty percent of the Tamil Christian community is lower or outcaste. Of these a significant majority are outcaste and at least eighty percent are poor rural Christians.[15] A reliable source to determine a historical benchmark is Joseph Elder's 1954 masters thesis in sociology from Oberlin College entitled "Caste in the Churches of Madura." Elder found that Christians in this area (where I also did most of my fieldwork) identified with twenty-eight different caste groups. Elder divided these castes into ten hierarchical divisions based on degrees of purity and pollution and the *varna* (Vedic) social divisions of Brahmin, Kshatriya, Vaishya, Śudra, and Avarna or outcastes.[16]

For the general purpose of understanding caste divisions among Christians in the Madurai area, Elder's study supports the evidence of a large conversion of outcastes to Christianity during the early twentieth century, and the gradual movement of a significant number to urban areas. He shows that, according to the 1901 Madras state census, approximately forty-five percent of the Tamils were very low (Śudra) castes or outcastes. By the 1950s in the Madurai area, at least sixty-five percent of Christians came from these low ranks (including Nadars).[17] Twenty-four percent were outcaste Paṟaiyars or Chakkiliyars, whereas only 3.9 percent of the general population of Madurai at this time were outcastes or tribals (Elder 1954: 69).[18] We may presume that the number of outcaste Christians in the Madurai area is even higher today, since many Nadars have moved to the larger cities like Chennai and Bangalore.

Class data in Elder's study shows that 37.2 percent of the Christian population was employed as white-collar (middle-class) workers or in occupations that required post-elementary school education (i.e., teaching or ministry). Post-college educated Christian professionals made up only 3.9 percent of the community, and capitalists (or business people) included 4.5 percent. When combining caste and profession, the percentage of each of the three major castes cited above who fell in this white-collar category are very close (Vellalars at forty-five percent, Nadars at thirty-six percent, and Paṟaiyars at 42.4 percent).[19] To be a teacher or priest in the Christian community was highly valued as it had always been among Hindus, as these were the traditional occupations of Brahmins. What is most significant is that by the mid-twentieth century, Paṟaiyars who were able, attempted to raise their economic and class status through entering the professions of teaching and clergy.

Although caste and class are separate categories, these identities often interact hierarchically (Dickey 1993, 7). I found that among Christians caste and class were at times conflated, particularly in cases of outright discrimination. For example, I observed that discrimination based on potential pollution (i.e., sharing a meal with someone) was more likely to be applied to someone of a different caste who was also of a lower economic status, while job discrimination was more likely to occur between two people of equal class but different castes. Thus it appears that among Christians it was easy to use class, as an overarching reason to discriminate when the victim was poor, although there may have been an underlying caste prejudice. When two people were of equal economic and educational standing, overt caste discrimination could come into play. An anecdote will help to demonstrate this experience.

During the last four months of my research I lived outside of the Tamil Nadu Theological Seminary in a Christian neighborhood near the CSI Cathedral and several Christian educational institutions. I moved into a newly built apartment above the home of a Christian, middle-caste, upper middle-class college professor. On moving day, Mary, my Paṟaiyar Protestant cook, helped me pack and clean. Mary had been my cook when I was an Oberlin Shansi Fellow at Lady Doak College where my new landlady was a professor. One of the first things I did when I arrived in Madurai to begin my fieldwork was to hire Mary to cook for me again. I also felt very close to her and her family and visited their home often. We ate together every day in my house and I shared many of my personal concerns with Mary. Emotionally, she was more like a big sister to me and she became an important informant in my study, as she sang classical *kīrttaṉai* in a typical village vocal style using a wonderful nasal quality. She was also fully literate. She had a high school education and her father had been a village catechist. Thus she was an important source for me of the experience of village Christians.

When Mary and I arrived at the new apartment, we began to do some cleaning before lunch, which we were going to eat at her house in the nearby slum. My new landlady, however, called me and asked if I would join her for lunch. With little hesitation or thought about its implications, I told her my lunch plans and asked if Mary could also join us. My landlady replied, "There won't be enough rice." I felt shocked by this response and torn about what to do. Against my own values, I thought it would be better that I eat with my landlady so as not to insult her and not to begin our relationship off on the wrong foot. So I asked Mary if it was all right if she proceeded alone to her home to eat lunch and I would join my landlady. Of course Mary agreed and we ate separately. With hindsight, I came to understand that the lack of sufficient rice was merely an excuse for my middle-caste, upper middle-class Christian landlady to refuse to eat with an outcaste, even though they were both Protestant Christians. I felt heartbroken at having not stood firm in my convictions. Middle-class Tamils always have and prepare enough rice, especially at lunch, just in case another person comes to their home and needs to be fed. Further, we could have divided the portion available into three parts in order to share this fellowship, or we could have run to the near by shop or restaurant to buy more, but we did not. Needless to say, this was the beginning of my observations of how many Christians outside the seminary continue to practice caste and class discrimination and segregation. It was also a transformative consciousness-raising moment for me.

Another significant incident of caste discrimination among Christians was related to me by one of my translators, Dr. Peter Raj. Peter is a Pallar Christian, who at the time had just completed his Ph.D. In a discussion of Christian caste relations in Madurai, Peter shared with me under great confidence that when he was an undergraduate at the American College in Madurai he had applied to be an officer in the Student Christian Movement organization affiliated with the college. The candidates were interviewed and chosen by a committee that included several middle-caste Christian faculty members. The first question the faculty asked Peter was, "Where are you from?" Peter replied, "Pasumalai," a Christian colony just outside of Madurai that had been the mission center for the Congregationalist American Madura Mission since the mid-nineteenth century. Then they asked, "Where is your father from?" Peter again replied, "Pasumalai." To the question "Your grandfather?" the reply was the same. The interview ended with these questions and he did not get a position as an officer. Later he came to understand that the faculty members, who had all been Nadar Christians, intended to appoint students who answered Tirunelveli or Nagarcoil to these questions, the areas from which most of the middle-caste Christian Nadars migrated in the last two or three generations. Both of these anecdotes suggest ongoing, direct, and subtle forms of caste discrimination within the Protestant Christian community particularly intended to psychologically humiliate the outcaste, whether one is also economically lower class or not.

CASTE DISCRIMINATION, CONVERSION, AND DALIT CHRISTIANS

Caste plays a significant role in social practice, particularly endogamous marriage, for Tamil Christians today. My informants claimed that caste preferences affected church pastorate committee elections, admission into choirs, Student Christian Movement elections, Bishop elections, job preferences in Christian institutions, seminary selection and financial support, decisions about whether one would invite another Christian into their house for a meal, and individual and ideological choice of music.

David Mosse, who studied the relationship between Dalit movements and Dalit Catholics in Tamil Nadu, found evidence, in a 1989 survey of "Social Discrimination against Dalit Christians in Tamil Nadu" by the Catholic Dalit scholar and activist Fr. Anthonyraj, of similar practices of discrimination and exclusion against Catholic Dalits. Anthonyraj draws a picture of ongoing segregation and separation of Dalit Christians in church practices that is similar to the life experience of Dalits, both Hindu and Christian, described above. These include segregated cemetery plots, church seating, separate reception of communion, exclusion all together from membership in upper-caste congregations, exclusion from participation in festivals through refusing outcaste tax contributions, exclusion from ritual ceremonies like feet washing on Maundy Thursday, or from roles in passion plays (Anthonyraj in Mosse 2005, 7–8). Finally, as I also observed among Protestants, Mosse notes that, despite their large numerical presence within the church, Dalits were "poorly represented on church leadership and governance structures such as parish or pastoral councils, finance committees or social service societies" (2005, 7–8).

Mosse interprets the continuation of these practices to be derived "in part from a complex (especially Jesuit) mission history of 'accommodation' to Indian cultural traditions" (2005, 8). That is, accommodation and indigenization to the Indian cultural traditions of Brahminical Hinduism. These manifest both in caste segregation within churches as well as the hegemony of elite music and cultural practices as the only acceptable indigenous forms for use in the church.

If one only considers the total percentage of Christians in India (2.3–5 percent) or even the percentage in Tamil Nadu (5–6 percent) one might conclude that the great efforts of so many mission societies to convert Indians produced little more than a drop in the bucket. But once one considers that eighty percent of Indian Christians came from the outcaste and Śudra ranks, and that many of those initiated their own conversion during the mass conversion periods of the late-nineteenth and early-twentieth centuries, Christianity's significant appeal to those oppressed by the caste system becomes apparent (Webster 1992 and Manickam 1988).

Contemporary Dalit scholars as well as scholars of the history of religions argue that Christianity's appeal to outcastes was so strong that entire families, kin groups, and caste *panchayats* (village-based governing bodies) decided to convert. This was especially true between 1871 and 1901 when the Christian population in the Madras Presidency increased by ninety percent (while it increased only twenty-two percent in the general population). Oddie (1991, 153) concludes that this dramatic increase was primarily the result of the outcastes' attraction to missionaries as patrons. Outcastes perceived missionaries as a potential source of support for their growing awareness of a discourse of human rights and their sense of equality under the British legal system as well as their mounting rejection of dehumanizing treatment by the upper castes[20] (Oddie 1991, 159). Outcastes increasingly turned to missionaries as patron protectors instead of, or in addition to, upper-caste Hindu landlords who traditionally played this role, for conversion at the height of British colonialism was a means to upward mobility for the lower castes (Kent 2004). During this period, missionaries advocated for Dalits in court, provided them opportunities for education and medical care, and provided special refuge for widows, all rare possibilities in Hindu society.[21]

While there is some evidence of outcaste conversion resulting from spiritual motivation in this earlier period, many converted because of the economic and social patronage of missionaries. However, within generations after the initial conversion, spiritual faith grew within the Dalit community. This is evident in musical composition and practice. Yet one wonders why so many outcastes remained Christians when they continued to face caste discrimination within the church. Furthermore, after converting they often faced greater hostility from landlords who feared that they would opt out of their traditional Hindu caste/economic and ritual duties such as agricultural labor and drumming for upper-caste funerals (Oddie 1991, 161).

It may have been the ideology of Jesus' preferential treatment for the poor manifest in the nineteenth-century social gospel mission movement and the humane treatment by some mission societies that kept the lower-caste Christians committed (Cox 2002, 238–239). Dalit theologian M. Gnanavaram asserts, "Jesus Christ is the supreme reference for God's preferential option for the poor and the oppressed through his life, death and resurrection. This . . . becomes the hermeneutical key in liberation hermeneutics. This option, in our context in India, concretely means option for the Dalits" (Gnanavaram 2001, 59).

It is difficult to determine the early impact of mission teachings about the essential equality of all people in Christ. However, oral history and scholarship supports the assumption that this principle at the least provided a sense of hope in the gospel message, and at the most, "an ideology they could utilize in their opposition to higher-caste Hindus" (Oddie 1991, 161). Sathianathan Clarke argues, on the other hand, that the mass conversions were a means for Dalit communities to escape the centuries of caste and class oppression that defined their past in order to forge a liberated future. Conversion was an opportunity "to enter into a new and transformed symbolic framework" (1998: 43–44). That is, while outcastes may have heard and seen the Good News of Christ in the missionaries' message and actions, the indigenized Indian Christian theological and liturgical context, influenced by Brahmanical Hinduism, "was a ready made caste Hindu symbolic world" in which they could now actively participate, and that held greater value than their village religious practices (ibid., 44).

The story of Theophilus Appavoo's great grandfather's conversion in chapter 2 provides a case of rational dialogue between convert and missionary as well as an example of the mission providing economic opportunities—in this case, employment for the convert as a butcher of meat for Europeans. It also exemplifies a Paṟaiyar family that eagerly embraced "sanskritized" or religiously elite Christian culture in the early twentieth century, yet eventually engaged in a critique of the limits to the culturally libratory potential of this Christian karnatak music and upper-caste theology.

The sustainability of the social gospel movement led by missionaries, particularly into the twentieth century, faced difficulties as indigenous churches became independent from mission societies. In particular, they were criticized as not "Indian" enough by Hindu nationalists, which led to even greater Sanskritic indigenization by Indian Christian theologians. Indian Christian leaders from multiple Protestant denominations and their missionary supporters formed the independent and ecumenical Church of South India in 1947, the same year India gained its independence from Britain. In both state and church contexts, traditional social elites, particularly Vellalars, took charge of institutions and moved into positions of power. While a small number of outcaste converts had become teachers, catechists, and eventually priests by mid-century, the majority remained poor villagers. As Mosse points out, "the post-Independence consolidation of church structures, the disappearance of the 'away-from-home' radicalism of the foreign missionary, and the reassertion of patterns of rural dominance, meant that Christian conversion failed to provide rural Dalits with any sustainable route to social advancement" (2005, 3).

Mosse argues that the historical Dalit conversions and the resulting Dalit Christian communities do not represent a "sustainable social movement against caste" (2005, 5). He asserts that contemporary Catholic priests and activists found inspiration instead in the progressive ideologies of the Communist, Ambedkar, and Dravida Munnettra Kazhagam (DMK) movements. It was not until the last quarter of the twentieth century that they began to transform their ministry and engage in local caste and class movements. However, I believe we need to examine the Christian contribution to and influence on these various secular movements especially in the realm of music and culture, to get a more thorough understanding of the roots of the contemporary Dalit movement.[22]

In the Protestant camp, Sathianathan Clarke critiques the lack of focus historically on Dalit cultural resources and religion by Indian theologians. Yet while he emphasizes the importance of oral theology among Dalits today, he ignores the early roots of Dalit theology expressed through music and even through the medium of karnatak music, or Christian *kīrttaṉai.* Because of their compliance with upper-caste Hindu-influenced or sanskritized theology at the turn of the nineteenth century, the Dalits were, according to Clarke, "helpless and marginalized." He asserts that they did not understand that their embrace of sanskritized theology as a move toward participation in a venerated upper-caste symbolic world and means to class status *could be* an expression of "subaltern agency to forge a kind of transformed subjectivity" (Clarke 1998, 44).

In contrast to Mosse and Clarke, I argue here that the mass conversion of Dalits, in addition to their musical expressions, in as early as the nineteenth century were significant acts of resistance and protest that reflected a caste consciousness among outcastes and encouraged a critical attitude to challenge their social conditions.[23] The adaptation by Dalit Christians of upper-class cultural values and theology may not have been a means to change the structure of cultural hegemony, but was a significant critical response within the Dalit Christian community to their conditions in the society and the church. This response was especially evident through the outcastes' attempt to use and perfect upper-caste culture through the practice of *kīrttaṉai* and karnatak music. The best example of this is the Pulaya (outcaste) *kīrttaṉai* or lyric heard in Nagarcoil, Tamil Nadu as early as the 1880s.

> **Our Slave Work is Done, Our Slave Bonds are Gone**
>
> *CHARANAM (VERSE) NINE:*
>
> They diligently taught letters, arithmetic and hymns; made us clearly see the path to heaven, and set us therein.
>
> *PALLAVI* (REFRAIN)
>
> Our slave work is done, our slave bonds are gone, for this we shall never henceforth forsake Thee, O Jesus! (Webster 1992, 33)[24]

This *kīrttaṉai,* which Christians referred to with the genre term "lyric," was likely in karnatak or light karnatak style. Yet its author subverts the domination of the upper-caste master (landlord) with the assertion in the text that s/he has learned to read and do arithmetic as well as sing his karnatak-style music or—perhaps even superior—the missionary hymns.

As this lyric demonstrates, Dalits were not passive receptacles of missionary welfare as the common stereotype "rice Christians" (used to denote the significant numbers who converted in the early twentieth century) purports.

Paraiyar families, such as that of Rev. C. S. Daniel, consciously pursued their own conversion during the mass movements in western Tamil Nadu. Following the family's conversion, they enrolled their young boys in mission boarding school in order to attain the knowledge of letters, arithmetic, and karnatak *kīrttaṉai* that they believed would free them from their slavery (Sherinian 1998, 298–300). Mission policy and upper-caste hegemony prevented Dalits from outwardly bringing the empowering aspects of village symbolic culture to their new religion, such as the singing of Christian folk songs in the church building.[25] Thus the acts of agency by late nineteenth- and early twentieth-century Dalits can be understood as the historical sparks that ignited the Dalit Christian cultural and theological movements in Tamil Nadu, for the following reasons: 1) the conversion of outcastes was self- or community-initiated, not a result of direct missionary persuasion; 2) outcastes understood that social and spiritual liberation was available in Christianity; 3) they showed that they could adopt (and sometimes perfect) upper-caste Indian Christian culture, and many proved that they could become teachers and preachers (caste occupations formerly held only by Brahmins). To borrow Audre Lorde's metaphor, while one may not be able to dismantle the master's house with the master's tools (Lorde 1984), that is, undo caste oppression by adopting upper-caste theology and music, sometimes the first step toward gaining the self-esteem to forge an empowered subjectivity is to prove to yourself and to the master that you can use his tools as well as he. While mimesis was the first step in disrupting this cultural hegemony (Bhabha 1994), we will see the important role that the critique and reformation of music played in the eventual transformation of values and identity from sanskritized Paraiyar to Dalit Christian that occurred in the lives and work of Rev. Theophilus Appavoo and many other middle-class Dalit activists and theologians who initiated the Dalit theology movement in the 1980s.

CLASS MOBILITY AND AESTHETIC MARKERS

Class is an important sign of Dalit identity reformation that is often layered onto caste and creates ideological divisions within the community. Sara Dickey (1993, 11) has shown in her work on the reception of Tamil cinema in Madurai that values and aesthetics play as significant a role in creating opposition between classes as economic inequalities. I have argued elsewhere that among Tamil Christians, the evaluation of musical style is significantly tied to issues of class (Sherinian 1998, 2005a, and 2007). Here I build on this work to show that as a small percentage of Dalit Christians have been able to move up in class status, they have rejected village culture (and all its negative value associations with untouchability) embracing instead the elite culture of the upper castes, particularly indigenous classical or karnatak music.

Seventeenth-century Catholic missionaries borrowed upper-caste elite cultural resources and Sanskrit language to make themselves and Christianity more attractive to local elites, while eighteenth-century Tamil converts began to create their own indigenous classical Christian music. They drew on karnatak music, which developed from the eighteenth century under upper-caste non-Brahmin courtly patronage in small temple/court cities such as Tanjavore (Subramanian 2006; Peterson and Soneji 2008). Some landowning, Vellalar caste members who were part of this milieu converted to Christianity and synthesized classical musical elements such as the *kīrttaṉai* form, the raga melodic system, and tala rhythmic cycles with Christian poetry and beliefs to create Christian karnatak music. In the early twentieth century, as a few outcaste Christians were able to become middle-class teachers and professionals they too embraced this genre as an expression of their class mobility.

Some middle-class Dalits have also embraced Western Christian practices such as hymnody, but not to the same degree as other castes such as the Śudra Nadars who worked closely with British missionaries. For middle-class Dalits who are also solidly urbanite, it was often not easy to embrace folk music as a means to a liberating expression, for they had internalized the middle-class ideology that folk culture is degraded. Further, this music sonically reminds them of the degrading personal experiences of oppression in the village. A significant difference from this pattern is seen in those Dalits who studied at the Tamil Nadu Theological Seminary with Appavoo between 1985 and 2005. Many of these individuals came from English-speaking communities in the large city of Chennai (Madras Dioceses of the CSI). Appavoo's close mentorship and treatment of these students as members of his own family—what I call the practice of "one family/one shared food"—made the difference in his students' understanding and adaptation of his ideology about the potential of folk culture to liberate Dalits, therefore helping to reconfigure their internalized middle-class shame. His strategy was to undermine the Victorian propriety of middle-class Indian identity using village cultural idioms reframed as Dalit culture. As Appavoo introduced his students musically and theologically to the use of genres such as folk lament or *oppari* we saw an empowered reengagement with both Dalit culture and the feminine. Further, he challenged class division within the Dalit community using anti-caste and gendered sonic terms.

GENDER OPPRESSION AT THE CORE OF DALIT IDENTITY

Dalit activists and theologians have argued that women's experience of oppression and their liberation has to be actively addressed at the core of the Dalit movement and that women's full participation in the struggle is essential (Raja Selvi 1997; Faustina 1997). In the words of Dalit movement leader and writer of the Indian constitution Dr. B. R. Ambedkar, "The progress of the community is dependent on the progress of [its] women" (Devasahayam 1997, 28). In this study of music as Dalit theology, caste is not *the* overarching category of oppression; instead caste, class, and gender are intimately and inseparably linked. Devasahayam describes the relationship between caste and patriarchy as an "irrevocable bond" (ibid., 30). M. E. Prabhakar (1997, 79) analyzes the intersection of caste, class, and gender hierarchy in "the organizing principles" of the Hindu-Brahmanic religio-cultural traditions and social order arguing, "caste, production and reproduction have constructed a closed structure to preserve land, wealth and property, women and ritual quality within it." This preservation is dependent on control of women through matrilineal succession and maintenance of the purity of caste. That is, "The honor and respectability of men is protected and preserved through their women" (ibid., 80). Furthermore, in Brahmanical philosophy women's general nature is constructed as sinful, an ideology that is carried into Indian Christianity particularly in relation to women's menstrual "impurity" which is commonly used to justify their ineligibility for ordination.[26]

Evangeline Anderson-Rajkumar (2004) describes how the strands of casteism, sexism, and the politicization of the body are interwoven in Hinduism and need to be deconstructed in Indian understandings of Christianity. She focuses on the substance and function of blood and the Hindu ideology of blood differences as "a common experience of suffering under the ideology of purity and pollution" for both women and Dalits (2004, 103). While these beliefs of impurity are founded in Hinduism, she shows that Indian Christians upheld them as a means to control women's bodies and to alienate Dalits. She argues it is necessary to reverse this construction in order to "recover the life-giving aspect of blood" (ibid., 103).

Gender oppression takes on specific and complex qualities for Dalit women and is expressed in various ways by their own male community members along with members of the upper castes. These are usually landowners who, with the blessings of Manu, the Hindu lawgiver, can rape lower caste women (and men if it is their desire) without retribution. Ironically, Dalit women's impurity does not seem to matter when the upper-caste male chooses to transgress the caste lines through the violence of rape.[27]

PARAṬṬAI'S APPROACH TOWARD GENDER

Women's experience and their perspectives on such issues as impurity and violence were essential for Appavoo in his production of a holistic theological hermeneutics of liberation through folk music and teaching. His music reflects the transformative impact his female students, the women in his family, and female villagers with whom he worked have had on his gender consciousness. The feminist consciousness that Appavoo instilled in his male Dalit students is also significant, as is the negotiation of gender oppression that his songs facilitate with villagers.

Paraṭṭai composed both sacred and secular Dalit folk songs that address the status of women and have had significant impact on networks of women's rights and Christian activists. He was also intimately concerned with the relationship between caste, gender, and class. His songs that address these issues include "Ammāḍi Kuṭṭi Poṇṇē" (My Girl) (see appendix 2 for lyrics) and "Otta Saḍa, Reṭṭai Saḍa" (One Braid, Two Braids) (PURL 0.4). He also addresses God as both mother and father in most of his songs and his liturgy.

While Appavoo and others have integrated the construction of God as mother/feminine in songs and worship practice, Dr. Gabrielle Dietrich, professor of social analysis at the Tamil Nadu Theological Seminary, asserts "we may not gain much if we address God as father and mother as long as the division of labour between mothers and fathers in day-to-day life remains unchallenged" (1993, 3). Understanding the links between the struggles of caste, class, gender, and the organization of the family—that is, the fundamental roots of oppression in social structures—is the first step toward creating a relevant indigenous feminist theology (ibid.). Understanding the historical constructions and shifts in gender ideology in Indian Christianity is also essential to addressing the participation of women in music in the present context.

GENDERED TAMIL CHRISTIAN HISTORY

Like caste, gender has not remained a stagnant construction in Tamil Christian history. In *Converting Women: Gender and Protestant Christianity in Colonial South India*, Eliza Kent (2004) has demonstrated the changing construction of gender in the Tamil Protestant churches among the lower castes since the nineteenth century. She argues that evidence of conversion as well as the community's status and power in relation to other groups was measured by women's gender behavior. The shifts in gender construction after conversion manifested particularly in more restrictive behavior, such as less public participation in music, as converts appropriated and combined both Victorian mores of enclosure, self-restraint, and self-denial that limited women's behavior, and similar Sanskritic patterns of acceptable "upper-caste" behavior by women (Kent 2004, 18). Kent describes the new gender ideology among Tamil Christian converts as a "discourse of respectability . . . articulated in moral statements about space, mobility, self-restraint and sexuality . . . [which] tended to narrow the already restricted range of behaviors and choices deemed appropriate for women" (ibid., 4). Yet, while these new refined behaviors clearly appear more restrictive from a contemporary feminist perspective, they were adopted with the intent to undermine the caste, class, and gender ideologies that justified oppression by upper-caste landowners and elites (Kent 2004, 5).

I have shown elsewhere that among middle-class Dalits and Nadars a restrictive feminine mindset still exists today and is specifically expressed in the practice of music (Sherinian 2005b).[28] Moreover, it is against these constructions that theologians like Appavoo have attempted to reclaim the empowered feminine aspects of village goddess religion and culture to infuse new life into Christian culture and worship. Kancha Ilaiah (1994) has shown that "Dalitbahujan" or Dalit and lower-caste Śudra women have relatively more freedom and influence in their domestic spheres than many middle-class women, particularly because they often earn a significant portion of the family's daily income through agricultural work or, more recently, through construction. Among the *Saṅguḍi Paṟaiyars* (white-shell-bangle Paṟaiyars) from the Dharapuram area of western Tamil Nadu, whose traditional occupation was cottage industry style "small weavers," bride price or *pariyum* (not dowry) was the common pattern as it was necessary for the groom to replace the daughter's productive labor in the family with the price of a loom.[29] Thus if one isolates gender in the Dalit village context, it is a sign of economic worth and value among Dalits compared to upper-caste women, even though Dalit women are still traded as commodities among men. Yet when economic impoverishment and caste oppression are factored in as inextricably related to women's status, degrees of women's value seem relatively inconsequential. The significance of this analysis, however is that it points to a model/source of potential equality for women in Dalit culture and religious practices, in the construction of the *Amman* (Mother) deity in village contexts as an independent feminine force, and through the relative economic equality between the sexes particularly in the village domestic sphere. Many Dalit feminist theologians hope to incorporate this history and contextual practice into Dalit theology and contemporary Christian social practice along with economic and caste justice.

WHICH TAMIL LANGUAGE?

When I first began my study of Tamil Christian music, one of my colleagues, who is a Brahmin from Tamil Nadu, asked me "which Tamil" I intended to study. The difference clearly mattered and, as I was to discover, is a significant social identity marker for Tamil Christians, as significant as, and intricately related to caste, class, and gender. Five types of Tamil language can be distinguished in Tamil Christian music: 1) a medieval literary style of sanskritized Tamil called *manipravalam,* into which the Christian Bible was originally translated by the early 1700s and in which many Christian karnatak *kīrttaṉai* were composed; 2) *sen* [pure] Tamil or high literary Tamil cleansed of its Sanskrit elements primarily in the twentieth century and used in contemporary sung liturgies in karnatak style; 3) *koḍuntamiṟ* or standardized Tamil presently used in school textbooks and the 1994 edition of the Tamil Bible; and 4) *pēccu* or spoken Tamil which is differentiated by regional dialects. A fifth type, which I describe as Christian liturgical Tamil, contains a number of terms from Sanskrit and Tamil which have been adapted to mean something very specific in a biblical or theological context and often quite different from a non-Christian or mainstream Tamil milieu.

The Tamil language is one of the strongest markers of Tamil identity. Tamil Christians and Christian missionaries have made significant contributions to the development of Tamil literature, the historical knowledge of the language, the movements for pure de-sanskritized Tamil, as well as the independence of the Tamil people from North Indian hegemony (see Ryerson 1988).[30] De-sanskritized Tamil, and more recently, spoken Tamil, have been utilized as distinguishing characteristics for particular styles of indigenized Tamil Christian music. Furthermore, sanskritized Tamil, *sen* Tamil, and *pēccu* Tamil represent distinct social standpoints of class and caste in this study.

The foundation of my education in Dalit theology involved understanding the triple axis of oppressed identities of caste, class, and gender that village Christians faced. Furthermore, understanding the devaluation of spoken Tamil and folk music was intimately tied to these identities. Appavoo brought the intersectionality of these as well as several other identities together in a neo-Marxist analytical method that informed his music. He therefore accentuated the grounding of identity and aesthetic codes in socio-cultural context and meaning.

A HOLISTIC STRATEGY FOR LIBERATION

Appavoo applied a neo-Marxist approach to a critical analysis of Indian society as a strategy to create a Dalit theology that addresses oppression in all socio-cultural areas. He argued that "whether it is oppressive or liberating, theology is a way of life in Indian tradition. God is linked with every aspect of life" (1997: 283). Thus grounding theology in a system that takes into account all aspects of society and culture is essential to interpret both the Bible and the socio-cultural context of the oppressed.

Appavoo's holistic social analysis is based on the Marxist categories of economics, politics, social structure and ideology. To this he has adds the post-Marxist categories of psychology, the environment, gender, and spirituality, calling this system EPSI-PEGS. Appavoo interrogates the subject (theological, musical, social) on all of the EPSI-PEGS levels to get a more complete picture of its social context and meaning, and to prescribe the means to address issues of oppression. For example, he locates the root of Dalits' *ideological* oppression in the dominant concepts of pollution and fate (karma). He quotes Antony Raj: "The worst crime caste has committed against us, has been to teach us to hate and pity ourselves."[31] He then applies this analysis to hegemonic constructions of Dalit religion and communication systems.

> All aspects of our culture are pejoratively spoken of. Our deities are called devils, demons, and evil spirits. Our communication paradigms are called unscientific, primitive, and illogical. These oppressions have made Dalits internalize the oppressor's culture (Appavoo 1993, 33).

Appavoo understood that ideological oppression falls under the rubric of culture whereas *psychological* oppression, another of his core concerns, focuses on the individual and self-destructive "shame consciousness." Psychological oppression attacks self-respect and psyche to the extent that it prevents involvement in protest or political movements (particularly by middle-class Dalits) because it "would be a declaration of . . . lowly origin" (ibid.). In these ways, both ideological and psychological oppression have alienated Dalit Christians from the transformative elements in folk music and village religious culture. Thus although some Dalits have improved their social class status, they have still have internalized caste and gender oppression.

Appavoo's EPSI-PEGS analysis is intended as a means to achieve transformation of the whole person: body, mind, and spirit (Appavoo 1993, 4–5). He argues that the body is liberated through economic and political justice as well as gender equality; the body is liberated through access to knowledge, a healthy psyche, and a belief in human potential; and the spirit is liberated through the attainment of religious equality in the eyes of God, the church, and society. Only after applying this holistic analysis to the hierarchy of musical styles and value in Tamil society did Appavoo come to his belief that folk music style was the means to transmit and internalize his theology for Dalit Christians. Understanding the historical process of the indigenization of Christianity through Tamil music will provide an overarching view of the historical and cultural context in which Appavoo came to create his music as Dalit theology.

BOOK ORGANIZATION

The structure of this book reflects the process of production, transmission, reception, and re-creation that frames my understanding of Appavoo's Dalit Christian folk music as dialogical (re)creative praxis. Part 1: Production, is a macro view of the Tamil Dalit Christian context, the context of music production at the Tamil Nadu Theological Seminary, the historical shifts in music production and use within this community, and the relationship of community structure to hierarchies of musical value. I also address theoretical issues of indigenization, musical value, and advocacy in ethnomusicology. This is followed by a micro view of the changes in Christian musical use by five generations of Appavoo's family. This family biography reflects the larger patterns of music use in the Christian community and demonstrates instances of individual negotiation. This is followed by an analysis of the process that led to Appavoo's consciousness that Tamil folklore/music could be the means and medium for an effective Dalit liberation theology. I show the contradictions and contestations between social identity, theology, and musical style choice as well as the history of musical indigenization that led to Appavoo's use of folk music. Through entwined narratives of Appavoo's family and the Protestant Christian community searching for a liberating Christian musical identity, I frame Appavoo as an actor creating and transmitting transformative music in dialogue with the struggling Dalit community. Part 1 culminates with a description and analysis of the three core tenets of Appavoo's musico-theology: *oru olai,* universal family, and a strategy of reversal. I provide the analytical and interpretive means to show how folk music can serve as an oral system of transmission and re-creation in its ability to provide cultural identification for and a means to theological (re)-creation by those who use it. Finally I engage in a comparative analysis with African American and feminist theology focusing on the theme of community, in part to elucidate the promise and limitations of Appavoo's theology (Townes 1995; Jones 2000).

Part 2: Transmission and Reception, is an anthropological analysis of the transmission of Appavoo's music through his relationships with students and the musical processes I observed through fieldwork at the Tamil Nadu Theological Seminary. There are three areas that I observed and participated in during my fourteen months of research in 1993–94: the production and transmission of songs, the experiment of *oru olai* (communal cooking and eating), and the transformation of community members into Dalit activists. This study proposes that the key to successful transformation lies in human relationships founded on a common commitment to the use of music, social action, and a theological conviction based on equality and sharing. I look more closely at the dynamics of "relationships founded in transformative music and food," as a model for both the fieldwork process and my ethnomusicological biography of Appavoo's life in the Tamil Dalit community.

Part 2 continues with an examination of the complex and sometimes "messy" reception of Appavoo's music by villagers to gauge the assertion that Dalit folk music *can* be a spark of transformative change for the oppressed. When one steps into the ethnomusicological complexity of reception on the ground one sometimes encounters a disjuncture between ideology and practice, intent and effect. My particular focus is the incomplete transmission of Appavoo's goals of the intersectionality of class, caste, and gender liberation. I conclude that the stronger the foundation of the church and secular Dalit movement that creates a context for reflection on these issues and action related to "secular" needs (such as water, electricity, caste problems) at the particular site, the more likely I was to find shifts in consciousness and thus the "successful" transmission of the integrated message of liberation in Appavoo's songs. This analysis provides early signs of the dynamics and potential for reception as Dalit activists internationalize the Dalit Liberation Movement. Specifically, I focus on how Dalits have used critical performance on the global stage to create a unified, universalist platform for identification and affinity.

1

HOW CAN THE SUBALTERN SPEAK?

Musical Style, Value, and the Historical Process of (Re)indigenization of Tamil Christian Music

People perform social identity through music. Thus musical value can encode both powerful and degraded social value. Over the last four hundred years, through multiple waves of culture contact and local internal negotiations, Tamil Christians have (re)indigenized Christian music, making conscious style changes in performance practice to encode shifts of power and social identity. Understanding the historical indigenization process of Tamil Christian music provides insight into how and why Theophilus Appavoo turned to folk music as his chosen medium for liberating theological production. It clarifies how he re-indigenized Christianity to the cultural resources of Dalit Christians in a context in which the devaluation of folk music paralleled the devaluation of outcaste people. The indigenization of Christian music in the Tamil context provides a model of the subaltern, re-sounding empowerment through theology in the church and greater society. Re-indigenization of Christianity to a Dalit theological identity through music is subaltern practice and praxis.

The first step to theorize subaltern musical practice is to recognize that the people who use and produce this music see it as meaningful. Tuning our ears to Dalit music forces the discipline of ethnomusicology to reconsider the valuation and power dynamics of our previous engagements with South Asian musical objects, subjects, and ideology. It necessitates deconstructing the illusion of value-free scholarship we have brought to the field in the last forty years through the almost singular study of classical practices in South Asia. Further, it provides an opportunity for greater dialogical engagement with those who create and use Dalit music in order to more fully understand its meaning in their lives. Deconstruction of disciplinary musical value in ethnomusicology through this case study of music as Dalit theology can provide theoretical perspectives for advocacy anthropology, specifically for Christian contexts, to understand the cultural process of production of theology. For the comparative field of history of religions this case shows the importance of musical processes in the study of the indigenization of religion. Finally, for Dalit historical studies it contributes a unique model of the ethnomusicological biography of a Dalit Christian culture broker.

MUSICAL INDIGENIZATION AMONG TAMIL CHRISTIANS

Christian indigenization occurs when individuals and communities interact under specific conditions of power to consciously choose and combine cultural characteristics that reflect, embody, and transmit the meaning of a Christian theological message through the cultural identity of the people who use it. Successful indigenization leads to a locally meaningful socio-spiritual experience for the indigenizers, or members of the identifying culture.[1] The significance of the indigenization of Christian music as a potentially transformative tool lies in the correlation between the identity of the music and the cultural identity of those for whom Christianity is to change. Furthermore, when the tools of communication are in an accessible local medium the music is infused with indigenous meaning and power.

Tamil Christians have produced an array of indigenous Christian musics in various local styles and forms that reflect the social diversity of their community. That is, musical style references local Tamil social identities, especially of class, caste, and language. These identities in turn reference a dynamic of cultural exchange between various Christian mission societies and sub-communities of Tamil Protestants, as well as specific actors brokering the process of culture contact. Margaret Kartomi (1981, 232–233) defines "the complete cycle of positive musical processes set in motion by culture contact" as "musical transculturation," but argues this term should be applied to "the processes of intercultural contact, not to the varying types of results" (ibid., 233–234). The application of Kartomi's terminology in the Tamil Christian context leads to an analytical distinction between musical *transculturation*, and the variety of local manifestation of Tamil Christian musical *indigenization*, or results that have

Table 1. Indigenization Taxonomy: Categories of Indigenization and Musical Style

Cultural Value	Inculcation of the Hegemonic	Translation Indianization	Assimilation	Christianization of Indian form	Acculturation
Power dynamic of indigenization	**European music** use reflects a larger movement towards Westernization and identification with Britain and the US as well as the values of capitalism, materialism, 19th century evangelical Christianity and upward class and caste mobility. Missionaries saw it as civilizing. Can be critiqued as imposition of or conscription in hegemonic colonial or local elite values.	**Western music** aesthetic is valued and maintained, but at the cost of destroying the meaning and poetic structure of Tamil language. Missionary still has the power of liturgical imposition and valuation. It continues to be used as the dominant genre in urban liturgies today. Rarely used in rural churches partly because most lack finances for an organ.	**Mission determines which indigenous style and aesthetic is appropriate** and suitable for Indian Christian worship and that the Sanskritized classical should be transmitted to villagers. With no theory or performance practice, classical style becomes folk simplified. Continued influence of harmony creates fusion.	**Influence of post-independence Dravidian movement which was anti-Sanskrit, but elite led.** Combines classical music and language considered to be elite indigenous Tamil. It is used to create songs and liturgies. Elite (non-Brahmin) and middle-class educated Indians make these decisions without direct missionary influence.	**Indians questioning both Western and elite Indian values reclaim and revive pre-Christian and village indigenous traditions.** Combine with and parallel early Christian Middle Eastern social context. Construction of Christianity not mainstream Western but returning to perceived original ideology of Jesus as liberationist.
Styles given value by Western mission and local elites	**Western Music and English Language** ***kīrttaṉai* when transmitted in karnatak style to lower-caste villagers inculcates them in local elite musical values.**	**Western Music with Tamil Language: pāmālai, *ñanappāttu and choruses. kīrttaṉai* when domesticated into folk style and village performance context, maintaining Sanskritized Tamil.**	**Classical Indian Music (Karnatak) and Language (Sanskritized Tamil) 3 *kīrttaṉai* types:** 1) Classical concert style 2) Western/karnatak fusion, organ dominated becomes light style. 3) Folk vocal quality and unaccompanied in villages. Retention of raga.	**Classical Indian Music and High literary Tamil Language:** *Tamil isai vaṟipāḍu* **Songs by V.P.K. Sundaram** ***mel isai* by D. Francis and Thomas Thangaraj**	

Styles considered inappropriate or degraded by local elites and mission.			**Light Music & Simple Written Tamil** Performance practice is a fusion of Western pop harmony and simple Indian ragas. A mix of E/W instruments. Inappropriate for church service until recently because associated with secular (love) music of film culture. TTS light music songs included here because high literary Tamil may be more accepted by educated and liberal people. Pentecostals use light music in their services, which represents new indirect missionary influence. But, power to decide aesthetic is held by heavily Western-influenced Indians.	**Folk Music & Spoken Tamil** Indigenous theological content from perspective of mass of Dalit and lower-caste Indian Christians who live in villages. Challenges cultural evaluation by elite caste and classes as degraded and inappropriate for church service because associated with the lower castes and classes.

occurred from the sixteenth century to the present. Both the process and results involve extra-musical dynamics of power and value. Distinguishing between the two in analysis serves to differentiate colonial and elite domination from local indigenizing agency.

Thus the ongoing process of the indigenization of Christian music over time in a single context can be continually transformative. T. M. Scruggs uses the term *re-indigenization* to describe a process of "renovation from within of an already established religion . . . [or] . . . a reinterpretation of important tenets within a single religion"[2] (Scruggs 2005, 94). In the Tamil Christian context described below, liturgy is re-indigenized from karnatak classical music into the moods, language, and musical elements of Tamil folk music. In a few cases, we also observe that single texts of karnatak-style *kīrttaṉai* have been recomposed to Western, folk, or light music styles to articulate changes in the culture, social identity, and religious needs of Tamil Christians (Sherinian 2007a).

Steven Kaplan's (1995, 10–23) model of Christian indigenization in Africa has been the most influential in ethnomusicology (see Scruggs 2005; Barz 2005; and Sherinian 2005). To understand the spectrum of indigenized Tamil Christian musics that have been created from 1606 to the present in Tamil Nadu I draw on Kaplan's framework. This indigenization taxonomy goes beyond missionary initiation to delineate the balance of power within the social strata of the Tamil Christian community and between missionaries and Tamils as manifest through musical values. This results in a layered taxonomy that applies the indigenization categories to song styles and genres on the horizontal axis, yet considers the indigenization process that determines the cultural value of particular styles and those groups of people with whom the style is identified on the vertical axis. The vertical axis contains two divisions which refer specifically to the use of the particular style of indigenized music in a liturgical setting: styles given value by Western mission and local elites, labeled "appropriate," and styles considered "inappropriate" or degraded by missionaries or local elites. The description of various types of Tamil Christian music below references this taxonomy to elucidate the power dynamics of indigenization and re-indigenization within the social and historical context of Tamil Christian music use (Table 1).

Tamil Christian music can be divided into three major groups: (1) English-language hymns and choruses using Western instrumentation; (2) *pāmālai* and *ñanappāttu* (Western hymns translated into Tamil while retaining the English or German tunes and meters); and (3) indigenous Christian music sung in some form of Tamil and using musical styles, poetical forms, and instrumentation that express culturally contextualized Christian hermeneutics. These indigenous styles include karnatak (classical or light classical), folk, and light music, the latter fusing Western pop with Indian folk and light classical music elements (Innasi 1994). Musical "style" as it references the category of indigenous Tamil Christian musics refers to an idiom (unit) of characteristic recognizable musical elements (or codes), performance procedures, and contextual purpose, use, and meaning.[3] The musical codes are structural, functional, and rhetorical and cannot be separated from their contextual use and meaning, all of which are affected by the dynamic processes of performance and historical change.[4] As a particular combination of clothing and physical behavior are commonly thought of as markers of social identity, I understand the combination of particular musical elements like rhythmic patterns, vocal timbre, instruments, and performance procedures (the structure of a style) as a musical package that is identified aurally as a musical style. As a functional device, musical style has a communicative presence, and as rhetoric it garners associations with particular subjects or ideas: here caste, class, denomination, and location. Thus the cultural arrangement of sound codes in this context I refer to as musical style identity.[5]

Next I elucidate how the three musical categories described above and the various musical style identities within them have been indigenized and re-indigenized by Tamil Christians in the historical process of their social identity (re)formation. I analyze the type of indigenization that each musical style references within the indigenization taxonomy and the meanings each may simultaneously have for different subsections of the Tamil Christian community.

INDIGENIZED CHRISTIAN STYLES

English-language hymns and choruses using Western instrumentation are indigenized in Tamil Nadu only insofar as they have been adopted as symbols of class mobility, modernization, and Westernization by lower-caste Christians, particularly people of the Nadar caste who were converted by British Anglicans. The process of inculcation of Tamil Christians to the English language, British manners, and musical systems by the Anglican missionaries beginning in the 1820s eventually led to strong affinity for the organ and four-part harmony by many lower-caste Christians. Through adaptation of and association with this hegemonic colonial culture, lower-caste Nadars in particular hoped to gain status vis-à-vis local upper-caste/class elites (Brahmins and Vellalars).[6] While identification with colonial powers is used to express agency against local elites (to claim equal or higher status with them), the category "inculcation in the hegemonic" implies a necessary complicity by lower castes both with missionary beliefs that their village goddess religion was "heathen," and with the upper-caste ideology that village culture (folk music) was "degraded" (see Sherinian 2002). Yet, as stated above, this can also be an assertion of upward class mobility.

Complicity with the devaluation of folk culture and its association with socially and economically marginalized peoples have been the greatest challenge for Dalit liberation theology. Christians who have successfully raised their class status through identification with Westernized and local elite forms such as English hymns, and have attempted therefore to shed the stigma of untouchability, have been particularly resistant to the use of folk style, spoken language, or village cultural symbols in liturgy because of the negative associations of these cultural markers with their past identity. While those in this category make up the privileged top ten percent of the Dalit Christian population, the majority of Dalits still live in villages and have minimal ability to understand the English of these hymns.

Indigenization as translation is best represented in this context by the genres *pāmālai* and *ñanappāttu*. These are Western hymns translated in the early eighteenth century into sanskritized Tamil that retained their English or German tunes and meters. They reflect the restatement of Christian doctrine and terminology in local, although elite Brahmanical and literary Tamil, languages, and idioms (Kaplan 1995, 13–14). The Western music aesthetic of these genres is valued and maintained at the cost of rendering incomprehensible the meaning and poetic structure of the Tamil language. Furthermore, until the 1950s the missionaries retained the power to impose the use of, and imbue greater value upon, these genres over any other in formal Church liturgies and hymnals. In most urban Protestant church services today one will still commonly find that three of the four pieces sung are *pāmālai*. The continuing importance of these genres in urban churches can be attributed to the nostalgic association with the missionaries and Western values that these genres carry for middle-class Christians. As described above, alliance with these missionaries provided many outcaste Tamils opportunities for social and economic mobility (education and jobs) as well as the development of their self-esteem.

The introduction of indigenous karnatak music from Vaishnavite or Shaivite (Brahmanical Hindu sects) devotional practice into Tamil Christian worship illustrates the assimilation of local features to make the message of the Christian ritual more comprehensible and acceptable, particularly for upper-caste Indians (Kaplan 1995, 15–16). Catholic and Protestant missions from 1600 to the early 1900s encouraged the use of the karnatak style and genres in the sanskritized language of the caste/class elites as the favored local aesthetic for indigenous composition by converts. Approximately ten percent of the Protestant community is upper caste (mostly Vellalars or non-Brahmin landowners) who identify directly with this elite culture. As early as 1714 Christian *kīrttaṉai* by Vellalar converts were first printed under the supervision of German Lutherans to be used in their mission in Tranquebar and eventually Tanjore (Lehmann 1956). In 1853 the American Congregational missionary Edward Webb published a collection of over one hundred *kīrttaṉai* by the Vellalar Christian composer Vedanayakam Sastriar (1774–1864). After learning the *kīrttaṉai* directly from Sastriar in 1852, Webb and his Tamil catechists then disseminated the new Tamil hymnal to lower-caste villagers who lacked previous direct exposure to this elite cultural genre. Thus while the Christian *kīrttaṉai* represents "indigenization as assimilation" for upper-caste Christians, for the lower castes it was the means to inculcation in hegemonic Hindu cultural values. The transmission of Christian *kīrttaṉai* to non-elite people led by the missionaries reflects the conscription of these villagers into the musical values of the classical genres, particularly the previously inaccessible system of raga (melodic mode) and the linguistic system of *manipravalam,* sanskritized literary Tamil. Furthermore, today the meaning of the sanskritized Tamil texts of the *kīrttaṉai* is even less intelligible to most Tamils whose vernacular was purged of earlier Aryan influences through the Dravidian movement beginning in the 1940s.

Use of *kīrttaṉai* by the lower castes represents a two-tiered historical process of the indigenization (and re-indigenization) of Christianity.[7] My analysis here considers the complexity of local social stratification that is essential to understanding the dynamics of indigenization of Christian music in south India. By the mid-twentieth century, *kīrttaṉai* experienced a process of musical "indigenization as translation" in some villages where lower castes began to accompany the words of *kīrttaṉai* with the stylistic idioms of folk melodies in similar modes, call and response forms, and rhythms. In urban areas *kīrttaṉai* went through a similar process of translation influenced by interest in Western harmony. Over the last 150 years the tunes for Christian *kīrttaṉai* have primarily been transmitted orally within communities that have had little access to classical karnatak music grammar. As a result, many *kīrttaṉai* have become simplified using only a skeleton of the original raga (lacking complex ornamentation or *gamaka*), and through using the Western tempered tuning system (major and minor modes) particularly with the introduction of harmonic accompaniment on the organ since the 1940s. Through such a "folk music strategy" of simplification in urban churches, ironically the *kīrttaṉai* have gradually been Westernized using simple diachronic melodies instead of karnatak modes.

One could argue that this is musical re-indigenization for accessibility. On the other hand the sanskritized lyrics of the *kīrttaṉai* have remained codified and unchangeable for most Tamil Christians.[8] Thus Christian *kīrttaṉai* lyrics contain very little theological meaning to most Tamils beyond their symbolic (superior) value as a "Christian karnatak tradition."

After Indian independence and the formation of the Church of South India in 1947, Tamil theologians and composers began to combine elements of *Tamiḻ Icai* (Tamil karnatak music) and desanskritized or *sen* (pure literary) Tamil to create socially conscious indigenized songs and liturgies.[9] Many of these theologians (of the generation just before Appavoo) were influenced by the anti-caste, anti-Brahmin, and anti-Hindi ideology of the Dravidian movement that attempted to raise the status of Tamil culture and literary language. This resulted in a body of sung liturgies called *Tamiḻ Icai Vaḻi Pāḍu* (TIVP) performed sitting on the ground in call-and-response *bhajan* style accompanied by *tabla* drumming typical of participatory devotional contexts throughout India. These liturgies exemplify "indigenization as Christianization" of native rites and practices, as the musical form and linguistic style remains Tamil while the content has become Christian (Kaplan 1995: 16–17). While the TIVP supplants Shaivite and Vaishnavite theological influences and sanskritized Tamil with a more socially progressive Christian theology, the use of literary Tamil and karnatak music style continues to preference the values and cultural experiences of socially and culturally elite Tamil Christians. The message of *sen* Tamil liturgies is the first step in the construction of a socially conscious subaltern Tamil Christian theology, while the linguistic and musical medium of transmission remains hegemonic.

Music for TIVP was what Appavoo's teachers had composed before and during his time as a seminary student in the 1970s and early 1980s. Exposure to the TIVP provided him a model for a sung liturgy that included a progressive theology, indigenous musical forms, and non-sanskritized Tamil. The next step in the progression toward a liberating musico-theology for Dalits was for Appavoo to create a TIVP liturgy in folk (*girāmiya*) music style and spoken Tamil language with theological perspectives that reflected village Dalit identity and hermeneutics. During the same period however, Tamil Evangelical composers used Christian light music to attract Christians and new converts, distancing the oppressed from a socially liberating message.

Tamil Christian Evangelists have used "light" or popular music since the 1950s to attract gospel convention audiences of all classes and castes and to communicate a message of "prosperity theology," which many liberation theologians derogatorily refer to as *āsīrvādam* or blessing theology. *Āsīrvādam* theology promises that the reward for faith will be economic prosperity. However, this highly individualistic and capitalist ideology does not address the limitations to opportunity imposed on oppressed people, and offers no means for addressing worldly problems embedded in hierarchical social structures.

Light Christian music can be understood as a form of Christianization of the music style of film (Bollywood/popular). Furthermore, it is a translation of Western (capitalist) prosperity theology through integration with familiar native features of popular music. Appavoo critiqued light music as pacifying (referring to it as "whiskey theology") because, while it uses the language of, and is directed toward, the masses of Christians and non-Christians, he believes it lacks the means to enable cultural or social empowerment.[10] Instead of encouraging action against oppressive social structures, he believes prosperity theology transmitted through light music style (played on expensive electronic keyboards) supports the status quo middle-class values that continue to remain far from the potential reach of the target audience.[11] Evangelists use lively rhythms and simple, catchy Western tunes to attract converts and those Christians who have not been "saved." They ask people to demonstrate their faith by donating significant sums of money in return for prayers to save them from their earthly problems and the assurance of a place in heaven after they die.[12]

In contrast, Appavoo campaigned against prosperity theology because it reinforces lower-caste people's internalized beliefs that they are impure from sins committed in previous lives (a reinforcement of the ideology of karma), and that they can only hope for a better existence when they go to heaven after they die. Many light music lyrics are taken directly from the Bible without adding indigenous poetic interpretation. Recomposition of these lyrics, the indigenizing folk strategy that Appavoo argued is necessary for the production of a liberating theology, therefore, is not encouraged by the Evangelists who produce light music. Thus although one might argue that light music style is a form of popular (i.e., mass) urban folk music, the biblical (fundamentalist) lyrics of Christian light music discourage transformative indigenization.

APPAVOO'S *GIRĀMIYA ISAI VAṞIPĀḌU* AND FOLK MUSIC STYLE

Appavoo's *Girāmiya Isai Vaṟipāḍu* or *Village Music Liturgy* exemplifies "acculturated" indigenized Christian music (PURL 1.1) (see Appendix 1). Acculturated Christianity assumes a positive attitude toward native institutions, not an attitude of Western cultural superiority. Moreover it involves a desire to preserve or even restore indigenous forms (Kaplan 1995, 19–20). Appavoo and others who have created Christian folk music question the inculcation of both Western and elite Indian values in Christian music. The former is rejected for its colonial condescension, which negates the power of village practices, and the latter is rejected for the indigenous principles of social hierarchy, which it reinforces. In the Dalit theology songs and liturgies, village cultural and religious elements are reclaimed, using their powerful local meanings and cultural perspectives to (re)interpret the Bible in ways often considered culturally parallel to early Christian or Jewish social contexts.

Girāmiya pāṭṭu (village song), *nāṭṭupuṛa isai* (music of the countryside), or the more vernacular and sometimes derogatory *nāṭṭupāṭṭu* (country song) or *nāṭṭupuṛapāṭalkal* (countryside-songs) all translate as "folk music" in English.[13] *Makkal isai,* which translates as "people's music," is another political term for "folk music" used by Dalit-oriented arts festivals since the early 1990s to redress its devaluation by upper castes and the elite. The language of folk music is inevitably *pēccu,* or spoken Tamil. Many upper castes (and those moving into the middle class) still consider this vernacular dialect of villagers, as well as folk music in general as *cōccai* (degraded), while Dalit Christian activists claim it carries the cultural life blood of villagers and is a primary means to create a liberating theology in folk music by the oppressed.[14] Tamil folklorists who are peers of Appavoo, such as Vijayalakshmi Navaneethakrishnan, Pushpavanam Kuppusamy, and K. A. Gunasakaran, have inspired new interest in folk music since the 1990s through books and recordings, and thus have improved its status at least among academics.[15]

A notable example of the negative discourse of folk music value to which Tamil folklorists responded is in the musicological writings of Professor P. Sambamurthy (1984, 105 and 114). Sambamurthy calls folk songs "rustic and uncouth," while he values classical music as "essentially intellectual music" of the upper castes and classes (1984, 140–141). Furthermore he declares, "the function of folk music is primarily entertainment . . . [and] the themes of folk songs are never serious . . . [while] classical music has a purpose higher than mere entertainment" (1984, 141). Some of Sambamurthy's musicological writing may be considered outdated. Yet I have observed in interactions with classical musicians and in the media many examples of folk music considered *cōccai,* or degraded. There is a famous scene from the 1986 Tamil film *Sindhu Bhairavi* directed by K. Balachandar in which JKB, a Brahmin karnatak singer, is challenged to sing karnatak songs in Tamil. His response is that all Tamil songs are folk songs, using the term *nāṭṭupāṭṭu* (country song) and that singing these would turn his concert stage into a sewer. These constructions reflect the parallel devaluation of untouchables as people and their culture as worthless and degraded that is still a common sentiment. The *Girāmiya Isai Vaṟipāḍu* (*Village Music Liturgy*) by Appavoo, the Dalit Arts Festival at the Tamil Nadu Theological Seminary in Madurai, as well as the People's Arts Festival in Tanjore (1993) are excellent examples of music and forums in which evidence for the degraded value of folk music was articulated and challenged, and its value reconstructed by folklorists and theologians (Sherinian 1998).

While some types of folk music are used today by all castes and classes of people in urban and rural spaces (e.g., lullaby), use of these genres are primarily a village cultural practice maintained by lower castes as a means to support their labor, to communicate news, to celebrate festivals, to practice religion, and to protest oppressive conditions of untouchability, poverty, and gender discrimination.[16] Furthermore, Tamil folk music is characterized by subgenres that are associated with rural and agricultural contexts or functional activities, such as driving a bullock cart, drawing water, or rowing a boat. Each genre in turn has a distinct set of mnemonic syllables and corresponding tune-types as well as a rhythmic and dance patterns by which it is identified.

The process of folk music reclamation in the Tamil Protestant and Catholic churches began in the 1980s. As its main Protestant proponent, Appavoo advocated that village folk culture is both an appropriate vehicle for Tamil Christian ritual and the necessary *musical* vehicle for the transmission of Dalit liberation theology. He determined through an extensive study of Tamil folk music that it is precisely colonial and upper-caste elite devaluation that gives folk music its liberating protest function (Appavoo 1986). Thus he intended to encode the values of protest and the transformation of oppression into Christian worship through folk music songs and liturgies.

Appavoo defined folk music as music that is economically and socially accessible, drawn on community skills, participatory, potentially re-creative, treated as un-authored, and orally learned. It uses spoken language and a musical syntax with which poor and oppressed people are conversant (Appavoo 1986, 8–22). Appavoo also asserted that the meaning of folklore generally "lies not in creation but in dissemination" (ibid., 13). Thus folk music and its meaning were not defined by stylistic (formal) musical elements, but by its purposeful use to reconstruct a positive identity, to protest oppression, and to communicate experience and feeling relevant to the life of the community (ibid.).

In his own creation of folk songs and liturgy, Appavoo drew upon rural musical moods, functional genres, instruments, stylistic devices, agricultural metaphors, and elements of Dalit religions and politics. With these he sought to create a participatory liturgical context where the message was primarily communicated through the heart and emotions. This was signified musically through mood and rhythm, which he believed were the key structural elements to the transformative power of folk music. The lyrics helped create musical moods through painting nostalgic rural images and through emotional shock engendered by using "unrefined" language.[17] Appavoo also consciously drew on the linguistic accents of spoken Tamil to create dramatic emotional responses in performance. He employed folk melodies that include distinguishable mnemonic syllables (such as *tā na na nē*) that marked particular genres including boat song, *oyilāṭṭam, kummi, cintu,* and lullaby. The common folk rhythms, which further enlivened his songs, were often set to a layered six beat pattern with cross-rhythmic tension of duple against triple meter. Folk instruments heard in performance of Appavoo's music include drums such as the paṟai (frame drum of the untouchables), the rubbed hour glass-shaped *uṟumi* associated with the village goddess, the *tabla,* as well as the double reed *nāgasvaram* and the bamboo flute. The timbres of instruments and voices used in his recordings were typically raspy or nasal, intending to evoke and even venerate the ambiance of the rural context, particularly Dalit worship and festival.

In Tamil village religions, empowerment occurs through rituals in which folk drumming invokes or induces possession by the deity allowing emotions to be directed into action. The primary musical means for this invocation are not Sanskrit slokas, but *paṟai* drumming.[18] Yet the *paṟai,* and the drummers who play it, are more commonly thought of by upper castes as polluting because the drum is a necessary ritual accompaniment for upper-caste funerals.[19] Appavoo's most radical act of musical indigenization has been to bring the *paṟai* and its driving syncopated rhythms into a Christian liturgy that reclaims it as valuable and respectable, rather than associating it with pollution and degradation. Through reclaiming the content and form of folk culture, Appavoo similarly constructs Dalit status to non-polluting and esteemed; he therefore intends to empower the oppressed within Indian Christianity to resist the values of the local elite and missionaries who consider their music and its message an unworthy form of Christian music and theology.

Appavoo's primary contribution to Christian indigenized music in India is to question the use of elite karnatak and Western music especially by rural Dalits as a means of transmission of theology. Appavoo consciously set his songs within folk music genres and styles, challenging the four-hundred-year church practice of only using Western style hymns and indigenous classical karnatak music. He therefore reinforced a positive sense of identity and engaged the people in the reevaluation of their cultural resources as liberating not only through lyrics, but also through sound and mood. Appavoo spearheaded the reform of the practices of the Church of South India rural congregations, providing them an "acculturated" repertoire and model for the transformative use of Tamil folk music. The possibility for Appavoo's music to be "incorporated" (Kaplan's final category of indigenization) from the local Tamil context to a more cosmopolitan or global level is being realized through this work and through the distribution of his recordings, especially through Anglican Church and Dalit networks (Kaplan 1995, 23).

THE SUBALTERN SING: MUSICAL RE(INDIGENIZATION) AS SUBALTERN PRACTICE

For three hundred years (from 1706), powerful members of the Tamil Protestant churches have constructed Tamil Christian identity and theology through the practice of karnatak and Western music. The introduction of folk music by theologians and a folk music process of re-creation of Christian music and theology by Dalit villagers since the 1980s have created what Sherry Ortner describes as "slippages in reproduction, the erosions of long standing patterns, . . . moments of disorder and of outright resistance"; that is, "subaltern practice theory" as the reformation of socio-musical identity (Ortner 1996, 17). Theology as sound creates a new subaltern musical voice in the Church, in Indian politics, and as examples of people's agency to be understood in relation to other literature on social movements and alternative media (Rodriguez 2003). To subaltern studies Dalit Christian folk music redirects and *answers* the question, "Can the subaltern speak?" (Spivak 1988). I argue one must listen for the resistive expression of Dalits not as speech, but as song. The Subaltern Sing! And they re-sound their empowerment through Dalit musico-theology.

Through musico-theological (re)indigenization that engages the sonic power of the divine through folk drums, rhythms, and sounded communication idioms, Dalits are changing Christianity, Christian theology, and their identity as a form of resistance to systems of caste, class, and gender that oppress them. They create, re-create, and practice Dalit theology as the action of singing. Folk music is an "alternative practice . . . that becomes the basis of resistance and transformation" (Ortner 1996, 18). While the secular academic term for this in anthropology, as demonstrated by Sherry Ortner (1996) and James Scott (1985, 1990), is "resistance studies," the alternative practice of theology through Tamil folk music in the context of Tamil Dalit Christian lives and praxis is the remaking or transformation of identity called by Appavoo and other theologians *viḍutalai* (liberation). Indeed the Dalit Chrisitian context blurs the secular/sacred distinction, as religious discourse is simultaneously socio-political, economic, and gendered.

The Tamil Christian context as described above reveals two different strategies of cultural resistance in the process of lower castes and Dalits indigenizing Christian music. The reclamation of local folk aesthetics challenges both foreign and local cultural hegemony. The use of European hymnody or elite karnatak music by lower castes and outcastes, on the other hand, challenges local caste/class exclusion while simultaneously representing an uncritical embrace of hegemonic culture. Both strategies associate the hierarchical value of musical style with the hierarchical value/ranking of the social categories of caste and class. Embracing the hegemonic in the form of Western hymns or *kīrttaṉai* has involved rejection of village identity because of its association with or reminder of the experience of oppression in the village. However, the strategy of reclaiming folk culture is potentially holistically transformative in a psycho-spiritual sense for Tamil Dalits, because it is based on empowered identification with village cultural idioms.

Identification with village culture and the reevaluation of these cultural resources as worthy of use in Christian liturgy was a significant transformation in the life and career of Appavoo. It was also a necessary transformation for me as an ethnomusicologist of South Asian music. Indeed reflection on this choice helped me recognize the need for a structural reevaluation of our choice of subjects in research and teaching within the discipline of South Asian ethnomusicology as well as our contribution to the replication of local hierarchies of musical value and thus the devaluation of marginalized South Asian peoples.

MUSICAL STYLE, ADVOCACY, AND DISCIPLINARY HEGEMONIES

The practice and performance of Dalit Christian Tamil folk music is engaged theological praxis. I found its study to require that I be fully aware of my role as an activist ethnomusicologist. That is, engagement with marginalized and politicized South Asian musics has the potential to change the way we do ethnomusicology in South Asia (and other locales dominated by elite court practices). It forces us to deconstruct local hegemonies of musical style and our discipline's contributions to the construction and perpetuation of them, and thus a self-reflexive consciousness of our choices and stance. It promotes a holistic method of social analysis that includes caste, gender, and class along with religion, ideology, and economics. It shifts the object of study from the formal analysis of virtuosity to transformative musical meaning/action and makes possible primary field relationships that are dialogic and less hierarchical. Finally, understanding music *from* the margins, such as Dalit Christian folk music, inverts South Asian ethnomusicology's perspective of the hegemonic system that places a hierarchy on the valuation of musical style and musicians. This approach gives us the opportunity to understand the importance of sound—indeed the politics of sound—and what the sound of Dalit Christian music accomplishes; why musical sound is not only an accompaniment to, or vehicle of theology, but is *itself* theology.

This theoretical and methodological stance of engaged musical scholarship I describe above evolved from my study of Dalit Christian folk music as theology. Its primary benefit for ethnomusicology is to reverse our obsession with the classical practices and upper-caste performers/*gharānās* (lineage). It also generally contributes theoretical perspectives on advocacy and dialogical production of theology through music to the anthropology of Christianity.

Ethnomusicologists housed within the Western music academy since the founding of the discipline in the 1950s have always played a role as musical advocates for whatever non-Western tradition in which we specialized, but the degree to which we were and continue to be conscious of the subjects of our advocacy—the agents, sound, and ideology—deserves further analysis. Many South Asian ethnomusicologists are the students of the great masters (or agents) of karnatak and Hindustani music. As a mrdangamist (barrel drummer), I include myself in this category along with many others who first studied classical music and then chose to work with more marginalized musics in South Asia.[20] We are taught to give all reverence and support to our guru. And often, we learn explicitly or otherwise not to ask questions about the social meaning of the music, for to ask questions *is to question* the guru. Our task is to learn by observing and replicating: By extension, we replicate the status quo of musical caste and class hierarchies. We all to often write about the historical and contemporary greatness of our gurus and their *gharānās* (lineages); we sponsor their world concert tours, and use their musical virtuosity as case studies for musical analysis in our research and in the classroom. Though often ambiguous and unconscious, these practices *advocate* for the elite culture brokers of South Asian society. Ambiguity is present when scholars of South Asia fail to consciously articulate the privileged cultural position of these musical and human subjects or neglect to interrogate our own role in propagating the local values associated with these musics. To avoid fully contextualizing a music culture, or to overlook the critical analysis of the identities of the people—of caste, class, religion, and gender—who transmit the music in South Asia, is highly political as it replicates South Asian hierarchies of musical value.

In South Asian ethnomusicology, the dominance of classical court and concert musics—Hindustani and karnatak—over popular and folk, parallels the hierarchy of social value in South Asia in general. In order to understand the dynamics and politics of advocacy in South Asian ethnomusicology we must confront the local socio-political identity of musical style as well as the contribution of colonial dynamics and scholarship to the construction or reification of these hierarchies. This study shows how the hierarchy of musical value in Tamil society is reconstructed and reproduced among Tamil Christians. Folk music scholar Jesudasan Rajasekaran described the devaluation of folk music and musicians that he observed in the 1970s when he first began to study folk music.

> The status of folk music and also musicians was very very low. They are not even considered as people that they [the middle classes and castes] can move [with], they can go about and talk to, or have any interaction with. Because they are only used for occasions where they are required, that's all. If it's a *karagam* dancer, Mariamman festival comes, okay, we pick them up. That is all. The rest of the time these people, they are just on the fringe. They are not very much part of the society, not like the karnatak musicians or any other light musicians or temple musician. That's another hierarchy that is in this thing. Just like in this community the caste hierarchy is so strong, even [in] the music they have a hierarchy (J. Rajasekaran, interview, February 15, 2009).

Rajasekaran's analysis highlights the local homology between the hierarchy of class and caste in South India and the hierarchy of value placed on genres and styles of music and dance, with folk music at the very bottom below classical karnatak, temple, and light or popular film style musics. Another vignette that reinforces this way of thinking and visceral feelings associated with this value came from a Brahmin karnatak mrdangam artist who said that simply hearing folk music made him feel sick to his stomach (pers. comm., Aaron Paige). Thus the untouchablity and unseeability of the people who play various genres of folk music is extended to the "unhearability" of their instruments and sound of their music. To address advocacy from the perspective of marginalized South Asian music and its cultural politics and to therefore bring the music of lower-caste, outcaste, poor, tribal, and rural people to the center of academic inquiry, we first need to deconstruct the subject of South Asian ethnomusicology to scrutinize how scholars have perpetuated this local hierarchical representation through research and teaching choices.

At the 2004, fifty-forth annual Midwest Conference on Asian Affairs in Minneapolis, the Japanese historian and Pulitzer Prize winner John Dower explained that modernization theory, which gained popularity in the 1960s and 1970s, immersed the academy in the idea of value-free scholarship. He argued that indeed modernization theory was not value free, but highly political and ideological. He explained that this apolitical, disengaged approach to academics was rooted in the 1950s McCarthy era and resulted in the purging of scholars from the Asia field and the subjection of those who were practicing "politically engaged" modernization theory to surveillance and great fear. In his book *Threatening Anthroplogy* (2004), David Price discusses the effect of these sanitization politics on anthropology arguing that during the Red Scare and Cold War of the 1940s and 50s, social activism by academics, particularly for racial justice, received the greatest scrutiny from government agencies like the FBI.

Did such scrutiny and the ideology of value-free scholarship affect the choice of subjects pursued by South Asian ethnomusicologists? During the Cold War period when the U.S. was politically aligned with Pakistan, and India with the USSR, studying Indian classical music and culture was certainly the least threatening choice a cultural anthropologist or ethnomusicolgist could make.[21] However, there were also "domestic" reasons for this choice, founded in struggles over musical value within the music academy where most ethnomusicologists were situated from the 1950s to 1980s. The singular focus on classical musics in South Asian teaching and concert presentation throughout most of the mid-twentieth century had as much to do with an interdisciplinary need to compete for acceptance with the eurocentrism of music departments and the ("value-free") ideology of virtuosity and perfection of the Western musical canon. The study of elite court and temple cultures of Asia more easily validated and facilitated the study of non-Western music during the early years of the discipline (1950s). The history of this eurocentric hegemony, however, can be traced back further than the 1950s to Western colonialism and racism of the nineteenth century, as well as orientalism of the eighteenth century.

Focus on "the great cultures" of Asia by ethnomusicologists is an example of the continuation of Indology and eighteenth-century orientalism, which Thomas Trautmann (1997) calls "Indomania." One of Trautmann's primary examples is the work of Sir William Jones who studied Sanskrit, arguing that it was a civilized European protolanguage, in some respects surpassing Latin and Greek in the development of its grammatical system (1997, 39). Furthermore, in 1784 Jones wrote what I call, drawing on Trautmann, Indic ethnomusicology's foundational "Brahmin-musical-mania" texts with his treatises on Indian classical music entitled *On the Musical Modes of the Hindus*. Indeed the use of the elite karnatak genre of *kīrttaṉai* as the basis for an indigenous hymnody among both high and low caste Indian Christian converts by 1714 reflects the practice of "Indomania" by the German Lutheran missionaries Bartholomew Ziegenbalg and later C. F. Schwartz. It was not until the height of imperial colonialism in the mid-nineteenth century that the eurocentric brand of orientalism Trautmann calls "Indophobia" was perpetuated by British missionaries, leading to the promotion among converts of four-part harmonic Western hymnody in English over the modal and odd-meter based indigenous genre of *kīrttaṉai.*

Among scholars, however, Indomania for elite practices continued in the nineteenth century. Augustus Willard wrote one of the earliest English treatises on North Indian Music in 1834. This was followed in 1914 by A. H. Fox Strangways's early prototype of comparative musicology, "The Music of Hindustan," and the work of two twentieth-century Protestant missionaries: Emmons White, who published *Appreciating India's Music* in 1957 (and who worked closely with contemporary karnatak theorist Sambamurthy, and in the 1970s with karnatak ethnomusicologist John Higgins), and H. A. Popley who drew on the earlier work of Fox Strangways and Captain Day to write *The Music of India* in 1921. These missionary and civil servant scholars wrote detailed analyses of the classical raga systems as well as some transcriptions of folk and Christian songs. Many of them conducted field studies that resulted in detailed transcriptions in Western notation and first-hand experience through personal study with a teacher. While these works contain subtle traces of ethnocentrism, rationalistic comparison, generalization, paternalism, and the impetus to scientifically codify structural procedures and performance practice, they generally wrote with a great respect and appreciation for karnatak and Hindustani systems. The obsession (particularly by Fox Strangways and Popley) with scientifically and practically "knowing" the classical systems, particularly of pure Indian melody, however, strongly affected the later focus and methods of South Asian ethnomusicology primarily on musical structure and theory without regard for cultural meaning and context.

In his analysis of the contemporary Hindu fundamentalist movement, historian Thomas Bloom Hanson argues, "the Brahmanical high scriptural tradition . . . [was] regarded as the classical center of the Aryan-Vedic high civilization" (1999: 65). The scholarship of early proto-ethnomusicologists like Sir William Jones, supported by the Indomania of scholarly communities such as the Asiatic Society of Bengal formed in 1784 and the larger colonial project, produced and structured the concept of a single classical Hinduism organized around a central high culture and extending across the subcontinent as a "great tradition." It also extended this value hierarchy to the structuring and production of Western knowledge of elite Indian musics. The "great traditions" of karnatak and Hindustani musics with their shared "ancient" theoretical foundations in Sanskrit texts like the *Natayasastra* (100 AD) were understood to stretch across the continent and empires of South Asia as a single musical system that only diverged in the thirteenth century with Islamic influence. Hanson argues that "the construction of a great tradition allowed . . . intellectuals to classify and order the vast mélange of cultural differences in the subcontinent into systems of core and periphery exclusion and inclusion" (1999, 66). This has led to our categorization of both Hinduism and musical practices as either "great" or "little" traditions (Babiracki 1991: 70).[22] The imagination of India as mystical, spiritual, ahistorical, and ancient was reinforced by exclusive focus on the "true" modern Indian cultures of the classical practices, those "oceans of knowledge" within music that no single person can ever fully comprehend (Hansen 1999, 67).

The promotion of a unified high classical culture by scholars further supports the politics of Hindu fundamentalist organizations like the Bharatiya Janta Party (Chatterjee 1993). Until the 1990s we uncritically and unconsciously continued to employ orientalist Indomania in ethnomusicology. Like Jones, who advocated for Sanskrit, we found ourselves promoting the complexity of raga and tala in an effort to compete with musicologists' claims for the superior complexity of Western harmony. We rarely analyzed let alone critiqued the influence of elite Brahmins as our teachers, translators, and field assistants on our constructions, valuations, and representations of Indian music. It was not until Matthew Allen's work (1998, 23) on the history of karnatak music and nationalism that an ethnomusicologist deconstructed the "classicist discourse" of karnatak and Hindustani practices as a strategy by elite culture brokers to compete in a comparative cultural framework established by Western colonial powers. We have also uncritically supported the postcolonial state's singular patronage of classical arts institutions leading to the codification of classical arts as national arts at the exclusion of regional and folk practices. Only since 2007 has there been a significant shift in the Indian state's support of anything but classical arts. For the last five years the middle-caste progressive Tamil Nadu state government has promoted the Chennai Sangamam festival, which brings over 1,500 folk musicians to Chennai during Poṅgal (harvest) season for a week of performances throughout the city.

In the present Indian political context, does it matter what our musical object is and how we represent it in South Asian ethnomusicology? Does it matter if we focus solely on elite culture, or if we strive for more nuanced understandings of caste divisions and diversity within elite culture, or if we examine the dynamics of more marginalized practices? With Hindu nationalists dominating Indian politics, the media controlled by the upper castes, and restrictions made on the ability for foreigners to study or lecture in India on subjects of Indian politics, human rights, communalism, Dalits, and religious minorities, it clearly does matter to the Indian government (Overland 2001). If we limit our construction of Indian music to uncritically examining the classical traditions and avoid embracing marginalized South Asian musics and their cultural politics, I believe we are supporting, if not fueling, the Hindu fundamentalist political and cultural constructions of an authentic, ancient, continuous, and fundamentally unified Indian culture.

Engaging with and advocating for marginalized South Asian musics provides a new mode of understanding, seeing, and strategizing. African American feminist bell hooks (1984, ii) calls this "an oppositional world view," seeing the margin and the center from both the outside in and inside out. To recognize the marginalized, or to tune in and listen to the marginalized, hooks advocates a holistic, yet oppositional perspective that maintains a critical awareness of the separation between margin and center and the cultural forces that create this separation, while the practitioners at the margins are empowered to acknowledge that they are "a necessary, vital part of the whole" (ibid.). In this book, the methods of value inversion, neo-Marxist social analysis, dialogical field process, and self-reflexivity provide the foundation for an oppositional ethnomusicological method that places marginalized musics and people at the center, while ultimately providing a more complete picture of Indian society.

Here I propose that we recognize three levels of advocacy within South Asian ethnomusicology: the musical sound; the ideology transmitted through the music; and the agents who produce, use and propagate the music. Marginalized sound is music in motion created and re-created in performance to facilitate the socio-political and religious needs of transformation for the oppressed. Appavoo's *Kuttam Uṇaruṟadu* or "Repentance or Realizing of Sin" from his *Village Music Liturgy* exemplifies a way to advocate for village musical sound, the ideology of Dalit theology, and the Dalits who have produced, transmitted, and reproduced it (see Appendix 1, Transcription 2).

***Kuttam Uṇaruṟadu* (Repentance [or Realizing] of Sin)**
From *Girāmiya Isai Vaṟipāḍu* (*Village Music Liturgy*)
Composed by James Theophilus Appavoo
Translated by J. T. Appavoo and Zoe Sherinian

LEAD: SOLO CALL
Kañjikillāma sanam kāñji keḍakkumpōdu
When people suffer without even simple *kañji* food
Añji añji saṉam aḍimaiyāyirukkumbōdu
When people become slaves of fear,
Anīdiya eduttu pēsāma ellārum ēttukiṭṭirukkumpōdu
When all accept these injustices without protesting,
Ēllārumdānē sāmi kuttavāli, kuttavāli
God, is not everyone a sinner?

Appavoo composed the "Kuttam Uṇaruṟadu" or "Repentance of Sin" as a result of his personal experience coming into a Dalit class consciousness through understanding the Christian theological implications of inequitable distribution of food resources in modern Indian society. The hermeneutical biblical analysis that inspired this consciousness came from a poor teenage Dalit girl he encountered in his rural theological education class. The class had discussed a passage of the Gospel of St. John, "We are one body in Christ. We are in one food." Appavoo asked the class, "What do you think of this passage? Are we in one body, one food?" The young Dalit girl replied, "Annan [big brother], what did you have for breakfast?" Appavoo replied, "I had *iddlies*" (a middle-class breakfast of steamed rice cakes and vegetarian curry). The girl said, "Oh, I had *kañji* [rice gruel] and my neighbor had nothing" (Appavoo 1992). Appavoo recounted that, "this helped me realize that we were not all *living* in one food."[23] For Appavoo, this analysis from the perspective of the most marginalized in Indian society, a poor Dalit girl, "questioned all the theological arguments over issues such as transubstantiation, consubstantiation, and memorable feast" (ibid.), and signified to him that everyone does not actually partake in *one* food. The girl's contextual interpretation brought the scripture alive and became the basis of Appavoo's central theological tenet of *oru olai* (literally "one pot"), or the practice of communal eating and shared labor as a daily Eucharistic lifestyle to address hunger in Dalit communities and to unify the oppressed.

As the Dalit girl taught Appavoo the "Dalit" meaning of the Eucharist, he in turn transmitted these ideas as Dalit theology in song to his seminary students through dialogue and the experience of *oru olai* or communal eating at the Tamil Nadu Theological Seminary (PURL 1.2). Appavoo consciously chose specific folk genres to encode the meaning of sections of his liturgy. For example, in the "Kuttam Uṇaruṟadu," by incorporating the characteristic wailing gestures of *oppāri* lament that fall into dissonance from the tonal center to the seventh pitch of the scale on the final phrase of the solo call ("ellarumdānē sāmi kuttāvāli kuttāvali," (God, is not everyone a sinner) he mourns the structural sins of society and aurally validates the worth of folk music considered degraded or *cōccai* (see Appendix 1, Transcription 2, Fig. 1) (PURL 1.3). This is also seen in the Confessional section of the "Repentance of Sin" as a social and musical gesture of antagonizing [*virōdicci*] God and other people, literally falling away from the light (see Appendix 1, Transcription 2, Fig. 2). The folk lament genre *oppāri* is commonly associated with untouchables who wail and play paṟai for funerals. Their performance and its association with the pollution of death typically reinscribes their untouchability (Green 1997; Clark-Deces 2005). By recontextualizing *oppāri* in Christian liturgy, Appavoo reverses that untouchablity and unhearability of *oppāri.* He reinforces a positive empowered sense of identity and engages the people in the reevaluation of their cultural resources as liberating not only through lyrics, but through sound and mood.

The Rev. Benjamin Inbaraj, a former student of Appavoo's who worked closely with Dalit congregations and social action groups in the Maduranda-gam area of Tamil Nadu, believes that through the "Kuttam Uṇaruṟadu" or "Repentance of Sin," Appavoo radicalized the concept of sin for Dalits. Appavoo, he believes, has shifted from a theology of personal sin as found in the Church of South India (CSI) liturgy to a corporate sense of responsibility for the social sins of injustice, particularly hunger, slavery, and fear. The normal CSI practice of the confession of sin instills a sense of guilt in congregants: both Christian guilt from sins such as lying or stealing, as well as Hindu karmic guilt, or sins inherited from ones previous life and thus the reason one is born an outcaste. Inbaraj recounted that, "before going to the altar for communion they [the congregation members] want to set right their relationship with God." He believes that Appavoo's "Repentance of Sin," however, radically alters this approach and relationship.[24]

> So whenever a Dalit congregation uses this part of this liturgy they don't feel guilty because it is all their experience. *Kañjikillama* starving is their experience. Being afraid, *anji,* of the slave master, that is their experience. Being beaten up, being the subjects of injustice, that is their experience. So they are not guilty. So actually this liturgy should be sung by the upper-class Christians [more] than these [Dalit] people. And when these people [Dalits] sing this liturgy they are concientized [sic] [that] . . . starving is not God's will. Being afraid of [the] slave master, of other human beings is not God's will. And accepting the unjust social system is not God's will. [But] standing up *for* justice *is* God's will.[25]

Inbaraj regularly uses Appavoo's *Village Music Liturgy* to orally transmit these radical new concepts of sin back to Dalit villagers. The result for him has been much more active participation by, and dialogue with village people. Through song and sermon, dialogue has also led to the people's reflection upon their own experiences of oppression and their sharing of examples with him in the middle of the sermon. This process raised intellectual questions as well as answers that the congregation pondered through biblical reflection as well as musical creation. Furthermore, he recalled that the mournful quality of *oppāri* lament used in the "Repentance of Sin" moved Inbaraj's village congregation to great emotion, facilitating the cathartic release of the guilt that society assigns to their condition (Inbaraj ibid.) The transmission of Appavoo's "Repentance of Sin" demonstrates that the dialogic communication process in this network of Dalit liberation is one of multidirectional exchange. The songs and sermons of the transmitters are constantly informed, altered, and reformed by the folk music transmission process.

Thus to advocate for Dalit folk musical sound is to understand the wailing cries of *oppāri:* lower-caste women protesting against their oppression through lament. To advocate for the study of marginalized instruments like the untouchable paṟai is to understand its contested meaning. In Tamil village religions, empowerment occurs through transphysical rituals of possession by the *sāmi* (deity). The village deity possessing or "coming upon" a villager allows even the weakest members of the community to gain power both physically and emotionally. Emotions such as anger and fear are not pacified but rather channeled into action. The key to inducing this possession is the power of paṟai drumming. Upper castes believe the paṟai has the power to transmit the soul to the next incarnation, yet they consider the drum, and the drummers who play it as polluting. Dalits, on the other hand, consider the transformative power of the goddess to reside in the sound of the paṟai, which induces the power to walk over fire without being scorched, to take on the goddess, and to speak her truths (PURL 1.4). It is the materiality of the instrument and the musicians, which are the problem in the physical world of the upper castes. The sound of the paṟai is transformative for both, while only in death for the upper castes. For Dalits, the sound keeps them alive in the struggle of the here and now.

The motion of marginalized music is felt in the ebb and flow of call and response among people working together rowing boats, pulling buckets of water, and thrashing the fields. Semiotic empowerment also comes from hearing folk tunes and folk drums in the Tamil films of Ilaiyaraja, a music director who was born a village Dalit Christian: the sound moves from the margin to a powerful position at the center of popular media. Is this sound actually physically marginalized? It comes out of the *cēri*—the distant ghettos of wasteland on the edge of the village where untouchables are forced to live. But its soundscape crosses the geographic boundaries of pollution and purity. As lament it crosses the walls of the house to be heard as protest by all (Greene 1997). However, this music will remain marginal inside and outside of India unless we take it seriously as meaningful and powerful, not as mere "entertainment" as constructed by Indian musicologist P. Sambamurthy (1984, 141).

If we reverse the hegemonic value of South Asian musical elements, we hear the layered rhythm of drums made of cow skin, not the melody of raga sung or played on the *vina* by Brahmins (Wolf 2000, 910). These upper castes traditionally played chordophones instead of drums (made of skin) or aerophones (that involve saliva) because they wanted to avoid contact with polluting elements (Allen 2000, 389). Reversing the value of Indian sound object leads us to focus on the purpose and function of the sound in society, not on the formal structure, *lakshanas,* or mathematics of the music. This also dialogically engages the ethnographer and culture-bearers more fully on the meaning of the music as a subject being created.

The second level of advocacy is for the values communicated through the music, either through the musical style or through the text. An ethnographer might personally distance him/herself from a carrier of the message while advocating for the general message or style of the music. However, when one has a critical relationship and shared values with one's primary field consultants, one can disagree with aspects of their ideology or method while agreeing with their message.

To analyze the power and impact of Dalit theology constructed and transmitted through Tamil folk music, I study the dialogical nature of its transmission process as re-creative praxis. Christopher Small (1987 and 1998) has argued that music making, or "musicking," is a shared activity of sound production that is meaningful and useful to people. Music is not an object, but an active creative process grounded in social contexts and human relationships. Meaning stems from the activity of music making in human relationships. My research shows that the meaning of the creation of theology through folk music for Dalits of India is part of the process of *viḍutalai* or "liberation" from being dehumanized, starved, raped, and untouched. Gunadayalan, a Dalit activist with the Social Action Centre in Madarandagam, who studied rural theology with Appavoo and then transmitted his songs to villagers while working on social justice projects, claimed that:

> Paraṭṭai's [Appavoo's] music is the people's music, particularly the oppressed Dalits' music of liberation. This self-employment scheme has divided [the women] into two groups, if they start singing Paraṭṭai's songs together they will have commitment and unity. This is the way for unity. We can say clearly that no ward member or president or any other person can deliver the people. There is no chance for that, we have to make them think about and find solutions for their own problems. They have to initiate the struggle. Then only it will be successful. We have so many successful examples in our village. We have handled many problems and solved them.[26]

Gunadayalan's assertion of the power of Appavoo's music to unify people and lead them to reflection and action to solve their own problems resonates with Black theologian James H. Cone's description of the transformative power of the praxis of liberation theology. "Liberation is not a theoretical proposition to be debated in a philosophy or theology seminar. It is a historical reality born in the struggle for freedom in which the oppressed recognize that they were not created to be seized, bartered, deeded, and auctioned" (Cone 1997, 142). The liberative theological meaning folk music has for Dalit Christians directly mirrors that which ethnomusicologist Mellonee Burnim has asserted is contained in the meaning and impact of spirituals for enslaved African Americans: "to perform the spiritual . . . was to wage systematic warfare on the institution that imposed the chains of bondage. To sing the spiritual was *to be free*" (emphasis mine) (2006, 61). To use folk music style, metaphors, and resources from rural culture, and to assert a positive Dalit identity in Christian songs challenges the church to reform its liturgy to the culture of rural Dalits, and, as James Cone asserts, take "the oppressed and their liberation as the theological point of departure" for reflection and action (Cone 1997, 46).

Meaning in this study is not *only* located in the transformative experience of the individual, but in the transformation of relationships through the sharing of music. I apply Tim Rice's dialogical ethnographic method by foregrounding the process of interaction, particularly among Appavoo, his students, and me that has led to the creation of this ethnography (Rice 1994). I do not want to mask this crucial process of dialogue through my authoritative voice. My intentions stem from lessons learned from Appavoo, particularly his motivation to downplay the "authorship" of "his own" songs by putting them in the re-creative style of folk music. Furthermore, by using the pen name of Paraṭṭai, he encourages a sense of "messing with" or making trouble with the status quo. The production of this ethnography as an ethnomusicological biography is also meant to foreground Appavoo as a specific speaking and acting subject, not a generalized Tamil Dalit (Rice 1994, 11). I use the method of locating statements of belief through referencing specific individuals. Thus I emphasize the authorial presence of my field colleagues through the integration into my text of their direct speech (Qureshi 2007, 4). By "acknowledging the dialogic character of the research . . . [I] open up the possibility of a polyphony of perspectives that displays culture 'as an open-ended dialogue of subculture, of insiders and outsiders, of diverse factions'" (Clifford 1988, 46, in Rice 1994, 12).

Finally, engagement with politically conscious music, such as folk and marginalized music, can be facilitated through a dialogic relationship between researcher and subject. I have found this requires the researcher to place his or her political cards face up on the table. Tim Rice (1997, 118) proposes that ethnomusicologists move beyond the structuralist notion of analogies and homologies in the analysis of musical performance in culture to focus instead on questions of "cultural relationships between the selves who make music in culture." Fieldwork conducted in dialogue with marginalized communities must be founded upon the shared values of social justice and the understanding of music's role as a tool for change. If trust is established through action and behavior—not proof of musical ability—a mutual flow of ideas and shared music making in a transcultural relationship is possible.

The third element of advocacy in music is ideology. To study advocacy and marginalization from the perspective of Dalit folk music, understanding the political nature of the message is paramount. Most folk genres (even lullabies) can be political and resistive—a means to voice oppressed experience, identity, and protest. If an ethnographer is engaged with marginal musics, it is more than likely that s/he will advocate for the oppressed people who use and produce the music along with its sound and message. On the other hand, one may not be completely enamored with the sound or form of the music, yet still support the message bearer. Or perhaps the aesthetics of the music are meant to repel and repulse. The music is understood as a vehicle for communicating a message about and from the people with whom the ethnographer has a close relationship. Though the message may not always be one with which the ethnographer is in complete agreement, s/he may be convinced that the people need her "academic" or personal support. However, in most cases in order for the ethnographer to consciously advocate for the people, it is likely that s/he has taken as her own, or is convinced of the intrinsic cultural or even moral worth of the needs and message of the people. The music then is an essential means of communicating these people's ideas.

Analyzing all South Asian musics holistically or interrogating the repertoire of a community from multiple perspectives can provide a much more complete picture of the cultural contexts of South Asia. Further, inverting the hegemonic Indian and Western musical values systems that privilege individual art to instead focus on elements that are important to the cultural purpose of protest and social change for a group, will not only allow us to fully understand the meaning of marginalized musics, but also the musics of elite culture, like Christian *kīrttaṉai*. Finally, if we embrace music and musicians in a dialogic relationship of musical exchange and flow, as people making transcultural music in motion, the status quo of oppression cannot be maintained. Or as Appavoo's song says, "The powerful peoples' position will be destroyed. Trembling they will fall."

A close look at the musical history of Appavoo's family in the next chapter outlines Appavoo's transformation from a proponent of Christian classical karnatak music to Paraṭṭai, the most vocal advocate for folk music as the most effective music to facilitate Christian liberation for Dalits. This ethnomusicological biography locates the specific dynamics of musical change in the individual and family unit to demonstrate that Appavoo is not simply a reflection of his community, but a catalytic node in an interactive network of change and resistance.

2

SHARING THE MEAL

A Dalit Family's Dialogue with the History of Tamil Christian Music, 1850–1994

***Virundu Parimāṟuṟadu* (Meal Sharing Song)**
From *Girāmiya Isai Vaṟipāḍu* (*Village Music Liturgy*)
Composed by J. T. Appavoo
Translated by J. T. Appavoo and Zoe Sherinian

LEAD SPOKEN:
Vāṅga ellām tayārā irukkudu
Come, everything is ready!
CHORUS
Tiruvirundu viḍutalai tandiḍum arumarundu
Holy meal, the rare medicine that liberates

1. *Mantiramāyamilla mariccavarai neṉacci*
It is not magic or illusion, not the feast given
Tandiḍum virundumala sāttira saḍaṅgumalla
in remembrance of the dead, or the rituals of *sastirams*

2. *Sondamuyaṟciyālē vandiḍum mīṭpumalla*
This meal is not redemption that comes through our own efforts
Tandiramāha deva aruḷpeṟum lañcamalla
It is not a bribe given to attain the divine grace deceptively

3. *Aṉṉakki mēlaṟaiyil āsānām iyēsu sāmi*
It is the best medicine, ground that day
Aṉaittunōy pōkkiḍavē araiccu vacca nalmarundu
in the upper room by the great native doctor, Jesus the Divine One

4. *Nittiya vāṟvu tarum uttama kāyakalpam*
It is the medicine, *kāyakalpam*, that gives everlasting life
Pattiyam pahai maṟandu pahundu tiṉṉum sōṟu tāṉē
Its diet requires forgetting enmity, sharing rice, and eating together

In the "Virundu Parimāṟuṟadu" (literally, "meal exchange"), or "Meal Sharing Song," section of the *Girāmiya Isai Vaṟipāḍu*, Appavoo creates a contemplative atmosphere of tension and release for a total sensory experience of the Eucharist. He emphasizes three themes: (1) the transformative concept of grace given freely; (2) the possibility of unity and thus liberation through *oru olai* (Eucharistic lifestyle of communal eating and shared labor), with the condition that people give up their differences, such as caste; and (3) positive identity reassertion for Dalits through associating Jesus with traditional village roles like the native doctor or *āsān*.

The lyrics of the "Meal Sharing Song" delineate what this meal *is* and what it *is not* using metaphors of promise. The chorus—*tiruvirundu viḍutalai tandiḍ um arumarundu* ("holy meal, the rare medicine that liberates")—defines the meal as bringing liberation, *viḍutalai.* Appavoo's specific emphasis here, which reflects a shared ideology with most Dalit theologians, is liberation from the illusions of Brahmanical Hinduisms and the false promises of Evangelical Christianity. These are two important themes that reflect the shifting trajectory of Appavoo's musical life, which I describe in a subject-centered ethnomusicological biography below focusing on how Appavoo (re)creates himself and his music through dialogue with the Dalit and Christian communities (Rice 2003, 157). To practice this meal regularly is to be in Christ. Earlier in the "Lord's Prayer" of Appavoo's liturgy, he says God's name means "let there be liberation." Jesus and God are liberators, and participation in the holy meal facilities liberation. Thus to be in Christ is to be in *oru olai* or deep communion with others through shared labor and food.

The chorus of the "Meal Sharing Song" is set to a triple meter and its melodic range covers only a minor third in step-wise motion facilitating easy transmission (PURL 2.1). The eighth-note plus quarter-note figure that happens twice in the first and fifth measure with chant-like melodic movement of a minor second give the chorus a pondering rocking movement (see Appendix 1, Transcription 3, Fig. 1). The rhythmically contrasting phrase *viḍutalai tandiḍum* ("liberation given") then stands out, articulated by four driving eighth notes and three quarter notes in measures 3 and 4 (see Appendix 1, Transcription 3, Fig. 2). This two-part melodic phrase in the chorus contains the folk melodic pattern of tension and release (also used in laments). The first half of the phrase (mm. 1–2), which slides down to the minor seventh (D) from the tonic (E) seems to ask the question (see Appendix 1, Transcription 3, Fig. 3), "The holy meal (*tiruvirundu*), what is it?" While the second half (mm. 3–6) resolves on the tonic in measure 6 with the answer, "freedom giving medicine" (*viḍutalai tandiḍum arumarundu*) (see Appendix 1, Transcription 3, Fig. 4).

The first two verses reject any association of *oru olai* with the magic of Brahmanical religion, or the blessings promised by fundamentalist Evangelical Christianity. In verse 1 the phrases *mantiramāya* ("magic or illusion") and the "rituals of *sastirams*" reference Brahmanical traditions and Brahmanical Christian theology and practices. Rejecting Brahmanical "magic," Appavoo believes the real magic is sharing.

Verse 2 emphasizes that people cannot control or manipulate their redemption or God's grace through giving bribes (*lañcam*). This is a critique of *āsīrvādam* (blessing) theology as practiced by Evangelists in India who encourage people to give money in exchange for an agent of the mission to pray for them. This assessment stems from a belief among progressive Protestants that the grace of God is freely given and available to all. Rev. Benjamin Inbaraj, one of Appavoo's students, challenged the common understanding among the middle and upper castes that the oppressed condition of Dalits is due to their own sin and that they need to seek God's redemptive grace. He argued that Dalits are living active embodiments of God's grace in their forgiveness and loyalty toward others—even toward those who oppress them.[1] While on the one hand this perspective constructs village Dalits as passive and naïve, Inbaraj supported his ideas with a story that reflects a culture of generosity, the desire for mutual sharing in a non-monetary economy, and the ultimate dependency of the elite in society on the lower castes for labor and the products of the earth.

> Job was a Dalit Christian of the Arcot Lutheran Church in Bethanayakankuppam village near Neyveli. He was working for a dominant cast landlord. Though he was a landless laborer, he took a piece of land beside his landlord's farm for tenant farming. He had sown seeds and the plants had grown up to the level to need transplanting. As there was no well or motor pump for irrigation, he was dependent on the *kanmai* channel for irrigation. But during the crucial phase of transplantation the *kanmai* went dry and the expected monsoon played truant. Desperate, he approached his landlord for water from his well, but he was refused by the landlord. Dejected, he came home and prayed to the Lord to take care of his crop. That night there was a heavy downpour. The next morning he was in his small farm plucking the *naṭṭu* from the seedbeds and tying them in bundles of five hundred. Then he saw his landlord walking on the *warappu* to and fro. When Job asked what brought the landlord there, he said, "I do not know how to ask you, I am ashamed. I need some *naṭṭu* for [my] field. I will buy some from you if you can give them to me." Job replied saying that if he [the landlord] needs *naṭṭu* he will tie them and keep them on the bank, as much as he wants,

> so that his workers can come and take them, "but do not talk about the money!"[2]

Inbaraj interpreted the living grace in Job's life saying, "I think here Job *is* God's Grace in person. I would not agree [with the idea] that Dalits still need to know God's grace." In other words, their generosity and forgiveness in the face of injustice personifies God's grace.[3]

In the third verse of the "Meal Sharing Song," Appavoo portrays Jesus as a native doctor, or *āsān* (teacher), grinding the medicine, or *kāyakalpam*, of redemption and grace in the upper room. Throughout the liturgy Appavoo raises the status of the local people by placing Jesus and God in roles as farmer, political leader and native doctor. Here, the medicine of *kāyakalpam* (which keeps one young) represents redemption and social liberation, but its ability to cure requires a special diet of forgetting enmity (i.e., caste differentiation, as we see Job exemplify above) and eating shared food; that is, "being in Christ" or practicing *oru olai* as one universal family.

In the verse, a mood of contemplative tension is articulated over two measures of triple meter through a twice-repeated rhythmic cell of two-beat duration (a quarter, plus two eighths) starting on the second beat of measure 7 (see Appendix 1, Transcription 3, Fig. 5, mm. 7–8). The tension of this pattern against the three-beat meter is then resolved on the last beat of measure 8 (see Appendix 1, Transcription 3, Fig. 6). The percussion accompaniment played on the tavil barrel drum contributes to the tension by playing a contrasting regularized unsyncopated pattern emphasizing the first beat of each measure (see Appendix 1, Transcription 3, Fig. 7). The rhythmic tension of the melody is finally resolved with three quarter notes in measure 13, but trips the listener again by moving to a $\frac{6}{8}$ feel of an eighth note triplet, followed by two eighth notes against the tavil's straighter $\frac{3}{4}$ feel in the last measure (see Appendix 1, Transcription 3, Fig. 8). The melody of the verse also creates tension by moving between the fourth and fifth (A and B) in the first three sets of phrases (mm. 8–13), but resolves to the tonic (E) through the fifth, fourth, and second notes of the scale in the last two measures. Thus musically Appavoo creates both rhythmic and melodic tension throughout the verses that is only completely resolved in the last phrase of the last verse, mm. 13 and 14, when the question "what is this holy meal?" is answered with the phrase *pahundu tiṉṉum sōṟu tāṉē*, "sharing rice and eating together," or *oru olai*. Here, the power of the word is necessary to resolve the musical and rhythmic tension.

The addition of a communion song in this liturgy allows Appavoo to clearly define what *oru olai* is and is not through a musically contemplative mood. The music reinforces the congregation's participation in the experience of sharing in rural-style communion of *kañji* (rice gruel) and *kañji* water. As his student Johnson Jebakumar articulated, these songs have a "*girāmiya maṇam* [rural or rustic smell] emanating from them."[4] Thus Appavoo communicates his message of Dalit liberation through *oru olai* on multiple sensory levels simultaneously: kinesthetically, visually, aurally, and through the palate. Appavoo preached that as herbal medicine requires a special diet, *oru olai* is a disciplined practice grounded in liberatory Dalit values, not elusive Brahmanical magic or Christian fundamentalist false promises that rob Dalit people of their penchant toward protest.

The oppositional stance against both Brahmanical and Evangelical theology within the "Meal Sharing Song" also reflects the changing musical alliances that Appavoo encountered before discovering the emancipatory potential of folk music and cultural identity as a means to Tamil Christian worship. While Appavoo was born into a family milieu in which classical karnatak music was greatly appreciated, he eventually rejected the elite association of this music as he rejected the magic of *sastirams* (Hindu incantations) in his liturgy. As a young performing musician he was exposed to Evangelical *āsīrvādam*, (blessing) theology through the medium of light or popular film music style. After observing class differentiation between the meals offered to Evangelical worship leaders and those given to common attendees at meetings, Appavoo rejected both the message of "blessings" and the style of light music as hypocritical and based on false pretense. He doubted the validity of the expressions of salvation that he observed and felt that the Evangelists were cheating the people out of their money offerings with the hope of promises that were materialistic and could not be fulfilled. After studying what at the time was called freedom theology at the Tamil Nadu Theological Seminary (TTS) and working directly with poor villagers, he came to embrace the liberating elements of folk music and culture such as *oru olai,* the potentially empowering aspects of village culture like herbal medicine, and the grace of a unified community. He also demonstrates the possibilities of a fuller sensory experience in liturgy.

THE APPAVOO FAMILY DIALOGUE WITH THE HISTORY OF TAMIL CHRISTIAN MUSIC, 1850–1994

The Rev. Dr. James Theophilus Appavoo (1940–2005) was one of the most influential Tamil Dalit composer/theologians, leading the process of reform of theology and liturgy in the Church of South India in the late twentieth century. Over the course of his career he was primarily a teacher, first of English and then of theology and communication studies.[5] He retired in May 2005 from TTS after teaching there for twenty-six years. His creative accomplishments were both oral and written. He published the book *Folklore for Change* (1986), as well as multiple articles, stories, recordings, songs, radio broadcasts, dramas, videos, and street plays. In his creative work, theology, and teaching, Appavoo exemplified the liberationist ideals of equality, justice, and sharing. He challenged and changed the practice of Tamil Christian music through creating a Dalit cultural identity transformed from six generations of family musical practice: a historical dialogue that both reflects and disrupts the history of Tamil Christian music.

Theophilus Appavoo was born on March 9, 1940, and raised in Cuddalore, a coastal town on the Bay of Bengal in the Cuddalore (formerly South Arcot) district of Northeastern Tamil Nadu. Appavoo was of the Pariayar (outcaste) *jāti* and described himself as "a town Dalit, whose exposure to folk music was very late."[6] Northern Tamil Nadu has a very large population of both rural and urban outcastes. Paṟaiyar make up twenty percent of the population in the South Arcot district (Clark-Deces 2005, 5), whereas scheduled castes are only about six percent of the population statewide. His family had very little experience with village culture and folk music partly because they had not been involved in agricultural labor since at least the 1850s and because the urban churches did not encourage the use of folk music. They were, however, talented karnatak musicians for several generations, reflecting an access and exposure to classical culture available to middle-class urban Christians that many rural Dalits did not have. However, his family was also exposed to and enjoyed singing some urban folk music.

Appavoo's folk music disrupts the top-down production and practice of Tamil Christian theology and musical liturgy, and in the hands of Dalit villagers, its reproduction is resistive and transformative. Anthropologist Sherry Ortner posits a subaltern subject involved in shaping her/his world, emphasizing the role of "practice" in changing structures (1996, 11, 17). Folk music practice is a re-creative system that is changing the identity of Christian music and theology. How is Dalit agency constructed and enacted as liberating through the practice of music? Through music, Dalit Christians are changing Christian theology and their own identities as a form of resistance to the greater systems in the church and society that continue to oppress them.

Dalit Christians make up seventy percent of the Church of South India today, and many of their ancestors experienced a radical identity transformation through conversion three to five generations ago. Despite this transformation, it has taken much longer to radically change Tamil Christian music and liturgy in order to reflect the cultural identity of the majority of its adherents. Through on-going processes of indigenization defined by shifts in musical style, language, and theology directed by politicized Dalit agents like Appavoo, the identity of Tamil Christian culture reached a point of metamorphosis in the late twentieth century.

The historical shifts in musical practice over five generations of Appavoo's family of musicians correlate with, counter, and construct the shifts in musical style of the Tamil Protestant Dalit community from 1850 to the present. This involves three historical narratives: the history of Christianity and its indigenization in India; the history of Tamil Christian music and its use in the construction and constraint of Dalits' transformative potential; and the history of a Dalit family and its musical practice in dialogue with the Christian community. The themes of colonial modernity, castism, class mobility, and shifts in cultural value through the discourse of musical style are central to each of these stories.

Through these entwined narratives of Appavoo's family and the Protestant Christian community searching for a liberating Christian musical identity, I claim Appavoo is more than a reflection of his community, or an embodiment of a wider musical sensibility (Terada 2000, 463). He is a catalytic node in a dynamic network of change and resistance. By listening to the biblical interpretations and social needs of villagers, composing folk music, and responding to the feedback of villagers about his music, he is an actor in dialogue within an oppressed community struggling to realize their liberating Christian voice through transformative song (Danielson 1997, 2).

How does an ethnomusicologist tell the life story of an individual in relation to the history of musical practice by a community? If ethnomusicologists treat music as the product of cultural processes of human interaction that construct culture, then ethnomusicological biography is a means to understand socio-historical processes of self-authoring in community through the story of musical change (Rice 2003, 157). Ethnomusicological biography will undoubtedly serve, as Stuart Blackburn says of the collectively authored texts of Tamil folklore, as "a counter weight to the widespread 'myth of the solitary genius,' which underlies some life-historical research" (2004, 206) and most works of historical musicology. My focus here is not to highlight some special qualities of theological and musical genius that set Appavoo and his family members apart from their urban Dalit middle class community or poor Dalit villagers. Instead I am interested in the "slippages in reproduction" (Ortner 1996, 17) in relation to the larger community narrative or "cultural constraints and generic logics" which contradict the patterns of identity and musical practice among Christians creating possibilities for personal change, assertion of status, and radical transformation of Tamil Christian culture (Blackburn 2004, 206). How did the moments of transformation, upheaval, and resistance to castism and classism in the life history of this family create the possibility for Appavoo, his ancestors and his contemporaries to change the practice of music in the Church of South India? Upper-caste members of the church (in negotiation with missionaries) constructed, transmitted, and reproduced Christian theology and music over four hundred years as a hegemonic discourse. Through alternative music practice Dalit Christians in the twentieth century (along with some of their forbearers in the nineteenth) have changed Tamil Christian music and their personal identity as Christians as a form of resistance to Western and upper-caste theological hegemonies and oppressive cultural systems.

In their anthology *Telling Lives in India: Biography, Autobiography, and Life Histories,* David Arnold and Stuart Blackburn question the perception that Indian society is dominated by collectives of caste, kinship, and religion (2004, 19). They counter this view of life history as the history of the collective by focusing on the significance of individual agency and of the self. Yet they find that "life histories do not consistently or unambiguously reveal the isolated, autonomous, individual self." Instead they reveal a complex and subtle negotiation between the self and the community. They argue that "Indians present individual lives within a network of other lives and that they define themselves in relation to larger frames of reference, especially those of family, kin, caste, religion, and gender" (Blackburn and Arnold 2004, 19). While Appavoo was certainly a cultural leader of great influence, his life and the creative changes he strove for took place within a dynamic dialogical network of family, teachers of different castes, seminary students, Dalit and feminist activists, and Christian villagers, who were (and are) negotiating changes in caste, class, gender, and religion through music.

Virginia Danielson's (1997) biographical study of the twentieth-century Egyptian music star Umm Kulthum provides a close model for this case. In both contexts musical practice is dialogical, involving a cycle of production and reception that transforms the music as well as the producers' identity. Composition and performance of Tamil Christian folk music in dialogue with villagers transforms Appavoo's identity to become Paraṭṭai and reconstructs his music through the oral transmission/reception/feedback network with villagers to remain liberating and thus meaningful.

Contemporary Dalits and both Indian and foreign anthropologists have created a handful of biographical accounts of twentieth-century "untouchables" in India, most of whom were poor villagers who internalized and at times resisted their oppressed conditions (Freeman 1979; Moon 2001; Viramma and Racine 1997). Arnold and Blackburn's critique of the biographical discourse on Indians begs the question of whether there are historical examples of lower-caste negotiations between the self and community. Dilip Menon provides evidence of negotiation and transformation of self and community through the Malayali untouchable Potheri Kunhambu's (1857–1919) novel *Sarasativijayam*. Menon argues that nineteenth-century untouchables wrote themselves into modernity using the Malayalam novel and Christianity (2006, xiv). That is, conversion to Christianity was an act of cultural criticism that allowed lower castes to reinvent both their notions of community and notions of self in a context of colonial modernity that subsumed the latter to the former. Significant to this analysis is that while religion is often dichotomized from the modern secular individual, Menon argues that the colonized subaltern uses the Christian abolitionist reform ideology, to assert the hope for a "yet to be realized" humanity and rights. Furthermore, Kunhambu's means for the reinvention of self is the "modern" aesthetic form of the novel. But Menon argues that the novel in this case is not a sign of the modern in India, only the *hope* of a new configuration of self and community (ibid., 105). Indeed the author, Kunhambu, advocated the conversion to Christianity "as a cure for the social evils besetting Hinduism, though he himself never converted" (ibid., 78). I take this argument further in the biography of individuals within Appavoo's Paraiyar family and within the Tamil Christian community, to argue that they used the oral medium of Christian music to transmit Christianity to untouchables, as a means by which they protested caste and Western hegemony, reinvented themselves, and ultimately reinvented Indian Christianity several times over in the course of five centuries. From Appavoo's perspective, the style or medium of music and its association with an empowered identity determines the possibility that the transformation of self can become more than just a hope, but a reality.

Josiane and Jean-Luc Racine, who produced a musical biography of the Tamil Paṟaiyar singer Viramma (1997), cite Henri Moniot who calls such biographical work "the history of peoples without history" (Racine and Racine 2004, 257). The Racines go on to make the keen comparison between "mainstream perception which, in the colonial vision of the world, have for long excluded so many peoples from history, with upper-caste Indian perceptions, which have excluded Dalits from history" (2004, 257). According to both perspectives, the subordinate is judged as lacking cultural monuments and unable to produce anything of sustained value. The Racines discern that in both cases the criterion for value is the production of written culture and thus those who communicate primarily through oral mediums, whether using Brahmanic sastras or Dalit folk songs, suffer the same contempt (Racine and Racine 2004, 257).

Appavoo's story is an ethnomusicological biography as oral history of the life of Dalit individuals interacting within a family and community to create theology in the oral medium of music, and to transmit and receive back this music through a human transmission system that allows the possibility of emancipatory transformation. The historical narratives below combine oral ethnographic history with analysis of primary documents and secondary literature. My intent is to use these sources to weave together the narratives of the individuals in Appavoo's family with the story of Tamil Christian music in order to highlight how music has been a means to transformation, resistance, and new creative directions for Dalit Christians. This is ethnomusicolgical biography that, through the oral sources of life history and music, hears the subaltern sing their transformation.

CATHOLIC AND EARLY PROTESTANT MUSICAL ROOTS: 1535 TO 1820

By the 1880s when Appavoo's great-great grandfather Edward Appavoo converted to Protestant Christianity and became a member of the Reformed Church of America's Arcot Mission in the city of Vellore, Tamil Christian music had already gone through more than three hundred years of indigenization. Since the early sixteenth century, music had played a primary role in the process of transmission and indigenization of the religion and the expression of each new mode of Tamil Christianity in its specific historical context. Translation and vernacularization of the Christian message into Tamil dialects and musical styles were central to the conversion process (Sanneh 1989). Throughout this history, language and musical style continued to be markers of local identity, particularly of caste and class as well as aesthetic values. Music became a means of theological transmission, while particular styles of music transmitted the aesthetic and social values associated with three kinds of processes: mimetic association with the West; the aspiration to status through greater respect by upper-caste elites; and political self-recognition by the lower castes, or "Dalitization." Music then became a means of expression and transmission of indigenized theology and contextualized Tamil Christian identities. A basic understanding of the three-hundred-year history of the development of these musical, religious, and social identities as well as the key actors in this process is necessary to discern the values and musical practices into which Edward Appavoo converted in the late nineteenth century and with which his descendants negotiated over the course of the twentieth century.

From its beginnings in Tamil Nadu in the early sixteenth century, Christianity was associated with shifting caste identities that were expressed through local rites and music. The potential for protection by the powerful Portuguese from the economic abuses of Arab traders convinced most of the members of the Paravar pearl-fishing communities (considered untouchable) of Tamil Nadu to convert to Catholicism. Between 1535 and 1537 practically the entire caste converted; about 20,000 people were baptized en masse with little preparation or examination of faith.

Sent by the Portuguese mission, St. Francis Xavier reached the southern coast of Tamil Nadu by 1542 to develop the Christian knowledge and practice of these communities. With little comprehension of Tamil, he attempted to establish rote knowledge of the basic prayers, creeds, and commandments among the new Paravar and Mukkuvar converts. On the whole, the lack of missionaries and catechists left the people with very little Christian instruction, guidance, or discipline, except that a few boys were taken to school at the mission center in Goa (Thekkedath 1982, 186). The relative isolation of this converted community, however, set in motion the domestication of Christianity to local religious and cultural paradigms.

The nature of Christian worship among the Paravars was characterized as fearful respect for saints and virgin cult figures, and reverence of the Jesuit missionaries as supernaturally endowed tutelary figures whose power was personal and charismatic (Bayly 1989, 329, 399). The fusion of Christian hagiography and local goddess and warrior hero worship formed the basis of the Paravars' identity as Roman Catholics. Portuguese patronage in the form of political and social protection in turn bolstered the Paravars' sense of caste identity. Indeed Xavier helped shape their Christian caste culture by assigning the group's caste notables, or *pattangattis,* to serve as a kind of moral policing agency among Christians (Bayly 1989, 332). The lauded position of *pattangattis* was further affirmed by their central role in the ten-day Virgin festival.

In the Tuticorin festival of Our Lady of Snows, the Paravar caste *talaivan* (head man) processed on the sacred road around the church in front of the *tēr* (small mobile palace) containing the figure of the Virgin accompanied by music (most likely the double-reed *nāgasvaram* and large barrel drum called *tavil*).[7] This was a practice modeled on the Hindu Navaratri (nine-night) festival of the goddess Minakshi held in Madurai, in which Brahmin priests and upper-caste community leaders process around the great temple led by the same type of ensemble. As untouchables, the Paravars had played only limited roles in Brahmanical Hindu temple rites. As Christians, however, they took a central role in their own Hindu-style Christian festival. This self-understanding of an improved state was negotiated within the parameters of an accepted indigenous Hindu scheme of rank and honor and facilitated by adoption and reimagining of upper-caste Hindu ritual practices. This was not a disguised duplication of the Tamil Hindu system, nor an opting-out of the system. Instead it was a Christianization of the indigenous system that facilitated the improvement of the Paravar's status. Furthermore, their choice was validated and endorsed by the European church and colonial authorities (Bayly 1989, 346–347). Paravar Christian identity allowed for shifting power dynamics in social relations while the new religion became endowed with local ritualistic powers through attention showered on the powerful charismatic figures of the Catholic missionaries. Furthermore, the Christians were able to differentiate themselves from Hindus and Muslim fishing people, and to find themselves patrons among European powers. Above all, they created for themselves a ritual arena that improved their position within the region's wider scheme of caste rank and honor.

The earliest example of Indian styles and forms of music adopted to Tamil Christianity occurred in the early seventeenth century when the Italian Jesuit Robert de Nobili first composed Christian karnatak music in Sanskrit and Tamil to attract potential Brahmin converts to Catholicism. He argued for the "trickle-down" or percolation theory, also held by later missionaries, that the lower castes would be attracted to whatever the Brahmins adopted (Thekkedath 1982, 211). By mid-century de Nobili's mission had converted fewer than fifty Brahmins and seventy middle-caste Nayaks, while he had transformed himself into a Christian *sannyasi* (holy man) who sat in his house waiting for the interested few to engage with him. He used a strategy of complete self-inculturation. He studied Tamil and Sanskrit, which he described as "beautiful, copious and most elegant" (de Nobili 1607 in Kuriakose 1999, 45). He also gave up wine, meat, fish, and eggs, and modeled himself physically as a guru, living an austere lifestyle in the Brahmin quarter so that the Brahmins would receive and trust him like one of their own teachers (Kuriakose 1999, 45). De Nobili stayed secluded, admitting visitors with reserve, but then charmed people with his abilities to cite Indian literature "and by a great number of verses of his own composition, which he partly sang and partly recited with exquisite delicacy and distinction."[8] He also intentionally distanced himself and Christianity from identification with the Portuguese or "Parangis" (particularly soldiers), who were hated by the upper castes for their impurity in personal and dietary habits and thus held in the same disdain as the "untouchables" (Thekkedath 1982, 212). He claimed he "was by birth a raja, by profession a Brahman Sannyasi" or social elite from Rome (Thekkedath 1982, 216; Kuriakose 1999, 48). Yet, while he created his identity as a "Roman Brahmin" as part of his strategy of indigenization, de Nobili made the argument to his Jesuit critics that it was only a shift in cultural appearance to a self-sacrificing, scholarly Indian ascetic, while he maintained the inward difference of being Catholic (Kent 1999, 36, drawing on Allocca).

De Nobili was the most prolific and talented of the scholar/missionaries of the seventeenth century, writing more than twenty works in Tamil on theology and philosophy (Thekkedath 1982, 253). He relied heavily on Sanskrit as a source for Christian terms, which Neill (1985, 32) believes "saddled the churches in India with a number of artificial constructs." The result was the creation of a separate Christian liturgical Tamil that was unfamiliar even to educated Tamils and the use of the linguistic form called *manipravalam*, which fused Sanskrit and Tamil. De Nobili composed Sanskrit canticles, in the same meters as their Hindu models, to be sung by Brahmin Christians at weddings and funerals, as well as hymns in Tamil and Telugu (Firth 1983, 118; Thekkedath 1982, 253). Arulananddam, one of de Nobili's catechists, composed the *Life of St. Margaret* (approximately mid-seventeenth century) in elegant Tamil verse, likely one of the earliest examples of Christian compositions by a native Tamil (1982, 255).

De Nobili did not consider the Christian principle that all people are equal before God to be contradictory to the social hierarchy of caste (S. Rajamanickam 1972 in Thekkedath 1982, 55). He preached in his manifesto of 1611 that Christianity did not require anyone to "lose his caste or pass into another, nor does it induce anyone to do anything detrimental to the honour of his family" (Kuriakose 1999, 49). He allowed his upper-caste converts to retain many of the outward signs of caste such as the sacred thread and hair tuft. He legitimized them to his superiors by defining them as symbols of the "nobility of their family and not their worship or religion," which distinguished the Brahmins, the Rajas, and the merchants "from the rabble and lower classes" (Kuriakose 1999, 51). He also Christianized life-cycle rituals including marriage, burials, and the important Poṅgal [harvest] festival (Thekkedath 1982, 214).

Though de Nobili's Catholic mission extended beyond Madurai by 1630, it never had enough priests. By mid-century it primarily extended north of Madurai, while in the late 1600s some lower-caste Shanars (later called Nadars) were baptized in the southern districts. By the 1630s several (upper-caste non-Brahmin) Vellalars were converted in Tanjavur by the Vellalar Yesu Adiyan, one of the first catechists of the mission. Yet even with de Nobili's earlier strategy of focusing on Brahmin conversion there were always more "pariahs" who converted. In 1644 there were one hundred high-caste and 350 low-caste Christian converts at Tanjavur (Thekkedath 1982). By 1678 there were 70,000 Christians in the mission. The Jesuit missionaries themselves divided their ministerial duties along caste lines; particular missionaries worked exclusively with either upper or lower castes. They also kept the castes separate, either through separate churches or by creating separate spaces or services within one church.

Tamil Christians—and the foreign priests ministering to them—were often persecuted either as scapegoats during the many wars in the seventeenth century or because upper castes objected to their conversion.[9] One governor of an area near Kuttur even proclaimed that Christians who had converted from the upper castes "should be expelled from every village . . . driven to the *cēris* [colonies] of the pariahs, since they had sunk to the level of the latter by accepting the Christian religion. No Hindu was to have any intercourse with them, or touch their person or clothes, lest he should be polluted" (Sauliere 254–5 in Thekkedath 1982, 246). Christianity became equivalent to untouchability. Through the efforts of the missionaries, however, these Christians often sought and received protection from *nayaks* (small nobles) or other officials.

De Nobili remained in Madurai until his death in 1656. Whether or not his mission was successful in terms of numbers of converts, he created an indigenized style of mission and a model for linguistic fluency that other Catholic Jesuits followed in the eighteenth century (Neill 1985, 90, 277). As a foreign indigenizer primarily interested in converting the social elite, he appropriated the local elite styles and forms of music, laying down a model of indigenization that the Lutherans, like C. F. Schwartz who followed him, continued to encourage. Yet his embodiment as an upper-caste Indian disguised the contradiction between the Christian principle that all people are equal before God and the hierarchical violence of caste (S. Rajamanickam, 1972, 55, in Thekkedath 1982, 214). Later re-indigenizers, such as Appavoo, recognized the necessity of self- and cultural transformation into the elements of Indian culture that would be socially liberating, especially for the poor and the oppressed.

EARLY PROTESTANT MISSIONS

The indigenization of Christianity within the Lutheran Danish-Halle Mission from 1706 to approximately 1820 was marked by missionary translation of text and European hymnody and the creation of indigenous karnatak musical compositions by Vedanayakam Sastriar, an upper-caste Vellalar. Through his advanced education in the mission and his years of service to it, he earned the designation "fruit of the Tranquebar Mission" (Lehmann 1956, 157). The Lutherans also accommodated the upper-caste Vellalars' determination to retain caste. Practices of social and ritual separation were justified by the Vellalars through the creation of what Hudson (2000, 173) has labeled an indigenous "theology of pluralism." That is, all Christian people are unified by a common faith in Jesus, expressed by the congregation as united prayer and love for each other, but they live, eat, and sit separately (Hudson 2000, 173).

The first Protestant missionaries in India, the German Lutherans Bartholomew Ziegenbalg and Henry Plutschau, came to India under the auspices of the Royal Danish mission of King Frederick IV. In 1706 these two men arrived in Tranquebar (Tarangambadi), a small Danish colony (fifteen square miles) on the eastern coast of Tamil Nadu. They were followed later by two very important figures in the history of Tamil Christian music: Philip Fabricius in 1742 and C. F. Schwartz in 1750.[10] Throughout the eighteenth century, their form of German Pietism (from the University of Halle in Germany) spread slowly to Tiruchchirappalli, Tanjavur, Madras, Caddalore, and Nagappattinam and later to Tirunelveli. The mission initially had very little support from the colonial powers (i.e., the British East India Company), which maintained a hands-off policy regarding missions and cultural interference until 1812, nor the local Danish chaplains or Roman Catholic priests (Neill 1985, 28–29). Lack of support made it hard to convert many people; thus these missionaries focused on scholarly pursuits. The Lutheran Mission work in translation and hymnody created a strong foundation for, and musical links to, the British and American Protestant missions of the nineteenth century.

By the second decade of the eighteenth century, the Lutherans had begun extensive Bible and hymn translation into Tamil. Ziegenbalg created hymns that children used "according to the Malabar way of singing" and by 1714 published a hymn book with forty eight songs "which had only hymns in Tamilian metre [*tala*] and according to the Tamil scale [*raga*]" (Lehmann 1956, 26, 61). This indicates that upper-caste converts and assistants to the mission had likely been encouraged to compose indigenous karnatak hymns for liturgical and mission use by this point. They later developed a repertoire of German hymns translated into Tamil called *pāmālai* and *ñanappāṭṭu*.[11]

Indigenization through literary culture and classical music continued to reflect the prevailing priority during this period of converting higher castes and creating a sense of respectability for Christianity. While the Lutherans attracted few Brahmins, converts from the upper caste Vellalar community dominated the church. The missionaries referred to the Vellalars as "Śudras," denoting the lowest of the four Hindu *varnas;* however, the Tamil Vellalar community was characterized as a "generally well-to-do and sanskritized caste who constituted the dominant, literate, property-owning class in the many Tamil-speaking regions where the Brahman population was quite small" (Kent 2004, 16). Indeed the Vellalars brought the classical poetic and musical traditions of Brahmanical Hinduism, Tamil Śaiva *bhakti* devotion, and literary Tamil to Protestant Christianity. Conversion to Christianity, however, meant negotiation between Lutheran missionaries and Vellalars, who insisted on keeping their caste divisions and practice of ritual separation in liturgy and social interaction—their "theology of pluralism." While the missionaries stated that they "took great pains to lessen these prejudices [caste discrimination] among our Christians" (Hudson 2000, 47), they accommodated the Vellalars, allowing the practices of segregation in seating and, for a time, taking of communion with separate cups among their converts who coexisted in single congregations. They also consciously chose not to ordain the Paraiyar catechist Rajanayakan who had worked successfully for many years in the mission. The missionaries believed that if he were given the status of a priest, and thus allowed to administer the Eucharist to upper-caste Vellalars, it would "diminish the regard of Christians of higher caste for that Sacrament itself" (Paul 1967, 40).

The Vellalars were a slight majority in the Tranquebar mission by 1740 (Neill 1985, 43), although they formed a single but spatially segregated congregation with the Paraiyars who had traditionally acted as their servants, while the outcaste Pallars were bonded to upper castes like the Chettiars (Hudson 2000, 46). The court culture of the Maratha kings in eighteenth-century Tanjore was an important seat of Tamil culture and karnatak music, as well as a diverse cosmopolitan meeting ground. The most prolific and well known of the Protestant composers, Tanjore Vedanayakam Sastriar (1774–1864) and H. A. Krishna Pillai (1827–1900), both Vellalars, nurtured their Christian *kīrttaṉai* in this Tamil Śaiva milieu in which Vellalars "were the principal custodians of Tamil literary traditions" (Peterson 2001, 13).[12]

Vedanayakam Sastriar, who produced over 500 *kīrttaṉai* is a prime example of a Tamil Christian agent who had the cultural authority of his upper-caste background, the best in foreign theological education and mission support, royal patronage, and social and geographical access to classical Brahmanical culture during the golden era of karnatak music; his repertoire has continued to dominate the production and publication of indigenized Tamil Protestant music for the last two hundred years.

Vedanayakam Sastriar was born Vedanayakam Pillai in Palaiyamcottai, Tirunelveli district in 1774. He was the son of the Arunacalam Pillai, a Vellalar who worked as a Hindu priest and merchant in Tirunelveli (Gurupatham 1993, 11). Arunacalam converted to Roman Catholicism, became a catechist who in all likelihood used some of the 60,000 verses he wrote in his Evangelism and took the Christian name Devasagayam (Sastriar, Noah [1899] 1987). He later married a Chettiar (upper-caste) Christian named Jnanappu Ammal. In 1785, upon the personal request of C. F. Schwartz, Devasagayam committed his son Vedanayakam to Schwartz's care for further instruction in Tanjore. Subsequently Vedanayakam was sent to the Tranquebar mission to study Western theology, astronomy, anatomy, and mathematics (1993, 11). Schwartz encouraged Vedanayakam's composition and musical Evangelism, eventually employing him as headmaster of the seminary for catechists in Tanjore where he most likely taught his students to use Christian *kīrttaṉai* as a means of Evangelism, as his father had done (Hudson 2000, 113).[13] He became a schoolmate to the future King Serfoji II, who was also under Schwartz's tutelage. Vedanayakam later received Serfoji's patronage and in 1829 became a minister in the king's court after quitting his position in the seminary over caste and indigenization controversies with the recently arrived Calvinist Anglican missionaries.

The turn of the nineteenth century saw India governed by a civilizing agenda founded in ideas of Western enlightenment and Calvinist reform. This agenda emphasized individual rights and duties rather than the collective rights that frame much of Indian social structure (Hudson 2000, 185). After 1813, this aggressive Anglicizing agenda, which Thomas Trautmann (1997) calls "indophobia," was embedded in colonial state-supported mission policies, particularly those of the Anglican Episcopal hierarchy. This opened the door for missionaries to attack previous attitudes of cultural accommodation in both liturgical and caste practice. However, these policies took different forms and emphases in different mission societies. Conservative attitudes by British Anglicans toward indigenization, along with reformist anti-caste policies, contrasted with American Congregationalists' indigenization policies at mid-century that rejected the idea that civilization must precede Christianization in the conversion process. Thus while the Anglicans forbade almost everything Indian, the Congregationalists allowed and actively transmitted local cultural elements like the Christian *kīrttaṉai* in order to more easily Christianize converts through local idioms (Harris 1999, 3).

The Lutheran community came under the control of the British Society for Promoting Christian Knowledge (SPCK) in 1820, and by 1826, under the Society for the Propagation of the Gospel (SPG), initiating a period of Anglicization that brought swift changes in cultural policy and practice. C. T. E. Rhenius, a German sent to Palaiyamcottai in 1820 by the British Church Mission Society (CMS), initiated a conversion movement primarily among Shanars (later called Nadars) in the Tirunelveli area (Grafe 1990, 33). These young missionaries reversed the previous Lutheran policy of encouraging the creation and use of indigenized karnatak music. Further, they no longer accommodated caste divisions, particularly eating separately, sitting on separate mats in the church, and the separation of communion cups.

The Calvinist reformed ideology that valued stark simplicity pervaded the Tamil CMS churches, eliminating all signs of potential idolatry from pictures and crosses, as well as sensuality in ritual (Hudson 2000, 148). The Anglicans attempted to distance their churches from elaborate European and Indian Catholic traditions, which they thought the earlier Lutheran style reflected, and simultaneously, to eliminate anything that appeared Hindu. Indeed Rhenius eliminated the use of Tamil *kīrttaṉai* after 1827, preferring Western hymns (Sastriar 1829 in Hudson 2000, 152), and referred to the use of flower garlands in the church as a "heinous sin" (2000, 150).

Evidence of the Anglican shift in policy toward caste and indigenous Christian culture and the Tamil retort is found in Vedanayakam Sastriar's *Saditeratoo* (Explaining Caste) written in 1829.[14] Sastriar outlined four problematic changes or "cruelties" imposed on the Tamil Christian community, particularly on the upper-caste Vellalars: (1) The old (Fabricius) Tamil Bible translations were replaced with new ones produced by Rhenius that mixed literary and common Tamil; (2) festival celebrations were restricted and local flower decorating customs were not allowed; (3) Tamil music and *kīrttaṉai* were removed from worship and festival; (4) the right- and left-hand untouchable castes (Paraiyar and Pallar) were forced to unite, along with the upper and lower castes, into a single egalitarian Protestant "caste" that intermarried and inter-dined. Those who maintained their customary differences were excommunicated (2000, 148). The Vellalars saw these changes as an attack on important symbols of their Evangelical culture and identity that had been nurtured by Lutheran missionaries like Schwartz for over one hundred years (2000, 146). Their resistance led to deeper entrenchment in their upper-caste identity and its ritual expression in indigenous elite music and theology.

In defense of the refined nature of Vellalar Christian practices, Sastriar compared the simplicity, soft dynamics, and minimal use of instruments among Tamil Lutherans to the elaborate Hindu-like celebrations of the Catholics in a letter written in 1829:

> As Europeans like decent music such as organ, Violin, Flute, etc. harmoniously suiting the tunes of Hymns . . . so we like decent music which suits our Tamil songs such as Harp, Pipe, Guitar, Timbrel, Cymbal etc. and use them in such time thinking that it will be acceptable to God and agreeable to the tenor of the 150th Psalm etc. But we have never used those riotous music, which the

> Roman Catholics use in their festivals such as Arabe, Taboret, *Negasarum*, Tumtum, Horn, etc. and we wish never to use them. Thus, we sing to the Lord in our festivals only by small bell, Cymbal, rejecting even those musical instruments which we might use reasonably for fear of their loudness and this we do after the divine service is over. At the Church we sing only the songs without any music [instruments]. (Sastriar 1829 in Hudson 2000, 152)[15]

Describing the simplicity of the Christmas celebration, Sastriar again compared the Protestant traditions to those of the Tamil Catholics, saying the Lutherans clean and whitewash the church, use candles (a Western emblem), and conduct the service modestly, whereas Catholics celebrate "pompously" with comedy, fireworks, and the Arabic *taboret* (frame drum) (Hudson 2000, 149).

The Calvinist CMS missionaries lumped together indigenous rituals, music, and language traditions, judging them not just as too heathen, but as too Catholic. And they forbade practice of all of them. Sastriar clearly differentiated them, trying to argue his case for "quiet and unaccompanied" devotional indigenous music (*kīrttaṉai,* most likely) by distancing the Tamil Protestant traditions from the Tamil Catholic, but in the process reinscribed the indigenous "style" hierarchy—classical over folk—that these instruments and cultural styles denoted.[16] He says the Protestants do not use the *nāgasvaram* and various drums, likely the *tavil* and possibly the *tasa* or small kettle drum called the *tunumpu* (tumtum), two drums of the Paraiyars considered "degraded" by many upper castes. These instruments are associated with loud outdoor parades in villages and temples and are used by Catholics for the *tēr* (cart) festivals of saints,[17] but they are not associated with elite music as are the "flute and guitar" (possibly *vina*).[18] Sastriar's letter provides an example of resistance to the British mission agenda, which had become closely tied to the larger project of colonial Anglicization. Yet further analysis of his rhetoric of musical value reveals the local dynamics of caste hegemony being played out among Tamil Christians.

The elite qualities of Sastriar's musical elements and theology further articulate the differences among caste groups (Sherinian 2005a). Sastriar drew upon familiar literary forms, melodic types (ragas), and even borrowed tunes from Orthodox Hindu and Western songs to use in his Christian compositions. The Christian community knows best his five hundred compositions in the *kīrttaṉai* form, while he also composed a *jebamalai* (garland of prayers) in the *tevarm* style of Tēyamānavar (which fuses Tamil *bhakti* with Pietism). Furthermore, he used the etude-like form called *varṇam* and produced a dance drama called *Bethlehem Kuravañci* (1800), which drew on the important eighteenth-century *kuravañci* genre of Tamil literature. Sastriar used folk elements within this drama and some of his songs, but Peterson argues that they were "appropriated or translated from the folk milieu to be included in the [classical] cannon, alongside the 'non-folk'" (Peterson 1998, 40–41). Each of his *kīrttaṉai* was composed using a raga and tala, which were printed above the song text in various hymnals after 1853. The Rev. H. Popley, a Methodist missionary, transcribed the skeleton tunes of Sastriar's *kīrttaṉai* only in the 1930s. Thus the assumption by the publishers before this time was that one knew the raga grammar and could apply it properly to the performance, or that one had aurally learned the tune. Sastriar commonly employed the seven popular karnatak ragas in his compositions that his Hindu contemporaries used in classical compositions.[19] The American missionary J. S. Chandler (1912, 247–248) wrote that Sastriar was "not a composer of tunes, but he adapted his lyrics to any tune that he found anywhere; Tamil tunes, Telugu tunes, Hindustani tunes, Portuguese tunes, band tunes, even jig tunes were harnessed to his Christian lyrics."

Sastriar consciously indigenized Christian themes to traditional raga moods and *bhakti* sentiments. One of the best examples of his expression of *mādhurya* or *bhakti* love for Jesus is the *kīrttaṉai* (CLS 1988, ♯ 87) "Pārkka Mu-ṉam Varivēn." It is composed in the karnatak raga *usēni,* which was often used in the eighteenth and nineteenth century, and is still used today in dance and drama, to express erotic love and romance (Gurupatham 1992, 67). There are also aspects of sympathy that give the verse some of the quality of *sakhya* or friendship *bhakti.*

> *PALLAVI* (CHORUS)
> I shall come quickly to meet him—he who
> in my times of difficulty gave me safety
> the one who sympathized with me. (I shall come quickly.)
> *CHARANAM* (VERSE) THREE
> Christ whom I desire, my good shepherd,
> lover of my soul, my benefactor,
> from the net of desires, you lifted me up
> you protected me with love, my chief helper.[20]

The first line gives the indication of separation typical of *mādhurya bhakti.* The word for "lover," *nāyakar,* in line two of the third *charanam,* means both "lord" as ruler and "God" as supreme being as well as "husband." *Nūyaṉai* translated here as "benefactor," also means the love and affection of a friend. The word for desire in line three of the *charanam* is *pāsam,* a concept from Saiva Siddhanta (Saivaite Hindu theology). Sastriar expresses *bhakti* desire for God as lord, lover, and friend.

Sastriar was also facile in applying the appropriate raga moods (or *rasas*) to support the philosophical concepts in his Christian lyrics. In a *kīrttaṉai* expressing happiness over the birth of Christ, Sastriar uses *kapi* raga, sung to express moods of joy and devotion (Gurupatham 1992, 67). *Bupala,* a raga of morning devotion, was used by Sastriar to narrate the resurrection of Christ on Easter morning in the lyric "eṛandarulam ēsu svāmi." Sastriar laments the sufferings, passion, and death of Christ using *maukhari* raga to express a melancholy mood (1992, 67). Sastriar chose *mohanam* raga, often used to begin concerts, as a beginning adoration "taruṅam iduvē kirubai sūrum." *Churutti*, a raga of joy and praising God, is used to close Hindu concerts. Sastriar likewise uses it as a *mangalam* lyric or final blessing at the end of a liturgy. His lyric, "Yesu natanukku jeya mangalam," was sung at the end of many services I attended at the Tamil Nadu Theological Seminary and was a blessing lyric written for special occasions within his family. Whether he used a mood (*rasa*) of devoted love, joy, passionate mourning, or adoration of God, Sastriar chose the appropriate ragas of his day to carry the sentiments in his Christian *bhakti kīrttaṉai* appealing to people in Tanjavur and its surrounding villages. His theology, however, may not have transmitted as easily as his tunes.

While Sastriar's music and themes have been indigenously meaningful to a wide variety of Christians for the last two hundred and fifty years as a marker of elite Christianity, many of his theological idioms, borrowed directly from Brahmanical Hinduism, may be more difficult to grasp. A reception study conducted by Gurupatham (1992, 119–126) shows that in the 1990s Sastriar's *kīrttaṉai* still carried meaningful and relevant "teaching for a Christian life," and that Christians of all ages find "sweetness" in his ragas (often conceived as "tunes" in the Christian community). However, Gurupatham also shows that contemporary lay Christians find very little theological relevance in Sastriar's *kīrttaṉai* (1992, 127).[21] It is doubtful that the lower-caste and lower-class people of Sastriar's day, considerably less educated than those in Gurupatham's study, could grasp the theology of his lyrics, especially when he used complex philosophical concepts borrowed from Brahmanical Hinduism (a practice Śudras, or untouchables, had no access to) and communicated many of these in literary sanskritized Tamil. Furthermore, the culture and devotional style that colored his *kīrttaṉai* through images and metaphors was one of an upper-class and upper-caste man, a perspective to which most lower castes were completely alien (Sherinian 2005a, 147). Finally, Sastriar's theology legitimized the Tamil Lutheran practice of segregation of the lower castes from the upper.

THEOLOGY OF PLURALISM

Lutheran practices allowed Vellalars to maintain a physical separation that ensured their social security through continued relations (endogamy) with their

Hindu relatives (Hudson 2000, 182). The Vellalars argued on practical grounds that separation would also ensure that Indian Christianity would continue to grow through conversions from that population of relatives and through maintaining respectable status within the wider Hindu milieu, a society that literally gazed at them through the church windows.[22] The Christian Vellalars' use of sanskritized literary Tamil (*manipravalam*) in the Bible, elite karnatak music, and the maintenance of traditional hierarchical dominance and separation from the outcaste Paraiyars, afforded them respect in the eyes of the Hindu elite and the wider society.

Dennis Hudson (2000) proposes that the Vellalar Lutherans of the eighteenth century had devised an indigenous theology of pluralism. This is evident in Sastriar's *kīrttaṉai* that justify Christian caste hierarchies by combining Lutheran evangelical theology of the unchangeable state of the fallen and divided man on earth, and Tamil notions that castes have distinct and vulnerable natures. Because these natures are vulnerable, castes must remain physically separate in order to maintain their distinction. Therefore, although the members view themselves as one unified congregation with a common faith, they need to maintain the "natural" hierarchical order on this earth by not sharing food (and potentially *eccil* or saliva pollution) or sitting on the same surface. This would lead to attachment or inter-caste *paṟakkam* (habitual practice or similarity of personality) (Hudson 2000, 173).[23] Hudson defines this theology as "pluralistic" because it maintained a distinction between spiritual and physical realms and called for "the insistence that differing habitations within a single congregation be maintained . . . [Furthermore, this] can be understood as an expression of love, as an affirmation of the dignity of the other's identity along with one's own" (2000, 181). Absent from this discourse is the question of whether the untouchables felt that the theology and the church practice affirmed *their dignity* or that maintaining the status quo, one's place in the system, was simply a means to respect the integrity of those in power.

Sastriar's lyrics helped articulate the Vellalar theological identity that combined confessional *bhakti* with Christian Pietism's focus on human nature as inevitably sinful.[24] Sastriar legitimized the maintenance of social divisions on the grounds that humans in the physical realm are inherently imperfect and ignorant, yet through faith have the hope of grace and forgiveness for their fallen nature in heaven, the spiritual realm (2000, 170). Through his confessional *bhakti* style, Sastriar argued that a community united in love, like the Singi in his drama *Bethlehem Kuravañci,* could pray hard "without ceasing till your knees are black and swollen" in order to gain forgiveness for this human nature and overcome it through eternal life in heaven (Francis 1978, 11). Individuals must remain close to God, always pining for vision and to touch his feet, in order to have *paṟakkam* (habituation) with God's perfection. They should not assume that they could gain perfection in this world, so they must maintain the social differences that reflect the fallen nature of humanity.

The Lutheran missionaries made significant advances in indigenizing Christianity by ordaining the first Indian clergy and producing the first Tamil Protestant Christian hymns. Yet, in the process, they established the elite role of Tamil Christian teachers, preachers, and musicians among the Vellalars, the highest Christian caste. Sastriar's integration of indigenous karnatak music, *bhakti* theology, poetic forms and language, from Vaishnavite or Shaivite (Brahmanical Hindu sects) devotional practice into Tamil Christian worship illustrates the assimilation of local features to make the message of the Christian ritual more comprehensible and acceptable, particularly for upper-caste Indians (Kaplan 1995, 15–16). He adapted Christianity to his own culture and language: that of an upper-caste educated Vellalar. Although he borrowed tunes from both foreign and local sources, his original song lyrics are modeled on common karnatak raga aesthetics, Tamil poetic forms, and religious and dramatic themes of his day. Sastriar very successfully fused *bhakti* theology with Lutheran Pietism in ways that allowed the sense of personal devotion, common to both, to remain appealing to Tamil Christians. His *kīrttaṉai* are musically accessible to Vellalars because he indigenized Christian themes with raga sentiments and cultural constructions. He used popular ragas and kept his melodies simple. Yet his foundation in Brahmanic paradigms and Sanskrit kept his work theologically and linguistically distant from the common people. Although he used folk idioms, most likely for their broad appeal, his approach was a hierarchical indigenization or appropriation. His folk music did not reflect village or lower-caste values; instead he used the style as a medium with which to reach the people and replace their "superstitions" with foreign and possibly upper-class values and respectable belief systems.

After one hundred years of patronage and cultural accommodation by the Lutheran missionaries, Calvinist reform ideology was imposed on Indian Christians, requiring converts to eat and sit together as equals. Sastriar is a unique example of a culture broker who stood up to Calvinist liturgical changes, declaring them "cruelties" that, as he put it, were "changing the religion of liberty into bondage" (Sastriar 1829 in Hudson 2000, 153). Sastriar and the Vellalars argued against the equality of caste and for their necessary separation on both practical and theological grounds. After being excommunicated for refusing to follow these reforms, some Vellalars used their upper-caste status, so valued in the conversion policies of all the mission societies, to move from one denomination to another, settling at one point with the Leipzig Lutherans who allowed them to continue practicing caste separation and the karnatak *kīrttaṉai*. Some also separated themselves from the mission and its politics by developing community-based Christian practices outside official church congregations. In the process they reified caste identity among the Christian Vellalars and reinforced the hegemony of elite karnatak music and theology within their community.

INTRODUCTION OF ANGLICAN AND CONGREGATIONAL MISSIONS

Anglican mission societies had been present in India since the eighteenth century. The SPCK (Society for the Propagation of Christian Knowledge) was established in Madras in 1728 and had given the Lutherans financial support without controlling their policy. The first British Baptist missionary, William Carey, began evangelizing in Bengal in 1793. Yet the Anglican Episcopal hierarchy had no formal presence until the early nineteenth century and became official only after passage of the Charter of 1813 when the British Parliament agreed to open mission activity "among the natives." In 1833 the East India Company gave permission for free movement and settlement in India to non-Indian and non-British nationals, leading to the influx of international mission organizations.

It was in the first two decades of this century that the Tranquebar mission went into decline and there was a transfer of power from the Lutheran to the Anglican missions, particularly around Tirunelveli and Tanjavur. Furthermore, the Tamil mission field was divided geographically, leading to differences in caste concentrations, and thus creating denominational splits along caste majority lines. This was further aggravated because the missions/denominations held differing religious doctrines concerning the Eucharist and ministry and held differing "ethos regarding practical consequences, which arose out of the common conviction of the fundamental equality of all human beings over conventional caste practices" (Grafe 1990, 42).

The Anglican SPG and CMS moved into Tirunelveli, primarily converting those from the lower-caste Shanar or Nadar *jāti*, along with a smaller number of Vellalars, Pallars (outcaste), and Naidus (upper caste). The less conservative British Wesleyan Methodists eventually established a strip across central Tamil Nadu from Manargudi to Dharapuram. They stressed the conversion of "individual souls" and were the primary mission group among the mass conversion movements of untouchables late in the century (Manikam 1977, 113). The

American Board of Commissioners for Foreign Missions (ABCFM), a Congregational mission arrived from Jaffna in 1833, centered themselves in Madurai, and worked systematically in the surrounding towns and villages including Dindigul, Arappukottai, Tirumangalam, Palani, Melur, and Sivaganga, "with their independent spirit due to a revival among students in America" (Grafe 1990, 46). The majority of their converts were from the outcastes along with some lower-caste Shanar (Nadar) immigrants from the southern districts. The London Mission Society (LMS) in Kanniyakumari was composed of British Congregationalists (free church) who also worked among Nadars. These were followed later in the century by the Salvation Army (1883), and the American Missouri Evangelical Lutheran India Mission (1895).

ANGLICIZATION OF NADAR CHRISTIANS: THE "MODERNIZATION" OF RURAL *KĪRTTAṈAI*

The British missionaries, whose imperial Anglicization was intended to save Indians from their state of moral depravity, encouraged and tolerated indigenization much less than other Protestant missions. They focused their Tamil mission and Anglicization work primarily in the Tirunelveli area with the low-caste (polluting) Śudra Sanars, who later changed their name to Nadars. Known primarily as laborers, who "tap the toddy" from palmayra trees, Sanars converted in mass movements under the Anglican missions (SPCK) as early as 1802 (Kent 2004, 28). The motivation for conversion was partly to escape the tyranny of the upper-caste Vallalar Hindus, who were dominant in the area, through association with the British. Organist Emmanuel Jebarajan described it as a "welcome hope, to completely convert to Christianity" when the missionaries came.[25] The Sanars took full advantage of opportunities for "civilizing" and education in the English language, rarely questioning the agenda of inculcation to British values and Westernization that estranged them from most Indian expressive forms. Indeed according to the well known composer Rev. Thomas Thangaraj, many learned to sing four-part harmony or play the organ before they could read and write.[26] Christian identity and British identity were conflated in the cultural ideology and liturgical practices of these missions to the point of observing every detail of church life as carried on in England (Neill 1985, 275, 490). Emmanuel Jebarajan described his Nadar Christian identity and its association with cultural Anglicization in the following statement: "I think actually we can call ourselves Indian Britishers, because all are more British oriented: so much admirers of Christian missionaries. Therefore [we have a] complete Christian background: everything Christian, Christian to the rigorous extent."[27]

The Sanars used their association with the imperial powers to raise their caste and class status, emulating and simultaneously protesting against the upper castes who oppressed them. Eventually, as an entire community, they officially claimed Kshatriya (warrior/king caste category) descent with a change of their caste name to Nadar.[28] Ironically, while the Anglican missionaries worked against caste practices, the Nadars were able to retain and strengthen their communal practices, particularly through endogamous marriages and living in Christian colonies in the Tirunelveli area.

In the liturgically tradition-bound Anglican missions generally, there was less tolerance and encouragement of indigenization than in other missions. These policies resulted in a strong Nadar/Anglican block or caste/denominational resistance toward liturgical and ritual indigenization, such as the use of *kīrttaṉai*. They also generally maintained a negative attitude toward folk elements: cultural resistance that continues to wield strong influence within the Church of South India today.

THE INCULCATION OF PAṞAIYARS IN ELITE CULTURE THROUGH *KĪRTTAṈAI*

There have been outcaste or untouchable Christians in Tamil Nadu from the time of de Nobili's Madurai mission in the sixteenth century. Paravar and Mukuvar fisher people, who have at times been considered untouchable or at least very low caste, were converted as early as the 1530s by the Portuguese mission and St. Francis Xavier. Evidence of official contributions by outcastes and lower castes to music and liturgy is scant and again indicates the control of the Tamil Catholic and Protestant churches by the upper castes as priests, choir directors, and members, and lay council members until the mid-twentieth century.[29] However, while castism has always existed in India's churches, the opportunities for education, jobs, and healthcare that the missions provided have contributed significantly to raising the status of many outcastes.

In the nineteenth century, the Paṟaiyars and others under the American Madura Mission (ABCFM) also took advantage of opportunities for education and "moral" development, particularly as this mission strongly opposed caste discrimination. Unlike the Anglicans, however, the Congregational missions held more accommodating attitudes toward indigenous forms of liturgy and ritual. The Congregationalists were part of the faction of nineteenth-century orientalists who "promot(ed) education in the vernacular languages [and stood] in opposition to the 'Anglicists,' . . . who promoted English as a medium of instruction" (Trautmann 1997, 23). They encouraged their converts to develop vernacular and indigenous expressions of faith; however, the approved model for indigenization by the church institutions and the upper castes was karnatak music. Both missionaries and upper-caste church leaders considered local folk forms used by the majority of the converts, the Paraiyars, inappropriate for use inside the church.[30]

In 1853 an ABCFM missionary from Batalagunta, Edward Webb, selected over one hundred *kīrttaṉai* from Sastriar's book *Pata Kīrttaṉai* to compile and publish the first indigenous Tamil hymnal (Vedanayagam 1987). Sastriar spent one month in 1852 teaching the *kīrttaṉai* to Webb and eight of his Tamil catechists, thus facilitating the oral transmission of the raga-based tunes to village and lower-caste communities who had little access to this elite musical system (Webb 1852). In the Tamil hymnal, one finds the song text with its two- or three-part formal divisions, as well as the name of the raga (mode) and tala (time cycle) in which the tune is composed. There is no notation, so one must either know the tune or be able to construct one based on knowledge of the raga. With the exception of some folk theater musicians, few if any lower/outcastes had this knowledge in the mid-nineteenth century. Thus catechists and missionaries orally transmitted the tunes.

A descendant of Sastriar describes the events of that transmission.

> In 1853 a priest from Batalagunta, Reverend Webb, selected some simple ragas from Vedanayakam's book *Pata Kīrttaṉai*. Vedanayakam taught these to the Deva Uziyakarakal [catechists]. Webb then brought into common practice the use of Vedanayakam's song in the regular church service. He also brought these songs to press, helping Vedanayakam get published. When the lyric book was printed all 300 lyrics were Vedanayakam Sastriar's. With *venba* [a poetic synopsis of the message of the song] placed at the beginning and within the last stanza or line, his name Vedanayakam will appear [as in the tradition of Tyagaraja]. (Vedanayagam 1987)

Another account of these events is found in the 1853 letter from Rev. Edward Webb of the Madura mission to the ABCFM in Boston.

> With the consent of the mission I last month visited Tanjore, principally for the purpose of making a selection of hymns and anthems in Tamil metre, for public and social worship from the compositions of Vathanaikam, the Christian Poet of that place.-A class of young men, [8] catechists from the different stations of our mission, accompanied me for purpose of learning the tunes of the selected pieces—We returned after an absence of little more than a month.—The importance of giving our foreign Christians a Psalmody in national metres—set to national music has, I rejoice to see, been lately recognized by the missionaries of our society in Western Asia—We, as a body, are now, for the first time taking a step in the same direction. You are aware

> that the poetical forms of the Tamil language are almost miraculously elaborated, that every arrangement and collection of letters, syllables, feet, words, and sentences which in consonance with the genius of the language and the national taste, could increase the beauty or sweetness of the thought, have been made by their poets for more than a thousand years. In respect to elaboration of Poetical form—the languages of the West will not bear comparison with those of India—But foreign Protestant Missionaries, rejecting these exquisitely furnished, and withal indigenous metres—have adopted those of European languages—[reference to the genres *ñanappāṭṭu* or *pāmālai*] By this means they have cramped, stretched, and in various ways constrained this beautiful language into the most ludicrous proportions. If the devotions of our Christians have moved at all in this vehicle—it has been slowly and heavily—The music of Europe is certainly more sweet to our ear than that of the Hindu. Doubtless the science has attained a higher cultivation among us than among them—and if we were the Apostles of Music it might be our duty to attempt a national reformation in this particular. But, until the taste of the people shall become refined as missionaries—it is surely our duty to accommodate ourselves to them.
>
> In our own country, A Western Air sung in Western fashion would be as ill-adapted to express and to elevate the emotions of a polished and cultivated congregation in an Eastern City, as a chaste and scientific performance would be to kindle and fan the fervid flame of a camp meeting—. Have we not then greatly erred, in imposing upon our Christians a metre and a music with which they as Tamilians can have no sympathy? It has yet to be proved that their music may not become a medium for the effective expression of devotional feeling—No missionary has as yet, so far I know, thoroughly investigated the subject of native music—My own prejudices against it are receding as my acquaintance with it increases.
>
> We propose to publish a volume, which will contain 150 anthems, or poetical compositions in Tamil metre, adapted for divine worship, together with a selection of about 100 hymns in English metre, and a few passages from scripture appropriate for chanting. The work will, GW [God willing], be printed in the early part of the year. (Webb 1852, 440 in collection volume)[31]

The distinctions between these two accounts lies in the different intentions of the missionary and indigenous composer (or his descendant). Shem Vedanayakam indicates that the missionaries chose "simple ragas," implying that the corpus of Sastriar's work was more difficult, possibly too difficult for common and lower-caste Christians or not suited for circulation outside the congregation at Tanjore or Sastriar's family. Secondly, Shem Vedanayakam seems to emphasize that Vedanayakam Sastriar viewed this transmission as an opportunity to publish his work, convinced that his songs were effective given their use by the Tanjore community since the late 1700s.[32] It is also interesting to note that the mission granted Webb 30 rupees to purchase these lyrics from Sastriar,[33] likely giving the rights to and control of transmission of these songs to the missionaries.

Webb's account is an attempt to convince the home office to support the use of indigenous music in worship and mission. He uses several arguments. First, he separates the two roles of missionaries, as transmitters of religion and as transmitters of culture, highlighting the common conflation of the two in policies held by other missions, particularly the Anglicans. Although he couches his argument in the imperialist rhetoric that Western culture is inherently better than Indian. Writing of the missionaries' "scientific cultivation" and more "refined taste" than the Tamils,' he implies some sense of cultural relativity. Webb establishes that European music is sweeter to the ears of the missionaries than Hindu music and that the poetry of the two cultures can not be compared, yet he freely admits that with greater acquaintance his own prejudices against native music were receding. Furthermore, although he believes that exposure to Christianity and Western culture will refine the natives' tastes, he argues that it is the missionaries' *duty* to accommodate to the Tamils and by implication the Tamils' taste and culture. On some level he grants the Tamil Christians the human potential to grow in appreciation, something the upper-caste Hindus would not deem possible because of the essential difference in their nature. He shows great respect for the Tamil language and strongly criticizes the approach of previous hymnal translators who rejected indigenous meters and instead "cramped, stretched and . . . constrained this beautiful [Tamil] language" in the attempt to retain the Western tunes in the translated *ñanappāṭṭu* and *pāmālai* hymns. Finally, comparing a camp-meeting context to a proper Eastern church, Webb also makes a powerful argument for the functional or appropriate use of different styles of Christian music for different contexts, implying that particular musical styles bring out the emotion of particular cultural contexts. Thus he justifies the importance of Tamil *kīrttaṉai* to provide religious interest in the Tamil context. Webb's letter exemplifies the positive valuation of indigenous language, culture, and inherent worth of the (primarily lower-caste) people that would continue in the American Congregational Mission over the next fifty years, leading toward the formation of an independent Church of South India.

Within a few years, the *kīrttaṉai* repertoire was brought into common practice throughout the Protestant Tamil missions. Furthermore, *kīrttaṉai* were used throughout the nineteenth century as a means of Evangelism, particularly in the villages (Chandler 1912, David 1986, 67). A preaching session always began with *kīrttaṉai,* often as a way to attract a crowd, and "native helpers" developed techniques of punctuating their preaching with songs (Arcot 1903, 121).

In the early twentieth century, the *kīrttaṉai* were also used extensively as a means to fortify conversion in the Methodist and Congregational boarding schools that were heavily populated with lower-caste Christian village children. C. S. Karunakaran (in the 1940s) and his father, the well known Trichy Tanjore Diocese priest Rev. C. J. Daniel, and uncles all learned *kīrttaṉai* at the Dharapuram boarding school and Findley High School in Manarkudi. They were Paraiyar village converts who lived in the District Boys Boarding Home attached to the high school in the late 1910s.[34] Karunakaran continued to teach classical or original versions of the *kīrttaṉai* to village boys as warden of the CSI boys home in Karur until the mid-2000s (see Fig. 2).

The wide dissemination of *kīrttaṉai* with its elite musical form, modal and rhythmic systems, to the rural lower-caste Christian population resulted in a kind of elite Hinduization for villagers who continue to use *kīrttaṉai* as their primary liturgical song genre. The induction into Christianity through cultural material rooted in Vellalar Śaiva *bhakti* philosophy gave outcastes access to upper-caste/class culture. However, as contemporary Dalit theologians and historians argue, the untouchables' conversion to upper-caste culture estranged them psychologically from the liberatory aspects of their own folk culture (Appavoo 1986, 1997; Devasagayam 1997, xiii). These aspects include the elements of protest present in folk songs and the psychological/spiritual transformation possible through Dalit religious rituals such walking on fire, the ability of the parai drum to induce trance, or the sound of lament to provide catharsis. Reversal of this estrangement through official church sanction of folk-based liturgical material would not occur until the late twentieth century.

As secretary of the ABCFM, Rufus Anderson was instrumental in implementing policies that rejected the theory that civilization (particularly through Anglicization) must precede Christianization. Therefore the Americans were less interested in imposing Western culture on the converts in the form of English hymns, and realized that the use of Tamil *kīrttaṉai* in Evangelism and worship would expedite the understanding of the gospel and attract potential converts.[35] Their goal was narrowed to focus on conversion or "Christianization" including developing a native church that would be "self-supporting, self-governing, and self-propagating" (Harris 1999, 4). While this development laid the foundation for an indigenous Christianity, neither acceptance of the *kīrttaṉai* as aesthetically equal to Bach or Wesley hymns nor the rejection of cultural imperialism was part of this indigenizing project (Sherinian 1998, 121–122).[36]

The Tamil lyrics found "immediate welcome" in the American mission as well as others. On January 2, 1854, Webb wrote:

> The good effects which will result from the introduction into our churches of national tunes and metres are beginning even now to appear. The members of our village congregations already take greater interest in the religious services, where they are used; and many of the young men who were unable to read, are making efforts to acquire the art; so that they may sing more correctly and fluently. On my recent tour among the congregations in the Periacolum valley, I was surprised to hear several of the new hymns sung, where I had never heard singing of any kind before. The members had learned from manuscript copies obtained through the catechist. (Webb 1854, 150–52)

While encouraging cultural indigenization of music, particularly to elite forms, the Americans led the fight against the culture of caste in the church by incorporating and enforcing anti-caste policies among their converts. The question of caste, which had burned during the first thirty years of the British and American missions, was finally resolved in a consensus at the Madras Missionary Conference of 1850. The various Protestant missions, with the exception of the Leipzig Mission (which had taken in the non-reformist Vellalars), concluded that caste in the church was a grave scandal indefensible on any Christian grounds (Forrester 1980, 42). They agreed to implement common policies that "converts before baptism, and native Christians before confirmation, should be required to renounce caste; vigorous teaching on the evils of caste was to take place; and the 'love feasts' were recommended to all the missions for general adoption" (1980, 43).

The Americans introduced the "love feast" test of inter-caste dining in 1847. They had resolved that giving up caste implied a readiness to eat "under proper circumstances with any Christians of any caste, and to treat them in respect to hospitality and other acts of kindness" (Chandler 1912, 141). Converts were tested before receiving communion, and before being employed as teachers or catechists; the mission also encouraged the employment of pariah (untouchable) cooks in the boarding school (Chandler 1912, 141). Thus the defining act of Christian identification became the sharing of food as equals, a notable precursor to Appavoo's theology of shared communal eating (*oru olai*) in the late twentieth century.

While the radical measure of inter-caste dining resulted in many resignations of upper- and middle-caste church workers (including teachers) and suspension of thirty-eight of seventy-two catechists from the mission, the employment of pariahs as cooks in the boarding schools led to the admission of more outcaste students, increasing the population to almost fifty percent. Thus began a revolution of educational and other opportunities for this community in the boarding school system (Chandler 1912, 55); the mission also introduced the first school for girls in the district.[37] Beginning in 1849, the Congregationalists emphasized education in the vernacular to the extent that they taught theology primarily in Tamil in order to establish native clergy and teachers (1912, 246). Emphasis on vernacular language, local relevance, and autonomy were characteristic of Congregational philosophy. In the Tamil context this manifested as acceptance and encouragement of indigenous music expressing the converts' experience of faith,[38] as well as the concept of a "free order" of worship that was probably the source of later experiments with musical liturgies.

The Anglicans understood Christianizing and civilizing as a single package of language, music, liturgy, and Western values, whereas the American Congregationalists differentiated between the missionaries' two roles as the apostles of Christianity (reformist Calvinist) and the "apostles of music" (Webb 1852). They did not see their duty as centered in the reformation of indigenous musical taste, especially if local music could make their message more relevant and further their goal of transmitting Christianity.

The outcaste communities took advantage of the opportunity to adopt karnatak *kīrttaṉai* from the missionaries who transmitted it to villagers and to children in the Christian boarding schools, particularly those of the Congregational and Wesleyan Methodist missions of the early twentieth century. By emulating and adopting Brahmin and Vellalar Christian culture, these outcaste people hoped to improve their material and social status within what had become a *Christian* system of rank. Yet this cultural inculcation was not only a case of upper-caste imitation or identification with the tastes and values of the Vellalars.[39] Indian Christians did not undertake the transformation of their customs and practices in social isolation: they were responding to cultural pressures and expectation emanating from both Indians and Westerners (Kent 2004, 18). While the adoption of karnatak music on the one hand is a symbol of inculcating the lower castes in upper-caste values, for them it was simultaneously a sign of Christianization "in so far as Christianity favored the adoption of more . . . civilized usages" (Kent 2004, 230). Kent argues that "to Indians in the nineteenth century, Christianization was very much like Sanskritization, a move toward more respectable modes of behaving and conducting one's life based on an ideal embodied by the higher castes" (2004, 231). Further, unlike some other signs of respectable Indian identity that the lower caste converts adopted, (such as wearing the *kumadi*, or a hair bun worn by upper-caste men), the Congregational and Methodist missionaries completely supported the singing of the Indian Christian *kīrttaṉai*.

The first edition of the *Christian Lyrics for Public and Social Worship* complied by Edward Webb in 1853 included over one hundred *kīrttaṉai* by Sastriar. The overwhelming presence of his work reflects the Vellalars' ability to establish a social, cultural, and theological hegemony within the Protestant churches—a caste influence that would last until the mid-twentieth century. Vellalars controlled the positions of influence as priests, bishops, pastorate committee members, theologians, and choirmasters. As a result, they have had a tremendous impact on indigenized music and theology, particularly in the promotion of karnatak music as the ideal indigenized style.

It was not until 1890 that the first non-Vellalar pastor, B. Samuel of Manigraman, was ordained (Hudson 2000, 29). It was just after this period in the early twentieth century that the Tamil Hymnal began to include *kīrttaṉai* by lower-caste Christian leaders such as Rev. V. Santiago, John Palmer, G. Samuel, Mariyaan Ubidasiyar, G. S. Vedanayakam, L. Ponnusuvami, and many others.[40] Some of these were textually and musically simpler *kīrttaṉai,* perhaps designed for village congregations. However, basic training in karnatak music was beginning to be available to a wider spectrum of Christian composers and musicians. For example, the American Madura Mission sponsored a summer training course for its converts led by well known Brahmin karnatak musicians.[41] It was also common to hear concert style *kīrttaṉai* in devotional settings such as *kālākshēpam,* an epic storytelling genre or sung religious discourse that involves a lead narrator accompanied by an ensemble of instrumentalists. By the mid-nineteenth century, *kālākshēpam* had become a favorite form for worship and Evangelism adopted by Tamil Christians and singing missionaries such as Rev. Emmons White of the ABCFM. Interest in karnatak music was nurtured in Appavoo's father and grandfather in such a milieu.

FIVE GENERATIONS OF PAṞAIYAR CHRISTIAN MUSICIANS

According to family lore, Appavoo's great-great grandfather, Edward Appavoo,[42] likely born about 1835, converted to Christianity through contact with an American missionary named Reed in Vellore (a large riverside town in north-central Tamil Nadu) in about 1880. As a member of the Central Congregational Church of Vellore, he joined the Arcot Mission of the Reformed Church of America (established in 1853), a fairly conservative Calvinist society that preached individual salvation, the power of God in one's life, and the final authority of the Holy Scriptures.[43] This mission, under the leadership of the

Presbyterians William and Joseph Scudder, splintered off from the Congregational American Madura Mission (ABCFM) beginning in about 1854. The Arcot Mission shared many of the same policies toward caste and positive attitudes toward the use of *kīrttaṉai* as the ABCFM, while their emphasis was on preaching in Tamil, producing and distributing vernacular tracts and books, and educating their converts (Arcot 1903, 125). I have found no evidence of a missionary named Reed serving the Arcot Mission during this period. It is possible a Presbyterian or Congregational missionary in the area converted Edward Appavoo and then directed him toward the Arcot Mission congregation in Vellore for a process of "arduous preparation," possibly lasting three years (David 1986, 28).[44]

The oral history of Edward Appavoo's conversion (the only source that we have available for most Dalits) has been passed down through his family.[45] Theophilus Appavoo's narration of the conversion story begins with a chance meeting on the road, which led to a friendship and discussions of religion between the missionary Reed and Edward Appavoo. Edward owned an ox-driven *reklar* on which a worker stands behind the driver. Theophilus described this as "a symbol of a rich man" lending support to the probability of Edward's middle-class status. One day, Edward's cart overtook a horse-driven coach in which the missionary was traveling, frightening the horse and causing it to veer to the side of the road.

> So, this missionary got angry and he wanted to eat the ox. So he [Reed] called this man, "bring him." He said, "Your ox is very ferocious. So, you must kill [it] and I want to eat it," he said. "You sell it." He said, "No, I won't sell." By this conversation they cultivated some friendship between the two.[46]

Later Reed attempted to convince Edward that Christianity was superior to Indian religions. Edward first resisted saying, "Our God is also God. We don't want your God. Our God is a good God." Then Reed presented Edward with two glasses of water, one of which contained dirt. He asked Edward to drink the dirty water. Edward refused, saying it was dirty. Reed replied, "This is like your religion; it is basically good but it contains dirt such as idol worship. Christianity, on the other hand, is pure water."[47] The family lore says that it was this analogy that led to his conversion.[48]

After his conversion Edward Appavoo received several financial opportunities from Reed. He was given a book on butchery from America and asked to supply meat to the Europeans and missionaries in Vellore, a job a non-Paraiyar (or non-beef-eating caste) would not have taken.[49] Participation in "love feasts," in which all castes ate food together that was prepared by Paraiyars, was required by all converts in the Arcot Mission as a behavioral sign of conversion[50] (David 1986, 114). Indeed Immanuel David writes, "the entire renunciation of caste was an indispensable condition of church-membership as was the abandonment of idolatry" (1986, 114).

Edward also began to supply horses to the military garrison. At the Central Church in Vellore there is a plaque that indicates that Edward Appavoo donated a hearse cart for funeral processions (see Fig. 3; PURL 2.2). Theophilus believes that the fact of this donation and that he had land, is evidence that Edward was middle class and wielded some power in his community.[51]

The active signs of an anti-caste policy and equality in social interaction by the Arcot missionaries was certainly a taste of the social justice promised by Christ and that a few of these missionaries preached. Most missionaries did not consider the destruction of the caste system, through outcaste conversion, "as, per se, a dimension of their salvation or reason to save them" but only as a by-product of Dalit salvation (David 1986, 183). One exception was W. H. Campbell of the LMS who preached a bold position of action against the status quo or theology *for* Dalits (Webster 1992):

> Some brethren look on this movement with something akin to fear and suspicion, and dread any action, which would tend to make the people discontented with their lot. I have no sympathy with such timid doubters. Our Lord Jesus Christ took up no such position. Where there is injustice and oppression His message is not a message of peace but of war . . . as Christian missionaries, we are bound to do all that lies in our power to help these people to throw off their bondage . . . The great work for us is to prepare the people for the struggle which must inevitably arise, so that they may enter upon it with no low evil motives, but as Christian men whose only desire is to obtain what is just and right.[52]

Campbell suggested several methods to prepare the people for this struggle: teach them to use wasteland, attain economic independence from their rich neighbors, get an elementary education, and "lead them to the Savior, [for] he will make them free" (in Webster 1992, 184). Others like William Goudie preached that social work could not be separated from religion and encouraged hope and self-reliance in a preserving effort for Dalits to help themselves, not merely to bring charity to them (ibid.). These are the same basic actions Dalit theologians advocate today, which suggests that Dalit liberation theology in India has its historical roots in the work and ideas of these early missionaries.

The new awareness of hope and humanity found in Christianity also enabled the outcastes to abandon their traditional occupations long considered menial and degraded, and to migrate from the villages to towns for better jobs. In doing so, however, they also abandoned many positive aspects of village culture and religion. "Census commissioners . . . noted the decline in the practice of untouchability in urban areas and towards those Dalits who had left their traditional occupations" (Webster 1992, 78). Yet, even if they were financially middle-class as Edward appears to have been, outcastes continued to be psychologically and materially affected by the daily oppression of untouchability. For example, Gauri Viswanathan documents how the Dalit leader Ambedkar who returned to India with a law degree from Columbia University suffered the humiliation of clerks "hurling files at him to avoid being defiled by his touch" (1998, 211). While Edward may not have desperately needed the financial opportunities that the missionaries provided him, their offer included a sense of human dignity. For a low-caste people, who, according to the Laws of Manu were never allowed to hear the Vedas of Brahmanical Hinduism for fear of molten lead being poured into their ears (Doniger 1991, section 12 verse 4), missionaries offered them the Bible or "True Veda" as well as religious tracts, which David describes as coveted even by those who could not read (1986, 85). But the greatest opportunity for most was the chance to go to school and the possibility of getting a mission job later as a teacher, catechist, clerk, or nurse.

For an untouchable who was defined by Hinduism as born impure and sinful from deeds done in their past life, Christianity offered the possibility of salvation from sin, acceptance as a child of God, and the possibility of a direct relationship with God. The opportunity to leave the social stigma and ritual impurity of untouchability, to be considered an equal (David 1986, 112) in the eyes of God (if not in the eyes of many upper-caste Christians or imperialist missionaries), must have found a great deal of resonance with the majority of Christian converts. Upper castes, on the other hand, had much to lose in status and community through conversion (G. Viswanathan 1998).

Edward's conversion is unusual compared to those documented in recent writings on the history of "Dalit mass conversions" of the late nineteenth and early twentieth centuries. The early 1900s were marked by so-called "mass movements" of conversions among the outcaste *jātis,* particularly in the central western parts of Tamil Nadu near Karur and Dharapuram between 1913 and 1920 and around 1890 in the Arcot districts where Edward lived (see Manickam 1988; Forrester 1980). Some outcastes converted in response to the missionaries' compassionate famine relief in the late nineteenth century. For example, the 1877 famine in the Arcot district was followed by a mass-movement conversion in 1890 (Webster 1992, 58). Most of these outcastes were villagers who typically converted in caste-based clan groups after group discussion and decision over the religious and material benefits of Christianity (S. Manickam 1988; Forrester 1977; Webster 1992, 48). It should be clearly noted that it was outcastes who started the mass movements, not the missionaries (Webster 1992, 37; Manickam 1988). Many of these outcastes have been accused by Indians and other missionaries of being "rice Christians"; that is, they received economic help and a leaf of rice during the famine in return for their conversion (Forrester 1977, 42). Manickam argues, however, that most of the "mass conversions" occurred after the famines had ended and many represented the community's own initiative. That is, most of these group conversions were based on a joint family or clan decision or initiated through the influence of a community leader (Carman and Luke 1968, 214).

> Besides baptism for protection, material benefits and education . . . one of the strong reasons for their conversion was their ardent desire to liberate themselves from the oppressive caste system and to improve their social and economic status, for Christianity offered them a social gospel of emancipation. In the case of such Dalits who were putting up a grim fight for upward mobility and seeking a new identity, [Walter Fernandes writes] "Christianity came in as [an] outside element and functioned as an instrument of re-adaptation to changing circumstances." (Manickam 1988, 164–165)

Manickam (1988, 127) also cites the Methodist Rev. J. J. Ellis who worked in western Tamil Nadu who said, "Thousands of people came 'gate crashing' into the fold of Christianity as a social protest to the age-old injustice done to them by the Hindu society." The mass movements of rural Dalits into the Protestant churches in Tamil Nadu significantly changed the demographics of the Christian population: Between 1872 and 1931 the Indian Christian population quadrupled, while the Indian population as a whole increased by seventy-one percent and was largely rural (Webster 1992, 56). Indeed by 1931 five out of six Indian Christians lived in rural areas.[53]

While the historians emphasize that the rural mass conversions were group initiatives, the family narrative of Edward's experience further establishes a genealogy of intellectual reflection upon which Theophilus Appavoo, as a Dalit theologian, draws empowerment. It simultaneously contradicts the rhetoric critical of Christian conversion out of the desire for material gain applied to the "rice Christians." As was the case with many outcastes, however, Edward established a patronage relationship with the missionaries, through which he was able to enact and develop his business skills.

But what of Edward's music practice? Theophilus Appavoo tells us that Edward and his daughters were said to be good singers. As a middle-class Paraiyar

Christian, what music would Edward have practiced in Vellore? In all likelihood the large mixed caste and class congregation of the Central Church used both *kīrttaṉai* (indigenous classical) and *ñanappāṭṭu* and *pāmālai* (translated Western hymns) as published in later editions of Edward Webb's *Christian Lyrics for Public and Social Worship* (Washburn edited the eleventh edition in 1891).[54] In the villages and towns, preaching and singing songs were combined in various ways. Rev. S. A. Sebastian, pastor of the Vellore church, successfully used the method of presenting the message of the gospels through singing, interspersing song with explanation.

We know very little about E. Simon, Edward's son. Theophilus Appavoo never heard his grandfather Samuel speak of his father Simon as a musician. He only referred to him as a local doctor or *nattuvaitiyam*.[55] He was probably born about 1860, and likely converted with his father and the rest of the family in the mid-1880s.[56] Apparently Simon maintained his father Edward's middle-class status, as his son Samuel later sold land that belonged to him, although neither directly farmed it. Simon also educated at least some of the children (likely in mission schools) of his three wives.[57] Education in mission schools for Dalit children as boarders and day students was widely available. In fact, while some middle- and upper-caste Christians hesitated to send their girls to school for fear that it would be a liability to finding a suitable groom and that it would associate them with the lower castes, both outcaste girls and boys were highly attracted to the mission schools (Kent 2004 140–141). Yet those educated lower castes were still a small percentage of the larger outcaste population, as the 1931 census indicates that only 2.2 percent of Paraiyars in the Madras Presidency were literate at that time, although 15.7 percent of the Paraiyar Christians in Travancore (southern Tamil Nadu and Kerala) were literate (Webster 1992, 78).

Theophilus Appavoo's grandfather E. S. Samuel was born around 1886.[58] He ran away from school when he was twelve, settling in Cuddalore. He ran away because his teacher had beaten him and he had retaliated by throwing a stone at him. After completing only the fifth standard, thus only learning to read Tamil, Samuel declared he did not want to study further. Several Dalit biographies (Freeman 1979, 68) and autobiographies (Bama 2000, 17) describe how Dalit children were torn between being beaten by their teachers at school, usually for no more than being outcaste, and being beaten by their parents for not attending school. Those who did go to school were often segregated, or forced to sit on the veranda.[59] Samuel's move to Cuddalore however, did not break the close contact he had with his family. His grandfather helped him start a private horse-cart taxi business, driving customers between Cuddalore and Pondicherry, and later a butchery for poultry and beef.[60] When Samuel moved to Cuddalore he joined the Anglican church (SPG), a mission that included many upwardly mobile Nadars and emphasized English music, language, and culture. Later he married Danabakiyam and had three sons and six or seven daughters. His eldest son became the headmaster of a small elementary school in Cuddalore Old Town.

Samuel was a self-taught violinist and, to his purist son's dismay, even mixed both classical and folk elements. Besides hearing him sing and play "beautiful" Christian *kīrttaṉai* early in the morning and for family prayer, Theophilus fondly remembers that his grandfather Samuel also sang secular and somewhat subversive folk songs about love and factory work, especially when he had had something to drink. These factory songs criticized the foreign managers and owners for paying such low salaries to the Indians "who worked as hard as oxen." This is the first documented example of the use of folk music in the family's history, particularly as a conscious means of resistance not only to the elite, but to the systems of colonial modernity: it surely stood as a model for Theophilus in his later work with folk music.

Samuel did not know raga theory but played classical style by ear. Theophilus said the following about his grandfather:

> He can play anything he hears. And even the folk songs he used to sing with the violin. He played and sang at the same time. I was his pet grandchild so I had more of him. I also loved him very much. So . . . early morning he'll get up . . . and start singing [and] playing his violin. And he will sing songs, *kīrttaṉai* songs and all songs. He played all Christian songs at these times mostly *kīrttaṉai,* not hymns. He used to sing, then after 6:00 am he'll ask the whole family to get up. Whole family has to get up. There will be lot of quarrel. And he will even beat [his children]. (Theophilus Appavoo, Madurai, September 22, 1994)

This was the first of three generations in Appavoo's family to play karnatak music, mostly in non-professional devotional settings and the epic storytelling/religious discourse genre of *kālākshēpam.*

E. S. Samuel's son James David was born in 1912. He served in the military and then worked in a sugar factory, first as a clerk and then as a supervisor—a job that carried some middle-class respectability.[61] James David received formal training from a Christian karnatak musician while living with his aunt in the hill station of Oothy [Ootacamund].[62] He was a purist in musical grammar (or theory) and was so adept at keeping tala (cyclical rhythmic patterns) that he could keep two different talas simultaneously, one on each hand—a skill Appavoo referred to as acrobatics. He was so talented that in the 1930s he was offered a chance to become a singing actor for Tamil films made in Madras.[63] However, the upper castes who ran the industry insisted he change his name to one that did not identify him as Christian, and possibly by implication, as outcaste. The family story is that after a meditation with God sitting by a fountain outside the studio, James David refused to compromise his identity and returned home to work in the sugar factory.[64]

The 1910s through the 1930s were years of Indian nationalism, when Christians often were labeled as foreigners and the national subject was becoming Hindu and Brahmanized. The response by the developing Indian-led United Church was to officially associate Christian culture, especially theology and indigenous liturgy, with Tamil Śaiva philosophy and karnatak music. A. J. Appaswamy wrote *Christianity as Bhakti Marga* in 1928, and P. Chanchiah supported the Christian ashram movement. Sugirtharajah (1993, 1) refers to this nationalist upper-caste-identified domination as the "Sanskritic-captivity of the church." It was not until the rise of the Dravidian movement in the 1940s that the Protestant culture was able to embrace a local Tamil identity that was in any way critical of the prior Sanskritic hegemony. James David was in many ways a product and adherent of this cultural shift to karnatak musical hegemony in the church, while he ultimately refused to compromise his "Christian identity" for public musical assimilation and the possibility of fame and prosperity as a vocalist in the film industry.

Besides James David, no other family member studied music formally, although his sisters were very good amateur singers. Theophilus learned karnatak music informally from his grandfather Samuel, and then directly from his father. The ideology that drove James David's musical instruction of young Theophilus in karnatak music was that "the Brahmins think that only they can sing karnatak music, but we must prove that we can also sing karnatak." In retrospect Theophilus understood that this was his father's method of protest against caste and class oppression that denied Dalits access to and participation in karnatak music; but Theophilus argued later, "[it was] not the right way of protesting, because everyone has their own culture."[65] Theophilus felt that his father, like many middle-class Christians, did not question the valuation of karnatak and Western culture as superior to his own roots in Dalit culture. Theophilus saw a more liberating form of protest than competing on the oppressor's terms or as he says, "accommodating the oppressor's value."[66] Dalits, he believed, must instead reclaim and proclaim the value of their own culture against the hegemony of upper-caste and Western cultures.

James David wanted to compete with and confront Brahmins on their own terms. His inspiration was Kanchipuram Naina Pillai (1889–1934), a non-Brahmin singer of the Isai Vellalar (lower-middle) caste, who used difficult talas and ragas, Theophilus believed, with the intent to challenge the Brahmin instrumentalists. James David learned his acrobatic tala tricks just by listening to Naina Pillai. Theophilus described him:

> Naina Pillai is the one who the Brahmin players, violinist, mrdangamists (drummers) . . . have to worship before they [play], . . . because if they didn't respect him properly, he'll put them into trouble by singing difficult songs . . . he used to ridicule and put the Brahmin instrumentalist into problems by singing difficult talas and using difficult ragas and he'll switch over from, for example *mōhanam* [raga] set to *adi* [four-beat meter] tala to *todi* [raga] set in *rupakam* [three-beat meter].[67]

Naina Pillai's attitude is also a product of the mid-twentieth century Tamil Isai movement that was the musical wing of the anti-Brahmin Dravidian movement.

From the 1940s to the 1970s Karnatak music remained the canonized symbol for indigenous Tamil Christian music, although the rising waves of the regional Dravidian language movement and the Tamil Isai movement strongly affected Tamil Christian theologians, composers, and musicians. The Dravidian movement, or Self-Respect Movement, was most strongly active in Tamil Nadu between 1949 and 1972; it was part of the all-India movement of nationalism and non-Brahmanism (Hudson 1995, 114). The political roots of this movement were in the Non-Brahmin Manifesto of 1916 (Ryerson 1988, 77), and the South Indian Liberal Federation or Justice Party formed in 1917. They argued for and gained communal representation, fighting for economic justice as well as cultural rights. Periyar E. V. Ramaswamy was the founder of the Self-Respect Movement and leader of the Dravida Karagma (DK) formed in 1944. He preached vehemently against casteism, the subjugation of women, and the use of dowry and caste endogamy, and he encouraged widows to remarry (Ryerson 1988, 55).[68]

Many Christian scholars as well as common people joined the Dravidian political parties: the DK, DMK, and ADMK. Some even became atheists under the influence of the socialist ideology in these movements.[69] Ryerson (1988, i) refers to it as "the golden years of the Tamil renaissance . . . most Tamils underwent a cultural revolution in which they forged and articulated a regional identity—although that identity retained firm links with the past." Literary and linguistic study as well as translation had its roots in the Tamil literary renaissance of the nineteenth century and the work of many Tamil Christians and missionaries. Ryerson (1988, 60) claims it began with Bishop Robert Caldwell's 1856 publication of *A Comparative Grammar of the Dravidian or South Indian Family of Languages*.

The Tamil Isai movement under Rajah Sri Annamalai Chettiar brought to public recognition music by non-Brahmin composers including those from hereditary musician castes. It also was responsible for the development of the public music college at institutions like Annamalai University, which gave access to advanced training for non-Brahmin musicians. Many Dalits and Christians took advantage of these opportunities. The most famous untouchable Christian karnatak performer was T. Mariyanandam, an A-grade artist who had a regular karnatak music teaching show on All India Radio (AIR) Trichy in the 1950s.[70] While Chettiar, the founder of Annamalai University, is considered the founder of the Tami Isai movement, the Nadar Christian Abraham Panditar was one of the earliest proponents of Tamil Isai through his influence on the organization of All India music conferences as early as 1912 and through his book *Karunamita Sagaram* (1917).

The movement to purify Tamil of its Sanskritic elements had a significant influence on indigenized Christian music, literature, and Bible translation; the majority of the leading Tamil theologians of the mid-twentieth century are also famous Tamil scholars and composers.[71] These theologians wrote new music liturgies and songs, desanskritizing many of the Christian words and idioms and introducing new Tamil terminology particularly for the characters of the Trinity (Sundaram 1990, 190). Yet along with advocates of the Tamil Isai movement, they further classicized the performance of karnatak-style music among Christians while establishing the roots of the lyrics, music theory, and ideology of the music in Tamil culture.[72]

CONTINUING CASTEISM, VEILED BY ECUMENICISM

In September 1947, less than a month after India gained its independence from Britain, the Church of South India (CSI), the indigenous South Indian Protestant church, was formed by an alliance between the South Indian United Church (SIUC) and the former Anglicans of the SPG and CMS missions. Issues of church governance delayed unification more than official doctrine. This may have been due to an important and often overlooked factor. As Bishop Leslie Newbigin put it: "the CSI was largely based on family bonds of the majority of its leaders. 'Tirunelveli Christians,' mostly Nadars, had penetrated the higher ranks of most Protestant churches all over Tamil Nadu" (Grafe 1990, 74).[73] Nadar caste hegemony had further repercussions: Anglican traditions dominated in liturgy, interior church architecture and structure, and the preference for *pāmālai* (translated Western hymns) over indigenous *kīrttaṉai*.

The Lutherans (i.e., Vellalars) and the Baptists remained separate from this union. The CSI and Lutherans continued to attempt unification between 1961 and 1970, ultimately failing because they disagreed on continuation and role of the historic episcopate and who would be the legitimate church leaders. Very little has been written on these negotiations, particularly from the perspective of social history;[74] however, the distinctive social makeup of these two church leaderships leads me to theorize that at the core of these episcopate differences was the inability of the Vellalars (who controlled the Lutheran church) and the Nadars (who controlled the CSI) to agree to share power as bishops and priests. India's united church movement has been called one of the greatest experiments or examples of ecumenicism in the world. However, this perspective is based on a perception that denominational differences are the most significant factors separating Christians in India as in the West. I would argue that in spite of the ecumenical appearance of the CSI in South India, true unity has not developed because of caste differences within the Church.[75]

JAMES THEOPHILUS APPAVOO: FROM ANGLICAN TO EVANGELICAL TO ATHEIST TO THE PRIESTHOOD

In the midst of nationalism, Dravidianism, and the creation of the Church of South India, James Theophilus Appavoo was born in Cuddalore on March 9, 1940, one of seven children of James David and Mercy Clara. Theophilus's early years in the Cuddalore church were marked by subtle caste discrimination mostly from Nadar congregation members.

> Even I know karnatak music; my father is a good singer. When there is a carol service only those people [who] sing these hymns and other kinds of things they'll be there. They will give [allow] only one lyric [*kīrttaṉai*] or two lyrics and [for] that also somebody [else] will grab that chance and we will have to be there . . . at their command. They will take the lead and we may have to sing that [their choice of] song.[76]

Appavoo described and understood this negation of participation based on differentiation of those who identify with Western hymns (Nadars) and those who support karnatak-style lyrics or *kīrttaṉai* (Paraiyars) as not only caste but also class oppression. The Central Church in Cuddalore was an Anglican church dominated by Nadars, whom he felt deliberately gave opportunities such as choir participation, Bible reading, and election support to their own community members over all others, be they high-caste Vellalars or outcaste Paraiyars.[77] Most of these Nadars were teachers or merchants, comparable middle-class occupations to Appavoo's own parents whom he felt had lacked opportunities to participate liturgically or in the power structure of their church.[78]

This sort of discrimination was reversed when Rev. Honest Chinniah took over the church in the 1960s. Although a Nadar himself, he supported the underdog. At the time Appavoo did not directly name his oppression. But by encouraging Appavoo's musical potential, Chinniah showed him that someone from the Nadar caste could transcend their clannish behavior. This also renewed Appavoo's Christian faith, challenging feelings of atheism that resulted partly from his experience of casteism in the church.

Many adherents of the Dravidian movement were atheists. Appavoo's move toward atheism began in the 1950s during the height of the Dravidian movement when he was in his late teens and was spurred by a rejection of Evangelical Christianity. His parents had been swayed by Sara Navaroji's Pentecostal movement and stopped regularly attending the Anglican Church, which led to Appavoo performing Evangelical music.[79] Tamil Christian Evangelists and Pentecostals have used "light" or popular music since the 1950s to attract gospel convention audiences of all classes and castes and to communicate a message of "prosperity theology," which many liberation theologians critically refer to as *āsīrvādam* (blessing theology). Light Christian music can be understood as a form of "Christianization" of film music style. Furthermore, it is a translation of Western (capitalist) prosperity theology through assimilation with familiar native features of popular music. After becoming a theologian, Appavoo critiqued light music as pacifying because while it uses the language of, and is directed toward the masses, he argued it lacks the means to enable cultural or social empowerment. Prosperity theology does not encourage action against oppressive social structures, but supports the attainment of status quo middle-class lifestyles that continue to remain far from the reach of this primarily lower-class/caste audience.

During the late 1950s, Appavoo played harmonium for some singing Evangelists, including Paul Dinakaran, who was originally a Nadar from Cuddalore and who eventually became a very famous Evangelist. As Appavoo observed these preachers, however, he became quite skeptical of the lack of equality demonstrated by them toward the *visuvāsigal* (people of faith.)[80] Appavoo had several experiences while traveling with Dinakaran's troupe, which confirmed his suspicion that many people "faked being saved" and that the Evangelists were cheating the people, making class-like differentiations among them. These experiences solidified his identity as an atheist because he wondered, "If there was a God, how could he allow this type of cheating to go on?"

> I went with a famous preacher called Jivanandam. He took me [to Kanniyakumari] to play harmonium. He'll speak and sing then I'll play. But the next day I found that [only] we had very good meal. Because, at the time I was a teacher so I got [a good] meal and this Jivanandam and others got good meal, but other people [of faith], *visuvāsagal* they had only *kañji.* So that shook me because my parents always practice equality in our house, even [though] we had servants . . . everyone will get the same food. You know I didn't get this holy spirit, but I was given good food, so it is status, not even faith, it is some status . . . So these things there shook me and I decided there was no God, because these fellows are all crooks.[81]

Ironically it was this very unchristian experience of food being separated among "classes" of Christians, priests, teacher/musicians, and the common people that disturbed Appavoo to the extent that he "lost his faith." However, a similar consciousness of such inequality would later form the basis of Appavoo's own theology of sharing food in a Eucharistic lifestyle as a means to liberation.

CSI DOMINATION BY NADARS

By the mid-twentieth century, education, migration, endogamy, economic development, and unified identification with the British missions and crown brought great power to the Nadars. Raam Kumar Nadar (2004) argues that, "mercantilism and Christianity played crucial roles in facilitating the Nadar's upward mobility." The Nadars took advantage of British control of southern Tamil Nadu, which created new opportunities for economic development and urbanization initiatives (Nadar 2004). The most important figure, Kamaraj Nadar gained enough political capital to become Chief Minister of Tamil Nadu in 1954 and President of the Indian National Congress in 1963. Famous Nadar Christians include V. S. Azariah, the first Indian Bishop consecrated by the Anglican Church of England.

Many Nadars migrated from villages in the Tirunelveli area to towns and cities throughout Tamil Nadu such as Madurai and Cuddalore, taking with them, and in some cases introducing the use of, the *pāmālai,* or English hymns translated into Tamil, where the practice of *kīrttaṉai* had previously dominated in the CSI churches. By 1937, the Nadar priest and musician Honest Chinniah began the practice of accompanying *kīrttaṉai* with harmony on the organ at All Saints Church in Tiruchchirappalli, fusing karnatak and Western styles (Sherinian 1998, 238). By this time the Nadars posed a numerical and unified threat against the Vellalar Christians who had held the majority of positions of power within the Protestant community for two centuries. When the ecumenical Church of South India (CSI) was formed in 1947, Nadars ensured the dominant presence of Anglican hierarchical structures, particularly the use of English liturgy and hymnody in urban churches, and a continued ideological resistance toward liturgical and ritual indigenization. Many of the Lutheran Vellalars maintained their caste power by staying separate from the CSI unification, remaining members and leaders of the Tamil Evangelical Lutheran Church. Thus the Nadars further solidified their control of the CSI (Grafe 1990, 74).

The person who led Appavoo back to Christianity and had the strongest musical influence on him, besides his father and grandfather, was Honest Chinniah, a great "guru" of Christian karnatak music and the man who had first accompanied *kīrttaṉai* with harmony on the organ. When Appavoo was in his early twenties working as a young teacher, Chinniah became the priest at The Central Church in Cuddalore. Before this time the church was riddled with caste and class differentiation manifest in who was chosen for choir participation, Bible reading, and election support, and in differentiating those who supported hymns (Nadars) or *kīrttaṉai* (Paraiyars). As indicated above, Chinniah was a Nadar. Yet like a few of his caste before him, he had a strong interest in karnatak music, while most were highly Anglicized.

THE KARNATAK CHRISTIAN MUSIC GURU

Chinniah wanted to start a karnatak choir in Cuddalore and heard that the James family was very talented in karnatak music, but did not attend church often. Chinniah approached Appavoo to work with the choir. However, Appavoo was not easily (re)converted by this Nadar priest. He resisted, telling Chinniah, "I hate all priests."[82] Furthermore, Appavoo believed Christians could not perform karnatak music because he believed they had no ability to keep tala (or rhythm).

> Twice I escaped him. Then somehow he got hold of me and said, "Come you must join the choir." Then I said, "I will come, but these Christian fellows they don't know how to sing. They don't have a sense of tala. Without the sense of tala, how can we sing karnatak music?" Then Chinniah said, "Why don't you come and teach them?" This is something which touched me, because being Dalits we are not much respected in the church. Because my father was middle class and he was working in the factory they did give some respect to us, but not that [level of] respect given to the other caste people.[83]

Moved by the respect Chinniah showed him as a musician and teacher (while reinforcing Appavoo's father's ideas of karnatak music as valuable because of its virtuosic nature), Appavoo agreed to lead the choir. However, he reiterated that he was an atheist and would not be in church for anything besides the music (indeed, he would slip out the side door between songs). Later, when some powerful church members criticized the sound of Appavoo's choir, Chinniah stood up for him, saying that Appavoo knew karnatak music and that this was the way it should sound.

Chinniah began to break down the caste divisions within the church focusing particularly on the youth. After Chinniah came, Appavoo became "like a brother" to several Nadar boys. The community building work Chinniah did and the close inter-caste relationships Appavoo formed among the youth did not, however, extend to the entire congregation, and the Nadars eventually separated to start (and dominate) their own church. The separation of CSI churches by caste-dominated groups is a trend that has intensified since the 1980s. Appavoo analyzed it as an economic issue. As the capitalist system created a rising middle class, particularly among lower middle-caste groups like the Nadars and some Dalits, these communities reacted by becoming exclusionary.

> It's because they wanted to have some identity to fight this capitalistic oppression . . . you have to stick together. You feel you are alone. Because capitalism brings individualism. Then you stick to your caste group, to get some power. If you are an individual you don't get power. Then if you are caste-oriented then you have power, as a group. That's why the caste [mindedness] is growing. People said that capitalism will kill the caste. No, that has been disproved.[84]

In his mid-twenties Appavoo trained and conducted Chinniah's one hundred-voice choir.[85] They performed both classical karnatak and Western pieces but never used harmony to accompany karnatak forms as had been common practice since the 1940s. After his harmonic experimentation, Chinniah had became a purist regarding the separation of Indian and Western elements.[86] Appavoo studied Western music and conducting with Chinniah, and also Western music from a Catholic nun, Mother Peter. It was Chinniah who first encouraged him to compose; the results included difficult karnatak forms like *varṇams* and *kīrttaṉai* (PURL 2.3).

In order to spread the appreciation for karnatak music acquired from his father and Chinniah, Appavoo developed some interesting techniques of transmission.[87] Using a technique of associating each raga with a film music tune in which the particular raga was present, he taught his students to recognize ragas. This allowed him to show the main *lakshanam* or defining characteristics of the raga. He was so successful that the boys (Paraiyars and Nadars) joined a music *sabha*, an organization typically run by upper castes that sponsored karnatak concerts. Later he started his own fifty-voice young men's choir called the Christian Musical Association.

TRANSFORMATION TO CHRISTIANITY THROUGH MUSIC

Appavoo maintained his atheism until finally Chinniah asked him to come to a youth league meeting. Appavoo resisted but consented to engage with Chinniah in rationalistic theological discussions, which included talking about "freedom theology." Appavoo describes the issues they debated.

> Where God has given human beings freedom [so] they are misusing the freedom, that's why all the sins and sorrows, that kind of theology. Then he was talking about freedom of human beings to choose their own path. You should not pressurize your parents or the parents should not pressurize the [child], . . . he's a Nadar, the argument went on, then suddenly I asked him, he has three daughters, I asked him "Ok, suppose I love your daughter, would you give her in marriage to me?" I know the Nadars won't do it! Then he said, "No!," I asked, "Why, but you are talking about freedom and all that." He said "What man! My daughter should love you. If she loves you and he loves her why there is no objection. You cannot just claim her because you love her." [Zoe laughter] He knew that his daughter is loving somebody else. [More laughter]. That shook me, that answer shook me. I always expected that he'll become angry and drive me out. He said it in a very jovial manner, suddenly everybody laughed. It's a punch line, no "she should love you," you know, punch line.[88]

Appavoo was embarrassed that he had overstepped his bounds with this priest but appreciated and respected Chinniah for engaging him like a friend. This form of equal engagement between teacher and student would be an important model of dialogue in his own teaching later. Ultimately it was Chinniah's support for marginalized people that brought Appavoo back to Christianity.

> He does what he believes, very honest, his name is Honest and he is also very honest. Even a small *paisa* (cent) he will not take. So that [the way he led] his life made me think that there should be God, because there are people like him. And also his theology. But now if I reflect back, I think it is

> his life rather than his theology, which converted me. He doesn't have any discrimination, on the basis of class, or caste or anything.[89]

One day while Chinniah was meeting with a poor man to arrange a wedding date for the man's daughter, the collector came unexpectedly to see the priest. Instead of dismissing this poor man, which would have been common social practice, he asked the collector to wait, saying that this man had come a very long way. He offered the collector a seat on the sofa next to the poor man, finished the appointment and only then saw to the collector's needs. Appavoo was completely moved by Chinniah's lack of discrimination. He described his deep feelings of esteem for Chinniah: "so that kind of person, he was my, he is . . . still my guru."[90] Chinniah's invitation to Appavoo to teach and conduct his one hundred-voice choir, his willingness to teach him Western music, and his encouragement of Appavoo to compose in difficult karnatak genres as well as Appavoo's observations of Chinniah's fair treatment of poor people renewed his faith that someone from the Nadar caste could transcend divisive caste behavior.

The Christian guru/student relationship between these two men ultimately led to Chinniah encouraging Appavoo to apply for the ministry. Appavoo applied for sponsorship from the CSI Madras Diocese but was turned down because of something he had previously done that was not considered in "good character." A few years later however, when Chinniah was teaching at the Tamil Nadu Theological Seminary, he arranged a scholarship for Appavoo as an independent candidate. Thus it was Chinniah who brought Appavoo to TTS. Assuming he would not get selected as a minister (although he did later) Appavoo chose to study theology with the intention of teaching, a profession in which he was already accomplished by this point as he had taught English in a Panchayat Union and Government High School for thirteen years. Further he had acquired a diploma in education from the Government Teacher's Training College, Vadalore, in 1959 and a Bachelor of Arts in history and geography from Madras University in 1963.

APPAVOO AT THE TAMIL NADU THEOLOGICAL SEMINARY

When Appavoo arrived at the Tamil Nadu Theological Seminary in 1975 at age thirty-five to earn a Bachelor of Divinity, music practice at the seminary was dominated by a type of sung liturgy in Tamil karnatak music and desanskritized pure (*sen*) literary Tamil. The theology of these *Tamiẓ Isai Vaṛi Paḍu* (TIVP) was influenced by Marxist social analysis, feminism, and anti-caste politics. Thus while these liturgies supplanted Brahmanical theological influences and sanskritized Tamil with a more socially progressive Christian theology, the use of literary Tamil and classical music style continued to preference the values and cultural experiences of the social and cultural elite. Transforming the message of *sen* Tamil (TIVP) liturgies was the first step in the construction of a socially conscious Tamil Christian theology, while the linguistic and musical medium of transmission remained hegemonic.

While studying at TTS, Appavoo learned karnatak music from several non-Dalits. One was V. P. K. Sundaram, an award-winning karnatak music theorist, composer, and specialist of the fifth-century Tamil book *Silapadikaram*. Appavoo recognizes Sundaram as one of his teachers, although later they had ideological differences over issues of style and teaching method: Sundaram fully embraced karnatak music and pedagogical styles, while Appavoo eventually questioned them. Rev. Thomas Thangaraj, a theologian and well known composer of Christian light music, was also an important musical mentor for Appavoo, giving him opportunities to perform and compose. Appavoo played harmonium for Thangaraj's *kālākshēpams* and even performed on tour with him in Sweden and Sri Lanka. Thangaraj was also significant as a model of liturgical experimentation, bringing folk dance into Christian liturgy at TTS.

When Appavoo was a student at TTS in the late 1970s the annual carol service composers included V. P. K. Sundaram, Dayanandan Francis, Swamikannu (a Paraiyar and one of the best Christian karnatak musicians of his generation), and Thomas Thangaraj. M. Karunakaran, who was training to be the music instructor for the Madras diocese (under Bishop Sundar Clarke) and was teaching a music course at TTS, was also involved in the carol service. Students were rarely invited into the composition process for the carol service (until Appavoo took over in the 1980s). However, Appavoo, the student, was given opportunities to collaborate with Thangaraj and three other musicians. In 1978 Appavoo composed most of the music for the song "Ammā Mariyammā," while Thangaraj wrote the lyrics. Although it was in light music style, not folk, this was one of the first compositions in which TTS composers used simple Tamil in the style of Tamil poet Subramania Bharathi as opposed to strict literary Tamil. The song "Ammā Mariyammā" is about liberation, particularly of the poor. When shepherds ask Mary, "What is the meaning of your son's name?" she replies, "Liberator." When they ask, "Liberation for whom?" She answers, "For the poor, the hungry, the needy."[91]

RURAL THEOLOGY INSTITUTE AND EARLY FOLK SONGS

After finishing his Bachelor of Divinity in 1979 and becoming a priest, Appavoo joined the Rural Theological Institute (TTS's rural campus just outside Madurai) as a project officer for communication. One of his primary duties was to develop forms of communication media that would be locally meaningful to, and encourage expression from, the rural poor. One of the main goals of the communication department at TTS was "to identify and present local expressions in folk arts (dance, puppetry, music, story telling) in order to fight against cultural imperialism and to use them with new [religiously and socially liberating] content" (Amirtham and David 1990, 169). In the villages, Appavoo found that although people enjoyed karnatak music if they heard it on the radio or sang Christian *kīrttaṉai,* it was "totally useless for communication" of liberating social and theological messages.[92] While at RTI he spent much of his time organizing music groups and touring the area listening to folk musicians.

> I would go to the folk musician's house, sit and ask them to sing and sing, here, here, here. Bring it into my body.[93] When I was in RTI I got it, I got that composing talent within two or three years. I started writing psalms and other things in folk music . . . Wherever, whenever, there is some festival, some folk performance, I'll be there. I'll take my bicycle, go, stay overnight, come in the morning . . . That was a kind of learning experience, I wanted to learn. And I learned quickly.[94]

One of Appavoo's first folk songs was composed on the invitation of TTS Principal Samuel Amirtham for the inauguration of the RTI outdoor chapel and its new stone cross. Appavoo's "Pudiya Siluva" (A New Cross) was a call to the RTI students to "not simply enjoy their spirituality and closeness with God," but to take it as action into the villages to understand and aid the troubles (tears) of the poor people there. The metaphors of "a new cross for every new generation" and "a separate cross for every place" signify the importance in RTI's social and theological work founded in continually recognizing contextual needs and relevance (see Appendix 2 for lyrics) (PURL 2.4). The song is also a reminder that the cross is not just a piece of jewelry to be worn as a token of Christian identity. Its significance is the miraculous act of deep loving concern of God. This deep love, *taya palūvu,* literally means "heavy" in Tamil. As a metaphor it means that God's heart weighs heavily in concern for the people and also reflects the heavy stone cross slab with a heart inscribed on it in the new chapel at RTI. The expression of God's love becomes manifests in people's united action to alleviate suffering.

Composing in folk style and spoken language became popular in the mainstream Tamil music industry in the early 1980s, particularly through the domination of film composer Ilaiyaraja, another significant influence on Appavoo. In his song "Kottuk Kottā Kāssirukku Koḍimundiri Tirātca," Appavoo weaves together in rhyme the spoken form of every word in the first line of the verse, especially in the endings of the words.[95] Appavoo continued working with folk music by setting many of the Psalms to this style including "Āṇḍavanē Eṅga Āṭṭiḍaiyan" (The Lord is my Shepherd) based on Psalm 23.[96] One of Appavoo's first folk songs to directly address social struggles is "Pēccu Tandiramā?" or "Deceptive Speech?" He wrote it for an Independence Day ceremony at RTI to address the struggle of jasmine flower cultivators in the RTI area. "Pēccu Tandiramā?" references people's discourse about independence and democracy in contrast to the reality of workers such as the jasmine cultivators not having economic independence from exploitative middlemen. Appavoo described it as "Christian only in the sense that its problem is Christian. The approach is Christian."[97] That is, social justice and poor people's economic rights are inherently a Christian concern.

Soon after this, Appavoo wrote his first folk song that directly addressed the problems of caste prejudice and religious difference. "Villabara Saṇaḍaiyillē" (recorded on his cassette *Nimindu Naḍa* [Stand Tall], 1985) uses the bullock cart genre of Tamil folk music. Its lyrics ask people to "be sensible" about caste differences by naming the contemporary hypocrisy of social treatment or caste distinctions in different contexts (urban vs. rural, deities vs. people). The lyrics say, "When you go to Madurai you eat with anybody in the hotel. Only when you come back to the village you say all these things" (about separation of castes from eating together because of impurity).

Appavoo's early folk songs from the late 1970s and early 1980s do not necessarily use obvious Christian symbols or themes. However, they reflect Appavoo's RTI experience theologically in that they express his exposure to the realities of rural, social, and economic oppression. Furthermore, they express his growing understanding of the necessity for Christian justice work to support people's struggles.

By the mid 1980s after exposure to Marxism, liberation theology, and several years working with and fighting for the needs of villagers at RTI, Appavoo came into his own as a folk music composer. His was music that both addressed the social needs of poor village Dalits and transmitted a liberation theology message in a musical style that positively reflected their values and cultural traditions. He radically disrupted the practice of Tamil Christian music by retrieving previously rejected indigenous culture and infusing a positive attitude toward it, and questioning earlier assumptions of the superiority of both Western and elite Indian musical values (Kaplan 1995, 19–20). Appavoo further incorporated into his songs *Adi Samayam* village religious practices and politics, rural musical moods, stylistic devices, agricultural metaphors, and the rhythms of the trance-inducing paṟai drum in order to create a means for Dalits to reclaim their self-esteem, redefine their status, and reinvent themselves as worthy of human rights and respect. Appavoo defines his folk music as *Christian* indigenized music because it is liberating in content, musical style, and in the music's ability to be re-created through a folk transmission system by those who receive and use it. Active re-creation of theology through folk music defines liberation as socio-spiritual transformation.

GROWING DALIT IDENTITY

An important step in Appavoo's shift toward reclaiming Dalit culture as the basis of the content, language, and musical style of TTS songs and liturgies was the development of Dalit consciousness and pride among TTS students and faculty in the 1980s. The process of Appavoo's consciousness raising involved touring villages near Madurai, organizing music groups, learning folk music, and becoming friends with village people from the lower castes.

> I had to go to the village, sit with them, talk with them . . . I had a kind of natural tendency to talk equally with people. So, they started loving me, kind of adopting me, we had very good relations. Then they started talking about their problems, how they feel. It is mostly non-Dalits at that time, very few Dalits at that time. The castes were Tevars, Nadars, and Mupanars.[98]

These problems inspired Appavoo's new folk songs. He empathized with the poor and began identifying with and "feeling" his own Dalitness. Further, he began to understand his own caste oppression as a middle-class Dalit through feeling an affinity with the caste oppression of poor Dalits near RTI. Appavoo reflected on the process of his growing consciousness:

> If I look back I feel that it started from Cuddalore and slowly developed when I was studying here [at TTS] and started growing and growing and when I went to RTI, I was exposed to the caste system practiced there in the villages. Although I was not directly oppressed or denigrated, I found that

some of the Dalits are denigrated. So that made me kind of angry. That's why the song came [as a composition to me] the *villabara saṉaḍaiyillē* song; it is about caste.[99]

Appavoo's experience at RTI helped him identify his own feelings and experiences of oppression from his childhood. At TTS these involved the subtle kinds of discrimination that many middle-class Dalits experience. Appavoo's primary experience of discrimination was feeling as though he was not given opportunities, or was left out when others he considered much less talented were given opportunities to advance before him.

Appavoo spoke further about this process of identification with "Dalitness" particularly in the TTS context where a sense of regional identity (Madras, Kanyakumari, Coimbatore) often leads to caste separations. This was especially the case at the time of student elections. There was a caste bond particularly among the Kanyakumari Nadar students. The fact that very few Dalit students come from that Southern district encouraged and reinforced bonding of multiple caste/regional identities. When Appavoo was a student, the Madras Dalits also began to gather in private, but in this case to share their experiences of caste oppression, which included being derogatorily labeled "beef eaters."

Appavoo: There was this oppression in TTS when Samuel Amirtham was principal, [1969–1978]. Some of the Madras students, like the present secretary of Madras Diocese, S. D. Soundarajan, and others, they started having this feeling: "Because we are Dalits we are oppressed," and we had some kind of unity. Caste identity, you know, joining together.

Zoe: Did you use the word "harijan" [Gandhi's term for outcastes that Appavoo considered patronizing] at the time?[100]

Appavoo: [strong and gruff] No! We used our caste name. Ok, but with a little bit of shame kind of thing. But we were trying to overcome the shame, concept. We used to say, "Yes we are Paraiyars, what [about] that?"[101]

The term "Dalit" was just coming in to use by the mid-1980s in Tamil Nadu. In the late 1970s and early 1980s TTS faculty and students were conscious of caste issues and many scheduled caste Christians were beginning to identify more positively with their identity as Paraiyar or Pallar. Although there may have been some bonding across scheduled caste subcategories, they were not using the term "Dalit" (oppressed), which is more inclusive of all the oppressed and avoids subcaste differentiation. Instead, Appavoo says, they defined this consciousness as "getting village identity or identity of the poor."[102] Mohan Larbeer described that in the early 1980s terms such as slum, village, and poor all implied or directly meant those from untouchable communities.[103]

The essential difference between the category "Dalit" and "scheduled caste" is important here. Appavoo would not say, "I am a proud Paraiyar," as distinct and separate from other scheduled castes like Pallars as well as higher castes like Nadars. Instead he claimed with pride an identity as "Dalit" or person oppressed by caste or a person who stands against caste. Rejecting his former caste/*jāti* name, he embraced a chosen identity of Dalit and signified through it an active opposition to the entire social system that has created caste status and hierarchical oppression.

THE NEXT GENERATION

Appavoo created and disseminated Dalit Christian folk music for over twenty-five years through his teaching position at TTS. He nurtured, negotiated, and tested his music in dialogue with his students, his wife Dorathy, and his own daughters: Adrina born in 1972 and Neena born in 1975. Growing up in this situation, his daughters have taken on their own interesting mix of identities. Both are highly fluent in English, hold bachelors degrees in English and Science respectively (Neena holds an additional B.Ed degree) and were raised in the intellectual, questioning context of the seminary: experiences that are still available only to the cream of Indian society. Both young women could have done anything with their lives. And they have chosen to take on the ideology of Dalit liberation and the voice of Tamil folk music. Indeed they both played significant singing roles in the production of Appavoo's last CD project, *He Gives All Blessings,* in which he was able to use "typical" folk vocal and instrumental sounds including a highly nasal quality (timbre) in the voices. Furthermore, he only used acoustic folk instruments adding very little studio effects. While one would expect Appavoo's daughters to have the voices of classical or light music singers because of the upper-middle-class milieu in which they were raised, they have consciously learned to sound like typical villagers. Adrina has become a specialist in acupuncture (encouraged by her father's strong interest in natural and Indian forms of medicine) and had an inter-caste marriage with Paul Pushparaj, a Chettiar Hindu. Neena has followed a typical path of many middle-class Christian women, becoming a teacher and (Dalit) pastor's wife, working and teaching music among Dalit villagers with her added commitment to continue to directly spread her father's musical theology among them. Since his death in 2005, Appavoo's wife Dorathy has been working as a warden in a CSI hostel near the Andhra Pradesh boarder, enduring personal hardships to continue serving the needy.

In order for Appavoo to create "Christian" indigenized Tamil Music, he radically departed from his family's musical inheritance and the institutionalized practice of Tamil Christian music. While he drew from the agency and resistance of his ancestors he also took the process of cultural indigenization full circle to reclaim and reinvent his folk roots, incorporating them into Tamil Christianity through music to make the religion more socially, politically, psychologically, and spiritually transformative for the majority of its adherents. In the process of embracing folk music as a means of transmission of Dalit theology, Appavoo was forced to radically critique the effectiveness of karnatak music to transmit anti-hierarchical values of justice and sharing and thereby challenged his own inherited "sanskritized" Christian identity. Furthermore, while light or film music style has some of the populist elements of accessibility that Appavoo deemed essential to folk music (in this case, urban folk music), light music used to transmit prosperity theology among Tamil Evangelical Christians has only reinforced the music's middle-class materialist identity. The use of expensive Western electronic instruments and the dominant presence of Western forms and melodies keep light music inaccessible as a liberatory medium for Dalit Christians. Through Appavoo's contribution to the discourse of the value of musical style in the Tamil Christian community, the practice of music is forever changed.

CONCLUSION

Theophilus Appavoo's family musical history includes many significant slippages in the generic patterns of Tamil Christian musical and caste history that allowed for the possibility for him to create Dalit theology in folk music. Theophilus Appavoo's first Christian ancestor, Edward Appavoo, converted in the late nineteenth century as an individual through an intellectual encounter with a missionary, as opposed to most poor rural Paraiyars of his period who converted in clan or caste groups. Appavoo's father James David was just one of a handful of outcastes in the early twentieth century who were able to attain a high level of skill in karnatak music. Then, instead of becoming a professional musician in the film industry, he consciously chose to maintain his identity as a Christian and by association an untouchable. James David trained his son

Theophilus in karnatak music. After becoming an atheist, Theophilus may have never applied these skills to a Christian context if it had not been for his mentorship under the Nadar, Honest Chinniah. It was also odd that as a Nadar, Chinniah was particularly interested in karnatak music and furthermore that he had no regard for the Nadar caste tendency to discriminate against outcaste Christians. It was only through Appavoo's association with Chinniah that he regained a sense of faith, became interested in the ministry, and was ultimately accepted as a student at TTS. It was in the Marxist and Dalit milieu of TTS that his prideful Dalit identity was formed, that he began to deconstruct his experience of castism and his gender and class privilege. He also received further mentorship from higher caste musicians such as V. P. K. Sundaram and Thomas Thangaraj who were experimenting with the relationship of theology to various styles of music and ultimately, through his encounters with lower-caste villagers he was able to realize his theological path through Tamil folk music.

3

PARAṬṬAI'S THEOLOGY

Greeting God in the Cēri

Mr. Pitchai, a non-Christian Dalit landless laborer, described God from the perspective of Tamil village religious practice (or Adi Samayam, "original religion"), saying "God is part and parcel of life" (Appavoo 1997, 283). This inspiration for Appavoo, from one of his "best teachers of theology," led him to formulate an understanding of Christian theology from Dalit religions. He concluded that "theology in Dalit tradition is not just speaking or writing, it is life that is lived with God. Theological expression is not just verbal, it is expression of life" (Appavoo 1997, 283). From this understanding of theology as the action of holistic liberative living and his observation of Dalit religion, Appavoo asserts that worship is the primary means of theological expression for Dalits and should be an essential part of an emerging Dalit theology (Appavoo 1997, 283).

At the heart of Dalit Christian worship lies folk music. Appavoo described this when he proclaimed to me, "We are drumming our theology," referencing the reclamation of the parai drum and drummer as a symbol of Dalit cultural liberation that has occurred among Christians and in the secular Dalit movement in Tamil Nadu. Paṟai drumming had been considered the ritually degraded occupation of the Paṟaiyars, as members of this *jāti* were required to play for upper-caste funerals, thus associating the drum and the drummers with the pollution of death.[1] By bringing this instrument physically into the sacred space of the church building and using it to accompany his liturgy in folk music, Appavoo made significant steps toward reversing its associations with degradation, transforming the psyche of Dalits with a sense of healing pride in their culture. Indeed while Appavoo and his students had been using the paṟai drum in liturgies at TTS since the early 1990s, one of his students, S. Jebarajan, took this reclamation a step further. In 2003 he composed a *Paṟai Isai Vaṟi Pāḍu* (or Paṟai Music Worship) which required that all members of the congregation gather around a musician holding the paṟai drum during the passing of the peace (creating community through shaking hands and acknowledging each other's presence) and touch the instrument to reaffirm their commitment to working for Dalit liberation.[2] An esteemed theologian and TTS professor, who was a Paṟaiyar himself, had been attending TTS folk music services for many years in which the paṟai was played, but had never touched the instrument. The experience of doing so in this worship brought him to tears, producing a cathartic release of internalized shame.[3]

The first section of Appavoo's *Village Music Liturgy*, the "Greetings and Praise of God," lies at the heart of his construction of the Christian Trinity as it evolves from Dalit people. My analysis of "Greetings and Praise" is extensive because a complete lyrical, cultural, and musical understanding of this section is central to my discussion of the differences and similarities between Appavoo's Dalit theology and other liberation theologies. From the liturgical analysis will evolve a broader discussion of Appavoo's relationship and contribution to the history of Dalit theology and the Tamil Dalit cultural movement. Finally, I present a comparison of Appavoo's work and that of other liberation theologians in the wider global Christian context.

Appavoo's theology fulfills a holistic set of needs for the Dalit community. It is a means toward empowered cultural and religious identification for Dalit people and their cultural resources, in contrast to the hegemonic claims of inferiority, degradation, and inauspiciousness of the "untouchable" in Indian society. Through liturgical song, Appavoo reclaims Dalits and their culture as valuable, auspicious, and worthy, and uses this consciousness of an affirmed identity to build unity within Dalit communities. As a context for enculturated Christian worship, the liturgy is the means to (re)create spiritual, cultural, and psychological liberation. This occurs primarily through the transformative aspects of oral folk culture. The description of Appavoo's three theological tenets—*oru olai*, universal family, and a strategy of reversal—provide the analytical and interpretive means to show how folk music can serve as an oral system of transmission and re-creation. This is musical theology as a dialogical process of creation and re-creation. It is not a commercial product (like much Indian Christian music) nor is it associated with the individual identity of a composer or musician.

To analyze Appavoo's relationship to Dalit theology and Dalit cultural movements in Tamil Nadu, I articulate the steps necessary to create an orally based theology that can serve the functions of positive re-identification outlined above. These steps include social and religious analysis, theological interpretation, media integration, transmission, and reception. By comparing Appavoo's theology to feminist and womanist liberation theologies, I come to the following conclusions. While the trap of essentialization often becomes a hindrance within identity politics movements, the work of Emilie Townes (1995) and Serene Jones (2000) shows how the oppressed can reclaim liturgy as a means to empowered cultural identity while avoiding the pitfalls of essentialization without romanticizing community. However, the feminist call to critically interrogate the essentialist ideal of community and identity politics requires an examination of the limitations and risks of Appavoo's Dalit theological model. For example, the potential for aesthetic inflexibility of an identity politics of music and the potential for exclusion of non-Dalits from a communal context could limit the impact of Appavoo's goals to create a sustainable liberating praxis. This global dialogue also shows that worship can function as a means for the oppressed to create the community structure necessary to support an empowered identity. Further, as the re-creative nature of folk music facilitates liberative theological construction by Dalits, the creation of a liberative Christian community also necessitates a continual process of transformation or reformation, renewal, and "internal critique" that can happen through performance as praxis. Thus both the musical form/style of folklore and the community context are necessarily transformative in nature.

Sāmiya Vaṇaṅguṟadu (Greetings and Praise of God)
From *Girāmiya Isai Vaṟipāḍu* (*Village Music Liturgy*)
Composed by J. T. Appavoo
Translated by J. T. Appavoo and Zoe Sherinian

SECTION 1
Pettavarē olagattai paḍaiccavarē—ammayappā
O, parent who created the world, mama/papa.
Attaṉaikkum āṇḍavarē ompādam vaṇakkam
Lord of everything, we bow at your feet.
Mūttavarē mīṭṭeḍukka vandavarē—kaṉṉimari
O, the eldest one who has come to redeem us.
Petteḍutta pālagarē ompādam, vaṇakkam
O, child of Virgin Mary, we bow at your feet.
Suttattiru āviyarē sūriyarē—ottumaye
O, the Holy Spirit, the sun.
Kaṟṟuttarum vāttiyārē ompādam vaṇakkam
The one who teaches us solidarity, we bow at your feet.

SECTION 2
Āttukkuḷḷa ūttu taṇṇi sāmiyaruḷ nādā—pāva
You are the spring in the river, O divine one, gracious lord!
Ūttai pōkkum jīvataṇṇi sāmiyaruḷ nādā

The living water that cleans the filth of sin,
O divine one, gracious lord!
Sutta neyyi poṅga sōṟu sāmiyaruḷ nādā—pasiye
You are the pure *ghee poṅgal* rice, O divine one, gracious lord!
Nittam pōkkum jīvasōṟu sāmiyaruḷ nādā
The living rice that removes hunger every day,
O divine one, gracious lord!
Kāttula nī teṉṉaṅkāttu sāmiyaruḷ nādā—olaham
You are the breeze from the coconut grove,
O divine one, gracious lord!
Mottattukkum vīsum kāttu sāmiyaruḷ nādā
That blows for all the world, O divine one, gracious lord!

SECTION 3
Muttipōṉa sorakkā nāṅga sāmiyaruḷ nādāoḍacci
We are the overripe vegetable, the *sorakkā*
O divine one, gracious lord!
Vitteḍuttu vedappavaru nī sāmiyaruḷ nādā
You are the one who breaks the gourd,
removes the seeds and plants them!
Neruñcimuḷḷu neṟañca nelam sāmiyaruḷ nādā—ēṅga
We are the land full of *neruñci* thorns, O divine one, gracious lord!
Neñcaikkotti kaḷaiyeḍuppavar nīyē aruḷ nādā
You are the one who plows our hearts and removes the weeds, O divine one, gracious lord!

SECTION 4
Karugippōṉa kāṇappayiru sāmiyaruḷ nādā
We are the wilted *kāṇai* plant, O divine one, gracious lord!
Tuḷukkavaikkum vevasāyi nī sāmiyaruḷ nādā
You are the farmer who makes it sprout, O divine one, gracious lord!
Viruttiyillā paruttikkāḍu sāmiyaruḷ nādā—adai
We are the cotton fields that do not yield, O divine one, gracious lord!
Veḷaya vaikkum vevasāyi nī sāmiyaruḷ nādā
You are the farmer who makes them grow,
O divine one, gracious lord!
Ēreḍuttu vantavarē sāmiyaruḷ nādā—oṅga
O you who took up the plow and came, O divine one, gracious lord!
Pēreḍuttu pōṟṟī seyyiṟam sāmiyaruḷ nādā
So we take your name and praise you, O divine one, gracious lord!

Appavoo's *Girāmiya Isai Vaṛipāḍu* is a welcoming, inclusive ritual in the community spirit of Dalit festivals. Before the "Adoration" or "Greetings and Praise," seen above, the ritual leader has announced that all community disputes have been settled, and asks, "Have all the in-laws, brothers, and sisters come?" as the community gathers in unity as one family and all are prepared to participate (Appavoo 1997, 285–6). The Christian Trinity is then welcomed and adored in a way that reclaims the Divine in the local agricultural and social context. The congregation participates through openly praying and through the use of a sung responsorial format. The folk tunes, rhythms, and metaphors woven throughout the liturgy are easily recognized, while their use in this Dalit Christian theology context infuses the musical elements with new meaning of "the fruits of the spirit." These include "life, new vision, freedom, voice, new actions and [the search for] community" (Devasahayam 1997, xiv) (PURL 3.1).

The *Sāmiya Vaṇaṅguṟadu* ("Greetings and Praise") consists of four sections, each delineated through changes in tempo, by a variety of musical moods. Section 1 demonstrates how Appavoo uses music to articulate the core aspects of his indigenized theology. Using the same melody to describe the Holy Trinity (and their essential nature as equals, or "three-in-one"), Appavoo outlines his theology of the universal family, characterizing God as the bi-gendered parent (*pettavarē*), and Jesus as the elder brother (*mūttavar*) and son of Mary. Then, with a driving vocal and instrumental unity, he describes the Holy Spirit, the sun, as a teacher of solidarity.

The second phrase of each melodic couplet musically defines the quality of each aspect of the Trinity by emphasizing the following words with *ottuccol* accents off the beat at the end of the line that musically and conceptually join the last word with the next line: 1) *ammaiyappā*,[4] mother/father, lord of everything; 2) *kannimari*, the Virgin Mary's birthed child; and 3) *ottumaya*, the one who gives and teaches solidarity.[5] *Ammaiyappā* (*ammā*—mother, *appā*—father, as one word), for example is separated from the previous words with a rhythmic accent after the first beat and articulated with a pulsating series of four high melodic notes that then slide down into the beginning of the next line (see Appendix 1, Transcription 4a, Fig. 1). *Kannimari*, or Virgin Mary, is constructed from Appavoo's feminist standpoint as the independent bearer of salvation. Jesus was conceived independent of a man. Furthermore, there would be no salvation without Mary's consent to the angel Gabriel's request to bear this child and her willingness to risk social ostracism as an unmarried pregnant woman.[6] Rhyme patterns throughout become mnemonic devices in the folk transmission system, which help people to remember the words and thus transmit the ideas easily (Appavoo 1986, 106–107).

In the second couplet of the Trinity, Jesus is defined as *mūttavar*, or eldest sibling. Calling him *mūttavar* situates Jesus in Appavoo's theological kinship framework of the universal family as the eldest child of God and the elder brother "to us all." While he is unique in the human family as the eldest, Jesus is emphasized as human, not as a God who became human.[7] Appavoo says, "You are also one among us, my elder brother . . . You are the first, but you are also like me."[8] This kinship framework may also reflect the Indian religious practice of placing deities in a family structure; however, Appavoo wants to avoid any hierarchical social relations that practice might imply, such as the lower status associated in Brahmanical mythology with some popular Tamil gods like Murugan.[9]

Using the more gender-neutral term *pālagarē,* or child, instead of son in this section, Appavoo stresses Jesus' identification as child of Mary to give greater social prominence to his mother in a system that oppressed women. He argues that Jesus calls himself "son of man," not son of David, resisting identification with his Jewish patrilineage. It follows from this social ambiguity that Jesus intended to align himself with the third and lowest social level of Jewish society (the category of laypeople—beneath the priests and the Levites—which Appavoo compares to being a Dalit), thus undermining the Jewish social and purity system, and consciously placing himself outside of its hierarchy.[10]

Section 2 of the *Sāmiya Vaṇaṅguṟadu* introduces a jovial, excited mood, both melodically and rhythmically. Its lyrics combine Christian, Tamil, Dalit, and rural metaphors to create a positive and hopeful indigenous perspective on the gracious gifts of *sāmi,* the Divine One. In the first of three choruses, God is defined as "the spring in the river . . . the living water that cleans (or 'removes') the filth of sin."[11] Through rural symbols Appavoo calls on Christian Dalits to return to the life force of the land, to rural simplicity and beauty, to wash off the filth of sins (like classism and internalized casteism), and to reclaim rural Dalit identity as positive. These nostalgic rural images also help Appavoo to reach the minds and hearts of the middle-class urban Dalit, who has left behind the village and everything associated with it.

The second section continues using themes of rural purity, yet focuses more on culture. Appavoo presents a metaphor of *sāmi* (or Christ), the living Eucharist as "the pure *ghee poṅgal* rice . . . the living rice that removes hunger every day." Poṅgal is the Tamil harvest festival named for the sweet *poṅgal* rice that is cooked in a pot and boiled over to represent the promise of good fortune in the coming year. In villages, *poṅgal* is cooked and shared communally. With this metaphor Appavoo gestures toward the Eucharist as *oru olai:* shared communal food cooked in one pot. By describing the *poṅgal* rice as pure *ghee* [*nei*], Appavoo again attacks the myth of lower-caste culture as impure, replacing it with an emphasis on the rich delicacy and ritual purity of *ghee* (clarified butter).

In the Tamil context, the Western concept of Christ and the Eucharist as living bread is indigenized as the living rice that removes the daily hunger of poverty. Going beyond the simple cultural substitution of rice for bread to create an oppositional Dalit construction, Appavoo consciously uses the denigrated vernacular term *sōṟu* for rice instead of the more literary or Brahmanic *sādam*.[12] He reclaims the auspiciousness of Dalit culture and subverts the Brahmanic hegemony through fusing *sōṟu* with the more Sanskritic *jiva* (living) in a blasphemous marriage of the Brahmanical and outcaste as the primary Christian symbol of God: the Eucharist given with grace. Poetic emphasis on the word "hunger" (*pasi)* placed at the end of the phrase further identifies the Eucharistic sacrifice of Jesus toward the hungry poor.

In this second section, the word *pōkkum* is used in two contexts: the daily removal of hunger, *pasiye nittam pōkkum* (see Appendix, Transcription 4b, mm. 25-26) and the removal or cleansing of the filth of sin, *pāva ūttai pōkkum* (see Appendix, Transcription 4b, mm 8-9). The double use of this word, reinforced by its articulation with the same melody, ties these two ideas together in the practice of *oru olai*. Appavoo advocates that if people of different communities eat together communally every day, no one will go hungry. Moreover, through this radical action they will undermine participation in the "sins" of caste separation and private property.

In the third stanza Appavoo returns his congregation to a peaceful pastoral scene where they can feel the breeze from the coconut grove given freely as the grace of God and available for all to enjoy. Appavoo reminds us that God has already given people everything they need in nature, in contrast to the inequalities of modern urban life with its material necessities like fans, which are available only to those who can afford electricity.[13]

The happy, lively mood of the second section of "Greeting and Praise" that supports these positive rural images is primarily coded in the rhythm. Each duple-meter measure of the melody begins a half beat after the first beat followed by an accent on the middle of the second beat (see Appendix 1, Transcription 4b, Fig. 1). A feeling of bounding exuberance is produced through syncopated articulations on these "off-beats" in the vocal phrase followed by a feeling of drive through emphasis on the last two quarter notes. The tabla, paṟai, and *uḍukku* drums accompany this vocal phrase with a two-measure pattern of duple meter that supports the rhythmic accents in the voice through duplicating them or anticipating them (Appendix 1, Transcription 4b, Fig. 2 and Fig. 3). Important lyrics in section 2 (*ūttauttaṇṇi*, or spring [literally, "bubbling"] water, *teṇṇaṅkāttu*, coconut grove breeze, and *sutta neyyi poṅga sōṟu*, pure *ghee poṅgal* rice) (Appendix 1, Transcription 4b, Fig. 4), are emphasized through contrasts in range and wide interval leaps.

Section 2 of "Greetings and Praise" focuses on "re-claiming," Appavoo's strategy of indigenization for the liberation of Dalits. God's essence and God's freely given grace are represented as rural beauty and natural auspiciousness in order to re-associate village culture and animistic religion as positive and to encourage an ecological consciousness among the people. Appavoo's focus on food in this section represents the centrality of Jesus' radical action in table fellowship and highlights the perspectives of poor Dalit people.

In sections 3 and 4 of "Greetings and Praise," rural hardships of rot, pain, heat, and infertility are not romanticized, but in fact starkly spelled out as metaphors for humans who have made mistakes. They are encoded musically with melodic tension. Each couplet contrasts poignant rural images with positive images of God's grace as the nurturing *vevasāyi* (gender-neutral farmer) who plows, sows, and grows new life, bringing redemption and forgiveness for human mistakes and resolving the (social and musical) tension of painful misfortune. In the fourth stanza Appavoo shifts the mood back to the lively rhythm and melody of section 2 in order to lead up to and positively reinforce naming God *vevasāyi*. Appavoo reflected on the Dalit farmer as a metaphor for the divine: "I'm moved by that metaphor. I was really happy that I got that metaphor because we have only been thinking of God as father, the patriarchal father, only as king, the aggressive dominant king. *Vevasāyi* is a term that is used for both man and woman and includes a gender-neutral ending."[14]

The lyrics in section 3 ask the congregants to ponder their own sins. Accordingly, Appavoo slows the tempo back to the original measured pace and uses a $\frac{6}{8}$, compound meter to express an interior "depressed mood," as one would reflect upon what has been left undone (see Appendix 1, Transcription 4c, Fig. 1 and Fig. 2). The first couplet of section 3 reflects upon people's sins with the line "we are the overripe *sorakkā*." *Sorakkā* is a gourd-like vegetable that becomes inedible when overripe. Some, particularly Brahmins, also think it is an inauspicious vegetable.[15] Farmers do not, however, waste or throw away the overripe *sorakkā;* they either dry its shell to use it to hold water, or break the shell to get seeds for the next generation of plants. The message of this metaphor is that, like the next generation of seeds, God sees our potential and has use for us even when we appear rotten to others or ourselves. Appavoo also described the overripe *sorakkā* as a symbol for the third and fourth generation of Christians who have left the village, have become "soft" middle-class urban people (passive, rotten, and corrupted by materialism, selfishness, and individuality) and have lost the taste for *sorakkā* or village culture, and for liberating protest that is an essential part of folk culture. In a tone of hopeful faith, Appavoo asks God to break our shells and make us seeds to grow new *sorakkā*.[16]

The second couplet describes the land that grows *neruñci* thorn weeds, because it lies fallow or is left uncultivated. If these thorns pierce the skin they can be very painful. Furthermore, in Tamil literature such a desolate landscape carries negative symbolism. In Appavoo's liturgical context, God the farmer plows away the pain from our hearts, removing the harmful weeds. The phrase *karugippōṉa* when applied to a plant means that it has wilted or been burned by the sun. *Kāṇappayiru* is a type of legume (similar to adzuki beans) that needs very little water to grow, and thus does not wilt easily. If the *kāṇappayiru* does wilt, as Appavoo describes in section 4, the sun must be very hot. Such extreme heat is a metaphor for people's sins against others: people are hot with sin like the intense sun that wilts the *kāṇappayiru* plant. But God, as farmer, gives grace to make the people sprout again.[17]

The depressed mood created with the image of overripe vegetables, and the intense heat of sin in section 3 are musically reflected in a slow but driving $\frac{6}{8}$ tempo, minor second intervals, and a raspy folk vocal timbre sung in a high tenor range (see Appendix 1, Transcription 4c, Figs. 1-4, measures 1 to 7).[18] The two-line lyrical phrasing is also mirrored in the melody. The first line of the couplet that presents people's sin is characterized melodically with tension and lack of resolution ending on the second pitch of the scale (G) in measure 4 (see Appendix 1, Transcription 4c, Fig. 4). The second lyrical phrase of the couplet repeats the first two measures melodically but in the third measure of the phrase returns to the tonic/keynote (F) with the phrase *sāmiyaruḷ nādā,* giving a strong feeling of resolution to correspond with the lyrical themes of God's grace acting to save the people from their sins (see Appendix 1, Transcription 4c, Fig. 5, measures 12 and 16).

Section 4 returns to the lively mood of section two (see Appendix 1, transcription 4d, Fig. 1). The first and the third lines expresses themes of people's sins and shortcomings using rural metaphors of agricultural desolation: rot, pain, heat, and infertility. The second and the fourth lines (creating the first two couplets) contrast this impoverished hopelessness with a construction of God as a nurturing farmer who re-germinates, plows, and cares for the sprouts. This is a radical move to humanize God or Jesus to the status of Dalit, the most impoverished level of Indian society.

The third and final couplet (lines 5 and 6) of section 4 ends the "Greetings and Praise" section on a positive tone musically and lyrically. This time the two lines do not contrast the sins of the people with the saving actions of God, but reverse the order of focus. The salvation of Jesus is described first by evoking the sacrifice of the Dalit farmer who takes up the plow (the cross) for all others. The people follow, taking up the name of Christ as liberator to praise him. The substitution of the Dalit plow for the cross of Jesus, accompanied by powerful folk singing and playing in unison (see Appendix, Transcription 4d, Fig. 2, mm. 29–45), fully enculturates Christian faith and worship in the sacrifices and joy of Dalit culture. God is not only with Dalits, but *is* Dalit.

PARAṬṬAI'S DALIT THEOLOGY

Appavoo creates a Dalit theology that he argues is "Christian," as it is enculturated into a medium that intends to liberate the poor and oppressed through claiming them as valuable, auspicious, and worthy. Through this *Girāmiya Isai Vaṟipāḍu* Appavoo emphasizes that in India, in order for the untouchables to be liberated, their cultural resources must also be liberated. He endeavors to induce spiritual, cultural, and psychological liberation including the trans-physical power of paṟai drumming and rhythms, community participation in song structure, the emotional power invoked by folk language, metaphor, and melodic devices, and a folk transmission system that allows for theological re-enculturation. As such, Appavoo's work is a unique contribution to the Dalit theology movement, while it is in dialogue with the discourses and actions of other Dalit Christian and secular organizations. This chapter further explores the resonance of Appavoo's work in this broader theological and socio-political context. It also places him in relationship to the work of specific feminist and African American womanist theologians.

DALIT THEOLOGY MOVEMENT

The Dalit Liberation Movement in Tamil Nadu has had an intimate relationship with the Catholic and Protestant communities since the 1970s. The history of Tamil Christianity includes a missionary-led Social Gospel movement against caste oppression that extends back to the mid-nineteenth century (see Oddie 1991 and chapter 2). As seventy percent of Tamil Christians are scheduled caste or Dalit, and eighty percent of those are still poor landless laborers living in rural areas, both the contemporary and historical human rights concerns by the Tamil churches may appear obvious. However, the cultural rights of these people to claim a valued rural identity reflected in liturgy and theology has only been embraced officially since the late twentieth century.

The term "Dalit" reached Tamil Christian theologians and Christian activists by the mid-1980s and led to the development of a body of literature on Dalit theology. The academic establishment of the Dalit theology movement began at the United Theological College Bangalore in April 1981, with a lecture entitled "Towards a Sudra Theology" by A. P. Nirmal. Kottapalli Wilson used the term "Dalit" in 1982 in his *The Twice Alienated Culture of Dalit Christians*. The Church of South India Bishop M. Azariah (the first Dalit Bishop in the Madras Diocese) brought the term to an international forum in 1984 to raise international Christian concern about the contemporary problems of Dalits.[19]

One of the most striking problems for Christian Dalits is that the Indian government does not afford them the same degree of compensation (quotas in government jobs and educational seats) as nominally Hindu Dalits.[20] In 1994 Bishop Azariah led the march to Delhi to fight for compensatory rights—affirmative action and quotas in education and government jobs—for Christian Dalits equal to those offered to "Hindu" Dalits. Dalit Christians have also been actively involved in the international struggle for Dalit human rights and recognition of caste discrimination. More recently many Dalit Christians participated in political demonstrations and performances at the 2001 United Nations Conference on Racism in Durban, South Africa, and the 2004 World Social Forum in Mumbai (see chapter 6).

VERNACULAR INSTITUTIONS AND DALIT THEOLOGY

TTS and the Gurukul Lutheran Theological College and Research Institute in Chennai, both vernacular Tamil Protestant seminaries, are the strongest seats of Tamil Dalit Christian cultural activism and production of Dalit theology today.[21] In 1985 Gurukul was reconstituted as a research institute intent on contextualizing theological education as a means to achieve the vision of the gospels in the socio-economic, political, religio-cultural context of contemporary India. Gurukul's new programs included Women's Studies, Dalit Theology, Social Analysis, Human Development, Communication, and Ecology (Rajaratnam 1997, ix). In 1987 Gurukul was also the first seminary to create a department of Dalit theology.

Since 1980, TTS has been a center for a Paulo Freireian style rural theological education, called TECCA (Theological Education for Christian Commitment and Action).[22] This dialogical approach to theology intends to "motivate [the laity] to Christian action in the world . . . with a thrust for a ministry of social justice" (Amirtham 1990, 127, 129). Rev. Honest Chinniah, director of the TECCA program in the mid-1970s, concluded that rural TECCA was a powerful symbiotic channel through which "the rich treasure of the folk culture of the villages and the vernacular theological venture of TTS began to meet each other" (1990, 131). TECCA was also the seed of Dalit theological production through folk music with its emphasis on transmission through a re-creative musical system. As the director of TECCA for eight years in the 1980s, Appavoo spearheaded this movement of reform.

TTS and Gurukul have been the center of the creation of Dalit theology, particularly those examples expressed through music and developed in dialogue with rural laity. Theologian Rev. M. Thomas Thangaraj describes the oral expression of theology as making "singable theology" or the "rediscovery of hymnody as the source for [self-consciously] theologizing, and [as] an instrument of theological education" (Thangaraj 1990, 112).

In the late 1980s, the Board of Theological Education of the Senate of Serampore College (which controls all theological colleges in India) revised the curriculum of theological education at the Bachelor of Divinity level to be more inclusive of the disciplines that support the creation and dissemination of Dalit theology such as Social Analysis, Communication Studies, and Women's Studies. However, TTS had many years before initiated several of these new directions in theological education. Indeed, in 1980, TTS inaugurated their department of Social Analysis headed by German Marxist theologians Rev. Bas Wielenga and Dr. Gabrielle Dietrich.

To provide a place where its initiatives in theological reflection and social action among poor Dalits could be further developed and given institutional permanency, TTS created a Dalit Resource Centre in 1989.[23] From the mid-1990s to 2007 the Centre produced an annual Dalit Arts Festival that served to fortify and recommit the community to the Dalit cause. It also served as an important means of transmission of the Dalit liberation theology message through music (Amirtham and David 1990).

The CSI Diocese of Madras includes a department for Dalit Concerns with most of its directors educated at TTS. Some have worked to build and support secular organizations like the Social Action Centre in the Madurandagam area, and to bring Christian Dalit laborers together with secular unions. Further, Bishop M. Azariah who served the Madras Dioceses through the 1990s has been one of the most outspoken proponents of Dalit rights locally and internationally. Another significant symbol of the relationship between the Dalit movement and the churches was the leadership of the Tamil Nadu Dalit Liberation Movement (DLM) in the early 1990s by Danny Gnanasakaran, a Lutheran priest who studied and taught at TTS. Many factors have contributed to the rising consciousness, change, and action among Dalit Christians and changes within the institutions of the CSI. Among these are over two decades of the institutionalization of Dalit theology and concerns at TTS, public events like the Dalit Arts Festival that transmit the message of Dalit liberation, leadership and action by individual culture brokers, and building a strong network of activists.

DALIT THEOLOGY IN CONVERSATION

Sathianathan Clarke (1998, 45–47) points to five necessary steps in the development and implementation of a Dalit liberation theology which I have expanded upon here: (1) an analysis of power dynamics in society that goes beyond economics to include religion and culture; (2) the study of Dalit religion and culture; (3) theological reflection upon these studies; (4) integration and transmission of theology into an accessible praxis, necessarily in an oral form, that has a direct effect particularly on rural Dalits; and (5) the reception of this continued dialogical interaction with this community for feedback and improvement of the theology. He emphasizes further that all of these steps should be dialogical and the medium should be oral.

While Clarke most strongly delineates the first four steps above in his own work, Appavoo is the only Dalit theologian to my knowledge who has most successfully followed all five of these steps with particular focus on the creation of a method and medium that facilitates the integration of theology into an accessible oral praxis, and a transmission system that supports the continual reconstitution of the theology to remain adaptive and thus liberating.

Very few Indian or Dalit theologians have actively turned to non-Christian Dalit religions (Adi Samayam, or original/indigenous religions, as Appavoo calls them) as a source for an empowering symbolic and ritual framework for Dalit theology. Indeed Indian Christian theology has been grounded in Brahmanical theology for several hundred years. Clarke and Appavoo are the most notable to enculturate Christian theology through Dalit religions. Re-indigenization of Christianity in this way is described by T. M. Scruggs as "the (re) assertion of localized aesthetics once linked to a different set of religious beliefs . . . by drawing upon local cultural models hitherto prohibited from use in such a context" (2005, 92 and 94). Sharon Welsh further outlines the necessary genealogy in knowledge reclamation and consciousness raising to create a theology grounded in the beliefs and practices of the oppressed.

> To state that liberation theology is an insurrection of subjugated knowledge means that the discourse of liberation theology represents the resurrection of knowledge suppressed by a dominant theology and a dominant culture. Further analysis involves three elements of genealogy: (1) the preservation and communication of memories of conflict and exclusion; (2) the discovery and exposition of excluded contents and meanings; and (3) the strategic struggle between the subjugated and dominant knowledges. (quoted in Clarke 1998, 48)

The least developed area of Dalit theology is an analysis of Welsh's third point: a socio-cultural analysis of strategic struggle between the subjugated Dalit religious elements and dominant Brahmanical Hindu and Western theological ideology. I would add to this the analysis of oppressive class, gender, and caste perspectives within dominant theologies. An examination of the impact of Appavoo's theology on Dalit villagers begins to address these issues (see chapter 5). First however, I will describe Appavoo's primary theological tenets in greater detail and then discuss the ideas of specific Dalit theologians that resonate with Appavoo's ideas or that differ distinctly.

THEOLOGICAL PURPOSE

Appavoo's broad theological intent is to reclaim Christianity in general and to reform Tamil Christian ritual in particular as a means of social liberation for the oppressed, regardless of religion. His particular target audience is poor Christian Dalit villagers, many of whom are third-generation Christians. The primary intention he held for his musical theology was to be a means of psycho-spiritual transformation of the self-esteem of Dalits, lower castes, the poor, and women. His secondary purpose was to "change" the hearts and minds of Indian Christians and non-Christians who continue to practice the corporate "sins" of caste, class, and gender oppression. Appavoo's theology of sin advocates corporate responsibility to eradicate the social distinctions that separate people, leaving so many hungry, enslaved, and afraid. Thus "conversion" has nothing to do with one changing one's institutional religious affiliation, and everything to do with changing the socio-cultural values that will fundamentally transform the hierarchical structure within the Christian community and the society at large. These values prevent people from creating relationships of love and sharing; Appavoo instead advocates relationships founded on, or striving for, the Kingdom values of justice and equality in this world, not economic, social, and religious interdependence forcibly born from hierarchical, caste-based systems of slavery. To accomplish these goals requires radical action on all social and cultural levels—that is, total liberation. He suggests that the primary means to this process is through the practice of poor people eating communally: practicing *oru olai*, a daily "Eucharistic" lifestyle of sharing food and the labor necessary for its production.

PARAṬṬAI'S THREE THEOLOGICAL TENETS

Paraṭṭai's Dalit theology includes three tenets: 1) to live in a Eucharistic lifestyle of sharing food (*oru olai*); 2) to be in one universal family with God as the bi-gendered parent of all; and 3) to employ a critical analysis strategy of reversal or inversion of hierarchical values based on the praxis of Jesus and Neo-Marxism or EPSI-PEGS. Appavoo's conception of total liberation is articulated though his EPSI-PEGS system. EPSI-PEGS—economic, political, social, ideological, psychological, environmental, gender-based, spiritual—is an acronym for a holistic analysis of oppression on all of these levels.

Besides dialogical transmission through teaching at TTS, Paraṭṭai has used music, stories, and dramas to most successfully articulate and transmit his theology.[24] He has also communicated his ideas in scholarly articles (Appavoo 1992, 1993, 1994a) and orally to me through hours of formal interviews and informal conversations in our ethnographic dialogue between 1993 and 2005.

Paraṭṭai communicates his theology both in lyrical content and musical medium. While the transmission of the message through the lyrics is essential, the values of his three tenets are contained within the system of folk music sound and performance. The corporate worship values of unity and sharing are encoded in call-and-response techniques, community participation in leading the service, and transformative empowerment through musical and theological recomposition (Sherinian 2002).

ORU OLAI

Through exposure to the perspectives of Dalit people's materiality, Appavoo realized that the Eucharist needs to be a daily living practice of communal eating and shared labor that liberates people from social and economic injustice. In chapter 1 of this book, I recounted the dialogue between Appavoo and a village Dalit girl in a rural TECCA class concerning I Corinthians 10:22 (which describes the church as one body partaking in one bread) that led him to develop his theological tenet of *oru olai.* The girl's analysis that class divisions in the society led to stark differences in the quality and quantity of what one is able to eat every day raised Appavoo's consciousness to the Dalit meaning of the biblical passage. That is, Christian theology as action needs to lead to the restructuring of the social system that creates and delivers food to those who put the most labor into its production, yet who so often remain hungry. With the goal of creating a communal eating system among the poor, the Eucharist became *oru olai,* [the] "common food of the universal family" (Appavoo 1992 and 1993).

Appavoo has created an origin myth for *oru olai* in which he synthesizes affirmative qualities of both Tamil folk culture and Christianity in a mythical past in order to prescribe his vision for the present and future. It is a universal revolutionary vision intended to transform, empower, and create action and possibility. It is also a vision that includes all castes living harmoniously, but only by undermining the hierarchies of caste and gender dependency that reinscribe the continuation of oppression.

> Once upon a time people were living without any problems. No one owned any property. There was a famine and everybody came together to pray to God. God came and asked them what they wanted. They replied, "We have nothing to eat." God said, "Come on." He had a stick in his hand and started breaking holes in the earth. From one hole came rice, from another hole came fruits. Thus, all good foods came. Then God told them, "Come on, I have blessed the earth, so you go on, eat!" And everyone went to the holes or pits, big pits. They collected this fruit, which made them happy.
>
> One fellow was very weak . . . he was also lazy, but he was very intelligent. He found that it was difficult to get food. He had to work, no? He had to go down and get the food. So he made a plan. He called those who are very strong, the big fellows, and said, "Why are you talking to *that* fellow, he belongs to a different caste? God came to my dream and said that all these pits belong only to you, not to the other people." Then, the strong fellows put fences around these pits and declared that it was their *sottu,* or property. The other people were confused by the use of this new word they had never heard or spoken. Then this [weak] fellow replied, "God came and he gave me this word." The other fellows replied "No! God never comes to an individual person: he always comes when people are gathered. How come

God came to this particular individual person?" Then the strong people beat them up [those who were questioning], saying, "No, we should obey, there is no argument. You have to obey God's word."

So these people also prayed to God. The strong fellows also joined because they were afraid if they didn't God would punish them. And then because all of them were together, God once again came. He asked, "What is the problem?" And they said, "We don't have enough food." So, He took the stick and put holes in the sky. From one hole milk came pouring, from another hole honey came pouring, from another hole even chocolates came pouring. The people were very happy. They put vessels under each hole and started collecting the food.

Then, once again this fellow, the intelligent fellow (let us call him Brahmin), this intelligent fellow said once again, "No! No! These fellows shouldn't touch these vessels because they are not our caste." The people replied, "What!? This is a new word once again." He said, "Oh ho [you see] it's a word which God gave to me." So, these strong fellows once again joined together and drove the weaker fellows away from the vessels, where they had built a fence around it and said, "This is our *sottu,* this is our property."

The people were suffering. Then they divided each person according to his or her strength into various castes. There was some fighting and those who were defeated were made low caste. The low caste, weak people were not getting any food. The weak people joined together and prayed to God. They prayed and prayed all night but God didn't come. Then they went to sleep. That night after all of them went to sleep God went to each house and destroyed their stoves (*aḍuppu*). All stoves, wood stoves, even gas ovens. God destroyed everything. There was only one oven left, the one which was in front of the deity's place where they used to cook food to worship God.

In the morning all the people got up and went to cook. They found that their stoves were destroyed. So they started fighting, asking, "Who destroyed them?" Then a boy discovered that there was only one oven that was not destroyed, the one in front of God's place. Everyone rushed to that stove to cook their food.

Again there was fighting over who should cook first and who should cook second. Then an old woman came, her name was Paraṭṭai [Appavoo's folk pen name and a name common for both men and women]. She said, "Hey, what foolish people you are, you cannot cook all at one time. So start cooking in one big pot." Some people agreed, some people didn't agree. Those who agreed were powerful [unified] and they started cooking. They had a very good meal because it was very tasty. Different items [types of rice] from many houses were put together. It was very tasty. That small group decided to cook as a collective. The others tried to cook in separate stoves, but God had destroyed all the stoves so no new stove could exist. Even if they built a stove it would disintegrate. So slowly people started coming [together] because of the food. This group was eating better food because they were putting everything together.

Before this happened, everyone would go to market separately. Now only one person went. Thus, they didn't pay much for the buses.[25] So, there was no money paid to the bus companies. They went to the wholesaler and bought things cheaply. So, their food was very excellent food. And so the other fellows, other thin fellows, they slowly started joining this group as well. And now they found that these fellows were eating very good food, even 5 *star* chocolates from Cadbury.[26]

So, there are three groups. Those who are very weak (I mean Dalits), backward castes, and forward castes. The second group, which symbolizes the backward castes, also found that this [communal eating] is something worthwhile. They are even eating chocolates, . . . and women are very free. So, a few women from this middle group, they declare to their men, "We are going to join them whether you come or not." But the men argue, "No! No! They belong to different castes." They (the women) replied, "Oh, that is a new word which has been given by this *individual* fellow, we never believe that God will speak to individuals.[27] "So, we are going to join whether you come or not." And women and children started joining them and men had to come because there was no one to cook their food. So both the thin and middle group, and the other fellows, they just started joining. And now they are eating very excellent food. And they refuse to come to work in the pits. And the rich fellows who got used to just eating, not working, slowly they also started joining. Then lastly this fellow, the Brahmin fellow, he is not a Brahmin, the *wise man*. The wise man had nothing to eat now. There are no rich people. Everybody has to join this group. So he started repenting. Then he found out that these people do not work. So, he went and asked for forgiveness from these people. They said, "Ok come, we also invite you [to join us], you were also our brother once. Only you invented all these words and separated us. But you are our brother. Come. You should have told us that because you are very weak, you cannot work. We would have given you food. You need not work; we will give you food, but don't create all these problems!" Then, they all were united and they worshipped the deity. And God came this time and asked them, "What do you want?" They said,

"Destroy all the stoves, whenever somebody tries to build separate stoves." And on that day they killed about a thousand goats and had a very good meal. God also enjoyed the meal.

Zoe—Not briyani [Christian holiday food], ah?

Appavoo—I don't know. (Both laugh). See this is what we emphasize—not fighting, but pressurizing in a different manner. Make people join.[28]

Oru olai literally means "one pot" or cooking vessel.[29] In Tamil culture it also has the broader connotation of home unit or joint family. Appavoo's visionary myth proposes an *oru olai* society: a community in which the fundamental and most valued commodity is human labor, not personal property (Appavoo 1992). *Oru olai* is a synthesis of three communal practices: the shared labor and eating practices of the Indian joint family, the festival practices of Dalits, and the values and practices of the first-century Christians (Acts 4:32). Appavoo worked out the details of this societal structure in prayer and discussion with several rural theological studies groups in villages near Madurai during the mid and late-1980s. In this proposed society the individual only owns that which he or she needs for daily life plus a little savings (1992, 6). Power is based on the theological model that Jesus came to serve, not to be served (Matthew 20:24–28). Power and responsibilities are shared on a rotating lottery system. Power is attained through working, not ordering others to work (1992, 8). Thus, Appavoo maintains, if individuals want power they will not hesitate to work.

The essential action of this *oru olai* system is sharing food produced through sharing power/work and responsibility. Appavoo believes that sharing food leads to growth in other areas. He argues, for example, that as more people and labor are involved, the quantity and quality of the food grows, the environment is preserved, and there is less gender oppression, which facilitates individual growth. Based on the model of Jesus who shared food at the Last Supper, Appavoo argues further that sharing not only involves property, food, power, status, and joy, but also suffering as Jesus shared food with the expectation of his impending death. Thus if all must share the burden of individual sufferings, people will work to prevent others from suffering.

Social relationships in an *oru olai* community are constructed on the model of a family with God as the common parent. Appavoo (1992, 7) speaks of this system as truly being "born again," because within it everyone, including the oppressed, loses their "origin of flesh, that is, [their] caste . . . and [their] private property inheritance." All people inherit "all the gifts under the sky," from a common parent—God.[30] However, the most important healing element created through Appavoo's concept of universal family is psychological "liberation."

> The most important of these liberations is the removal of shame from the Dalits. In the *oru olai* society, there is nothing to be ashamed of our birth because we are born again as children of God. There will be a dynamic and healthy conscience of self-confidence because all are important in the new society and inherit a great number of relatives. (Appavoo 1992, 13)

The *oru olai* myth can be interpreted as both an origin myth to explain the inequalities in Indian society as well as a Christian myth explaining the source of sin and its redemption through the coming of the *oru olai* system (the Eucharist and the sacrifice of Jesus). The primary purpose of Appavoo's *oru olai* myth is to reverse the psychological attitudes that the Dalits hold: low self-esteem and shame toward their culture. He focuses this action of reversal on two primary structural elements of oppression—caste and class—reframing their origin in language introduced by the Brahmins or Aryans. In the myth he emphasizes that the Brahmin invented the words "caste" (*jāti*) and "property" (*sottu*), they were not given to him with religious legitimacy from God. Then Appavoo shows how the non-Brahmin upper castes—the strong group (landlords or Tamil Vellalas and Counders)—have economically reinforced and empowered these systems.

Paraṭṭai focuses on Dalit religious beliefs, more than specifically Christian ones, to deconstruct the Brahmanical ideology that legitimizes the oppression of Dalits. Three times in the myth he states that the Brahmin could not have independently received the ideas of caste and private property from God because, in Adi Samayam religion, Dalits believe that God only comes to people when they are gathered as a unified group to worship or conduct a festival.[31] He uses this prescriptive myth to delegitimize the Brahmin's power as not divinely ordained and communicates the essential practice and belief that, in united gathering, God freely and equally provides all that is needed to everyone. Furthermore, God's gifts include free will, which may lead an individual or group to oppress others. Appavoo stresses that structures of inequality are created not by God (or because it is God's will), but by people. They are located in the church and in divisions of the wider social structure. Appavoo preaches further that the problem lies with Dalits, because many, especially those who have become middle class, have forgotten to worship as a unified group or universal family devoid of subcaste divisions, sharing food communally as they practice in festival and times of need; indeed he advocates this is the proper way to worship God (Sherinian 2002, 36).

God's generosity continues in the myth with gifts of milk and honey from the sky, even after the "strong fellows" hoard the first gifts (fruits of the earth) as private property, thereby creating a class structure. He confirms that Brahmins may be intelligent and that the "strong fellows" may have strength and power (a reference to Tamil upper and middle castes who controlled property, the military, and political power through violence as kings), but he emphasizes that the ability to work in unity, as the Dalits do in the fields of these strong fellows, is a greater source of power.

Appavoo emphasizes in the *oru olai* myth that when people divide themselves into castes and classes, creating suffering, God is not pleased and thus will not come when they pray. They must be united as a community. However, like the coming of Jesus who established a new way of living in community, the wise old woman—Paraṭṭai—teaches the people to cook together with one pot. That is, she introduces the *oru olai* (Eucharistic) lifestyle. The fact that the food, which contained ingredients from many houses, was much "tastier" symbolizes that life is more meaningful and plentiful when people share in a unified community.

The *oru olai* myth further focuses on the dynamics of dependency operative within the hierarchies of caste and gender. Appavoo emphasizes that the oppressed subject (wife and Dalit) actually holds essential power over the oppressor (husband and Brahmin) because the oppressor depends on the oppressed to cook/produce food. Consequently, if society is structured so that the labor required for food production is most highly valued, and thus all share equally in labor, then these hierarchies should not exist. More importantly, Appavoo uses this example to make the oppressed Dalits aware that their power is located in food production. He further exemplifies this by outlining the method by which lower-class people can avoid middlemen agents through cooperative systems.[32] Appavoo's message to Dalits is that they can reclaim their own power by choosing not to participate in the system of food production for Brahmins or the elites dependent on their labor, instead uniting in a self-sufficient system in which they produce only enough for their immediate purposes and not enough to support the wealth of a non-laboring group. This prescriptive system of self-sufficiency uses grassroots economic pressure to force those with power to change their oppressive values.

At the end of the *oru olai* myth Appavoo portrays a pitiful character: the wise man (the Brahmin) with nothing to eat. This ironic reversal, a theological hermeneutic strategy, suggests that the wise man is not actually "street-wise" or in this case "village-wise." Dalits "own" the wisdom to survive, particularly to feed themselves. This is revealed by their shared "community skills," including music and transphysical religious experience. In the end, Appavoo encourages an attitude of sympathy and forgiveness toward the oppressors from the "weak fellows" and women who have formed an *oru olai* community. However, an element of protest conditions the forgiveness in that the oppressors must repent and give up their sins of separation. In our interviews, Appavoo made it clear that he does not hate the Brahmins, but thinks that their religious and social practices are narrow minded. "You cannot hate the people who are foolish. I think all these Brahman scholars are foolish. They don't know what is good for them [or for the larger] community."[33]

Appavoo uses the *oru olai* myth to resist the "foolish" practice of degraded naming essential to oppression. The Brahmin is accepted back into the community, but on the condition that he not perpetuate a discourse of caste difference. In her retelling of the legend of the Ibo slaves who walked on water to flee back to Africa and thereby escape slavery, womanist (Black feminist) theologian Emilie Townes describes the empowering theological practice of the oppressed collectively defining themselves and "controlling who names us" (Townes 1993, 114). Townes argues that folkloric mythology, whether reflections of truth or not, functions for womanist spirituality to pass on "legends that affirm strength and righteous agency in the miasma of oppression," especially in its manifestation as colorism or intercommunity casteism based on a hierarchy of skin tone (ibid., 115).

ORU OLAI IN PRACTICE

The practice among Tamil Dalits of eating food communally is an essential element of religious festivals. In the festival context, people worship as a group. If there is an unresolved disagreement within the community, no festival will be celebrated. Appavoo criticizes that Dalits do not worship together daily, arguing that if they worshipped daily by establishing a lifestyle of food sharing they would be less oppressed. Appavoo's vision, of course, is not to have (in his words) "festival-style" worship on a daily basis with all the associated burdens festivals impose on the poor, but to incorporate rural Dalit festival worship *values* into a Christian Dalit lifestyle. He emphasizes, however, that as a lifestyle *oru olai* must go beyond ritual. Religious practice as strict adherence to ritual, he argues, prevents the practice of Christian values.[34]

In order for *oru olai* to move beyond ritual to be a living theology, it needs the support of living practices that actively free people from social and economic injustice. "Being in *oru olai*" necessitates prioritizing human relations above money, and taking the risk of offending the oppressors who would object to the self-sufficiency and empowerment afforded by this lifestyle.[35] Movement toward *oru olai* is a slow process. Appavoo explains that it has to reflect a change in values, not just a desire for economic liberation or improvement, which is a primary challenge to Indian evangelical theology.[36] "The food is really Christ, so if you are in Christ, if you are eating in common meal, if you are in *oru olai,* then you are liberated. In Christ we are all liberated."[37] For Dalits this action means pooling their financial resources and sharing the labor of food production. The opportunity to observe the experience of a group of Dalit people forced into an "*oru olai* situation" helped Appavoo understand that *oru olai* requires a change of values on multiple levels of human experience or activity (EPSI-PEGS[38]) and that through the practice of *oru olai* such value changes are possible.

In the late 1980s, the Dalit people of Allalaperi, a village seventy-five kilometers from Madurai, had been forced out of their village by upper castes because the villagers complained about the rape of a ten-year-old girl by an upper-caste Hindu. For many weeks they took refuge in the Dalit colony of a neighboring village and began to prepare and eat food communally. Appavoo traveled there after they had been sharing food communally for fifteen days. To his amazement people claimed they were not suffering.

> I went to a woman and asked her, "How are you?" She said, "I am very fine." [Paraṭṭai exclaimed,] "What, woman, how can you be fine? You are suffering! You are driven out! You have lost everything!" They [left] with only their dresses. Then she said, "Every day my husband [used to] find some fault with my food and beat me. But today he can't do it because the food is cooked by some other people. Every day I had to cook. But now I'm cooking once—only once in five days," [she said].
>
> Then I met one man and asked him this same question. He said, "I am fine, Pastor." Then I asked him, "How can you say that when you [have been] driven out?" He said, "Every day I [was] thinking of what to do for the next day's food." He used a very, very powerful word which is vulgar . . . He [was] thinking, "Whose penis will I suck for my next food?" A powerful expression, very powerful expression. Completely, I understood . . . He knows me as a person from the other culture, a professor. [He thinks], "Ah, he won't like these words" and all that, but in spite of this understanding, because of his feeling[s], he's using that word. He's relieved . . . of a very psychological burden. Very psychological. Now he says, "Now I don't think like that. The burden comes to me only once in five days, because the responsibility has been divided. Four people will be in charge for five days, then the next four

> people. So, now I am not worried because . . . every day I get my food. My wife gets her food and [my] children get their food. I have to pay only a small amount which I can easily work out and give."
>
> So, there were many things that liberate people if you think in terms of this EPSI-PEGS [holistic approach to social analysis]. Ah, many aspects, many liberative aspects are in this *oru olai.* That's why I say the main problem, the 2000 years of slavery, is due to our deviation from our original practice. That's [the] hypothesis . . . It's prescription not a description.[39]

Appavoo's observations of this forced *oru olai* situation extended his Marxist approach to social analysis to include psychology and gender. It stressed the following: liberation from the middleman allows growth in the form of better and/or more food (three meals instead of just two); communal cooking frees women from the gender-role obligations of cooking and from their husband's potential abuses; communal cooking frees workers from bonded labor and its potential abuses providing greater personal integrity in work. In his previous analysis he had primarily considered the economic benefits of such a communal system, not other empirical elements that bring liberation. "We think only about the truth of *happenability,* but we don't think about the *potential* of liberation."[40]

The *oru olai* experience of the Dalits from Allalaperi illustrates the potential of what some have critiqued as a utopian vision. Appavoo's response to this critique is to frame it as a radical necessity. That is, if people believe *oru olai* will solve their problems and they commit to it completely, it will work. He explains:

> At that time I was using the word *karaḍipatti* to denote the Kingdom of God. *Karaḍi* means "bear." In Tamil we have a usage, *karaḍiodarar,* which means "telling a lie" . . . the expression *karaḍiodaradu* means "telling something that is not possible." So, when I was talking about this *oru olai* and Kingdom of God, people started saying that it was *karaḍiodaradu.* And I said, "Ok, let it be *karaḍiodaradu.* We'll call this *karaḍipatti* [impossible town, town of a lie]. So, at that time I was not using the word *oru olai.* Instead, I was using the word *karaḍipatti.* "But, [I asked the people], do you want it or not? Even if it is not possible. Do you like it? Do you want it? Do you think that this will solve your problem?" Then they [would generally reply,] "Yes it will solve our problem, but it is not possible."
>
> Zoe—So at least some hope is there?
>
> Appavoo—Yah! Then I used to tell them. "Yes, some things are not possible." For example, if suddenly somebody died in Madras. Going to Madras from Trichy is very expensive for poor people. No? . . . they don't go easily . . . More or less, it is not possible because of their economic situation. But

> suppose someone dies. Some villager dies, or some marriage happens in Madras of their own [close] relative, then somehow you manage to go. You get money from here and money from there and you save some money. Somehow you go. [Why do you go? Because it is] needed; you must go . . . Then *karaḍipatti,* if you want *karaḍipatti,* then you go for it! Don't say, "It is possible or impossible." That is the argument I used to give at the time. But nowadays I talk about the Wright brothers, you know—human flying. That is the example I give now.[41]

Appavoo emphasizes that his theology is more prescriptive then descriptive, while these examples show that it is grounded in the observation and experiences of real life situations for the oppressed.[42]

THEOLOGICAL ISSUES OF *ORU OLAI*

The metaphoric Christian symbol of *oru olai* is both the risen Christ and the Eucharist. Appavoo emphasizes that in the Gospels when the disciples meet the risen Christ he always shares food with them (Luke 24:30–35, John 21:12–14). In fact they recognized him as Christ only when he started breaking the bread.[43] For Appavoo, Jesus is the living bread. He says, "Jesus Christ calls himself as living bread. Life means it grows, it is moving and it is growing. We call only those things as living. So . . . Jesus, he is food, he grows. You know [as] many people join [*oru olai*], the quality and quantity of the food also grows."[44]

Oru olai is also the lived Eucharist. Theologically, Appavoo moves away from a Protestant understanding of the bread and wine as lifeless symbolic reminders of Jesus' sacrificed body. He instead reclaims the Catholic concept of transubstantiation and Jesus as dynamic liberating life because in this experience of sharing food, people are liberated, given life.[45]

> Transubstantiation, it is transformation, the whole food. You know they [Dalit villagers] don't understand this bread and wine as symbols, but that, which is really Christ. The food is really Christ, so if you are in Christ, if you are eating in common meal, if you are in *oru olai,* then you are liberated. In Christ we are all liberated.[46]

Oru olai as a living practice is radically relational. It further requires unity, commitment, and accountability to relationship.

In a discussion with Catholic workers in Nagercoil in August of 1994, Appavoo communicated this lesson of Eucharistic action by saying that Jesus went to the people where they were, and ate what they ate. He concluded: "If two people do not eat the same food, there will be no love. The relationship won't last."[47] For Appavoo, eating the same food with one's family creates attachment;[48] it promotes relationships and de-emphasizes money and material goods.

On another occasion, Appavoo explained this concept using a metaphor of the "Church as One Body."[49] In a TTS sermon delivered as a skit (his common communication strategy) he explained, "If the church has a body there must be only one mouth. The limbs must not be separated. We cannot allow this to happen."[50] He described the connection between Christ and *oru olai* on another occasion:

> If you hold [Jesus] up it will attract everyone. That's what I feel when Jesus says that "when I am lifted up the whole world will come . . . I will attract everybody." The common meal [is] Christ. This *oru olai* [is] Christ. Because Jesus himself said, "This is my body and this is my blood." Which means that Jesus is this one *oru olai*.[51]

Although the sources for *oru olai* are found in both Christianity and Dalit religion, Appavoo firmly believes its practice should not involve religious discrimination. He does not want the symbols of one religion to alienate the poor of other religions and thus discourage them from accessing this liberating system. Thus he attempts to avoid borrowing religious terminology from either of the faiths and instead grounds his language in common spoken Tamil that he believes will not offend the poor. In this way he emphasizes that "*oru olai* is an attempt to de-religiousize" or perhaps secularize the Eucharist (Appavoo 1991, 1). His theological tenet of universal family most significantly emphasizes oneness across socio-cultural differences.

UNIVERSAL FAMILY

Appavoo's second central theological tenet is "universal family." In Appavoo's "universal family," all people are siblings born of the same parent's (*pettavarē*) womb.[52] Appavoo understands the Christian God as both mother and father, with feminine and masculine qualities. Here *pettavarē* literally means "parent who bore me," signifying the maternal womb. The goal for Appavoo is to prevent people's separation based on class, private ownership, or gender differences through creating a universal family which functions in an *oru olai* system to undermine these differences. Galatians 3:28 supports Appavoo's discourse that

"If you are in one family then [as in Christ] there is no difference between . . . man or woman, between slave and master."[53] In the Indian context *oru olai* is a radical concept because it intends to erase distinctions based on class, private ownership, gender, or caste differences: no person is separated from the family table because he/she is considered unclean. Appavoo explains that this "is very disturbing for the ordinary congregation, to ask them to be as one family, to share one food, to cook one food . . . [It] means . . . destroying this capitalistic concept of . . . private property. Ownership and exploitation and also the patriarchy."[54] The idea of universal family was generated from Appavoo's reflection on *oru olai* with village Dalits. It prescribes the familial nature of people's relationship with God, other human beings, and the earth, with all three of these relationships holding equal importance. Emphasis is placed on one's relationship with one's neighbor, for God is within this person. Evangelicals in India, on the other hand, tend to focus primarily on the individual's relationship with God over all else.

In a sermon to middle- and lower middle-class students (many of them Dalit), attending the 1994 summer music camp at TTS, Appavoo described the universal family and the need to analyze the social systems that separate people from this vision:

> Universal family means God is father [to] all, not just [to] Christians but [to] all religions and classes. To disrespect a brother is to disrespect our father. Do we care about the prostitute as our sister and the beggar and leper as our brother? If we accept God as our father, how are we using our talents? The father who gives singing talents—for whom are we going to use them? Are we only going to use them for ourselves? Like Cain, are we going to be without concern for our brothers? Do you have a feeling of separation from other Christians? Do you have a relationship with all other [types of] Christians? If among Christians we think that God is father, how did caste come? Is there a specific God only for Nadars or Dalits, Paraiyar, Pallar, Chakkiliyar, Vaniyar, Tevar? If we are all calling God "Father" [and we are separated,] are there many Gods? We are born again with Christ and God as father of all of us. Having accepted God as father, how did these difference come among us?[55]

In an attempt to subvert the rhetoric of caste-minded, middle-class fundamentalists whom he believes separate Christians into divisive class and caste groups, Appavoo defined "born again" in the context of universal family theology. He emphasized that practicing these forms of separation destroys the possibility of existing as one family and having a relationship with God as a common parent. To counter these social habits of separation he stressed that the students must have concern for the less fortunate (beggars and prostitutes) and those from different religions. In particular, they should express their concern through using their God-given musical talent not for their own benefit, but to help these others: musical action for social change. Thus, with the theology of universal family, Appavoo conceptualizes the relationship between people and God as parent to child. More importantly, he emphasizes the need to destroy class, caste, and subcaste divisions, especially among Dalits so they can be unified against their oppressors.

STRATEGY OF REVERSAL

The third element of Appavoo's theology is the concept and strategic action of reversal. He advocates several "reversals": of values, of social hierarchy, of the paradigms with which hegemonic institutions interpret the Bible, of the concepts of inauspiciousness, cleanliness, and purity, and of the metaphors used to understand Jesus and God. Appavoo's strategy of reversal or inversion is expressed most powerfully through reclaiming the use of folk music as a legitimate source for indigenized Christian liturgy in his *Girāmiya Isai Vaṟipāḍu*. These methods of reversal are applied to music first by indigenizing or rejecting Western elements. Second, both the form and content of indigenized Christian music are reversed from upper-caste/class karnatak style to Dalit village folk. Appavoo consciously uses instruments such as the paṟai frame drum associated with outcaste "pariahs," vernacular language, melodies, rhythms, and folk-music genres commonly thought of by middle-class pastoral and lay leaders as the degraded cultural antithesis of classical karnatak music or Western hymnody.

As described above, Appavoo defines Christianity and the key to liberation as an active reversal of values within an oppressive society, where the Kingdom of God is implemented through the practice of "Kingdom" values. In his Tamil folk version of the Lord's Prayer, Appavoo communicates his belief that the purpose of reversal should be the attainment of freedom. He replaces the line "Hallowed be Thy name" with the lyrics, "The meaning of your name is freedom." God is not just holy, but communion with God and fellowship with other people are the source of liberation.

Appavoo develops his strategy of reversal from both his interpretation of the communication methods of the biblical writers and the Dalit folkloric practice of inversion (or subversion) of the status quo through emancipatory "reinscription" and "remythologizing" (Clarke 1998, 108). Appavoo's biblical grounding of reversal lies in the metaphor of the Kingdom of God to be realized on earth. Paraṭṭai (the trickster) follows Jesus in "using the language of paradox and reversal to shatter the conventional wisdom of his time" (Borg 1994, 80). Appavoo, however, uses this language of "a total reversal of the known world"[56] in a musical context and performs acts of reversal through musical style choices as well as through text. Scholar of religion and culture Marcus Borg's (1994) description of Jesus' understanding of the Kingdom of God is illuminating.

> Jesus frequently spoke of the Kingdom of God in the language of impossible or unexpected combinations. The Kingdom, something great, is compared to something very tiny: it is like "a grain of mustard seed" [Mark 4:30–31]. Moreover, mustard was a weed; thus, the Kingdom is like a weed. The Kingdom is compared to something impure: it is like a woman (associated with impurity) putting leaven (which was impure) into flour [Matthew 13:33; Luke 13:20–21]. The Kingdom is for children, who in that world were nobodies: thus, the Kingdom is for nobodies. The same point is made by Jesus' meals with outcastes: the Kingdom is a banquet of outcastes, of nobodies . . . [Matthew 13:33; Luke 13.20–21] Moreover, the Kingdom is not somewhere else; rather it is among you, inside you, and outside you. Neither is it some time in the future, for it is here, spread out on the earth; people just do not see it. (Borg 1994: 80–81)

Appavoo's primary intent is for Dalits to reverse their cultural and psychological shame to proudly reclaim and re-engage with their culture and its sources of transformative power. Thus he rarely names Dalits or Dalit culture in terms of negation, focusing instead on their continuous active resistance through folk culture (Appavoo 1986). Other Dalit theologians, however, concur with Borg's description of outcastes as nobodies and Jesus' redemptive purpose toward them. For example, Samuel Rayan claims that:

> To these upper sectors of society the outcastes are nameless; they have no self and no identity of their own. They do not count, except, of course, when there is work to be done to produce wealth, to create leisure and the conditions for the development of culture, and to keep society healthy. They are *avarnas*, colorless and nondescript; or *pancamas*, those left over as it were after the four castes have been counted; or *antyajas*, last-born, as if they were an accident, an unwelcome appendix, an unwanted tail . . . But now these nobodies are beginning to name themselves, to show a new self-awareness, to find their own identity, and to claim their due place in society. They are beginning to call everybody's attention to their existence . . . They refuse to be *harijans*, that is, the people of the god of the upper castes and oppressors. They call themselves *dalits* (oppressed) . . . They are holding up for all to see a terrible truth

> Indian society has always sought to keep in the dark; India has shrouded in much pious and metaphysical verbiage the truth about the large-scale slavery, violence, exploitation, apartheid, and cruelty on which its proud culture rests. (Rayan 1992, 129–130)

Rayan recognizes the action of Dalits to name themselves and in so doing blatantly draws attention to India's oppressive social hierarchy. Few others have recognized the resistive elements of reversal through re-creation in folk culture, however.

Reversal of purpose becomes Appavoo's radical approach to both the understanding of social norms and traditional interpretation of biblical stories. His social goals are first to reverse the value of private property and money over human relationships, and second to reverse (and ultimately equalize) the hierarchies of class, caste, and gender. His theological goals are to reverse the metaphor of Jesus as king, portraying him instead as a farmer or working-class political leader who rides a working animal, the donkey.[57] Appavoo also attempts to reverse the patriarchal foundation of Christianity by interpreting the qualities of God as both masculine and feminine. He has found that interpreting Jesus' actions as efforts to primarily benefit the poor and oppressed challenge traditional Indian and Western interpretations that support status quo power relationships, particularly of class and gender.

> The Bible has upset everything, has turned the established norms upside down. That is the Kingdom of God. As in the wedding of Cannan where water was changed into wine. Those who came last [the poor and outcaste] were served the best wine. Why did Jesus say the time had not come? Because, affluent people would have finished it [that is, the wine, if he had changed it from water earlier].[58]

Appavoo and other Dalit theologians understand many of these hermeneutic reversals as returning to an original intention or purpose of Christianity as practiced by Jesus and his disciples in the Holy Land two thousand years ago. This historical move toward an original purpose is also part of the indigenization of biblical interpretation. The historical understanding of these theologians is that Christianity has been co-opted by the rich and powerful to enhance and support their dominant position over others. Tamils have inherited this co-opted Christianity from Western missionaries, particularly of the high Anglican missions, which most strongly influenced the form of the CSI liturgy. However, Dalits in Indian culture relate much more empirically to the environment, social practices, and daily lifestyle of the Holy Land two thousand years ago than they do to the middle-class British or urban Indian lifestyle, the paradigms of which have been used to teach them the Bible.

Appavoo cites the biblical story of the wedding at Canaan as an example of the strategy of reversal in the Bible. Appavoo reconsiders the story using his strategy of "purpose analysis" and in light of his tenet of reversals.

> Suppose there is a feast. What is the usual practice? First men will be served. Among men, V.I.P.s will be served first; collectors and engineers will be given first. When you serve the pastors and theology college lecturers first, what do you do? You will serve a lot of mutton. For the second group, the amount will be less. For the third group that comes to eat there is a very little *sambar* [vegetarian curry]. So, water will be added. Hindu *kurma* [vegetarian curry] will be baptized into Christian *kurma* [note: Christian *sambar* or *kurma* is often more watery than that of Brahmins.] So, for the third set of wedding guests, water is sprinkled; for the fourth group immersion baptism. Who will be served last? Those who are wandering and standing outside.[59] This is the practice of the world.
>
> But in the wedding of Canaan, water was changed into wine. Who was served the best wine? Those who came last! Who would have come in the end? Beggars and poor people. When Mary told Jesus that [the] wine was getting scarce, what did he say? He said that his "time had not come." Why did he say that? If he had changed it right at that time, affluent people would have finished it. Theological seminary professors and engineers would have drunk it. So, Jesus asked them to wait. There were six stone jars. They looked at them. They were empty. What does it indicate? The water there was kept to wash hands. If that had been emptied, it means that all the people have eaten. After all the jars had been emptied, Jesus came there and asked them to fill them with water. Then, it changes into wine. So here the custom is reversed. It is changed upside down. The best wine will [normally] be served only first but now it is ready for the last group.[60]

Appavoo thus applied his method of biblical interpretation that focuses on reversals of class and hierarchy, challenging authority and interpreting the biblical parables as advocating for poor and hungry people.

Appavoo's living theology requires that those in a universal family relationship, un-separated by the sins of class, caste, and gender differentiation, live in the prescriptive, radical, reversed lifestyle of *oru olai*. Values and hierarchy are reversed, creating a completely self-sufficient system of simple living, in which all are equal under a philosophy of sibling-hood where God is a common parent. Furthermore, Appavoo legitimizes the *oru olai* system as a reversal of middle-class material norms by interpreting the Bible as a document demanding the reversal of the power and status of the rich.

Appavoo's chosen mode of communication for his theological message reverses the Western norm of a written treatise. Instead he uses the alternative medium of human transmission through oral folk music systems that allow re-creation with every transmission. Folk music as a participatory medium is a reversal from the traditional Western or classical karnatak music used by Tamil Christians that are often not as accessible stylistically and textually (in English or sanskritized Tamil). A more detailed analysis of Appavoo's ideas in relation to other Dalit theologians who similarly focus on the use of libratory media from Dalit folk culture and religion offers a greater understanding of the possibilities of both theological theory and praxis for Dalits.

CONVERSING WITH DALIT RELIGIONS

Among the Dalit theologians I have surveyed, Appavoo and Rev. Dr. Sathianathan Clarke are the most similar in their commitment to the necessity of "systematically recalling and creatively remembering" (Clarke 1998) Dalit religions (or Adi Samayam) as the means for symbolic and material sources of liberation in Dalit theology. Clarke is a non-Dalit Tamil Christian committed to the liberation of Dalits. His mother Clara is of the Nadar (lower) caste and his father, Bishop Sundar Clarke (former Bishop of the Madras Dioceses of the CSI 1974–89), is of the Vellalar (upper) caste. Clarke comes from a long line of famous Tamil Christian Vellalar priests and church leaders including Aaron (the first pastor ordained in the Tranquebar Lutheran mission in 1733) and W. T. Satthianadhan, ordained in 1859 (Neill 1985, 42; Grafe 1990, 57).[61] Clarke is Appavoo's academic peer, although several years younger and of a higher-class background. These two theologians have had very little direct contact. However, I took a course with Dr. Clarke on Dalit theology in 1995 at Harvard Divinity School where he had just finished his dissertation and was preparing to return to India to teach at the United Theological College in Bangalore. This direct contact as well as reading his dissertation and subsequent book facilitated my detailed comparison of the two theologians.

In the mid 1980s before coming to Harvard for his Ph.D., and again in 1992, Clarke conducted ethnographic research on Dalit goddess religions (among non-Christian Dalits) in the Madarandagam area of Tamil Nadu while serving as a priest to several Dalit Christian villages nearby. I went to this area in 2002 to conduct a reception study of Appavoo's music among the same villagers and secular activists with whom Clarke had also worked a decade earlier. What surprised me most was the discovery that Appavoo's songs had been used by Christians in the area for years, including during the time that Clarke conducted his field research. Yet in his book *Dalits and Christianity* (Clarke 1998),

Clarke does not acknowledge the presence of Appavoo's songs as a form of oral Dalit liberation theology (which he advocates is essential for Dalit theology), nor does he investigate their impact on Christians. I determined that the impact of these songs was substantial, particularly through their use by the same members of the Social Action Centre of Karunguzhi with whom Clarke worked (Mr. Gunadayalan and Mr. Gunaseelan). I conclude that Clarke's focus has been theoretical while Appavoo has created, and seen the results of, a practical model for oral Dalit theology, its praxis, and its successful transmission.

In the comparison between Clarke and Appavoo that follows, I investigate several of their similarities and differences. In each of these areas, they have slightly different approaches and results that I explicate. They both critique the sanskritization of Indian Christian theology and instead focus on the power of orality and sound, particularly in the resources of folk music and instruments. Both have used dialogical experience in villages (and advocated for it) as the means to construct Dalit theology. The result for both has been the integration into their theologies of either the image or the empowering association of the village goddess. The more striking differences between Appavoo and Clarke lie in their approach to social analysis and reconciliation, which I believe reflects differences in their caste and class standpoints.

Indigenizing Christian practice and theology to the cultural values and expressions of upper-caste Brahmanical Hinduism has kept Dalit Christians in the shackles of cultural and psychological inferiority for over four hundred years. Clarke argues, "It is crucial to locate, recover and validate critique-based voices that are contesting the content and the process of the dominant and dominating religious discourse" (1998, 21). Further, both Appavoo and Clarke intend to garner the active and creatively constructive aspects of subalternity (Clarke 1998, 7; Ortner 1996). Like Kancha Ilaiah, who wrote *Why I Am Not a Hindu* (1994), both Appavoo and Clarke reveal Dalit religions as separate from Hinduism, and critique Indian Christianity as having "elude[ed] its responsibility of dealing with the culture and religion of a significant portion of its subaltern members who are not part of the Hindu community" (Clarke 1998, 18). That is, from first hand experience observing and participating in village goddess religion, which Appavoo calls Adi Samayam (old or original religion) instead of village "Hinduism," these theologians recognize the significant differences between Brahmanical Hinduism and these village practices. These differences lie in the emphasis on individual rather than communal worship, the deities worshiped (Vishnu/Shiva/Brahma and their consorts versus different independent goddesses such as Ellaiymman, goddess of the boundaries and protector of Paṟaiyars), the practice of vegetarianism versus sacrifice and consumption of animals, the focus on fire versus the importance of water and fertility, and the central practice of ecstatic transformative experience through pain rituals in Adi Samayam (Appavoo 1994a).

Understanding these differences and the potentially liberating aspects of Adi Samayam has helped these scholars recognize that the indigenization of Christianity to Indian culture has been to elite philosophies of Brahmanical Hinduism, and as Appavoo has clearly analyzed, to elite karnatak and Western musics, especially through the *kīrttaṉai* (Sherinian 1998, 524–534). Thus, while the church population is seventy percent Dalit and rural, the church has explicitly rejected cultural material of this population, such as folk music, investing instead in musical values associated with upper-caste and class status.

To re-indigenize Christian theology and music to elements of Adi Samayam religion for Dalit liberation requires rejecting the label "Hindu," the religious practices associated with Brahmanical Hinduism that carry elite values, and understanding the political process of appropriation that led to eighty percent of Indians being categorized as Hindus. The labeling of all indigenous religious practice on the Subcontinent or Indus Valley as Hindu began with the Muslim invaders in the first millennium and was further codified by European conquers by the middle of the second millennium. While religious practice was distinct geographically and socially throughout the Subcontinent, it was not until twentieth century with the introduction of religiously based separate electorates within a democratic representative system that a need for a Hindu majority emerged. The Dalit and Śudra population, previously segregated, considered outcaste, and forbidden to enter Brahmin temples (until the 1930s), was appropriated into the Hindu fold particularly to counter the potential threat of a Muslim voting block.[62]

Most of the historically recognized writers of Indian Christian theology were upper caste, and several of them Brahmins. As a result, Indian Christian theology has been heavily sanskritized and "non-representative of the symbolic interaction of the whole community" (Clarke 1998, 35).[63] While the best known Tamil theologian A. J. Appaswamy (1891–1975) wrote treatises such as *Christianity as Bhakti Marga* (1928), which directly drew upon Hindu concepts, Brahmanic cultural domination has most thoroughly occurred through music, especially through the transmission and use of the karnatak-style *kīrttaṉai* repertoire (Sherinian 2005a, 2007). Since the early nineteenth century the *kīrttaṉai* of the upper-caste Vellalar composer Vedanayakam Sastriar were disseminated across all of the Protestant mission societies and denominations. Through the *kīrttaṉai,* Dalit and village Christians in turn were inculcated into hegemonic sanskritized Christian cultural identity and its elite cultural symbols, becoming estranged from many of the empowering elements of the symbolic world of Adi Samayam.

Clarke makes a significant contribution to Dalit theology through his critical assessment of the Sanskritization of Indian Christian theology, his assertion that theology has a necessary task of advocating for the role of the oppressed in the process of creating theology (1998, 21), and his advocacy for the potentially liberating elements of Dalit religions that challenge the historical devaluation of Dalit religions and culture to Indian Christianity. His analysis of the need for multimedia oral-based theology asserts the necessity for both liberating theological content and medium.

> It is not simply enough for Indian-Christian theology to champion the inclusion of the subaltern communities; it must also create space for their particular mode of expressing and communicating their reflections. Through a history of representation in which Dalits have been prevented from using the 'sacred' mode of the written word, their rich communal religious reflectivity is expressed in non-textual/non-scriptive forms, i.e. music, painting, dance, weaving, song, architecture, etc. Dalit communal symbolic interaction is thus a multimedia configuration. If Indian-Christian theology wants to critically reflect on the dialogical symbolic intercourse that is all-inclusive, it must go beyond the text and language in its traditional sense. Theo-logia (literally, words or language about God) in India, thus, ought to become inclusive of theo-graphia and theo-phonia. (Clarke 1998, 22–23)

Unfortunately Clarke's contemporary analysis and anthropological research does not recognize in Appavoo's work the existence of, and theoretical foundation for, exactly what Clarke advocates: an oral-based Dalit theology.[64] Furthermore, while Clarke's historical analysis correctly constructs a picture of the lack of a systematic Dalit theology by lower-caste Indian Christians until the 1980s, he appears unaware of Webster's evidence of late nineteenth-century "Dalit Christian Theology" in Punjabi and Tamil Christian hymnody (Webster 1992). Webster's analysis shows resistance to oppression by outcastes as well as their construction of God as the source of divine compassion and deliverance in bhakti-style hymnody. Webster cites a Pulaya lyric (written by 1883) referred to by Sherwood Eddy as "an old slave song heard in the Pulaya congregation in Nagercoil" which includes the verse "they [missionaries] diligently taught letters, arithmetic and hymns; made us clearly see the path to heaven, and set us therein."[65] Both of these "oral modes of expression" show an awakening of liberal consciousness and a sense of agency to take advantage of new opportunities and patronage, while the Pulaya hymn celebrates access to material deliverance: I would argue both are early examples of, in Clarke's words, oral "theo-phonia" by Dalits.

Clarke draws heavily on the symbols of orality from Dalit religion to create his Dalit theology and theories of orality. He understands Dalits as marginalized from the oral and written sacred word of the Hindus and attempts to reclaim the orality or divine sound of the Dalit drum in Christian theology (Clarke 1998, 123). While this is a significant theoretical contribution, he continues to codify his theology in a textual form that I fear will never be easily accessible or useable by the Dalit Christian community, and thus will not contribute directly to their liberation. On the other hand, I would assert that Appavoo was the contemporary exemplar of Clarke's theological intentions to reclaim Dalit orality. Further, Appavoo's songs carry on his mission through the network of activists that he created and musically trained as his students. Appavoo not only provides an orally based theology or theo-phonia in his songs and liturgy, he has developed a clearly articulated theory of theological transmission through the medium of folk music that has made his theology effective and accessible for Dalits.[66]

Both Appavoo and Clarke conducted systematic "fieldwork" in Dalit villages over multi-year periods in the 1980s to more deeply expose themselves to Dalit religious and cultural practices and, in the case of Appavoo, specifically to learn Dalit folklore and music. Their theological production with Dalit villagers was highly interactive. Both have drawn upon Paulo Freire's action/reflection methodology and mutually advocate that theology should be a shared dialogue evolving from group hermeneutic processes.

Clarke's definition of theology stems from these ideas: he says theology is "a critical and constructive reflection on human dialogical symbolic interaction in its attempt to make sense of, find meaning in, and determine order for living collectively under the Divine" (1998, 19). Appavoo's method of theological inspiration and construction was to work directly with village Dalit Christians through the TTS Rural TECCA program to learn villagers' contextual hermeneutics of the Bible as well as their music and folklore. Through this exchange he has composed songs and dramas that draw directly on the villagers' biblical interpretations as well as the folk vocabulary and grammar that he internalized through working with them for extended periods of time. Appavoo therefore built the necessary dialogical system into his theology by grounding it in the oral medium of folk songs that can, and have, been reconstructed by Dalit villagers. Clarke's work, on the other hand, is most useful as an anthropological understanding of non-Christian Dalit religious practice that has been integrated into a *textual* theological proposal which he hopes will "be liberative for the Christian Dalits," but that he admits must still be tested by them (1998, 208).

Appavoo has more easily been able to transmit his theology to villagers because of his association with TTS. From the early 1980s until his retirement in 2005 he spent his career teaching at TTS, a Tamil language, seminary that allowed him to directly facilitate the transmission of his "theo-phonia" through his seminary students who then transmitted it to the Dalit villagers whom they served as pastors. Through maintaining a strong "family relationship" with many of his students, and through his continual involvement in TECCA classes, Appavoo was able to receive both ideas for his musical theology and feedback from villagers in order to rework his ideas or musical elements to keep the theology relevant to their needs. It is through culture brokers like Appavoo that TTS has gained the reputation for excelling at grassroots, practical-level application of Dalit and feminist theology.

Clarke's primary teaching experience in India has been at UTC Bangalore, an English language, academically focused seminary attended by students from all over the country, most of whom return to serve either in English-speaking (and Western hymn singing), elite urban congregations. This situation cannot but distance Clarke from, and limit the direct effect of his theology on, the people who need it most: Dalit villagers and poorer Dalit theology students who may not be as facile in English.

THEOLOGICAL COMPARISON

While their methods of transmission and resulting theological impact have taken different trajectories, Appavoo and Clarke share similar theo-musical themes, and constructions of God. They both draw on aspects of the Dalit village goddess as a means to emancipatory empowerment. However, Appavoo constructs God in an agricultural image as *vevasāyi*, or nurturing farmer. Furthermore, for Appavoo, The Divine is *pettavarē;* the parent who bore us and who has both feminine and masculine qualities. With the term *pettavarē,* the mother is foregrounded as the bearer of the child. Further, his frequent use in performance of the sound of the *uḍukku* (hour-glass drum) aurally signifies empowering possession by the village goddess. In his song "Maṉasamātta" Appavoo references the protective qualities of the Paṟaiyar goddess of the boundaries with lyrics that describe whipping or driving away evil[67] (see chapter 4).

Clarke centers his concepts of theology of/as collective resistance in the Dalit Goddess Ellaiyamman: Mother Goddess of the *cēri* (untouchable village ghetto) boundaries. He focuses particularly on Ellaiyamman's quality as "an iconic representation of resistance" to the hegemonic assimilationist or conquering threat of Brahmanical Hinduism (Clarke 1998, 101). This goddess protects the Paṟaiyars' distinct cultural identity and religion. Further, her identity as unmarried and outcaste from the Hindu pantheon generates divine protective power that cannot be contained by caste Hinduism. Similar to Appavoo's emphasis on the re-creative power of Dalit Christian folk music, Clarke emphasizes the Paṟaiyars' use of the mythological origins of the independent goddess to "re-imagine their own communal subjectivity as a counter-history to the hegemonic one" of the caste communities and as a means to positive valorization (1998, 104, 107). Appavoo's theology does not rely on this form of symbolism. Instead his essential theological theme of collective resistance derived from Dalit culture involves community action of unity through sharing resources, particularly sharing food as *oru olai.*

The musical themes of both theologians center around folk music and drums. Clarke borrows the Dalit drum, "representative of the Divine" (1998, 119), "as a central religious symbol in communicating with the Divine" and thus "a symbol for emancipatory theography" (1998, 109). Appavoo, on the other hand contextually and sonically uses the divine power of Dalit drums (primarily the paṟai and uḍukku), and thus the aural power of the Dalit goddess herself, to articulate folk rhythms through his Dalit Christian liturgies and songs as the sounded *means to communication with* the Divine and to communicate a liberating Dalit identity. Indeed he directly re-sounds their Dalit empowered, valued existence for all to hear outside the church walls and *cēri* boundaries. In the lyrics of his well known Tamil song "Allēlūyā Allēlūyā," Appavoo directly refers to various folk drums and dances as the means to worship God.[68]

> Let's praise Him with the *uṟumi* ensemble [tension drum], the *periya* [big or paṟai] drum[69] and the *uḍukku* drum; the wailing *pamba,*[70] bells and hand claps.
>
> Let's praise Him with folk dances, *kummi, oyilāṭṭam,* and brave stick fighting. Come on woman, let's dance *kummi,* worship! Let's make a spectacle.

The principle thematic differences between these two theologians are their approaches to social analysis and to reconciliation. In his book *Dalits and Christianity,* Clarke focuses little on the nature of Jesus, instead centering on Jesus' praxis, his solidarity with the Dalits as deviants, "by reinterpreting the Christic presence as appropriated by the collective experience of the Paṟaiyar through the symbol of the [paṟai] drum" (ibid., 198). Clarke argues that as "liberator for the deviants," Christ has a posture of emancipatory resistance, while simultaneously maintaining a posture of emancipatory reconciliation that affirms that Jesus "does not cease to be saviour for the prominents" (1998, 6). Whereas his theological argument is one of Dalit collective identification with the emancipatory power of the goddess and the paṟai drum, he ultimately shifts away from identity politics toward a focus on liberating action to include non-Dalits. It allows those of the prominent community who cannot be Dalit to strive for salvation by being in affinity with Dalits.

Clarke openly locates his subjectivity as an elite Indian Christian and a non-Dalit. Furthermore, he stands in great affinity with, and advocates for, the Dalit community and their work toward liberation. He insists the advocacy function of his proposed theology "does not imply a silencing of other voices," that is, of the upper-caste Christians. Thus he proposes, "in Indian-Christian theology the caste communities' voices are [should be] in constructive and critical dialogue with the voices of Dalit communities" (1998, 21 and 22). I am in total agreement that dialogue and affinity are essential to Dalit Christian theology. Yet it must be pointed out that Clark's stance of reconciliation with caste communities in many ways reflects the needs of, and his position as, a "caste Christian." My critique is that he needs to articulate the complexities, particularly in relation to class and gender differences, of how this reconciliation would occur.[71] Further, he stresses that he has primarily focused on "fleshing out the caste dimension of subalternity" (1998, 7). Appavoo and many other Dalit theologians, in contrast, are purposely holistic, analyzing gender and class as core means of caste oppression *for* Dalits.

Appavoo concentrated minimally on issues of Dalit/non-Dalit reconciliation. Instead he focused on the dire needs of rural Dalit Christians to find a useful means to liberation and an empowered identity through their cultural resources. His consciousness was directed to a greater degree toward the gender and class hegemony within the Dalit community. This follows Sherry Ortner's position that within resistance studies and communities of resistance academics should focus on "the ambiguities and points of internal conflict within subaltern communities" (1995, 177). Appavoo not only directly addressed issues of class and gender in his theo-phonia, but, as a middle-class male, he was highly conscious about how he did so. The only deliberate caste-related expressions of reconciliation I have observed are found in Appavoo's *oru olai* myth, when Paraṭṭai Amma and the community embrace the Brahmin (i.e., upper-caste person) who (like the prodigal son) was "once also our brother." However, reconciliation with the Brahmin is conditional, based on the necessity that he give up his caste, his caste labels, and his practices of ritual separation based on pollution. It then follows that he will express that reconciliation by eating together with the rest of the community. Therefore all are empowered and unified through the collective resistance of *oru olai* against oppressive social structures. Along with reconciliation, those with greater status need to be self-reflexive about their role in the power dynamics of social change. Whether one is American or Indian, it is essential to understand the impact not only of caste difference, but of one's class, gender, racial, and national identity within the dialogue.

PARAṬṬAI'S THEOLOGY IN THE GLOBAL CHRISTIAN CONTEXT

Bringing Appavoo's theological perspectives into conversations with other liberation theologians helps us gain a wider understanding of the state of liberation theology in the larger global Christian context. Here I focus on Appavoo's philosophy of community in conversation with feminist and womanist theologians Serene Jones (2000) and Emilie Townes (1995) as well as with cultural theorist bell hooks.[72] Appavoo's theology of universal family, of corporate sin, and his use of neo-Marxist social analysis resonate with Townes's (1995) concept of a womanist spirituality of justice and Jones's (2000) idea of communitarian "bounded openness." His tenets of universal family and *oru olai* also parallel hooks's (1990) discussion of the chitlin circuit, or supportive Black community. Bringing these four visionary liberationists into conversation shows parallel strategies employed in different cultural contexts. It also provides a critical forum in which to consider the limitations of their prescriptive visions, while still providing the means to hopeful engagement for change.

I find several correlations in this conversation. All assert that the oppressed can reclaim and re-create folklore for liturgy as a means to create positive self-esteem and empowered cultural identity without romanticizing or essentializing the rural, the folk, or history. Worship furthermore, is a means for the oppressed to create the community structure necessary to support that empowered identity. The call by feminist theologians to critically interrogate the essentialist ideal of community and identity politics in general leads me to examine the applicability of Appavoo's Indian theological model outlining its limitations and risks. Finally, Appavoo's argument that Christian liberation theology necessitates a musical mode of transmission like folk music that is re-creative and thus liberatory is supported by the strategies of these womanist and feminist theologians. Furthermore, this global theological conversation can extend

Appavoo's musical thesis to argue that the creation of a liberating Christian community also necessitates a continual process of transformation or reformation, renewal, and internal critique that can happen through performance. Jones describes this as "a process of continued reformation"—lest the church community's "faith pronouncements and practices become destructive idols of its own creation" (Jones 2000, 159).

Appavoo's theology of universal family and his use of neo-Marxist social analysis to understand the social context of the oppressed resonate with the ideas of a womanist spirituality of justice theorized by theologian Emilie Townes in her book *In a Blaze of Glory: Womanist Spirituality as Social Witness* (1995). African American theologians created the term "womanist theology" from Alice Walker's use of the term "womanish" (Walker 1983), which describes a young Southern Black woman who is "precocious, inquisitive, stubborn, ornery, in charge and serious." She moves beyond prescribed cultural boundaries and socioeconomic determinants and is thus a threat to hegemony (Townes 1995, 9).

Townes describes womanist spirituality as inclusive, "concrete, particular, universal, . . . relentless, and self critical. In short, [womanist spirituality] is a social witness, but it is not monolithic" (ibid., 121 and 123). Community is central to womanist spirituality as the opposition to injustice. Its support of freedom counterbalances oppression. Womanist spirituality is a protest against the structural inequalities and evils of the status quo (ibid., 123). As Appavoo focuses the fight against injustice, oppression, and corporate sin in unified community with God as the common parent, Townes constructs God's purpose among people, and in turn one's accountability toward others, as a struggle for liberation.

> A womanist spirituality is drawn to question continually the inordinate amount of suffering that is the lot of the oppressed. Spirituality is challenged to a new awareness of God's presence within humanity as a liberating event. Situations of oppression do not reveal the mystery of God's love. The revelation of God's love manifests itself in work to end oppression. (ibid., 121)

In his "Lord's Prayer," furthermore, Appavoo declares that God, and relationship with God through loving relationship with one's neighbor, is the practice of liberation.

All four of the scholars compared here understand the theology of community as radically relational. For Townes this is "divine-human" community formed through the unconditional love of God, which is moving toward justice (ibid., 140). As we move into reconciliation with God, so "we are called to seek a reconciling relationship with one another . . . to stand in solidarity with God's will for a new heaven and a new earth" (ibid., 139). In her focus on the African American community, Townes says, "We make ourselves the oppositional Other, we turn to forms of self-hatred and self-destruction. Instead of critiquing and then working to eradicate notions of individualism, we forget our African past and seek to establish our lives as separate from one another" (ibid., 65). She understands womanist spirituality as a means to address internalized self-hatred, as it is grounded in self–other relation. That is, she reclaims the modernist dualist opposition of "otherness," reintegrating it from the margins to reconstruct difference within community as "an interactive interdependent spirituality of wholeness" (ibid., 66).

A crucial feature of womanist theology is to affirm African heritage, just as Dalit theology affirms Dalit culture and Adi Samayam religion. Townes calls on "the historic Black community of faith" committed to justice to help Blacks "re-member" or "re-call" a strong community identity through African and African American folkloric forms (ibid., 142). Townes draws the poetry for her womanist spirituality and its intellectual framework from the work of three Black female authors: Alice Walker, Paule Marshall, and Toni Morrison. Townes uses Baby Suggs's sermon from Morrison's novel *Beloved* that admonishes the oppressed to love their whole flesh or body. It is preached in a clearing to ex-slaves in the form of a call and response ring-shout, a circle of inclusion, as a way to reflect on the nature of being and surviving, a way to remember identity through dance and song.

> Womanist spiritual reflection demands that we stand up and dance with sometimes-twisted hips to the rest of what our hearts are saying. The reality of Black folk will give us the music to the song we must dance. To be called beloved is to do ethical reflection with the deeply held knowledge that we are not dipped, we are not sprinkled, we are not immersed, *but we are washed in the grace of God* [italics mine]. (ibid., 67)

Townes goes on to say, "This . . . sermon to love one's heart is an individual and a communal call to question the radical nature of oppression and devaluation of the self and the community in the context of structural evil" (ibid., 48). Thus self-hatred, particularly internalized racism and colorism, what she refers to as casteism, is linked to the loss of cultural identity.

Townes is particularly critical of the internalization within the African American community of destructive dominant structures like colorism, that is, "interiorized color consciousness that draws out the various shades of complexion among Black folk, hair texture, and physical features."[73] Townes addresses the need to reunify the African American community and Church divided by colorism. She shows that miscegenation leading to colorism was the historical determinant for class differences among African Americans and it "proceeds to rip us apart as a community of the Spirit" (Townes 1995, 101).

The experience of middle-class assimilation by the subaltern through the Church is common in both the Indian and African American contexts. Middle-class values are manifest through the adoption of hegemonic material, cultural values, and forms of worship. The prosperity or middle-class consumption theology that has resulted in both contexts reflects a cultural amnesia and alienation of the middle class from the potentially empowering aspects of their cultural roots in folklore.

Townes argues that the structural solution for the corporate sins of racism and lack of opportunities for the black underclass is a renewed call to organization for political and social change within the Black Church and a renewed sense of community accountability. This will require political and spiritual values of integration across African American classes. The agenda is to "broaden the vision of each class into one that eschews a mentality of relentless consumption for one of salvific redemption" (ibid., 138). Womanist spirituality will once again move the Church toward, not away from "a vision of communal hope and survival" (ibid. 138). Appavoo's *oru olai* vision of sharing so that all have the basics elements to survive resonates with Townes's call, and further, articulates a model for its possibility.

In her book *Feminist Theory and Christian Theology: Cartographies of Grace,* feminist theologian Serene Jones focuses on the creation of communities that are open to fluid, multiple identities, where the flourishing of women and all persons is ensured. She argues that they must simultaneously maintain "shared rules and a common sense of identity," communal integrity, and the possibility of exclusion of behaviors. Jones suggests this tension can be managed through "bounded openness" (Jones 2000, 135). She argues that in order to flourish, communities need room for resistance and openness to self-criticism allowing for individual agency and creative change (ibid., 151). However, like the Indian joint family and village caste group, boundedness offers "safety, trust, delight, mutual regard, and reciprocal accountability" (ibid., 126).

Jones sees bounded openness as a vision of the normative Church rather than a "blueprint for the hard, practical labor of constructing and sustaining Christian community."[74] She describes it as "a preliminary aesthetic of community" (ibid., 175). Indeed she uses performance metaphors to understand how the mimetic aspect of liturgy, ritual, and scripture "calls attention to the interpretive dimension of church life; as it imitates, it reenacts the story in the context of the lived experience of its present-day performers" (ibid., 157). Jones recounts how Joyce, a woman in her congregation who struggled with mental illness and low self-esteem, tearfully sang "Joy to the World" as a member of the Christmas pageant choir, and by envisioning herself an angel, transformed herself. Furthermore, she describes how Reggie, a homeless man in the congregation who played the inn-keeper, re-imagined the Christmas narrative by *welcoming* Mary and Joseph, unwilling to deny them (and thereby himself) a place to stay (ibid., 153). These contemporary American social outcastes redefined "what it means to be a community of faith" as they transformed the performance of Christmas and themselves through it (ibid., 154).

Bounded openness in church community reflects the dichotomies that feminist theorists and theologians have struggled with: classic rational liberalism versus communitarian approaches of radical difference, essentialism versus constructionism, universality versus radical situatedness, descriptive theory versus pragmatic utopianism, and identity politics versus normative commitments to the flourishing of an identity group.

As liberation theologians, Appavoo, Townes, and Jones ground their theology in the pragmatic, rational, concrete conditions of daily living for the oppressed communities that they serve. Yet as academics, they (and I) struggle against a "relativistic historicism" that can undercut the necessary "emancipatory visions" and emotion that create the hope necessary to continue to struggle for change (Jones 2000, 144). By comparing these theological ideas on community, I have shown the various ways all three theologians recognize the role and power that music, folklore, and performance play in creating bounded openness for communities, in creating the transformational, nurturing emotion necessary for people to take themselves from a state of oppression to renewed hopeful life.

For Appavoo, Jones offers a caution. In the messy process of creating actual *oru olai* community, the social and musical structures used to create community should remain flexible. Appavoo's Dalit theology is grounded in musical identity politics that reclaim "folk music" as the means for liberation that is most accessible and identifiable for Dalits. However, it will likely be necessary for those who apply this method to maintain a sense of cautious or conditional inclusiveness toward upper castes as well as toward the potential use of both popular film style music and elements of classical music. However, as these styles that encode upper-caste and material values are used in a space of universal family or open boundedness, their meaning may be recontextualized to encode liberative inclusiveness.

Black feminist cultural theorist bell hooks, who is not a theologian but a self-described "insurgent black intellectual," nevertheless reflects the general integration of spiritual and secular/political ideas of African American culture and philosophy in her writing. Her work on engaged pedagogy and liberative consciousness (hooks 1994) is a feminist development of the ideas of Paulo Freire found in his well known study, *Pedagogy of the Oppressed* (Freire 1970).

In her book *Yearnings: Race, Gender, and Cultural Politics* (hooks 1990), bell hooks titles her essay on the African American practices of community, "The Chitlin' Circuit: On Black Community." She defines the chitlin circuit very generally as "that network of black folks who knew and aided one another" (ibid., 38). Music scholars more specifically describe the chitlin circuit as a network of venues for Black performers performing before Black audiences, and a network of Black community members who, during U.S. racial segregation that reached back to the end of the nineteenth century and extended until at least the 1960s in the South, "provided room and board for a fee because hotels (unless black-owned) were not an option."[75] The use of chitlins (chitterlings), or hog intestines, the "pig leftovers that black folks got after the white folks ate high on the hog,"[76] as an emblem for community resonates with Appavoo's emphasis on Dalits proportioning to every family in the *cēri* both good and bad parts of an animal during *oru olai* festival occasions. It further metaphorically articulates the similar nature of racism with casteism that results in second-rate "leftovers" for the poor and oppressed. However, African Americans have reversed the value of chitlin scraps: what was once regarded as the cheapest food available would now be considered a soul food delicacy that is essential to festivals like Christmas.[77] In a similar move of social/theological reversal, Appavoo reclaimed the poor Tamil people's breakfast of *kañji* or rice gruel as the "body of Christ," replacing it for the Eucharist wafer when he led his Dalit village music liturgy. Shared simple food becomes materially more delicious and spiritually more valuable as the means to unify community.

Oru olai and the chitlin circuit communities extend the sharing of food to a network or web of those who may be strangers, yet share life experiences of discrimination, thus making them one family. Hooks describes this experience as "racial solidarity born of shared circumstance . . . that concrete relational love that bonded black folks together in communities of hope and struggle" (hooks 1990, 36).

Hooks mourns the loss of the chitlin circuit, arguing it is long broken by narrow patriarchal nationalism, middle-class assimilation expressed as self-sufficiency and rooted in internalized racism, and an identity crisis over "how we should struggle collectively to fight racism and to create a liberatory space to construct radical black subjectivity" (ibid., 36).

Both hooks (1990, 34) and Townes (1995, 91) draw upon Paule Marshall's novel *Praise Song for the Widow* (1983) to exemplify the personal crisis and community destruction that has resulted from African American middle-class assimilation. Avey, the protagonist in Marshall's novel, begins a journey home to her Caribbean roots and symbolically to her African spirituality. Townes describes this as "her middle passage back to her heritage and her spirit as she begins to estimate the cost of moving into a Black middle-class existence that is sterile" (Townes 1995, 91). In a dream that signifies the process of cultural remembering, Avey's Aunt Cuney "appears before her at Ibo Landing in Tatem, South Carolina. As she mutely begs Avey to come with her to again experience and respect the ritual of their communal heritage, her passivity turns to pleading" (Townes 1995, 91). In the ensuing battle between Avey's spirituality and materiality Townes refers to as a "transformation [from] death to grace" (ibid., 91), Avey "gain[s] [with the help of a community of others] the knowledge and the freedom of reclaiming a healthy heritage that enables her to have the necessary tools to face the dangers of assimilation and success for middle-class Black folk" (ibid., 118). Remembering and re-knowing the rituals and transformative power of a healthy communal heritage is the liberative message Townes draws from Marshall's writing.

Hooks illustrates Avey's struggle in less religious terms. Instead it signifies for her the loss of Black community and identity, especially through class assimilation. Her interpretation of the circumstances in the novel are that "the black couple is so intent on 'making it' economically in the white world that they lose the sense of who they are, their history. Years later, older, and going through a process of self-recovery, the black woman has the insight that 'they had behaved as if there had been nothing about themselves worth honoring'" (hooks 1990, 34). However, hooks employs very similar language to Townes to describe a necessary process of remembering Black folk culture and "rituals of belonging" that she deems necessary for the Black community's collective self-recovery (ibid., 39–40). She advocates that sharing stories, remembering history, family genealogy, and facts about the African American past is the catalyst for self-recovery (ibid., 39).

> A very distinctive black culture was created in the agrarian South, by the experience of rural living, poverty, racial segregation, and resistance struggle, a culture we can cherish and learn from. It offers ways of knowing, habits

> of being, that can help sustain us as a people. We can value and cherish the "meaning" of this experience without essentializing it. And those who have kept the faith, who embody in our life-practices aspects of that cultural legacy, can pass it on. (ibid., 38)

She advises renewing community through returning to relational love, and to rituals of belonging and Black communal feelings by "acknowledging one another in daily life," therefore reversing outright and internal racism as well as alienated individualism to affirm and recognize one another, instead of "aping the dehumanizing practices of the colonizer" (ibid., 39). And most importantly hooks declares "We need to sing again the old songs, those spirituals that renewed spirits and made the journey sweet, hear again the old testimony urging us to keep the faith, to go forward in love" (ibid., 40). For Appavoo such Christian folk songs are not only transformative, but as a medium created and re-created in the present they serve as the mode of resistance to oppression (Appavoo 1986).

Townes joins the chorus to assert that folkloric mythology, whether reflections of truth or not, function for womanist spirituality to pass on "legends that affirm strength and righteous agency in the miasma of oppression" (Townes 1995, 115). She sees the poetry of Avey Johnson's journey home as bridging the past with the present: "the remembered Patois of her youth that signaled a connection with those who have gone before and those who are yet to come." This renewed identity "helps maintain cultural continuity and wholeness in a context of oppression and injustice" (ibid., 92). Re-enactment of communal responsibility through practicing folkways and folklore leads to cultural pride, wholeness, unity, self-esteem and a liberated future.

Appavoo, hooks, and Townes all struggle to create a liberating vision for their communities in the context of middle-class assimilation by a relatively powerful Black/Dalit middle-class minority, particularly within the Church. The theology of and obsession with material gain has led to a loss of memory and alienation from the potentially empowering aspects of the "traditional Black folk experience" by the middle class (hooks 1990, 40).[78] Both Townes and hooks argue that remembering and revaluing the lessons of rural Southern community for the *meaning* that they held and that can be reclaimed, avoids essentializing them as passive reflection or nostalgic longing (ibid., 38, 40). Remembering and reclaiming is instead an action of "knowing and learning from the past, . . . a catalyst for . . . collective black self-recovery" (hooks 1990, 40). Further, it reflects an "awareness that humanizing survival strategies employed then are needed now" (ibid., 39). Appavoo understands this process as a proscriptive vision for liberation based on reclaiming the liberative elements of village culture to re-integrate into Christian theology and liturgy.

In an era in which Christianity in the U.S. and Hinduism in India has been co-opted by right-wing fundamentalists and conservative politics, this conversation among differently situated liberationists contributes to a larger theory of the relationship among performance, identity politics, feminism, and Christianity within oppressed communities. It shows that through performance, these scholars and their communities are expressing a moral agency and radical relational love of God and neighbor founded in justice. As Townes declares, "In times like these, love without justice is asking for trouble. When what we offer folks is a restricted diet of love and do not provide an equal portion of justice, we are only talking about a partial gospel—not a whole one" (Townes 1995). Conservative fundamentalism bounded by exclusivity and middle-class priorities only offers half the gospel meal.

4

ETHNOGRAPHY AS TRANSFORMATIVE MUSICAL DIALOGUE

Maṉasamāttayappā/Maṉasamāttayammā
Composed by J. T. Appavoo
Translated by J. T. Appavoo and Zoe Sherinian

PALLAVI (REFRAIN)
Show us the way to change our hearts, Oh, Lord our God!
The people must live in peace, Oh, Lord our Father, Lord our Mother.
ANNUPALLAVI
The demon gang has come like bedbugs and mosquitoes.
They have immigrated into the country and homes.
They are dancing and singing wildly,[1] causing fights.
So, you must come as quickly as possible to resolve this conflict.
CHARANAM ONE (VERSE)
The peace, which Gabriel talked about, that Christmas song,
has vanished into the air. It still has not come to us.
Even the coffee tumbler in the stall has arrogance and wickedness.
The caste devil is the vicious one.
You should scold and drive it away.
CHARANAM TWO (VERSE)
We think money is our god. It has become a barbarian.
We lay stones to divide the land into property.
It has become an evil devil.
Can we eat money, like rice cakes from old grandma's shop with lamb bone curry?
Oh! My dear Mother [God], not even knowing this we became fools.
Those devils created quarrels between us.
Oh, child,[2] Jesus, take the whip, come, come quickly to chase away these devils.
CHARANAM THREE (VERSE)
Oh, King of Kings!

> You ride on a donkey that carries loads on its back.
> We have plowing bullocks; ride on them and come quickly.
> The mad devil of power [authority] has come riding on a horse.
> It teaches us new methods of fighting with bombs, planes, atom bombs, warships and [it tells us to construct] all kinds of guns.
> Because of these conspiring devils, peace is gone.
> You take the brave cross to scare and drive away these evil things.
> Come, our king!

On a pleasant evening in mid November, 1993, a choir of seminary students, graduate student spouses, faculty and staff children of approximately age ten and up, faculty wives, and me, an American ethnomusicologist, gathered in the auditorium on the campus of the Tamil Nadu Theological Seminary. The auditorium was a simple multipurpose room with rows of ceiling-high windows on the sidewalls, a wooden stage at the far end, and a cement floor. We sat in the audience area on metal folding chairs, women on the left and men on the right, while various students and faculty taught us their compositions in preparation for the seminary's largest public relations event of the year, the annual Christmas Carol Service. For the composers and theologians at TTS, this was one of the most important opportunities during the year to make their liberation theology singable and to spread this song to a large audience of mostly middle-class, fairly conservative Madurai Christians. This year the TTS community hoped, through their songs, to change the hearts of those Christians who still practiced caste discrimination and social injustice.

The 1993 Carol Service theme was "Let's Make Peace." Appavoo convened the service, creating a show with musical pieces and short dramatic skits that asked the audience to consider the meaning of real peace. His song "Maṉasamātta" conveyed this question most powerfully in the complete process of its creation and transmission. Appavoo rehearsed and directed the choir, and he worked with student composers to fine-tune and arrange the music of the songs they had composed and submitted. He was assisted by Kavinesan Solomon, who was an excellent karnatak mrdangamist and singer as well as the son of Swamikannu, the former karnatak music teacher at TTS.

I attended all of the rehearsals, learning the songs as a member of the choir and observing the rehearsal/transmission process. Although the choir would write down the lyrics and *swaras* (indigenous classical music notation) particularly for the *citta swara* (pre-composed improvisation) sections of karnatak-style songs in personal notebooks, Appavoo simultaneously taught the melody and words orally. He did not teach the tunes using *swaras,* but occasionally reinforced the melody aurally on the harmonium. I sat on the women's side, while some of the teenage girls helped me quickly write down the Tamil lyrics as they were recited to us. I noted in my field diary (November 17, 1993) how amazed I was at how fast these kids, in particular, learned the pre-composed *citta swara* sections and memorized the lyrics to Appavoo's song. They also sang very strongly, without any hesitation or shyness. This generation of young people was the enculturated embodiment of TTS values. As young women, they boldly engaged in the creative and political process of bringing to life through their singing voices, TTS's progressive ideals of women's equality, environmentalism, Dalit rights, class equality, and the "change of heart" Appavoo described in his song.

On this particular evening we practiced Appavoo's folk song "Maṉasamāttayappā" which he had newly composed for the Carol Service. He had originally composed the first line of the *pallavi* (refrain) as a simple sing-songy melody followed by a quick shout-like response that named God combining the word *sami,* the gender-neutral term for deity that comes from Adi Samayam village religion, with the Christian term for Lord, *āṇḍavaṉ,* or "one who rules over."

> Show us the way to change our hearts, Oh, Lord our God [*āṇḍavaṉē sāmi*].
> The people must live in peace, Oh, Lord our Father [*sāmi-yappā*]

The tune of this refrain was simple and lively, with the last two words of each line shouted with great enthusiasm, and supported melodically by a quick jump upward almost an octave. This rehearsal was the second or third time we had sung the song. The teenage girls (daughters of staff) had learned the refrain well by now, and all of a sudden while singing the second line, a group of these young women shouted "*sāmi-yammā*" or "God our Mother." The rest of the women's side of the choir quickly caught on, gleefully singing "God our Mother!" every second line, while keeping "God our Father" at the end of the first.

As members of Paraṭṭai Annan's choir, these young women were not out of line with their textual re-creation. Appavoo applied the practice of re-creative folk transmission in his musical pedagogy. He both verbally and non-verbally encouraged changes in the lyrics if the choir members did not agree with his ideas. In this case, the women were moved to apply a feminist perspective, a central aspect of TTS discourse, to the song. Feminism at TTS focused on gender equality, social justice, mutual respect, gender experience in religion, and equal gender access to education and church positions as well as an active engagement by community members with both the poorest and most oppressed women as well as lower and middle-class Christians.[3] Feminist theology and organizing, along with Dalit theology, are also integral parts of the curriculum at TTS.[4] Thus retextualization of "Maṉasamātta" to construct God as bi-gendered was the theological realization or praxis of TTS feminist discourse. Instead of insisting that God be called "Father," Appavoo fully embraced this feminist theological re-creation of God as both mother and father proposed by the youngest women in the choir in a spirit of dialogical transmission.

Appavoo also allowed changes in the musical patterns if many choir members found them too difficult. For example, in the most classical-style piece in the Carol Service, Appavoo negotiated with the group as to whether he should take out a karnatak rhythmic element called *arai eḍuppu* (entering the song after a 1/2 beat syncopation in the first line).[5] Ultimately, he removed it because many struggled with its complexity.

Appavoo's dialogical teaching strategy facilitated indigenous theological creation through the folk transmission system that he argued is key to creating a liberating Dalit theology. As a dominant senior male professor in the community, he facilitated a participatory production process transforming the song to become truly folk (by Appavoo's definition), as it was (re)indigenized by the people to represent the voice and theology of the most oppressed of the community: the young (Dalit) women. This strategy is in keeping with Freire (1970), who maintains that the teacher who facilitates liberation "does not regard cognizable objects as his private property, but as the object of reflection by himself and the students. In this way, the problem-posing educator constantly re-forms his reflections in the reflection of the students" (Freire 1970, 68). Furthermore, Appavoo's dialogical teaching strategy was also in tune with the theology of internal change in the text and musical performance of the song "Maṉasamātta."

Recent theoretical work in ethnomusicology has emphasized an understanding of fieldwork as an experience of dialogical exchange of music and its values (Rice 1994 and 2003; Titon 1997; Barz and Cooley 1997; Araújo 2006; Qureshi 2007). Ethnography includes the self-reflexive experience and local impact of the ethnographer while focusing on the exchange, through musical practice, of cultural ideas and values. Conducting ethnomusicological fieldwork over the last eighteen years among Tamil Christians in South India, particularly working with Dalit Christian theologians and activists, has led me to define fieldwork in this context as a means to the creation of social change through transformative musical dialogue, and "the field" as those relationships that reveal or negotiate the shared values that contribute to that change. This process has also led me to conclude that when Dalit and feminist politics are the central practice of the music culture studied, critical dialogue leading to social change by all actors, including the fieldworker, is expected and must be taken into account in the ethnographic process.

Through discussions with Appavoo about the practice of feminist theology in the re-creation of his songs, he communicated that my presence at the seminary and my interactions with him and his students affected them as a reminder to live up to their progressive feminist values. Simultaneously, my observations and participation in music at TTS focused on the substantial impact Appavoo and his music had on his students, the seminary, institutions of the Church of South India, and on me. It is impossible to be close to Appavoo and seriously engage with his music without being drawn into political dialogue and, for most of his students, become transformed into activists for social justice.

During my fieldwork at TTS I participated in daily chapel worship, seminars, music classes, recording sessions, and political events, while doing intensive interviews about the production and transmission of Christian music. There were three areas in which I focused my observations and participation during my ethnographic research at TTS and among the Tamil Christian community: the production and transmission of Christian songs in indigenous styles, the experiment of *oru olai* (communal cooking and eating), and the transformation of community members into social activists.

The descriptions of musical transmission in this chapter focus on the context of seminary music classes and choir rehearsals as well as performance analysis of Appavoo's liturgy and songs in order to explicate the dynamics of the responsorial compositional process between him and his students. I focus on the song "Maṉasamātta," which the women students rewrote during the Christmas Carol Service rehearsals. Furthermore, I analyze the creation and performance of liturgies by Appavoo's students that were inspired by his musical ideology to show his impact and the variations on his model that they had produced. I then describe the praxis of sharing food through communal eating (*oru olai*) within the seminary and among a small group of my women friends. I conclude that it is the dialogic production and transmission process of liberatory theology through music, reinforced by the implementation of these values in the practice or *oru olai,* that is the means to the education and creation of committed activists. These students were the individuals who extended the transmission network, creating new nodes of socio-cultural liberation through their work with poor Dalit villagers.

TTS AND INDIGENIZATION IN CONTEXT

The Tamil Nadu Theological Seminary (TTS), founded in Arasaradi, Madurai, in 1969, is a microcosm of Tamil Christian music production. It is the center of the theologically institutionalized production and dissemination of Tamil Christian music for the Church of South India (CSI). Creating indigenized Tamil Christian music as a means of communicating a singable theology and as an interactive method of ministry has been an important task for theologians at TTS since it was founded (Thangaraj 1990, 115).

Indigenizing Christianity to be locally meaningful has been fundamental to TTS's mission in their training of ministers to serve the Tamil people.[6] Kambar Manickam, the principal of TTS during the early 1990s, explained the seminary's understanding of the need to support the culture of, and minister to, poor rural Tamils and the way in which the seminary's educational priorities reflect this. For Rev. Manickam and TTS, the Christian message is made locally meaningful through the struggle to extend basic human rights and dignity especially to poor village people. Therefore students' training is grounded in a liberation theology lived out through social and political work with the rural and urban poor.

> TTS's job is first of all to bring the rural poor people to become aware of their rights and needs and then to become conscious of their human dignity. Of course then the social and economic status has to be improved, but more than that, they should be given equal rights in a democratic society . . . There are millions of people suffering in the rural areas . . . As a seminary, we have our own methodology . . . [The students'] second year is the year of exposure. [They live] in different parts of the city, mostly in slum areas . . . bringing their daily experience into the classroom.[7] Then the third year is the year of involvement. They go on internship[s] [and then] come back and live in the villages . . . [We expose] our students to the Indian or rural reality . . . So the methodology is . . . to train our students in this pattern with the hope that when they go to the churches and actual field of work they will carry this experience and message to the people at large—the message of liberation through Christ.[8]

TTS is a vernacular-language seminary not an English language institution like many of the top educational institutions in India and many of the seminaries. It is organized upon the belief that use of the Tamil language and culture is key to the social and political empowerment of the Tamil people. Therefore both undergraduate- and graduate-level theology is taught in the Tamil language. Liturgies created at TTS are written using the grammar of literary Tamil poetry and performed entirely as music [the genre of *Tamiẕ Isai Vaẕipāḍu* TIVP], and Tamil music, art, and sculpture are promoted.[9] During the 1990s, the type of Tamil used in songs and liturgies at TTS was dominated by *sen* Tamil: a literary form from which most of the Sanskritic elements had been removed. Yet, while this linguistic form remains literary and elite, since the mid-1980s the stylistic focus of music at TTS began to shift away from using classical karnatak style toward using Tamil folk music. This reflected both the institutional priority of Dalit theology and the presence and popularity of Appavoo, who was becoming Tamil Protestant Christianity's most influential interpreter of Dalit cultural and theological expression. The result was that some theologians and students began to compose songs and give sermons using spoken (*pēccu*) Tamil, the language of folk music and of the poor villagers to whom they directed their theology.

As the focus of the indigenization of Christian elements at TTS shifted from the use of Brahmanical cultural sources to Dalit and rural sources, Dalit theology and its expression through folklore became a priority. Manickam explained:

> In most of the other theological colleges in India they teach a course called Indian Christian Theology and the Senate of Serampore also offers this course. But . . . in their courses they treat Indian Christian theology as an appendix to the so-called classical or Western theologies. They teach all Western theologies, then they add from the Indian Christian theology point of view. So, we wanted to change that kind of approach. Why should Indian Christian theology be called by that name at all? So, theology is theology, and theology done by an Indian or Tamil should be theology of our own people. And, the climax of this approach is the birth of Dalit theology. I feel it is the native theology born out of the context. Because in a church, which consists of mostly oppressed people, the need is a liberation theology.[10]

Unity was one of the central themes of liberation theology that the TTS community advocated and attempted to practice. The TTS community regularly participated in the ritual experiment of *oru olai* by producing and sharing food communally after Sunday services and on special occasions. Yet the people who live, pray, and sing within the walls of the TTS campus are also a microcosm of the wider Tamil Christian community with all its differences of social hierarchy, caste, class, gender, and geographic division. It is also a place where all four major styles of Christian music—karnatak, light, folk, and Western—and the social divisions that are reflected within them interact, are negotiated, create dissonant clashes, and struggle for ideological predominance. While there was clearly social and musical diversity within TTS, along with differences in the wider Christian community that separated people, Appavoo and others held the hope that the dialogical production of music and shared eating would be a means to unify the TTS community. Further, he hoped that through the seminary's attempt to transmit liberation theology to the laity in annual musical events like the Christmas Carol Service, a sense of commonality and affinity with the problems of oppression in society would be nurtured among the conservative Christian community that surrounded TTS.

CHRISTMAS CAROL SERVICE

Through participant observation in the 1993 Tamil Nadu Theological Seminary's Christmas Carol Service, I witnessed the dialogical production of music and creative exchange that unified the choir, and resonated throughout the TTS community particularly in the Carol performance. The transmission of Dalit theology through music and drama was one of many seminary activities that helped educate and transform the students and TTS community members into activists. The Carol Service was also a non-threatening means to negotiate musical style and theological content with the wider Madurai Christian community.

Late in the afternoon on the first Sunday in Advent, November 28, 1993, the palm tree-lined path from the front gate to the chapel of the Tamil Nadu Theological Seminary was illuminated with lanterns of all shapes and sizes. The Christmas Carol Service was an opportunity for the entire TTS community to come together in a creative endeavor. The lantern contest was also the annual opportunity for TTS to reach out to the larger Madurai Christian community by inviting them to participate in the artistic interpretation of the service's theme. Thus, for several weeks prior to the November 28 event, groups inside and outside of TTS applied themselves to create expressions of peacemaking while the Carol Service event itself became a celebration of community interaction and expression. Local church and Christian organizations constructed beautiful lanterns with a variety of visual expressions of peace and community building. For example, the TTS fellowship group in which I participated made a lantern in the shape of a globe with figures of people linking hands across the continents (PURL 4.1).

The service's songs were of many styles interspersed with karnatak-style *slōka* (religious) chants by Rev. Mohanraj Peter and the choir, Bible readings by TTS children, and dramatic vignettes written by Appavoo. As the crowd settled into their chairs in rows in front of the outdoor stage in the *mānadōppu* tree grove, Mohanraj Peter, the blind theologian, composer, and advocate for the handicapped, sang an opening Christian *slōka*. The college recording engineer, Ravi, then played a traditional karnatak *gītam* that had become the basis of a well known Christian hymn. However, he performed it on the electric guitar, imitating the sound of a *vina* by plucking individual notes on the strings on this long-necked chordophone and adding electronic sustain rather than strumming or playing chords. Kavi accompanied him on the *tavil* (barrel drum), the processional drum of the Hindu temple and village folk music (PURL 4.2).

To this Indian Christian processional music, the choir filed down the center aisle of chairs. They were dressed in white, like angels: little girls in white skirts and blouses, female youth in *churidar* (baggy pants and long tunic), and women in white saris, men and boys wearing white shirts and dark pants.[11] The choir sat in three rows on stage, the smallest cross-legged on the ground, taller students sitting on the ground behind them, and then a row of students and community members in chairs. Men and women were on separate sides but without space between them. The orchestra sat on stage to the choir's left, displaying an elaborate array of instruments and electronics. The conductor, Appavoo, dressed in South Indian *dhoti* and *jiba* (not "Western" pants as was common for urban Christian professionals), stood below the choir in front of the stage, taking the focus off himself while facilitating the Indian-style seating arrangement on the stage (see Fig. 6).

The Carol Service introduction lent a familiar yet modern karnatak classical setting for the mostly middle-class audience. Indigenous hymns in karnatak style, or *kīrttaṉai,* are commonly sung in urban churches signifying for the (majority) lower-caste Tamil Christian community that they have become sophisticated and civilized by adopting upper-caste cultural forms (Sherinian 2007). By the end of the service, however, the audience's sense of musical identity would be challenged and transformed.

Appavoo approached the theme of "making peace" by creating a musical and dramatic context in which the audience was asked to consider the meaning of "true peace." They were challenged to not settle for a superficial peace, conceding to "normalized" daily oppressions for survival, but to work toward real structural equality.

To transmit the message of making true peace, in place of a sermon, the third-year students staged a series of dramatic vignettes. Using several social situations (a fight between church factions while caroling, a husband beating his wife, and international negotiations) Appavoo asked the question: Is finding a momentary sense of security in an ongoing oppressive system really the state of peace that we want? To ensure that the message was clearly communicated, Appavoo pre-recorded the dialogue of the vignettes in the TTS recording studio with appropriate dramatic music coded in the background. He worked closely with students, training them to express, both vocally and physically, the kind of emotion he felt was necessary to communicate his message in this dialogue (PURL 4.3).

The most successful musical means to communicate the message of making peace was through the compelling metaphors, lilting folk rhythms and melody of Appavoo's song "Maṉasamātta." It was the choir's favorite piece of the Carol Service. Even the children told me how powerful and poignant they found its lyrics. The choir's identification with the message and style of the song was exhibited through the dynamic energy and emotion in their performance.

In "Maṉasamātta," Appavoo grounds his theology in the social analysis of the Dalit folk context. He considers the meaning of true peace as announced by Gabriel's song and brought by the coming Jesus in a context riddled with caste oppression, private property, materialism, class, division among the oppressed, and first-world ideological imperialism (PURL 4.4).

In the *pallavi* or refrain, Appavoo presents his theological position: to create peace among people in this world it is necessary for people to change their hearts, that is, their values of casteisim and classism and other discriminatory practices. He suggests that it is the people's responsibility, yet he asks God (mother and father) to "show us the way." He does not ask people to make this change alone, bearing all the responsibility, but reminds them to nurture the support of their community (not to allow divisive devils to threaten this unity). Furthermore, he reminds the people of their relationship with God who acts as a guiding, nurturing parent.

Appavoo set the *pallavi* to a folk-song style with a simple, lively melody and lilting folk rhythm in a $\frac{6}{8}$ feel. In live performance the voices were accompanied only by a simple electric guitar strumming a six-pulse pattern with accents on two-three and five-six, with the chords sustained for a measure or more on the keyboard; the melody was not duplicated on the instruments, yet the choir carried the tune with great strength, rhythmic vitality, and emotion.

The lyrics of the *anupallavi* and *charanam* (verses) use striking metaphors and ironic twists that force the listener to consider Dalit politics both intellectually and emotionally while also leaving room for humor. The *anupallavi* invokes a gruesome image: the Brahmanic caste system becomes a demonic gang that infests the country like bedbugs and mosquitoes invading from outside with a divisive social system. Appavoo derides the classical arts tradition by constructing a musical image of buzzing pests dancing and singing wildly, creating noise pollution. His underlying intention is to compare the buzzing sound of mosquitoes to the sound of fast vocal oscillations in karnatak music.[12] He asks God to come to earth to resolve the social divisions, thus encouraging his audience to turn to God and to positive aspects of folk culture and religion to find answers and creative action to fight these oppressions.

The first *charanam* (verse) continues Appavoo's focus on contemporary forms of caste discrimination and the discord (lack of peace) it causes. The line "Even the tumbler in the coffee stall has arrogance and wickedness" refers to the practice in many villages of coffee stall proprietors serving untouchables coffee in disposable coconut shells or glass tumblers rather than the metal tumblers used to serve higher castes. Furthermore, untouchables are forced to wash their own tumblers. Such discriminatory differentiation is intended to psychologically reinforce impurity, untouchability, and secondary status.[13] Appavoo calls attention to the tumbler as a code for caste discrimination, expressing the "arrogance, wickedness, and viciousness" of this devil.

The second stanza scrutinizes the social inequalities of class and private property based on materialism and the capitalist system that Appavoo argues serves only to fool the people into further dividing themselves. His lyrics suggest that money and capitalism have replaced religion, leading the people toward barbarism. Blind worship of materialism has made people (particularly the middle and upper classes) uncivilized, uncultured, and rude; this is a reversal of the former missionary critique of the low-caste/class people as heathen and undeveloped. Appavoo asserts that "modern" and Western "progressive" systems have turned people away from each other and from the values of unity and sharing that their former folk religion provided.

Appavoo uses irony to make the point that the primary concern of poor village people is still survival—they do not know the source of their next meal. He asks whether money, literally the paper and coins, can be eaten like rice cakes with curry from Grandmother's shop. He reinforces this irony by placing a dramatic falling slur at the end of the line. At this point during the song's performance at the TTS Carol Service the spirited teenage daughter of a staff member proclaimed the line "we have become fools." Appavoo's choice of a young woman's voice and this particularly precocious girl reflected his belief that folk music and folk religious practices are liberatory to such commonly suppressed voices, particularly during possession or physically transformative rituals. In Tamil folk religion, young women are often whipped using freshly cut *margosa* leaves to exorcise *pēy* (devils) from them or as proof of their possession by the Goddess (Nabokov 2000). At these times they are treated *as* the Goddess, thus their exclamations are respected as truth. Following this teenage girl's declaration, the choir returned almost screaming the lyrics in the higher octave, asking Jesus to exorcise the Devil with a whip.[14]

Appavoo often uses food metaphors to refer to the Eucharist, particularly the practice of *oru olai,* and as a poetic code for his primary social and theological strategy for the poor. He connects these images to women and village economic systems of food distribution and sharing, thereby advocating reconsideration of female-centered practices.[15] He warns his Christian audience not to foolishly and unknowingly reject them in favor of Western capitalism.

In the third stanza, the lyrics address local and international issues of power and class. Appavoo uses the metaphor of Jesus the king who rides the working people's vehicle, the donkey. Breaking the musical line and thus creating a momentary emphasis with silence, he reminds us that the donkey is the animal that carries the workers' loads. He then localizes this image further by inviting Jesus to ride the bullock-driven wooden carts, the vehicle of Tamil villagers. He contrasts this indigenized image of Jesus as a poor villager with "the mad devil of power" that rides a horse, the symbol of upper-caste, non-Brahman kings (Pandyans, twelfth to fourteenth centuries) in Tamil Nadu. The contrast is emphasized by a vocal jump to a high-pitched anxious wail. In the fourth line he shifts this embodiment of evil power to the "conspiring devils" of international power who take away the impoverished people's "peace of mind," duping them into focusing their precious resources on building "new" (i.e., modern) weapons of mass destruction. The musical mood accompanying this line becomes ominous with held minor chords and low eerie voices that describe all the new weapons. Then the choir again jumped to a screaming tension, crying out that all the peace is completely gone (*ellam pocca*) because of these devils.

The *anupallavi* and each *charanam* (verse) of "Maṉasamātta" end with a call to God to resolve these problems with a dramatic show of angry power: scolding, whipping, chasing, and driving away the devils. The choir reinforced this by almost screaming the words at a very high pitch. In these final lines Appavoo fuses two religious references: the exorcism of evil spirits in Adi Samayam (folk) Indian religious traditions (whipping the possessed), and the ultimate Christian "bravery" of Jesus taking the cross, a sacrifice so great that it drives away evil. Thus Appavoo gives equal positioning in the song structure to both rituals, Tamil village whipping and Christian crucifixion, as transformative bodily experiences of inflicted pain. This is Appavoo's means of raising the status of transformative village rituals, at least figuratively indigenizing Christianity to that context. After each of these lines the song structure returns to the *pallavi* that asks God to "show us the way to change our hearts." Although people ask God to solve these problems using great power and a transformative show of anger, ultimately, in order to transform the oppressive social system, they must change their own hearts, their internalized oppression and fear, and their negative feelings toward each other.

The theology of "Maṉasamātta" indigenizes Christianity to local folk socio-religious concerns in order to address the local impact of global power issues. Correspondingly, the TTS musicians fused local folk music sounds and rhythms with international electronic technology to negotiate the interaction of this global/local reality. In an elaborate percussion solo and using an accompaniment pattern that combines $\frac{6}{8}$ folk meter patterns with a funk groove, Kavi used the electronic timbral qualities of a sophisticated drum machine in a way that deviated considerably from Western sound. Instead his playing reflected the ability of a *tavil* master to mix subtly distinct tones into an elaborate layered pattern of rhythmic accents, tension, and groove. An urban Dalit musician trained in karnatak drumming appropriated a Western electronic medium to a Tamil folk acoustic performance style, transforming the aural expectations that the drum machine sound will encode westernized film music. Instead he reminded the sophisticated urban crowd of the transformative power of Indian folk rhythms and timbres. Through the compelling musical sound and message of "Maṉasamātta" Appavoo began to redirect the values of the middle-class urban Dalits away from material individualism and assimilation with urban elite culture toward a positive re-acceptance, and memory of, their village roots.

Many of the lower-caste Nadars and outcaste Paṟaiyars (or their ancestors) in Appavoo's Madurai Christian audience fled the social degradation of the village in the early to mid-twentieth century in search of the relative anonymity of urban life, particularly through attending Christian boarding schools, teacher training schools, and colleges. In the process they also rejected most everything associated with village life. This included the transformative cultural elements of folk music and religion especially as the cultural elite had labeled these degraded and the missionaries considered them heathen. Appavoo attempted to reclaim specific values and rituals of village culture. Through employing quick shifts of musical moods, folk instrumental patterns, spoken Tamil, and direct and metaphoric references, Appavoo strove to emotionally transport the urban middle-class Tamil Christians back to the village—an imagined world rearticulated as powerful and worthy through music (PURL 4.5).

Appavoo's strategy of geographic relocation of his urban audience through musical remembering was also a means to shift the purpose of Christian worship, to focus it on liberating the oppressed through Dalit, feminist, and class-consciousness. Reconstruction of the value of folk music was a necessary step in the process of transforming the structures, practices, and theological perspectives of the Church of South India to create an institution with its political and cultural resources centered on the liberation of poor village Dalits. By grounding Christian salvation in the social needs of the most outcaste of Indian society, Appavoo intended to transform the local Madurai Christian community, the Church of South India, as well as global Christianity from the inside out.

This is the power of music to evoke other spaces and times and to direct people's emotional attachments by redefining contexts, in this case reconstructing village life-ways and cultural elements as positive for an alienated urban middle class.

While this level of engagement with the reconstruction of theology and musical style only occurred a few times a year for the majority of the Madurai Christian audience who attended the annual Carol Service, the TTS staff, faculty, and students engaged in liturgical and community building experimentation every week. The weekly Sunday service and shared meal provided TTS members an opportunity to fully experience the meaning of Dalit theology through music, food, and full sensory participation.

LITURGIES, FOOD, AND MUSIC

Every Sunday evening the TTS community gathered for a community service led by a fellowship group, followed by a simple community meal in the *mānadōppu* grove. The meal was prepared and served by the students and faculty of the assigned fellowship group for that week. Appavoo described this weekly event as an experiment in *oru olai*. The TTS celebration of the Poṅgal (harvest festival) in January and other community celebrations also took on the flavor of community building, participation, and celebration in which music and food were a central expression of unity.

The Sunday evening service in the seminary chapel always included communion. Sometimes it took the form of a traditional CSI or Lutheran liturgy, but it was often a forum for liturgical experimentation led by faculty and usually involved a great deal of music. The karnatak-style Tamil music worship (*Tamiḻ Icai Vaḻipāḍu*), particularly Rev. Israel Selvanayagam's communion service, was performed several times during the year. Appavoo first conducted his newly composed folk or village music worship (*Girāmiya Isai Vaḻipāḍu*) communion service on Palm Sunday, March 27, 1994. It included a procession of folk drumming, singing, and palm swinging that wove throughout the campus, leading the community to gather in the open-aired indigenous style chapel at the center of campus (PURL 4.6). At another point in the year, a service led by Rev. Mohan Larbeer and the Human Rights Forum was held in honor of the "Year of Indigenous People." It explored and celebrated elements from indigenous Tamil ritual. They used *ragi* (local grain) and *kañji* water (rice gruel water) for the Eucharist elements, children participated, and inter-community reconciliation was emphasized. The church historian, Arthur Jaykumar, led another service on the history of particular hymns and lyrics. Every section of this service (confession, creed, etc.) was encapsulated in a particular song from the seminary songbook, or in a *kīrttaṉai* or *pāmālai*. Before each song, Jaykumar unpacked its meaning and discussed its history. Other sung services were led by the youth fellowship and the women's fellowship. The latter conducted a service written by the women's studies director, Rev. Margaret Kalaiselvi.

A special service celebrating International Women's Day was conducted on March 8, 1994. It was originally planned to include a procession of village women driving forty *māṭṭu vaṇḍis* (ox-driven open carts) through the city. This highly anticipated display of female presence had to be canceled, however, because the police refused to grant a parade permit. The day's events included the opening of an exhibition of artwork (posters, cartoons, etc.) expressing the oppression, concerns, and status of women. Women and men from TTS and from the wider Christian community attended the evening service. The women at the service were a more diverse group than I had previously witnessed. They included Catholic nuns, older Protestant community women (teachers and representatives of women's fellowship groups), the women and children of Arulagam (abandoned women who lived in a Christian group home), and some American women students and Tamil friends. Each person was given flowers and sandalwood as s/he entered.

TTS women faculty and students composed the liturgy. The rituals they chose were meant to reflect elements of women's daily lives. Participants exchanged flowers as a sign of love as well as a symbol of their responsibility to share the message of women's liberation, extending it to others in the wider society. Elements of women's lives mentioned in the liturgy included food, *kunkumam* (red powder), light, milk, bananas, and flowers. In the center of the chapel floor was a large *kuttuvilakku* (brass oil lamp). The congregation sat in concentric circles around it with the liturgy leaders sitting in the circle closest to the altar. I observed this circular liturgy formation one other time at TTS: during a folk liturgy conducted by Appavoo in which he introduced the song "Tāyi Tagappanārē" that refers to God as both mother and father. In both cases it seemed to create a more community-oriented focus with less separation between men and women than is common.

Although the liturgy was entirely composed and led by TTS women, they did not compose any of the music. In the organizational meeting, I had encouraged both composition and musical performance by women, but no one followed through on this suggestion.[16] At the service, I played mrdangam while Prem Kumar played guitar and another male played harmonium.

The service contained six songs. Participants entered to the singing of "Amaiḍiyil Iraivanai Kāṇuvōm," the beautiful light music song that describes seeing God in silence. A flute solo was played while a male and a female student lit the multiple wicks of the large lamp. One of the most powerful moments came during a liturgical section entitled *Peṇgalin Avala Kuralkal* (Women's Cries of Distress). They used the chorus of Appavoo's song "Ammāḍi Kuṭṭi Poṇṇē," which is an emotional call for women to rise up and fight their oppression, interspersed with vocal cries made by women seated throughout the chapel expressing women's problems in different social contexts (see Appendix 2 for lyrics) (PURL 4.7). Another song adapted to this Christian service by members of the Madurai women's rights movement, "Peṇṇurimai Iyakkam," incorporated images of music and food (see Fig. 4). It began with an image of processing women factory workers fighting for better working conditions. The central importance of food and liberating music in the lyrics made it easily adaptable to the TTS Christian context.

> We will march forward.
> The sound of agony of the countless women who have embraced death
> [from working as slaves],
> even that sound will form a part of our song.
> That song is for food, for the feeling of music, for the aesthetic
> [*kalai*—artistic] appreciation and for love.
> The hearts of those [women] who went before
> will know that we fight.
> That fight is to ask for food and flowering affection.[17]

The three other songs appropriately used in the Women's Day Service were "Tāyi Tagappanārē" (Oh, Mother and Father) by Appavoo, "Āla Poranda Poṇṇē" (You Woman Who Is Born to Rule) a folk song by Prem Kumar sung by three women students, and the final *maṅgalam* or blessing song.

Music's role in liturgy at TTS was vital, particularly in liturgies that directly addressed the social concerns of feminism, indigenous rights, caste oppression, and the embrace of Dalit culture. Liturgical music and ritual were also means to emphasize the central symbolic importance of food. In these services I observed a conscious indigenization of the Eucharist to the food ways of poor villagers or things in Tamil culture specifically associated with women. Experimentation with the symbolism of local village and feminine-identified food through Christian music, musical theology, and ritual empowered developing activists to hold their culture as worthy and provided them creative tools for composing their own liturgies. It also brought an important positive evaluation of the daily contributions of women toward sustaining life. The presence of local foods in liturgy made the ritual a full sensory experience of Tamil culture. For example, the use of *ragi* and *kañji* water reminded people of the taste of poor people's food and village culture. Associating these with the Eucharist, the sacrificial body and blood of Jesus Christ, further reminded the seminary students of the daily sacrifices of the poor through their agricultural labor to produce food for the rest of society while they often go with little or none. In an interview about Appavoo's "Confession of Sin," which begins with the line "people who starve without even the simplest *kañji* food," the poor Chakkiliyar people in the Mulanur area of western Tamil Nadu reacted with both sadness from being reminded of their predicament of often having to go without food and with great anger and resentment that while they produced food for others they were often left with only the worst broken pieces of rice (interview, Sakarvalasu Congregation, June 24, 2002). While starvation was not the present experience of the seminary students and faculty, ritual and music were means to create affinity between those Dalits whose daily reality is hunger and fear and the future priests trained by TTS to serve these communities. Weekly criticism services were an opportunity for students to bring together their growing affinity with the poor with their own experiences of oppression and impoverishment into ritual action.

CRITICISM SERVICES: RE-CREATION OF APPAVOO'S *GIRĀMIYA ISAI VAṞIPĀḌU*

Each Wednesday at TTS, a fourth-year student gave his or her final criticism sermon during early morning service, often creating their own liturgy or using it as an opportunity for extended experimentation. M. J. Rajaiah, a fourth-year Bachelor of Theology student from the CSI Trichy-Tanjore Diocese near Karur, modeled his liturgy and sermon on the style of Appavoo (who was his advisor) incorporating spoken Tamil, folk music, and a commitment to instilling more meaning in the liturgy of the rural parishes from which he came. While Appavoo used a pan-regional form of spoken Tamil that draws on a hegemonic Madurai dialect, Rajaiah wrote his own liturgy using the Coimbatore regional dialect to facilitate easy learning by people in his home diocese.[18] Indeed he claimed only the few educated villagers follow the CSI written liturgy from the prayer book, while this service would enable the illiterate majority to easily memorize and understand the language of the service.[19]

In the Lord's Prayer, for example, Rajaiah used several indigenous Dalit/village concepts in very simple spoken Tamil; these include *kuttam* and *tappu* for sin. He avoided using the term *rājyam* (kingdom), and instead used the metaphor of the *koḍi* (flag) as a symbol for the reign of the Kingdom of God. Furthermore, he used *kañji* instead of *appam* (bread) from the prayer book. Similar to Appavoo, he referred to Satan or evil as *pēy* and replaced the phrase "the Kingdom, the power, and the glory are yours" with "the flag, the good tidings, and the respect, all we give to you God." Throughout the service he also referred to God as our mother and father (*ammā* and *appā*). While Appavoo used many of these same phrases, Rajaiah emphasized that Appavoo's primary influence was the use of the bi-gendered, village religion word *sāmi* (God or Goddess) instead of *āṇḍavan* (Lord), which has upper-class overtones, or *kaḍavul*, a common Hindu term for God.

Rajaiah set a ritualistic folk mood for his service by using two *kuttuvilakku* (oil lamps) on the altar instead of candles. The liturgy was not sung,[20] but included Appavoo's song "Bumiyil Vāṟuṟa" (*Puttuyir Pāḍalhal*, number 8) as well as a special folk song "Pādam Nalla Pādam Ayyā" (The Good Feet, The Good Feet, Oh God) written and performed by Victor Prem Kumar based on the assigned biblical passage for Rajaiah's sermon: Isaiah 52:1–12. In this song, Victor Prem Kumar interpreted the passage (Isaiah 52:7) in colloquial language and style to emphasize Rajaiah's central point that the Good News is peace and justice for the oppressed. Rajaiah was particularly happy about Prem Kumar's song because he felt that its use of colloquial language made it easily understood by village people compared to the *kīrttaṉai*, which he says uses sanskritized Tamil.[21]

> *Tānē tānē tandana tānē tandana tānē*
> *Tandana tandana tānē.*[22]
> The feet the good feet, oh God.
> The feet that tell the [Good] News, oh God.
> The feet that speak of peace and give new life, oh God.
> Look at the top of the mountain, it is glittering beautifully!
> It speaks of the love of the king,
> your pure feet without dust, oh God.
>
> Shake off the dust well and get up my people!
> Untie the bondage and wait my people!
> Your king, who is the Rose of Sharon.
> He who redeemed you, was that easy?
> Clap your hands, beat the drum!
> Shout the song—the new one, new one!
>
> For all of the poor people the Good News was told.
> Rich, caste-conscious people have taken it.
> What justice, what justice is that?
> As king you came as a free gift.

Now they auction you off, selling you so easily.
Teach us to roll away this pride and realize
even a little of the truth.[23]

This passage from Isaiah references the beautiful feet of the Lord (a parallel image to that in bhakti worship), the messenger who announces peace and brings the Gospel's Good News. The first stanza contextualizes Isaiah within Tamil folk culture. The process of shaking off the dust and shackles of bondage involves the transformative experience of singing (or re-creating) a new song, clapping and drumming in Tamil folk religion. In the second stanza, the biblical experience of the Israelites being sold into slavery is indigenized to describe the Indian villagers' experience of having the free gift of Jesus (grace) and his Good News taken from them and then resold to them by rich Evangelists who further cheat people by asking them for money in exchange for blessings.

A choir of many of the best singers at TTS sang Prem Kumar's song for Rajaiah's service. The harmonium player accompanied primarily with a drone and a few simple chord changes and the tabla player played a folk-style rhythmic pattern. During the introduction men and women sang an octave apart while some tenors sang "seconds" (a major third higher than the melody). Men and women also traded phrases, and both employed Tamil folk vocal inflections and shouts. At the end of the phrase, they shouted "sing it" (literally, "put it"). They also emphasized the word *ayyā* (God) using falling oscillations between notes at the end of a phrase, and brief half-sung, half-spoken passage.

In his sermon, Rajaiah spoke about being deceived into accepting a false peace within oppressive systems. He asked, "If we are afraid and do not protest, what peace do we really have?" In the Hindu Brahmanical system finding peace and acceptance of one's status (as oppressed) is the essence of karma. By asking the questions "For whom is freedom? For whom is the Good News?" Rajaiah challenged the passive acceptance of oppressed status by poor people. When upper-class and upper-caste people dominate there can be no true love, no true relationship; if God rules there will be peace and justice.[24]

In the morning chapel service performance of "Pādam Nalla Pādam Ayyā," Prem Kumar indigenized or adapted the concept of using folk music (learned from Appavoo) to his own urban Christian light style by adding harmony and contrasting choral lines between the men and women. This created an attractive separate choral performance that was not as participatory for the congregation as Appavoo would advocate, but which was easy enough for a congregation to sing along or learn the tune in one hearing.[25] Both the music and liturgy in this example reflect the transmission to students of Appavoo's philosophy of using indigenized elements, particularly folk music and language. However, the style of the performance and language (dialect) is re-created for individual and contextual needs as determined by the re-composers.

After the morning chapel service, I greeted my women friends, clasping their hands and smiling. I congratulated the "performers" as did their classmates. After Rajaiah's service I told Prem how wonderful his new song sounded and asked him if we could translate it so I could better understand its meaning. He called me by my pet name, Subramaniyānai kutti,[26] and said that of course he would play it for me after music class and that he wanted a cassette copy of it from my video. We found that each could provide the other access to a form of media otherwise not readily available; a music transmission deal had been made.[27]

I packed up and walked out with Neena, Appavoo's youngest (seventeen-year-old) daughter who was one of my field assistants, to go back to my house and translate the service. The crowd of students headed toward the mess hall and the professors back to their respective houses for breakfast. It was a beautiful day. The rush of the music and message was alive inside each of us as we went to share food. Every once in a while I joined the students for a *dosai* or *iddli* in the mess, using the time as an opportunity to further understand the day's sermon and their opinions of it or to talk about the music. As we walked back to my cottage, faculty and staff children in blue and white uniforms greeted us with cries of "Good morning Auntie, good morning *Ākka* (big sister)." We passed the vegetable woman Vijay Lakshmi carrying her overflowing basket of shining red tomatoes, small purple *brinjal* (eggplant), and lady's fingers (okra) on her head. Her strong arms balanced its weight with every sure step. I asked her in Tamil to stop by today, to which she replied, "Ok, Sister."

Inside my cottage, Neena sat on a woven straw mat on the floor looking up words in the dictionary to translate for me from her notes while I boiled the milk and prepared our coffee. Sweet white foam mixed with rich dark brew to create the famous Madurai delicacy. My guru-*taṅgai* (little sister) began to teach me the Bible and Dalit politics: It was only through my TTS experience that I became more fully aware of the meaning of each of these and better understood how they interrelate. Neena always commented upon or critiqued the students' sermons; I soon realized how much her commentary reflected the ideas of her father. Appavoo taught his children well; they surely learned many of his ideas through his songs. Neena and I discussed terms like *nīdi* (justice) and *pōrāttam* (large protest)—TTS theological Tamil vocabulary. After translating her notes we came to conclusive agreements about the points of the sermon and also reviewed the choice of music and how the lyrics related to the sermon themes.

By 8:30 Neena was off to school and I had a few minutes to practice for my karnatak vocal lesson before jumping on my purple mountain-style bike, to ride a few blocks to the house of my vocal teacher in S. S. Colony. The younger boys who used the playground across the path from my cottage had noticed right away when I bought this bike and daily greeted me with "Auntie! Auntie! Just one round on your bike, Auntie! Please, Auntie!" I tried to be disciplined, but usually gave in. Upon reflection it seemed I had gotten to know people at TTS from the bottom up: kids and workers first, then students, and finally after several months the faculty. In fact, I did not interview the principal until the last few months of my stay.

As I built relationships at TTS through learning to share materially and intellectually, I discovered in my study of music and theology that Appavoo's primary means of transmitting his musical theology was through developing close, family-like relationships with students that would nurture a deeper understanding and commitment to his ideas. His primary means of developing these relationships was to maintain an open door to his home and to his table. Students, particularly Dalit students who needed support, knew they could come to Paraṭṭai Annan's house any time and have food with his family. He also became a mentor and guru-like figure to those who understood his vision and were prepared to walk his path of change. His home-office was always full of students, community activists, and other faculty engaging in creative ideas, writing songs, and generally making cultural trouble! Over the course of the late 1990s, when I was only able to visit India for shorter periods of time, Paraṭṭai's health began to worsen. But I noticed that this only brought more students to his home. He even held some of his classes in his house as his ability to walk deteriorated. It was this form of family relationship, where sharing food was a central practice, that Appavoo encouraged within the wider TTS family through weekly community meals after the Sunday service and through the practice of monthly *oru olai* that he introduced.

ORU OLAI: SHARING A MEAL

After the Sunday service, most of the community members would retrieve plates from their home or hostel, walk over to the *mānadōppu* (tree grove) and line up in front of the two steaming cauldrons, one with rice and the other with a vegetarian *koṛumbu* (curry). Members of that week's sponsoring fellowship group had taken their turn chopping vegetables or cooking and then served the community, often making jokes or greeting individuals as their gift of food was accepted. This was a simple but tasty meal blessed with a grace and shared sitting on the ground in circles of friends, faculty, staff families, and the women of Arulagam. After eating and visiting, we each washed our own dish at a large set of outdoor sinks and moved on to the night's tasks.

The money to pay for the weekly *oru olai* food was collected by the college accountant's office as a small percentage of one's monthly income; thus those who earned less, paid less. Some members, especially wives of a few male theologians or staff, did not attend. Others came to collect their serving and took it back to their homes. Furthermore, as is inevitable in most communities, some people tended to mix only with their known friends, or were shy or cliquish about extending themselves. However, in general I observed that the majority felt, and demonstrated through their participation, that it was a positive community-building event.

In the beginning of my second academic year at TTS (June 1994), Appavoo initiated a second type of *oru olai* event once a month on a Wednesday evening. It was different in several ways. First, it was voluntarily attended by approximately fifty people as opposed to the nearly two hundred who regularly came to the Sunday meal. Second, each brought rice from their own kitchen, brought it to the *mānadōppu* and mixed it into one pot (a true *oru olai*), which Appavoo always declared tasted better. Finally, the new experiment involved a more formal structure of singing songs and discussing a particular Bible passage; an opportunity for lay theological discussion similar to the TTS lay theological training program called TECCA. Thus the Wednesday *oru olai* event allowed people to participate spiritually and intellectually, as well as communally. It was not merely one group hosting the rest of the community in an environment in which people tended to separate into smaller groups.

In December 1993, TTS also sponsored a Christmas dinner for the community that involved full *oru olai* participation. That is, everyone in the community contributed their labor in one way or another to create the meal. The morning of the event, I found myself sitting cross-legged on the cement floor of the auditorium next to Principal Kambar Manickam helping him peal ginger for the Christmas biriyani to serve over two hundred people. The mounds of garlic, ginger, and chilies in the middle of a circle of chatting friends and colleagues was quite a sight. The meal was fabulous and followed by a festival atmosphere complete with a bonfire and dancing to popular Western and Indian music.

POṄGAL

Poṅgal is the annual Tamil New Year's harvest festival celebrated on the first day of the month of Tai in mid-January. It has a rural secular or cross-religious emphasis on blessing agricultural animals, and giving thanks to nature (particularly the sun) for a successful harvest. The festival name comes from the rice *poṅgal* cooked on an outside fire with milk and sweetened with jaggery (unrefined brown sugar). Most Hindus believe that if the rice boils over the sides of the pot it is a sign that the goddess Lakshmi will bring prosperity to the family.

Poṅgal is, from my observations, the festival most commonly and easily Christianized by Tamils perhaps because it is founded in nature worship. The indigenous celebratory feeling of this festival was apparent at TTS. There was more dancing, singing, and informal relaxed celebration typical of a village community than at any other event I observed over the course of my year there.

Poṅgal actually began on the night of January 14 with the collection of unneeded items from campus households that the students took to be burned in a huge bonfire. Led by the loud excited drumming of the *tavil,* students pulled a cart around the campus collecting old boxes and trash from the houses and hostels (PURL 4.8). This represented a form of community cleansing where the old year's household *kuppai* (garbage) was burned symbolically along with the *manasu kuppai* (heart/mind garbage) that had dirtied personal relationships. Burning the household garbage, cleaning, white washing and decorating one's house, as well as taking a special bath and wearing new clothes on Poṅgal morning symbolized a renewal of oneself, one's household, and the whole community for the New Year. Burning the garbage was accompanied by community prayers and singing of Appavoo's songs (PURL 4.9).

While it was still completely dark on the morning of January 15, male students, including the *tavil* player and a few faculty members, gathered in front of the chapel to begin a second procession to collect the Poṅgal *pānai* (round clay cooking pots). Each collection of cottages and hostels around campus had its own pot, which had been placed on the ground in front of a building in the middle of a beautiful *kōlam* (chalk drawing made by women). We moved from station to station praying, playing the *tavil,* and singing folk songs such as Appavoo's "Allēlūyā," "Āṇṇē Tambi Māppiḷḷē" (Big Brother, Little Brother) and Mohanraj Peter's "Āṇḍavar Iyēsuva Kumbiḍalām Vāṅga" (Come Worship Jesus the Lord) all songs about the extended family (and community) gathering to worship God in a festival context (PURL 4.10). Each *kōlam* was in a different style, some with intricate looping white lines and others with blocks of colored powder. The majority of those at this TTS festival utilized star shapes, which are a common shape that Hindus use regularly and Christians often use at Christmas time.[28]

As we collected the reddish-brown pots painted with white geometric designs, each was paraded carefully on the shoulder of a male student. In my entire year at TTS this was probably the most exciting and energy-filled event I witnessed. The entire community was involved. It was a meaningful event that could easily be Christianized, apparently creating little tension for any Christian who might feel that the use of a particular ritual was *too* Hindu. This is likely because most Tamils identify Poṅgal as a "Tamil" harvest and New Year's festival and not an orthodox "Hindu" event.

Finally, the parade gathered in the *mānadōppu* in front of the stage where individual firewood hearths for the pots had already been kindled (PURL 4.11). An elaborate colorful *kōlam* of a *poṅgal* pot with palm branches arching over it had been drawn in the middle of the ground. The women gathered there were dressed in festival saris, and others wore especially nice new clothes. As prayers were spoken, the pots were placed on the fires accompanied by *tavil* drum flurries intended to keep away any inauspicious presence.[29] Milk was poured into each pot, again accompanied by *tavil* flurries as the cooking began. The male students and *tavil* player gathered, sitting on the ground to the right, and began singing both TTS folk songs and other folk songs that were not specifically Christian (PURL 4.12). The songs did not reference the name of a deity such as *Mariamma* but instead used the general term *Amman* (mother goddess). A period of informal music making was followed by a formal program of folk songs and dances, dances to film music (particularly the 1993–94 hit film *Gentlemen* that exemplified the early music style of A. R. Rahman), and comedic skits by all sectors of the community, but especially by the children and youth (PURL 4.13). After an hour or more of entertainment, prayers and speeches, the sweet *poṅgal* boiled over (PURL 4.14). Along with stalks of sugar cane, it was finally passed around for all to enjoy (PURL 4.15).

The next day at the Rural Theological Institute, I observed Poṅgal celebrated in the style of a rural *pūja* (worship), but integrated with Christian prayers and songs. Cows and bulls, the animals on which rural people most depend for their livelihood, were decorated with brightly-colored spots of pink and green paint while the horns of the bulls were painted in blocks of white and blue or red and black and adorned with balloons[30] (PURL 4.16). While a pot of *poṅgal* was cooking outside, a Hindu-like *pūja* began in the cattle barn, which had been decorated with streamers of palms. In the middle of the earthen floor a *kōlam* of interconnecting stars had been drawn with white chalk powder. The non-Brahman *pūjari* (priest) conducted a typical Hindu ritual that involved breaking coconuts, blessing the *pūja* elements of flowers, betel nut and leaf, bananas, *poṅgal* cereal, and camphor with smoke and holy water, and then offering these to all present. The flame was passed around to the gathered community who held their palms in prayer position, reaching them out to the light and then bringing its energy back to their bodies. As this took place someone said in

Tamil, "Come on, please say it!" and suddenly another let out a high-pitched tongue-vibrato wail, or ululation, a rural Tamil tradition I had rarely heard. A younger person chuckled and the initiator again said, "Come on, please say it!" Then several people responded boldly. The master of ceremonies followed this by shouting a greeting of *Poṅgalō Poṅgal* (Happy Poṅgal!) to which everyone responded in kind. This was followed by Christian *jebam* (prayers) of thanks for all of life's blessings offered by Rev. Danny Gnanasakaran, the local Dalit Liberation Movement leader, and the spontaneous singing of Appavoo's "Tāyi Tagappanārē" (PURL 4.17 and PURL 4.18). This song was chosen because its second verse refers to the celebration of Poṅgal:

> In January (the Tamil month of Tai, which begins with Poṅgal) we have sweet *poṅgal*.
> But, Father, you are the life *poṅgal* overflowing.
> If we are true to that, we will find the path to life

And finally there was the sharing of more sweet *poṅgal*.

Poṅgal at TTS reinforced the transmission of music, dance, and the arts especially among the children of faculty and staff who had many such opportunities over an extended period of years to learn, participate, create, and express themselves in this nurturing experiential environment. After almost a decade has passed, several of these children of staff members and faculty have gone on to be activists who used the arts; one works with local youth raising their awareness about oppression through folk dance, another has worked with the Narada Dam project, and others have gone into the ministry. Immersion in expressions of Tamil folk Christianity at TTS also helped prepare the seminary students to introduce such festival practices in their own congregations, particularly in the villages, after they graduate. As the Dalit cultural revolution continues to expand within the church and greater Tamil society, these children and seminary students, many of whom were nurtured both directly and indirectly by Appavoo, have become leaders in this and other social causes.

DAILY REFLECTION OF MUSIC AND POLITICS THROUGH SHARING FOOD

After morning music class while students went off to courses in history, theology, Hebrew and Greek, I would often meet with Dr. J. Arun Raja Selvan, my primary field assistant. Arun and I spent hours discussing church politics, the Madurai congregations, Dalit issues, and Tamil literature and poets. He was also my Tamil teacher. While we worked, Mary, my cook and my *akkā* (big sister), would prepare *koṟumbu* (vegetarian curry) or meat, vegetables, and rice for our lunch. When it was ready, the three of us would spread a mat on the floor and share the meal, continuing the conversation throughout. During lunch I often jumped up to take notes or turn on the tape recorder. Mary also shared her experience as a lower-class urban Christian and sang us songs in her lovely raspy village voice, which was distinct from the urban polished middle-class vocal quality. She also showed me her personal notebook of Christian *kōlam* designs. She and her daughter would make Christian *kōlams* outside her suburban slum house every morning.[31]

YOUNG WOMEN'S *ORU OLAI*

In the early spring of 2004 I became friends with Jacqulin Jothi, a second-year student living in the women's hostel. Jacquie, a Dalit from Trichy, was studying for her Bachelor of Divinity with the intent to become an ordained minister in the Tamil Evangelical Lutheran Church. However, at that point the Lutherans did not ordain women. Much of our early friendship evolved around sharing food and an understanding of oppression, particularly that of Dalits and women. Indeed our first friendly encounter was when she shared a sweet with me on New Year's Day. Jacquie was one of the boldest, brightest, and most politically savvy young women I met in the seminary.

One hot March night when the electricity had gone off around campus and in the local neighborhood, Jacquie and I went up to the roof of the women's hostel to find some cool air and talk. Several other groups of young women who had the same idea sat chatting under the stars. Then Jacquie asked me if I had eaten. I admitted that in the midst of all of the evening's activities of filming a passion play I had forgotten. She offered to make me *dosai* from wheat flour and water. She cooked to the light of a candle in the hostel's simple kitchen while I enjoyed watching her skillful hands flip the pancake. Then she asked me "sugar or *tacalli* (tomato)." I said, "Okay, *tacalli*," and she proceeded to make a very basic *koṟumbu* of onions, tomato, and spices, just a few simple ingredients, but so tasty. It was this night that she taught me her Tamil *paṟamoṟi* (old proverb) grace: *Uṇavu koṇḍu uṟavu illē; uṟavu koṇḍu uṇavu āsīrvādam* (It is not the food that brings the relationship; it is the relationship that blesses the food).

Our sharing of food and politics soon expanded to become a women's *oru olai* joined by two other women seminary students, Adlin Reginabai and Christy. We started gathering in the mornings right after chapel service each bringing to share whatever we had to our "club": I brought my packet of milk and some coffee powder; Jacquie made flour and water *dosai* (pancake); Adlin shared some leftover *koṟumbu.* We prayed for each other and the day using Jacquie's *paṟamoṟi* grace and singing songs. We ate, laughed, and talked about liberation, thereby creating the new song that we would sing the next day. Later in the spring, I invited Adlin and Jacquie to my house for lunch several times along with my cook Mary and my field assistant Arun.[32] Our breakfast club soon became a lunch club. We all sat on my cottage floor in a circle on the straw mats eating and engaging in heated discussions about politics and music. And Mary, who was *akkā* to all of us, freely joined in.

Putting *oru olai* into practice at TTS as a large community and in small groups of friends was significant for both Jacqulin and Adlin both of whom went on to become ordained priests, graduate degree holders, and activists for women's and Dalit rights. In the mid-to late-1990s Rev. Jacqulin Jothi introduced the practice of *oru olai* to her Dalit congregation in the village of Vedal near Kanchipuram, while she also helped organize the Christian laborers of Vedal into the local unions. She and her husband, Rev. M. Enose, supported these actions for social justice and unity through teaching Appavoo's songs and folk music liturgy to their congregation accompanied by preaching on his theological ideas.

Community services and festivals were events at TTS that centered worship on experimental music production and the sharing of food: both forums for expressing theology and experiencing the message of the Eucharist. It was in the creative process of liturgy that *music as liberation* was developed and sounded, while *oru olai* was the primary practice of community that liturgy symbolized. The development of its students and faculty children into activists and transmitters of Appavoo's theology as music is the measure of TTS's success as an ideal community formed around the values of sharing, unity, equality, and participation (see Fig. 5).

Figure 1. Paraṭṭai Aṇṇaṉ (aka Theophilus Appavoo) wearing his "Paraṭṭai" cap and appearing in his disheveled trickster form.

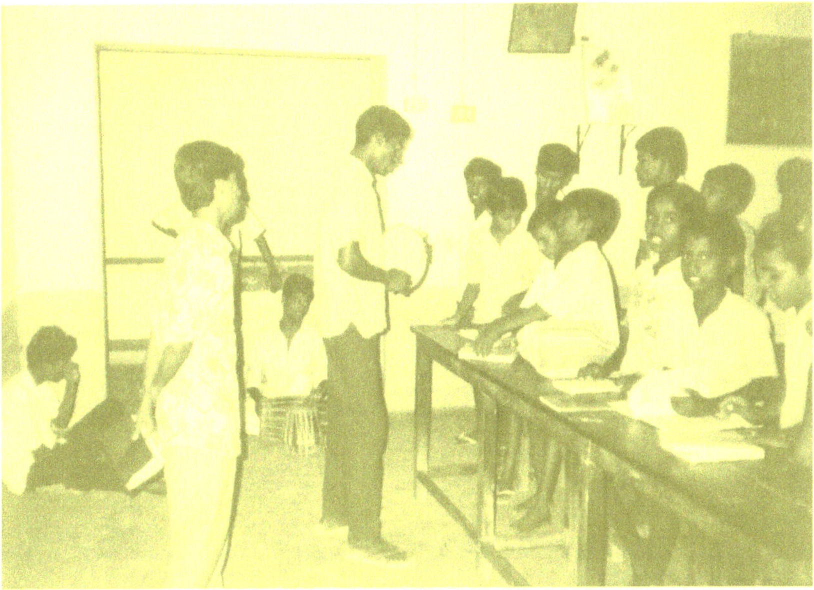

Figure 2. Village students of Headmaster C.S. Karunakaran, son of Rev. C. J. Daniel, sing *kīrttaṉai* in the CSI boarding school in Karur.

Figure 3. Horse-drawn hearse at the CSI church at Vellore. Possibly the one that Appavoo's great-great-grandfather Edward Appavoo donated to the church, or one very similar to it.

Figure 4. Appavoo's daughter T. Adri Paul conducting a parai workshop with members of the Madurai women's rights movement "Peṇṇurimai Iyakkam."

Figure 5. Students of Appavoo who are transmitters of his theology: Rev. Jacqulin Jothi, Dr. Zoe Sherinian, Rev. Benjamin Inbaraj, and Rev. Ebenezer Kirubakaran.

Figure 6. Rev. Theophilus Appavoo conducts the 1993 Tamil Nadu Theological Seminary Christmas Carol Service choir. The theme of the service written in Tamil is "Let's Make Peace."

Figure 7. Rev. Jacqulin Jothi and Rev. M. Enose and their daughter Eucharista.

Figure 8. Rev. M. Rajamanikam and his family, including his brother and mother, in Chinnadharapuram.

Figure 9. Rev. Francis Devadoss and his family in Uttukkottai.

Figure 10. The author and Rev. J. Theophilus Appavoo at an international conference on religion in New Delhi, 2004.

5

RECEPTION AND TRANSFORMATION FROM SEMINARY TO VILLAGE

In the small community of the Tamil Nadu Theological Seminary in Madurai where Theophilus Appavoo taught for twenty-six years there was no question of his significant impact: the use of his songs in almost every service and community event brought Appavoo's Dalit theology and an orientation toward Tamil folk culture to the heart of seminary life. He transformed the lives of Dalit and non-Dalit students as well as summer music school students and local congregations with a critical understanding of how Christianity in India looks and sounds when focused on social justice and cultural equality. However, during my fieldwork in 1993–94 the extent of his music's impact throughout the state of Tamil Nadu was not as obvious, at least from my perspective within the TTS community. While I observed the positive impact of the music during brief fundraising campaign tours, TECCA (lay theological education) classes, and student internships, it was not clear to me the extent of transmission and long-term impact resulting from extended use by village and town congregations, especially through the careful introduction and transmission of the music by Appavoo's students.

To determine the extended transmission and effect of Appavoo's music beyond the Madurai area, I conducted a reception study of his music among Dalit Christian villagers in several districts of Tamil Nadu in the summer of 2002. The following outlines the results of this study showing how Appavoo's students have used his music and how the Tamil folk transmission system facilitates recomposition of music so villagers can most usefully address their needs for change. As I have argued in previous chapters the re-creation of folk music is a means to transformative personal and social change. The transformation of the psychological and cultural basis of oppression occurs when Dalits draw on folk music, aspects of village goddess religion, and vernacular language, and when they are free to re-create the music as they see necessary in performance. Appavoo referred to this process with the phrase, "Yār vēṇālum, eppaḍi vēṇālum" (However one wants to sing it, sing it that way).[1] As an act of musical agency, re-creation reinforces a sense of value and self-worth among Dalits. The focus of this chapter is how Appavoo's Tamil Christian *girāmiya isai* or village folk music, which he intended to be stylistically, liturgically, and textually liberatory, has facilitated caste, class, and gender consciousness, and where it has fallen short or been re-created. I analyze the reception of one of Appavoo's best known songs, "Tāyi Tagappanārē" (Oh, Mother and Father), to reveal the process of dialogical rhetorical performance with his students and their village congregations that articulates a Dalit consciousness: that is, the interactive process of transformation of identity from being "untouchables," or known by a caste name such as Paṟaiyar, to claiming a Dalit identity and the importance of music in that process. I present the transformation of poor villagers through politicization, protest, and collective action in their negotiation with the construction of a Dalit identity and how Appavoo's music helps facilitate this transformation. I also describe the transformation of middle/upper-class Christians and those from the Nadar caste as they come to embrace Appavoo's theology of sharing and unification with the oppressed, instead of being solely concerned with their own rising class status and personal welfare, and the use of folk music in town congregations in this process. Furthermore, I describe how Appavoo's students nurture a commitment among the more privileged Christians toward helping the more unfortunate within their community. The significance of this reception study to the larger project is that it shows the degree to which gender and class are understood as a holistic part of the Dalit struggle, and when these identity differences within these subaltern communities threaten unified action.

Appavoo's primary strategy for the transmission of his theology in folk music was to engage in dialogic and transformative relationships with his students and with villagers. As his student Rev. Johnson Jebakumar describes, Appavoo lived his theology and provided his students an opportunity to experience it with him particularly in a familial context where everyone is encouraged to share food.[2] In the TTS context Appavoo's mentoring and engagement in critical dialogue in choir rehearsal, the classroom, and meals together at home shaped his students to become oral transmitters of his musical theology. Three case studies of his students below reveal their experiences of transformation through their relationship with Appavoo, their effect on his music and its use, and their experience working with village and town congregation members to transmit his theology. These are followed by an analysis of his song "Tāyi Tagappanārē" (Oh, Mother and Father), which provides a framework for the themes of reception of his music by villagers from several areas of Tamil Nadu.

TRANSMISSION TO APPAVOO'S STUDENTS: THREE CASE STUDIES

Reverends Jacqulin Jothi, M. Rajamanikam, and Francis Devadoss stand out as examples of active nodes in the transmission and use of Appavoo's musico-theology among village and town congregations, while each of these students is unique in the experience they bring to their use and interpretation of Appavoo's teachings as well as the quality of their relationship with him. Jacqulin Jothi was likely the most dynamic female seminary student of Appavoo's. Indeed he called her a tiger. Her skills in drama and oration, which she developed as a child, were revitalized and further nurtured under Appavoo's direction. She combined her dramatic skills with his theology of sharing, applying these in her determination to change the lives of Dalits and women by becoming an activist priest, a union organizer, and coordinator for Dalit concerns for the CSI Diocese of Madras. M. Rajamanikam is one of the most talented musical interpreters of Appavoo's theology. While he was not personally close to Appavoo, he absorbed many lessons through Appavoo's songs and his style of teaching, applying these in his work among Chakkiliyar Christians in western Tamil Nadu as well as in negotiations with town congregations over issues of gender, caste, and class perspectives in Appavoo's songs. Francis Devadoss, the folk music pastor, was first exposed to Appavoo's musico-theology as a young college graduate working as a clerk for a local village social movement organization. While involved with everyday people's struggles and social issues he saw the ability of Paraṭṭai's songs to bring empowerment and social change. This nurtured a commitment within him and gave him tangible skills to transmit his theology through music. These skills and his relationship with Appavoo have sustained Francis through the process of becoming a pastor who must negotiate these ideas among village and city congregations who are sometimes resistant to both Appavoo's liberating message and its "degraded" medium of folk music.

JACQULIN JOTHI: SHARED FOOD, SHARED LIVES

The Rev. Jacqulin Jothis's story is that of a woman born to a lower-class Paraiyar Lutheran family, nurtured in Dravidian oration by a politically conscious father, then discouraged and silenced by caste and class discrimination within a Brahman educational system. Yet, through the influence of Appavoo and her study of liberation theology at TTS, she reclaimed a voice of great strength that expressed an intense commitment to improve the lives of Dalits and women as she became one of the most dynamic preachers in South India.

After more than a dozen years of ministry, Jacqulin has refined and applied Appavoo's theology in a unique way with particular focus on women's issues. Her theological praxis includes unionizing Dalit Christian construction workers, establishing an *oru olai* practice among Dalit women that extended to the entire village community during festival times, organizing middle-class Nadar women to share their skills in teaching and counseling with more unfortunate groups, standing as a model for women's organizations as an ordained pastor who actively works for social justice, and inspiring her congregants with Appavoo's songs and a fiery preaching style that draws from his theology. Her impact among Dalits and women has not only sewn the seeds for long-term successful transmission of Appavoo's theology, but she has been able to permeate the middle-class/middle-caste Christian community in ways few have equaled or expected possible.

Jacqulin Jothi is also one of my closest friends: a friendship nurtured through the fieldwork process and beyond, but begun with a simple act of sharing food that exemplifies the essence of Paraṭṭai's theology. Jacqulin, more than any other of his students, helped me realize Paraṭṭai's understanding of the Bible and the praxis of Dalit liberation theology. She accomplished this through allowing me in-depth exposure to her own life, to her development as a pastor, to her work for social justice for the past fifteen years, and through maintaining with me a friendship of religious, political, and personal dialogue for which any person, let alone an anthropologist, can only hope to experience in their lifetime. While the fieldwork process has led to a deep friendship, it is her accomplishments against great odds as a Dalit woman and our shared values of feminism and commitment to spreading Paraṭṭai's ideas that have been the dialogic glue between us.

Jacqulin was a second-year student at TTS when I first met her in 1994. Her expressive abilities lie with drama and oration more than music, thus my early activities at TTS did not bring us into contact. Yet Jacquie's philosophy that "if we start with sharing, we never bother with which caste, which gender, which region or class (the other belongs to)" brought us together. On New Year's Day, 1994, Jacquie demonstrated this by reaching out to me, a "foreign student," to share a celebratory piece of cake. I was so impressed with her kindness and wise intellect after spending just a little time with her that I in turn bought a Bengali cotton sari for her on my trip to Delhi later that month. As our friendship developed we shared some important moments of emotional stress (experiencing sexual harassment on a train trip together), finding that we also shared similar feminist values and concern for women.

As our friendship deepened Jacquie taught me not only how to pray in Tamil but the purpose of prayer, which she understands as the ritualized expression of the relationship between God, people, and the creation. Together with a few other friends, including Adlin Raginabai, we formed within the women's hostel at TTS an *oru olai* subcommunity or breakfast club, sharing whatever each of us had to make a wonderful meal and to strengthen our friendships and commitments to such practices. It was within this community of Tamil women that we refined the application of Paraṭṭai's theology to everyday life.

At TTS, Jacqulin's dramatic and oratory skills were recognized and encouraged by Appavoo and other professors (PURL 5.1). She did not apply her skills specifically to music, but to women's folk poetic forms, like the *paṛamoṛi* (old proverbs), and to skillful preaching and social organizing, especially during her internship in Nagarcoil with women of the Catholic fisher communities. Through combining a refined understanding of Dalit and feminist theology learned at TTS with an activist's commitment toward women's issues, she honed her ability to become a charismatic leader in the fight for women's and Dalit freedom.

Jacqulin Jothi was not naive, unworldly, or unaffected by politics when she arrived at TTS in her late twenties, ready to be molded into the charismatic preacher she would become through her studies there. She brought with her both a unique background in Tamil oration and the experience of living with caste, class, and gender oppression.

At her birth in 1964, Jacqulin's grandfather blessed her, declaring that she would be a great person with a big bold personality. However, her father, John David, was not as happy that she was a girl, as she had three older sisters and he really wanted a boy. In spite of this (or perhaps because of it), he trained her in the skills of public speaking meant more traditionally for men. He also influenced her values of showing concern for the less fortunate. John David was a *panchayat* (village government) schoolteacher, whom one might describe as lovingly strict. He was known to often drag children to school when their parents wanted them to go to work in the fields.

In 1956 Jacqulin's father became a member of the political party Dravida Munetra Kaẓagam (DMK), a reformist party formed in 1949 that worked against the hegemonic imposition of Hindi on Tamil-speaking people and against Brahmanical domination. The DMK was at the forefront of the *Tamiẓ Icai* (music) and cultural renaissance as well as the creation of reservation policies and "rationalism and unity among non-Brahmins" (DMK official home page).[3] John David joined the DMK primarily because of the party's anti-caste policies and because they regularly helped the poor.[4] Furthermore, as a result of his DMK membership, like many other Christians of his generation, John David was a strong advocate of literary Tamil. The singing of light and folk-style music also had an important place at DMK rallies, however.[5] The confluence of religious, class, caste, and political identities was symbolized in the living room of the family's small cottage home in a village along the Kavari river outside of Trichy: hanging on the wall next to the picture of Jesus was a picture of DMK leader—Karunanidhi.[6] And, next to Karunanidhi, Jacqulin's brother placed a picture of the Tamil Bollywood actor Rajni Kanth, who symbolized the contemporary lower-class workingman's hero in Tamil Nadu.

As a ten year old Jacquie began training with her father in DMK oration. When she was twelve her father composed a speech about Karunanidhi and had her memorize it. But he did not stop there. He lifted her on top of a large rock "podium" and taught her how to deliver the speech using the hand gestures and expressions typical of DMK orators. Young Jacqulin then delivered her speech about the greatness of Karunanidhi in front of the leader himself at the Trichy Town Hall. She spoke for more than fifteen minutes having memorized ten pages of text. It was unusual for a child, let alone a girl, to do something like this. However, John David understood his actions as part of the DMK doctrine that women should "come forward." Jacqulin also says that "he took me to the hotel (restaurant) and gave me whatever I wanted, he encouraged me like anything."[7]

This early training and support led Jacqulin into drama and speech competitions in which she represented her school throughout the district, won prizes, and continued to develop her skills. She was most involved between ninth and twelfth standards when she attended St. Anne's Higher Secondary Catholic School in Trichy. Her father continued to guide her and her teachers also expressed admiration for her speaking abilities.

When Jacqulin began studying economics at Seethalakshmi Ramaswamy College, a Brahman institution in Trichy, her experience of receiving encouragement from her teachers began to diminish. She did not, however, fully analyze the social meaning of those changes until she studied for her Masters of Theology in social analysis years later. In one college class, Jacqulin had trouble with the teacher whom she felt favored the Brahman students over the darker skinned non-Brahmans. Once Jacqulin skipped class because she did not like the atmosphere of the classroom. However, she did not follow the proper procedures to get permission for the absence and the teacher scolded her cruelly saying she had no manners. Soon after, in class, the teacher asked for a volunteer to read some Tamil prose.

> Jacqulin: Then I stood and I started reading. [But], she could not bear my voice. Because that voice irritated her, it seems. But, I read boldly. This [was a] good voice. All the up and downs in my voice. Wherever I need to put emphasis, I emphasize the word. Comma, then full stop. Everything I did well. But, she did not encourage me to read. She suddenly stopped me and told me, "Oh your voice is so irritating [to] me! Please can anyone [else] volunteer to read that?" And again one of the Brahmins stood and started reading. [She had] a feeble voice, [a] weary childish pronunciation. She could not break the sentence [properly] because she is 'very good in English,' it seems.
>
> Zoe: Umm. But, not in Tamil.
>
> JJ: But not in Tamil! [I am a] *pakka* (typical) Tamil girl. I was bought up in village school . . . My father trained me in all the Tamil words. I thought it was because I was not economically sound . . . But, after that [I realized] it is also because I am Dalit . . . That is why she discriminated against me . . . Now only I realized because I am Dalit, I was discriminated against in my college time. At that time I could not recognize that.
>
> ZS: So, what effect did it have on you? How did it change your behavior?
>
> JJ: After that I didn't want to involve myself in reading at a common public place. Also I didn't want to involve myself in any competitions. I pulled myself [from them]. Just I read and I did my exams well. That is all. I was not involved in any activities in the college.
>
> ZS: So no drama?
>
> JJ: No drama. No elocution competitions. Even I didn't sit among the students and watch. I hated to be in that cultural hall. Simply I come and go. I concentrated on my studies. That is all.
>
> ZS: So then, you had an experience at the end, when you were going to graduate. A Dalit teacher . . .
>
> JJ: Yeah. In my third year at the farewell function. The teacher, I don't know her name. She belongs to the economics department, I think she is head of the department. It seems she is Dalit. Might be. At that time she asked someone to do some drama or speech. Then I gave a speech and she said, "Oh, you have the good voice! You have so much potential. So much talent. I don't know why you did not [get] involv[ed] in speech competi-

> tions and drama. I did not notice that you had such kind of potential." Like that she approached me like anything. But, what to do? That was final [year] B.A. in our college.[8]

Jacqulin's experience with class and caste discrimination at Ramaswamy College silenced her, keeping her from contributing her talents and being fully involved in the community. However, her previous training in oration and drama gave her a foundation of self-esteem, on which she would later draw to recover her voice. As Appavoo's cassette called *Nimindu Naḍa* ("Stand Tall") makes clear, most outcastes have been beaten down in ways such as this that cause them to physically shrink back into themselves carrying their head down. Jacqulin's reaction of isolating herself also shows the experience behind the stereotype that many upper-caste people hold that education can be offered to untouchables, but they do not posses the innate nature to be able to develop themselves through its advantages. Jacqulin Jothi, however, survived this Brahmin college and her experiences soon improved.

After college Jacqulin became a warden in a Lutheran Hostel (boarding school) for girls. Here she had her first taste of preaching and sharing the narratives of the Hebrew Bible with students, developing and applying the morals she understood within them. The opportunity to preach sparked an interest in pursuing a Bachelor of Divinity, which her father again actively supported by going directly to the Bishop to get his approval for her candidacy for seminary when Jacqulin told him of her intent.[9]

It was through her studies at the Tamil Nadu Theological Seminary and opportunities given by professors like Appavoo that Jacqulin molded her voice into a theologically trained tool for social justice and change. Appavoo identified her dramatic skills, casting her in one of his plays as a Tamil village *pūsari*, or priestess. She embodied the strength of the village religious leader wearing her long hair loose and holding neem branches. He was further impressed by her abilities to analyze and articulate inter-caste problems in a public forum of seminary students and faculty. When the TTS faculty dismissed the students' concerns about inter-caste division among people involved in a dispute at the Rural Theological Institute as "fear for their personal safety," Jacqulin got up to address the entire group. She clarified that the students were not afraid, but ready to stay at RTI, they just wanted the sub-caste problems to be settled. Further, they felt that the faculty were making it worse by not admitting that it was an internal Dalit sub-caste issue (between Paṟaiyars and Pallars).

Paraṭṭai was very impressed by Jacqulin's boldness to speak, articulating the problems that divided the Dalit community.

> Then, after that meeting was closed Paraṭṭai was very happy. He stood at the entrance (with a smiling face). Then, [as I was] about to [come] out of the room, some of the classmates and staff were standing [there]. And then he said, "Give way to Jacqulin, this tiger is coming." Then I said (humbly), "No, I am not a tiger." That gave me a kind of encouragement. Those who fight for justice, he encouraged those people. He never said, "This woman should not talk like this." So, he encouraged the women. If they have enough boldness to question authority, or question for justice, he always encouraged people.[10]

It was during her internship organizing Catholic women on the costal areas near Nagarcoil in May of 2004 that Jacqulin was able to try out her new skills of feminist organizing and liberation theology. Her internship also exemplified the successful transmission of TTS theology to one of its students and her successful application of the theology through preaching, organizing, and performing music and drama in her internship context. Jacqulin, and the fishing community women with whom she worked, in turn, contextualized the theology in ways that expressed their own needs. Paraṭṭai's secular feminist songs were very useful in these endeavors.

Her internship assignment was to organize the women of the Anbiyam community fellowships in villages in the Kolachal area. These groups were part of larger community-based networks formed through a Catholic program called Basic Christian Communities.[11] The Basic Christian Communities (or BCC) were groups of thirty families in each village that gathered together regularly to share their problems and actively support each other in their struggles against casteism, for access to facilities, and to address women's issues. The local Catholic priests, nuns, and lay organizers also held regular workshops for youth and women that often included the use of training in folk arts for empowerment. Working mostly among Mukkuvar, Paravar, and Nadar caste groups, Jacqulin consolidated the Anbiyam women's groups on three levels and at the end of her internship organized a daylong conference of music, drama, empowerment, and networking attended by representatives of the women's groups from the entire district.

She organized these women's Anbiyam groups around the issue of the effect of male alcohol abuse on women and families, as this was a devastating problem among the local fisher communities. With the flare of a fiery preacher and the use of feminist songs composed by Paraṭṭai, she inspired and motivated women to design creative forms of protests. For example, in Mīdalam village the women, with police support, conducted a protest march down the center of the village to the toddy (alcohol) shop, tearing it down, and chasing the proprietor out of the village. This did not have a long-term effect on their husbands' access to alcohol and resulting abusive behavior, colloquially called *kuḍikku aḍi* (having drunk, they hit), but it did empower the women to fully realize their ability to publicly unify and protest the financial, psychological, and physical effect that long-term drinking had on them and their families.

The liberating songs that Jacqulin taught the women were mostly from the BCC *Anbiyam Songbook*, which included Paraṭṭai's "Otta Saḍa, Reṭṭai Saḍa" (One Braid, Two Braids). This is also a song that our friend and colleague Adlin has used in organizing the Madurai women's movement groups. "One Braid, Two Braids" praises women's traditional gender roles, such as cooking and sewing, saying that they provide the knowledge and means to create a new egalitarian world that has been torn apart and become rotten (see Appendix 2 for lyrics). Moreover, the fisher women themselves created very humorous and thus transformative skits in which they ridiculed their drunken husbands and gave voice to their own painful experiences. Jacqulin's internship provided first-hand contact with the problems of oppressed women and gave her a manageable project: organizing an event that would foster greater unity at both local village and regional levels. The unity created among the women in the context of sharing, praying, singing, and dramatizing their experience gave them the community support and motivation they needed to organize to solve their own problems.

During her Bachelor of Divinity studies at TTS, Jacqulin met Enose Magimaidoss, a Paṟaiyar from the Madras Diocese of the Church of South India (Chennai). Jacqulin and Enose married on April 9, 1997, after they graduated in 1996 and she worked for a year as a researcher in the department of Social Analysis at TTS. The progressive Dalit Bishop M. Azariah of the Madras Diocese then offered to ordain Jacqulin in 1999 and she became one of six female priests in the CSI Madras Diocese, while continually regretting that her own TELC church refused to ordain women. Indeed Jacqulin wrote her Bachelor of Divinity thesis entitled "Women's Ordination in the Tamil Evangelical Lutheran Church" on this struggle. Enose comes from a devout, middle-class, English-speaking Paṟaiyar family and finished a Bachelor and Masters degree at Madras Christian College before going to seminary: a typical profile of young CSI priests brought up in the Chennai city area. Furthermore, he is as fervent as Jacqulin about promoting social justice in the world and was a student of Paraṭṭai's and follower of his theology (PURL 5.2). It was undoubtedly the shared goal of creating social justice through ministry that brought the couple together. However, it was Enose's strong musical abilities, influenced significantly by his father who was skilled in Christian karnatak music, that helped facilitate the easy use and transmission of Paraṭṭai's songs and liturgy in the couple's work in the village of Vedal and in Pondicherry at St. John's and St. Luke's churches (PURL 5.3).

In 1997 Enose was assigned to a rural Dalit pastorate near the town of Kanchevuram. The couple spent their first five years of ministry living in the village of Vedal where their congregants were almost all poor Paṟaiyars. I had the opportunity to visit them twice (once at Christmas and once at Easter) while they lived in Vedal, and to visit the village again in 2002 after they had moved to Pondicherry (PURL 5.4).

Jacqulin and Enose's work in Vedal included experimenting with the application of Paraṭṭai's theology of *oru olai*. This involved Jacqulin's work to unionize both male and female Christian Dalits from Vedal who worked in the construction industry. Second only to daily wage agricultural work, construction has become a significant occupation for both rural and urban untouchables in the modern economy. Organizing this sector has been an important part of the women's, Dalit, and Christian liberation movements. Women typically do the manual labor of carrying bricks and containers of sand or cement on their heads within the construction site, while men are normally the masons: a skilled job that pays significantly more, but requires less hard physical labor. Jacqulin found that the primary impediment to organizing these laborers was their Christian beliefs. She explained,

> If you are part of the union you have to protest. You have to struggle. That means it is an anti-Christian attitude . . . because . . . Christians are taught to obey authority. We should not protest. We should not lead the group to raise question[s] against the injustice. Obey! Obey your parents! If your parent beats you, obey him. You don't ask okay, "I am not worthy to get beaten." You should not raise [objections] like that. Still now, this [is the] Christian attitude. They never protest . . . And also [they believe] it is not the duty of the priest to unionize the people.[12]

The people in Vedal were very clear that the duty of the priest was to serve them as their spiritual father and mother: to give communion, to preach the word of God, and to conduct the services including Holy Communion and marriages. They did not consider it the duty of the pastor, especially a woman pastor, to unionize the people or to be involved in social work. They would assert that this was the work of political parties. Jacqulin's approach was to teach them about the government facilities that were rightfully available to them. For example, she told them that the government provided pensions for construction workers who can no longer work, while only a few of the workers had any inclination that these retirement pension schemes existed. She also clarified that while the people tended to believe that the *Church* should step forward to provide such support, the Church did not have near the ability to provide this assistance as did the government.

> Jacqulin: Then we started explaining to them, if you can form a union or if you can form this organization, workers union, through that you can register yourself and you can get benefits from the government.
>
> Zoe: Wasn't there also maternal benefits?
>
> JJ: Yeah, maternity. After long fighting only these women have got the maternity benefit. Before that there was [only] old age pension.[13]

In her work unionizing the Christian construction workers in her village, Jacqulin employed Paraṭṭai's song "Uruppadiyar Oru Kāriyam." She explained how the song encourages protest and unionizing through reflecting on poor people and women's common experience and communicating Paraṭṭai's theology in vernacular language that needs little to no explanation.

> We cannot get crops if we simply leave the field.
> If we do some work, we will get something.
> The child cannot get milk unless she cries.
> Then only the mother understands that she is hungry and will give food.

Jacqulin interpreted the lyrics saying, "If we simply sit at home, the government will not come forward and do any welfare. If you want anything, we have to protest. We have to come forward. We have to lead the group. Then only we can get whatever we want."[14]

It was a real shock for the villagers to see a female social organizer. Yet Jacqulin explained how her general efforts to help the people had the secondary effect of encouraging women's organizing and empowerment.

> Jacqulin: See, already in Vedal there is a women's group. When we entered, [however] they are not visibly coming out and doing their work. They never exposed themselves. Simply they registered themselves. Some of the leaders will go to the office and come. After I revealed myself, I [got] involved in the unions and all, they came to me saying we are also working with that women's group. Can you come and join with us? Can we jointly do some program? Like that they came up. After I [got] involved, so many women got encouraged to participate in some other women's group.
>
> Zoe: So you acted as a role model.
>
> JJ: Yes, because they understood okay, this is not a sin, this is not wrong to work with the women's group. Because pastor herself is joining and unionizing the people, "What is wrong [with that]?"[15]

Jacqulin's work with women in Vedal eventually led to an experiment in *oru olai*. She encouraged her women's fellowship group to practice *oru olai* for a church festival by collecting a small portion of rice from each household and cooking it in a common pot, sharing the labor to produce the food. They ultimately decided to collect the ingredients for *iddli* (steamed rice cakes) and chutney instead of a rice meal, as poorer quality, cheaper rice that was available among the villagers was better for making *iddli*. Each family also contributed a portion of the oil, chili, and spices needed for the chutney. The festival was a great success and the women had enough food to feed not only the Christian congregation members, but also the entire village, including the Hindus. The women were quite skeptical in the beginning when Jacqulin suggested this common fellowship meal idea to them, but in the end were excited about how well the strategy worked. It brought both the women within the fellowship group and the entire village together in the experience of shared table fellowship.

Enose did his part to reinforce the theological praxis of the festival by training the choir to perform Appavoo's entire *Girāmiya Isai Vaṛipāḍu*. As described in previous chapters, this liturgy in Tamil folk music includes several sections that articulate and reinforce the theology of *oru olai* (Lord's Prayer, Greetings and Praise, Repentance of Sin, and the Meal Serving Song). The choir performed the liturgy with great community appreciation and participation followed by the shared meal (PURL 5.5).

While they were in Vedal, and soon after the birth of their daughter, Jacqulin and Enose visited Paraṭṭai. It was the first time that he saw their daughter. He held her and asked what her name was (see Fig. 7).

> We said "Eucharista" and he immediately said "Oh oh, *oru olai*!" We did not realize before that (Eucharista) also means *oru olai*. Okay, we know about *oru olai*. We proclaim that to the village. But, suddenly, he caught that "Oh you named her as *oru olai*, very good. Eucharista means *oru olai*." Because Paraṭṭai puts his *whole heart* in the *oru olai*, or the communion, community and all that, so he can relate all the things [back to the idea of] community.[16]

After five years in the Vedal village, Jacquie and Enose were transferred to two large town parishes in the former French colony of Pondicherry. Jacquie was the priest for St. Luke's and Enose for St. John's, while Jacquie also ran the women's fellowship group at St. John's. The majority of congregants at both churches were middle- and upper-middle-class Nadars who had migrated north from Tirunnelvely and Nagarcoil to work as managers in the textile industry, dry goods industry, and as nurses and doctors in this urban area. Focusing her work particularly with the women and youth of these two congregations, Jacqulin created a significant transformation within this community toward the active concern and welfare of poor people in Pondicherry, particularly street people and those in the fisher communities severely affected by the tsunami of December 26, 2004. It was the conscious use of Paraṭṭai's songs at church functions, special services, and Bible study that helped Jacquie and Enose transmit Paraṭṭai's theology of action for social justice among their congregants. It was a significant accomplishment considering that their congregants fit the Tamil Christian demographic of conservative, urban, middle/upper-class Nadars who are generally the most resistant to liberation theology, to doing social work among Dalits, and to the use of folk music in the church.

> Zoe: Many people think, "Oh, these songs will never catch on among the urban elite of the Christian community," but it sounds like it did [among the Nadars in Pondicherry]?
>
> Jacqulin: Yeah, yeah! We cannot deny. I can say boldly. Definitely the urban class sang [these] because of the meaning of the song. Not simply the music.
>
> ZS: The folk [music]?
>
> JJ: The meaning of the song is very much appreciated [among them]. Because they are elite . . . they know some songs, no [if] it is meaningful or [not]. They compare, no?
>
> ZS: You are saying they actually use their intellect?
>
> JJ: Ah!
>
> ZS: And they see that this is powerful, a deep kind of poetry.
>
> JJ: Yeah, yeah!
>
> ZS: So they actually connect with it intellectually.
>
> JJ: I think so, because in cities they always like the Berchman's song. Pentacost[al] song, *chuma* [simply] blessing, blessing, like that. But, those songs don't have that much meaning.
>
> ZS: They recognize that, they are smart enough to recognize?
>
> JJ: Because of the music and all. But these [Paraṭṭai's] songs [have good] music and also meaning.
>
> ZS: Right. And they don't object to the music? Do you ever hear people say, *Aiyo, nāṭṭu pāṭṭu, vendān* [Oh no, we don't want to use folk songs].
>
> JJ: *Illē, appadi, teriyale* [I am not sure]. But Enose did the *Girāmiya Isai Vaṛipāḍu.* At that time they welcomed.[17]

In Pondicherry, Jacquie and Enose introduced Paraṭṭai's songs to the congregants through Bible study classes, a strategy that directly challenges the critique from fundamentalist Christians that Dalit theology is not biblically grounded. Enose often sang Paraṭṭai's songs solo and the parishioners would inevitably say, "It was a nice song, teach us, Pastor teach us, we want to learn that song."[18] The songs "Tāyi Tagappanārē," "Māṭṭukkoṭṭil Reḍiyācci," and "Bumiyil Vāṟuṟa" became favorites in the Pondicherry congregations especially for Christmas gatherings and the Christmas carol service. Jacquie and Enose even printed the lyrics to these songs in their cottage prayer meeting songbook. Jacqulin exclaimed, however, that the "hit song" in the community was "Inikkāda Tēnumilla" because its musical elements were "so good" and because of its metaphorical reference to communal eating through the description of the common behavior of crows sharing their food with each other. She explained, "It's kind of *oru olai,* you know." Thus, through introducing these songs by contextualizing them in biblical and theological understandings and through Enose's strong musical performances, the Pondicherry urban congregations came to appreciate them.

In one children's Christmas carol service Enose prepared the choir to sing "Māṭṭukkoṭṭil Reḍiyācci" (The Cowshed is Ready), but they feared it would not be well received by the congregation. Jacquie explained that they worried that the congregation members would be very sensitive to the words of this song that proclaim "Christmas illē, Christmas illē" [there won't be Christmas]. Jacquie explained further that, "If someone says Christmas, they think it is auspicious." They worried that it would create a "bad mood" or an inauspiciousness toward Christmas, something to which everyone was looking forward. But, in the end, people listened to the whole song. They realized that the lyrics warned that there would be "no Christmas" or anything else if we continue to destroy nature.[19] How did Jacquie and Enose know that the people understood the point of the song and appreciated it? Jacquie explained, "Because they did not raise any questions. Okay, they appreciated. They always like to sing 'Tāyi Tagappanārē,' 'Māṭṭukkoṭṭil Reḍiyācci,' and 'Bumiyil Vāṟuṟa.'" In most town congregation contexts if the members objected to the theology, lyrics, or style of new music that was being introduced they would not hesitate to communicate this to the pastor (see Rajamanikam case study below). But, in this case, their lack of questioning was a sign of acceptance. Indeed Jacqulin believed that the women tended to appreciate these songs more than the men. Perhaps it was her consistent and meaningful social action with the Pondicherry women's fellowship that laid the groundwork for the acceptance of these radical ideas and the openness toward putting them into action through social work: starting a school for street children and conducting tsunami relief work among the fisher people near Pondicherry.

On December 26, 2004, a massive tsunami hit the east coast of India and Sri Lanka. In Tamil Nadu hundreds of fisher communities living along the coastal area between Visakhapatnam in Andhra Pradesh and Kanyakumari in Tamil Nadu as well as up the west coast to Ernakulum in Kerala were badly affected. At least nineteen villages in the Pondicherry area were affected (Sewa, 2). This was one of the second hardest hit areas along the coast. This included 43,000 people affected and 599 deaths (UNTRS 2007, 1, map). Fatima Burnad reported for the Asia Pacific Forum on Women, the Law, and Development that in Tamil Nadu 12,000 people were killed, 650,000 displaced, and 5,000 injured. Seventy-five percent of those killed were women and children and the Indian government estimated that total financial losses, including material and livelihood, were estimated to be $1.2 billion (UNTRS 2007, 9). The majority of those who suffered from the tsunami were from fishing communities who are generally under the category of backward castes (BC) and most backward castes (MBC). However, about one-third were from outcaste and tribal groups who also participate in inland fishing and crabbing, as well as landless agricultural laborers whose livelihood was affected by the inundation of sand into coastal agricultural areas by the saline waters (UNTRS 2007, 9 and 14).

The third-year United Nations Tsunami Report recommended the following regarding long-term non-material impact, particularly the need for psychosocial support:

> One of the least measurable impacts though is the effect that the catastrophe has had on the human mind and soul. The disaster took away lives, caused injuries and destroyed families, homes, and livelihoods. There are long-lasting effects on families due to death and injuries, for widows, single parents and their children, orphans, children separated from their families, the elderly, and the disabled. It is essential that recovery and rehabilitation work also focus on the long-term needs of the affected population in a holistic way. (UNTRS 2007, 9)

The Church of South India Madras Diocese has been actively involved in tsunami recovery work since 2004 and has made special efforts to provide psychological counseling to the victims (David 2007, 2). An assessment study that Jacqulin and Enose produced soon after the event helped recognize this need. Within hours of the tsunami, youth members from both Jacqulin and Enose's congregations were on the scene offering help. Within days they began an assessment study to determine the people's opinions of what sort of help they needed the most. It became clear that this type of tragedy was unlike any other the fisher and Dalit communities in this area typically encounter, as the losses simultaneously affected everyone in the community, and one of the greatest needs was consolation and counseling.

> In that village, among the women, sometimes they say the counseling idea is . . . [a] Western thing. The Indian people, they never trust in counseling, especially in the fisher folk community and Dalit community. [There is] no need for counseling because if they have any distress or any agony they will not keep [their feelings] inside. [Normally, if they have] husband and wife problem . . . Simply they shout at [each other] like anything. "Po da, va da," as Bama (the Dalit writer) said, using all the filthy words . . . they simply said, [and] everything gone. But, at the time of tsunami, everyone [was] having the same problem. They cannot shout at . . . all men and women, neighbor's house. Some [had] not lost their loved one, but lost their material things. Like that everyone, each and everyone, [was] affected. At that time they cannot shout at each other, they cannot think [of] each other. They try to console each other so that they can get hold [of] the problem inside. Because the husband is crying, so the women cannot shout at him. At that time the counseling group went, these people they cried.[20]

Jacqulin and Enose also used Paraṭṭai's songs to bring a sense of hope to the tsunami victims, and they networked with TTS in Madurai to send their street theater group to help address these needs. Furthermore, TTS sent counseling trainers to teach the women's fellowship group at St. John's Church skills in counseling that they have since continued to use to help the affected people, especially the women in Kalapet village near Pondicherry. Through the efforts of the CSI Pondicherry congregations and their pastors, Jacqulin Jothi and Enose Magimaidoss, both the tsunami victims and the CSI Pondicherry congregants were transformed.

Continued sharing through counseling and attempts to provide help that the tsunami victims believed they needed has led to meaningful relationships between very different religious, caste, and class groups. That is, between the middle- and upper-middle-class Nadar Christians of the Pondicherry CSI congregations and the lower-caste and -class Muslim, Hindu, and Christian fisher communities who live along the coast near Pondicherry. In a 2008 interview with Jacqulin we ended our discussion with reflection on Paraṭṭai's theology.

> Jacqulin: Most of the Paraṭṭai's ideas are based on sharing.
> Zoe: Yes, definitely.

JJ: He started one thing [but] it will [always] end up with sharing, or it's connected with sharing, or it starts with sharing. *Su̱ri su̱ri* [it goes around and around].

ZS: It comes back around to sharing.

JJ: Jesus' main theology is sharing. God so loved the world, God gave his only son. God shared his or her love through his son to the world. *Illē?* [is it not?]

ZS: Um!

JJ: Jesus shared his whole life, ended his life on the cross sharing his own body.

ZS: And where does relationship come into that, *u̱ravu* [relationship]? What is the relationship between *u̱ravu* and sharing?

JJ: Which one comes first, that is the question?

ZS: [big laugh] Sharing leads to relationship or relationship is a means to sharing?

JJ: [If] relationship leads to sharing, it won't give much meaning, but sharing leading to relationship, its gives more meaning.

After ministering in the town of Pondicherry and its nearby villages for ten years and serving as coordinator of the Department of Dalit Concerns for the CSI Diocese of Madras, Jacqulin returned to TTS in 2006 where she completed her Masters of Theology in Social Analysis in 2008. She focused her masters thesis on the history of the women's movements in Tamil Nadu and its essential relationship to other movements: a thesis that she has lived in her ministry and social work in rural and urban areas. Jacqulin and Enose have shown that Paraṭṭai's theology can be successfully transmitted to both poor rural Dalit and middle-class town Nadar Christian congregations. They have been able to nurture unity within and beyond these communities: unity among workers, unity among women, and unity between classes and castes that cannot easily be broken after they leave. Their work has also shown that *oru olai* can be practiced successfully, at least on special occasions like festivals, within rural communities that include both Christians and Hindus. Jacqulin's work can be seen as a tremendous accomplishment for a Dalit woman in India and a female pastor in the CSI, especially as she has modeled the feminist ideal of strength in Appavoo's songs. But what is most significant is that Jacqulin and Enose have understood and sewn the roots of cross caste/class relationships, the assertion of rights among the oppressed, and the sharing of personal and emotional resources that the Dalit and women's communities so need and will continue to nurture on their own.

M. RAJAMANIKAM

While eating beef their voices laugh like the Dharapuram wind,
blowing sand in the faces of the high castes.

M. Rajamanikam presents a significant case for this study of the transmission of Appavoo's theology as folk music and its transformative effects both on Appavoo's students and their village and town congregations. First, it shows that successful transmission of Appavoo's Tamil Christian folk songs is facilitated most easily by priests or activists who know music and the qualities of folk style well, and who can easily introduce these songs through performance and thereby capture the attention of the people. In particular, it is the ability to correctly emphasize the lyrics with the stylistically appropriate musical stress that Rajamanikam has mastered. Second, this case shows that a close personal relationship between Appavoo and the transmitter-student appears to be an important factor in assuring a successful transmission without compromise to Appavoo's theology for a town congregation. But for villagers it is not as necessary for successful transmission as they appear to easily be able to identify and embrace the aspects of the songs that reflect village culture. Finally, Rajamanikam is significant in that he is among a small handful of former students who extensively use music to convey Appavoo's Dalit theology and politics, thus staying committed to the medium of transmission in which Appavoo believed his theology was most effective.

While Appavoo's influence on Rajamanikam was formidable, their relationship was more distant than that which Appavoo had with other TTS students. Rajamanikam's shy personality was likely the primary reason for this. He observed and learned from Appavoo from a distance, while Appavoo did not realize the critical impact he had on him. This detached relationship may be one reason Rajamanikam was willing to compromise some of Appavoo's class perspectives in the process of negotiating changes in the lyrics of the song "Tāyi Tagappanārē" with a town congregation. In addition, although Rajamanikam was from a very poor family of Paṟaiyar tea plantation laborers, he developed keen skills in elite karnatak music. After studying with Appavoo his attitudes toward karnatak music were transformed as he came to see the value in Tamil folk music, particularly as the best means to communicate Dalit theology, while his understanding of the interrelationship of caste, class, and gender may not have been as thoroughly refined.

During my year of fieldwork at TTS in 1993–94, Rajamanikam was actively engaged in music. I knew him as an extremely proficient harmonium player with skills in both karnatak raga and Western harmony. These abilities were likely the result of his upbringing in Volpary, a quaint hill station on the Tamil Nadu side of the Western Ghats. The formidable British and American colonial and missionary presence around the Volpary tea plantations and within the hill station culture resulted in a vibrant practice of both karnatak Christian music and Western choral and keyboard practice. Although Rajamanikam's parents were coolie day laborers, they held strong middle-class aspirations that manifest in the desire to study and perform both of these styles of music. A similar pattern can be seen among the Paṟaiyar Christians in the Dharapuram plains area (Sherinian 1998, 297–304).

Rajamanikam's mother was a tea estate laborer in Volpary for most of her life. She moved there from Pallani (which is at the base of the hills) with her own mother when she was one year old and at age eleven started working in the fields. She worked for fifty-five years until she took voluntary retirement in 2000. Rajamanikam's father and his aunt also worked in the fields. One of seven children, three of his siblings worked in the estates. One brother was promoted from coolie worker to supervisor in 1998. Another brother is an electrician in Pallani, and his youngest brother is a missionary for the Indian Missionary Society (see Fig. 8).

Rajamanikam was born and raised in Volpary. He was the first member of his family to go to college. After graduating with a Bachelor of Divinity from TTS in 1994, he took his first posting in a small, but famous village near Karur called Perunkarunaipalayam (the village of great grace). This village was the first village from which outcastes (primarily Paṟaiyars) initiated their own conversion during the mass conversions in western Tamil Nadu beginning about 1910 (Sherinian 1998, 297).[21] Over the course of the twentieth century many of those Paṟaiyar families took advantage of educational and other opportunities offered them by the British Wesleyan Methodist missions and the American Congregational missions to become solidly middle class today. Rajamanikam's family appears to be an exception among Paṟaiyars from this area in that they have only moved out of the lower class in this generation. It may also be that his family converted later or that there are still a greater number of lower-class Paṟaiyars living on the tea plantations than in the plains below: the work of picking tea continues to require intensive manual labor. On the other hand, as evidenced by the demographics of the rural congregations with whom Rajamanikam and his colleagues in the Revival of Rural Congregations program and the CSI Trichy-Tanjore Diocese work, most of the plains Dalits who are still poor today are of the Chakkiliyar outcaste community (also called Arundhatiyars). Indeed Rajamanikam's congregation members whom we met in the village of Arangapalayam were primarily poor Chakkiliyars, whereas a greater number of middle-class Paṟaiyars lived in the town of Chinnadharapuram.[22]

Most scholars believe that the Chakkiliyars migrated to Tamil Nadu from Andhra Pradesh around the seventeenth century as servants to other Telugu-speaking land-owning immigrants such as the Reddiyars and the Telugu kings (Viswanathan 2005, xvi). They are known primarily as leather workers (shoe repairmen) and are considered the lowest on the Tamil outcaste hierarchy. We found that Chakkiliyars in western Tamil Nadu, who spoke a Telugu dialect, also played the paṟai drum, while some who Rajamanikam worked with had attempted to distance themselves from the polluting associations of the instrument in order to raise their social status.

While his upbringing gave him middle-class aspirations, Rajamanikam has fully integrated and applied many of Appavoo's lessons about the value and use of folk music in his ministry. It was his experience with Appavoo as a third year student at the Rural Theological Institute (RTI) of TTS that transformed Rajamanikam's musical direction.

> I cannot sing well. I didn't have much interest in folk music. When Annan [Appavoo] taught us in RTI, I began to [easily] pick up Paraṭṭai's songs. They were very interesting. From RTI, I learned "Olakattula Kuḍuttu Vassavaṅga" (Who is the Blessed Man?).[23] When Paraṭṭai Annan begins to teach songs, he will . . . how can? . . . I don't know how to express the words. He will completely come to that situation. When Appa [Appavoo] sings he doesn't raise his voice or he doesn't sing very loudly, without any extra . . . strain. He used to sing slowly/quietly (*mēduva*), but with depth. That is so very good. That is what has attracted me. But I won't show this to him. I used to stand at a distance and admire him. Like this there is such a man (I would think) [chuckles]. I am going to do M.Th. [Masters of Theology in Communication] through him. I am thinking of . . . [focusing on] folk only. It is my proposal.[24]

Rajamanikam had a clear understanding of the musical and performance elements that create the type of convincing and communicative folk song that Appavoo intended. He understood that the musical style of a song bears as much significance to the transmission and reception of a liberating meaning in Dalit and feminist awareness songs as does the linguistic meaning of the text. Thus if the semiotic meaning of the music's sound does not parallel the meaning of the lyrics, it will affect its reception and usefulness as a tool of transformation. Rajamanikam made this understanding clear to us in his criticism of the production of Appavoo's cassette *Māṭṭukkoṭṭil Reḍiyācci* and in particular his song "Ammāḍi Kuṭṭi Poṇṇē." In the production of this cassette Appavoo was unable to maintain close control of the music's recording. Thus a cinematic female vocal sound, similar to the Hindi background singer Lata Mangeshkar's high, thin, domesticated virginal style, arranged by the studio director, enabled a contradictory interpretation to the message of female strength intended in the lyrics of "Ammāḍi Kuṭṭi Poṇṇē" (Sherinian 2005b). This girlish sound reinforces women's oppression, especially among the urban lower-caste Christian community that aspires to middle-class status reflected in a domesticated femininity, or what Eliza Kent (2004) calls a "discourse of respectability" developed in the Protestant Tamil community since the mid-nineteenth century as a necessary marker of one's successful conversion to Christianity.[25]

Appavoo had great success raising caste, gender, and class consciousness among Dalit villagers. However, he was also challenged by the aesthetic dominance of Westernized film sound (and this high thin female vocal style) that pervades the Tamil Christian community therefore reinforcing a model of femininity that is not highly empowered or feminist: a standpoint that most Dalit theologians and activists advocate for women.

The lyrics of "Ammāḍi Kuṭṭi Poṇṇē" express an intimate relationship between the narrator and a young girl who is the subject of the song (see Appendix 1; PURL 4.7). This girl is constructed as a personification of the powerful freedom-giving folk genre of *sindhu* or *sindhu kāvaṭi*. Appavoo considers it a "freedom-giving song" because of the empowering protest quality he believes is core to Tamil folk music. In the refrain he employs the highly feminist term *āṇavattai* meaning male chauvinism, arrogance, or dominance, asking the young girl to kill this oppression. The narrator declares that when the Virgin Mary spoke with the angel Gabriel and agreed to bear Jesus, becoming an unmarried pregnant woman, she risked ostracism in early Jewish society. Appavoo uses the Virgin Mother metaphor as a model of boldness and risk necessary for women to emulate in order to stand up against the limitations society places on them. In the next line, male dominance is constructed as the devil (*pisasu*), using a term from lower-caste village religious practice that Appavoo often uses to reference casteism rather than the Evangelical *settan*. The narrator asks *tāyi* [mother], referencing Mother Mary or perhaps God as Mother, to drive away the demon, as Jesus drove demons away, or as a priestess in rural Dalit religion might cast out *pēys* (unsettled souls of the dead) with neem leaves, or even through whipping and pain rituals.

The first verse constructs the practice of receiving dowry as shameless, unchristian behavior especially as practiced by Evangelicals (many from the middle-class and -caste Nadar community who often demand very high dowry) and in general by Christian priests, catechists, and teachers. He ends the song by declaring that women should be encouraged and supported, for they are favored by God and deserve social justice. Salvation through Jesus came from Mary taking the risk of being an unmarried pregnant woman and going through with the birth. Appavoo's message is that such bold risk-taking action by the oppressed will ultimately bring down the powerful, reversing the structure of dominance in society and ultimately lead to equality. While these lyrics are a highly feminist and a powerful rereading of a well-known Gospel story, the cinematic style of music to which the lyrics have been set by the music producer in this recording has undermined the musical construction of a strong femininity and the Dalit feminist message of the lyrics.

Māṭṭukkoṭṭil Reḍiyācci (*The Cow Shed is Ready*), recorded in 2000, was a highly produced studio recording sold on cassette, which generally uses a light music or Tamil film music style arrangements. When Appavoo was recording this cassette, he fell ill. He had also previously had some disagreements with the music producer over various issues in the recording process, became fed up, and handed over control of the musical arrangements. The result was a very different, if not contradictory, arrangement of the song "Ammāḍi Kuṭṭi Poṇṇē" from the strong feminist message that Appavoo had intended.

This version of the song begins with a bamboo flute solo and the sounds of a baby crying. One is reminded of a lullaby. But the most striking contradiction to the lyrics is marked by the quality of the female singer's voice. Its timbre, like the flute, is airy and light. The singer puts little emphasis on the key liberatory lyrics, and most importantly, her range is a high soprano, typical of film singers. The most distinct mismatch of lyrics and arrangement is the line "endiri endiri, viḍutalai tandidum sindunī," or "Get up! Rise up! You are the freedom-giving *sindhu* song." There is absolutely no emphasis on *endiri* (get up) or *viḍutalai* (freedom). The background instrumentation is further sprinkled with bell-like tones from a synthesizer. While there is a synthesized *nāgasvaram* and *uṟumi* drum sound under the male narrator's voice and later in the instrumental interlude, there is little evidence of the kind of percussion accompaniment to the voice typical for a *sindhu kāvaṭi* folk song. There is also little vocal emotion on the line "The people who are teaching the Bible are shamelessly getting dowry these days." The result is a kind of pacification one might expect from a lullaby and the undermining of the feminist message of the text.

Rajamanikam's reaction to the entire cassette was that it was "an atrocity." He felt totally dejected finding changes in tune and stress, places where the dynamics decrease but he believes they should not, and places the pitch and intensity should rise that are missing. In our conversation about the cassette, Adri (Appavoo's daughter) agreed saying that in those particular places it "stays straight." Rajamanikam analyzed further that the arrangement for "Ammāḍi Kuṭṭi Poṇṇē" created a very ordinary (*sārdāraṇa*) message, that they sang the song very casually, "like an entertainment song," not a social awareness song. Rajamanikam felt that the original way that he had learned the song in TTS was very good, as the particular stress given to specific lyrics made the song more applicable and appropriate to the context of women's oppression.[26]

> Rajamanikam: I was about to write a letter to Appa saying, "Annan, how is it that your cassette was made this way? Have you given your approval for this [production]?"
>
> Adri: [laughs] How come you have given your permission for this? Actually, Brother, it was me who was supposed to sing it.
>
> RM: Oh ho, is it so?
>
> Adri: But exactly on that day, I had flu. No one in the family participated and as a result, Appa got very upset. And he didn't concentrate anymore on it [the production].
>
> RM: When I heard [the song] I thought if they had let me sing, I could have sung in Annan's way [style], the way Annan taught.

Besides being inspired to use folk music in Christian liturgy, Rajamanikam understood the difficult strategies and processes by which one might compose musical theology from the people's perspective. "Paraṭṭai has identified the songs from the people. The ideas are there within the people. It is very hard to get it back from the people and write songs. [But], Paraṭṭai has done that work. So, that [is why] we have admired the songs of Paraṭṭai." Rajamanikam was further able to articulate the process of theologico-musical inspiration from rural culture. "He taught us: whenever you go to villages, see the situation of the people. Observe everything from the people. Try to write [about] the people, those who are leading the life that [these ideas come] . . . from."[27]

Rajamanikam further understood from Appavoo that it was the priest or theologian's role to identify the aspects of the local culture and religion that are liberating and then ascribe Christian meaning to them (a form of Dalitization of Christianity). He applied these lessons as well as the concept of folk re-creation to his own compositions. Indeed, more than any of his other students whom we encountered in our reception study, Rajamanikam's engagement with performance and composition led him to change Appavoo's lyrics and write his own compositions based on Appavoo's songs. Specifically, he adopted genres that Appavoo had used, like *temmāṅgu pāṭṭu* (sung while doing field work and in street theater), to his own Christian composition: something only a few of Appavoo's students have done.

In one such song, Rajamanikam introduces a social theme that Appavoo rarely explored: the necessity of those who speak publicly about being blessed with financial security to show concern for their ailing elder parents.

> If money, degrees, and positions come, our relationships, affection, and everything will fly away.
> If property and inheritance comes to us, we will think that is heaven.
> As magic and cunningness cannot be hidden, God also knows your heart.
> You will always be in his sight. Do not forget this.[28]

In this song Rajamanikam is critical of the hypocrisy with which many middle-class people, who claim they have been blessed (and often saved), approach their relationships with their ailing parents by sometimes choosing to put them in institutions for the elderly instead of caring for them at home. He emphasized that

> blessings from God means loving each other, sharing, living in the village with one's parents. If you give a chance to material blessings you will lose everything. The result is that they have no real peace in their homes, their lack of loyalty towards their own parents is a sign of hypocrisy towards God, and their public show of being blessed is a scam.[29]

He also resented situations where people pretended publicly that there was harmony in the house when there was no real relationship present. "So I preach to them in the word of God, you love your neighbor, you love your parents first. Whenever you avoid loving your parents you are against God. You are hypocrites." Rajamanikam drew on the mood of pathos from *temmāṅgu paṭṭu* and from Appavoo's song "Inikkāda Tēnumilla" to communicate through his song a sense of warning to younger people who may have a neglectful apathetic attitude toward the care of their elderly parents.

In our interview with Rajamanikam, he tried to substantiate that his changes in the lyrics of Appavoo's song and adaptation of his tunes in several cases followed Appavoo's philosophy about the liberating aspects of the folk process of re-creation. To confirm this in a humble way, Rajamanikam asserted that he did not sing Appavoo's tune "correctly," to which Adri replied, "It's not [about being] correct. It's up to you. You sing it correctly. How the song comes to you, 'Yār vēṇālum, eppaḍi vēṇālum.'" Here Adri used the old Tamil saying (*paṟamoṟi*) that Appavoo used to encapsulate his theory of folk re-creation: "Whoever wants to do it, however they want to do it."

Another example of changes in tune that Rajamanikam practiced was his continued use of a re-created version of Appavoo's song "Āṇḍavanē Eṇga

Āṭṭiḍaiyan" (The Lord is Our Shepherd), based on Psalm 23, that he learned before coming to TTS. Rajamanikam's version is a bit straighter, and the tune has a call and response feel where its melodic contour dips down. It maintains a major tonality more than Appavoo's original version, which uses a fall to the minor 7th at the end of most phrases (see Appendix 2 for lyrics; PURL 5.6). Rajamanikam changes the tune of the fourth line in the second stanza to give it a feel of resolution from the previous three lines. Further, in the third stanza the tempo doubles in Appavoo's version, yet stays the same in Rajamanikam's. The differences in Rajamanikam's version, particularly the lack of the minor 7th and the maintenance of tempo, brings less tension and urgency to the song's arrangement and to the words of the psalm that are used to call on the Lord for support in situations of great fear. Its musical setting seems to correlate more closely to the passivity of a sweet light music song. He was not exactly sure where he first heard this song and thus describes it with the Tamil phrase which is equivalent to oral transmission: "It comes in the air and I heard it."[30] Rajamanikam continues to teach this re-created, lighter version of Appavoo's song because it is the version about which he first felt passionate.

VILLAGER'S REACTION TO APPAVOO'S SONGS

Rajamanikam's experiences transmitting and using Appavoo's folk songs among village Christians, particularly the Chakkiliyars with whom he worked in western Tamil Nadu, was very successful. He described how surprised and pleased they were to find Christian songs composed in folk tunes when he sang Appavoo's songs on visits to towns and villages. Rajamanikam also found Appavoo's songs very easy to transmit. He described how villagers were able to memorize the tune in one practice session, while he teaches the words step by step, taking perhaps two or three times. But, by the third time he says, "they will completely pick up." The specific songs of Appavoo's that Rajamanikam said people learned easily included "Āṇṇē Tambi Māppiḷḷē," "Inikkāda Tēnumilla," "Aṇṇātte Aṇṇātte," and "Māṭṭukkoṭṭil Reḍiyāccu," which he says even his five-year-old daughter sings often.[31]

The song "Tāyi Tagappanārē" was also a favorite of village people. Rajamanikam sang it whenever possible, and, to his knowledge, none of the villagers ever initiated any changes in the lyrics, unlike in his town congregation. He described this satisfaction with the song by explaining that within the first few lines of the refrain the people sing "cas illē miragatiri" (we have no money, we cannot bring candles). "Thus they meet their everyday problems in the line of the song. It is more appropriate to the people. It speaks the people's problems." As the song continues they sing "ottumayā ottumayā" (unity, unity).

> The oneness is more meaningful in the villages. We'll see oneness only in villages. [In] town we will not see. In villages there will be dependence, [on] a neighbor. People are mingled. If there is a death in the family, the total village will not go out. Everyone will come and mourn. Sit with the people. So, oneness is a tribute to God. That is what they are thinking. That itself is an offering. And they believe they are already doing it. "We don't have money, but we live in unity." They feel that this is their offering. The church is mostly getting money from the people. This was their . . . usual . . . regular habit. But this song teaches [a] different theology. Money is not more important. Your unity is much more important than your offering. Your unity is a more meaningful offering than the material offering. They feel they already live [in] unity. They automatically feel their own action in front of God . . . So that is "*kannikai*" [offering] says Paraṭṭai. It has come as a new idea for the church. At that time only I asked, "Are you in unity?" "We are all unified pastor," [they answered]. "Are you helping each other?" "Yes we are, Pastor." This only is the offering . . . even to buy a candle, we don't have money, but we have come for the worship service. "But, are you unified? Are you living with your parents happily? Is there happiness in your life? Are you united and truthful in helping others to get through their suffering?" "This is the offering, enough, go with happiness." This is what Paraṭṭai's song says.[32]

Besides reflecting their village cultural life ways, the song "Tāyi Tagappanārē" confirmed deeply for villagers that the values of helping each other and unifying in times of trouble that they commonly hold *were* the fulfillment of their Christian duty. Furthermore, through the theology in his songs, Paraṭṭai reversed the karmic and Christian concept of sin being the result of one's own action as a poor untouchable. Rajamanikam and Adri had the following discussion about this:

> Rajamanikam: Wherever you see Appa's [Appavoo's] song, he never calls these oppressed people as sinners. If you look carefully and ask "Who is he saying is the sinner?"
>
> Adri: The oppressor.
>
> RM: It is those people who are oppressing that he calls sinner. Daringly he will say this. "You are the sinner." This we can see in his songs.
>
> Adri: Yeah, that "Āṇḍavanē" song ["Āṇḍavanē Nī Emakku Koṭṭai"].

> Adri and RM: "*Nī emakku, koṭṭai kallu koṭṭai*" [You are like a fortress of stone for me].
>
> RM: *Akkirama kāranukkō sāṭṭai muḷu sāṭṭai* [But for the wicked (unjust) you are a whip with a thorn].
>
> Adri: In that song it will come "Paṟivāṅgu sāmi yeṟai rattatta" [Take revenge against them, *Sāmi,* the people who shed poor people's blood, beam the spotlight on those sinners.] In the middle, he scolds them as "mundagalē" bloody fools . . . scolds them as this, no! [chuckles then continues to sing] [He will listen to the cry of the poor; get angry with you, and destroy your glamour].

Rajamanikam clearly understood the tenets of unity and corporate sin in Appavoo's theology and applied it successfully in the villages, especially among Chakkiliyar Christians. However, he found more difficulty in the acceptance of some of Appavoo's strategies of raising class consciousness among town congregations. That is, Appavoo purposely chose specific terminology within his song lyrics with which he knew the town people or middle-class people would feel uncomfortable. As Adri explained, "They do not want to be reminded of their past. We used to say, bring them back to their roots," or to village culture.[33]

The most conscious and significant change that we found in the lyrics of any of Appavoo's songs was a change to "Tāyi Tagappanārē" that Rajamanikam made with his town congregation in Velacovil as a result of their discomfort with lyrics that referenced village life ways. This was a middle-class, lower-caste congregation of teachers and their children who through two generations of boarding school education had become college and even graduate school degree holders. Their class mobility, however, had led to the rejection of village values and lifestyle in favor of westernization and urbanization as they ran away from the caste oppression associated with the rural environment. Their reaction to "Tāyi Tagappanārē" was generally positive. They had little problem with the way Appavoo mixed socio-political issues like Dalit and gender consciousness into the song. But they took exception to the line "You made us your flock of sheep, but they cut us up and make biriyani."[34] They strongly rejected the use of graphic metaphors from domestic and village life, like butchering animals. They felt such images were inappropriate to sing about in church. Rev. Rajamanikam explained this middle-class perspective:

> Cutting the goat, cutting the meat into pieces, making biriyani, all these things feel . . . unchristian, out of the church. . . . They said, "What is this, Aiyya? Why should we talk about these things [common household and worldly things], cutting goat, making biriyani? . . . People will come to the

> church only for praying and hearing some good things. . . . Cutting and eating is not necessary [to talk about in the church]. You go to your house. Your house is there; cut, eat and drink, sleep. Church is not the place to talk about these things."[35]

Butchering and eating meat was not only considered inappropriate to sing about in church, but more specifically it was too graphic or frank for the passive spiritual setting that protected the fragile status of these newly middle class Dalits. Rajamanikam said that members of the Velacovil congregation told him, "It is not compulsory to make the change, Aiyya [Pastor]. But, it would be better if you changed it." This was *not* a decision Rajamanikam took lightly as he understood the depth of theological meaning that Paraṭṭai put into every line of his songs, yet he also understood Paraṭṭai's theory of re-creation and thought perhaps the parishioners could contribute something to the song.

> I concentrated very hard. In this place it should not be changed [I thought]. Even though they are changing the words, the thoughts [ideas, meaning] should not be changed. Night and day I pondered this. I thought a lot about this. I wondered whether they [the congregation members] could also contribute something. They said one or two words. For the other words I sat, thinking that the meaning should not change and I wrote this.[36]

The result was that two lines were changed. Here are the lines in the original:

> *Āṭṭumandai ākkiyē enkalai veṭṭi kariyākki biriyāni señci*
> *Kūtta sukkā vamuvalumē señci susāma tiṅgkira sūddantān atikam*
> You make us your flock of sheep. But they cut us up and make biriyani.
> They fry us like a side dish and recklessly eat us. Oh father, you are the only true shepherd.

Rajamanikam's rewriting was as follows:

> *Āṭṭumandai ākkiye enkalai atakki oḍukkaṟ saiṭṭaṅ kuṭṭam*
> *Akāna āsaikalai kāṭṭi mōsak ku iyila metāvākat taṟṟam*
> We are the flock of sheep controlled and oppressed by the devil group.
> They slowly push us into the ditch while showing desirable glamorous things.

In this rewriting Rajamanikam combines a direct political and biblical approach using words like "control" (*atakki*) and "oppressed" (*oḍukkaṟ*) that come from political movements, while consciously avoiding graphic domestic metaphors of butchering, frying, and eating. Furthermore, his use of the phrase "saiṭṭan kuṭṭam" (devil group) has Evangelical overtones that appeal to his middle-class audience. Although he asserted to us that the oppressive satanic forces are "political people and prosperity theologians," the latter being Evangelicals, it is commonly known that this phrase "saiṭṭan kuṭṭam" is typically used by Evangelicals and is not as threatening or harsh to a middle-class audience as Appavoo's original (pers. comm. Jacqulin Jothi). The second line that describes people being fried up and recklessly eaten was intended by Appavoo to point the finger at those powerful forces in the Church who exploit the poor. Rajamanikam feels that he maintains that intent by also pointing the finger at people who exploit the poor and who push them to desire unnecessary material goods. He further addresses the class tension that many Dalits feel as they are duped by the media to desire material objects, while their opportunities are limited and their oppression formidable.

While most of the changes in lyrics that we observed over the course of our reception study were slight, Rajamanikam's rewriting shows that it is not only the poor who can change the lyrics of folk music to meet their social needs. Middle-class Christians also feel the freedom to change folk lyrics to reflect their needs for a more conservative Evangelical theology. While this change is evidence of a middle-class Dalit consciousness and subjectivity, it is not the "re-creation with a purpose connected with the life of the folk" that Appavoo intended (Appavoo 1986, 15). The biting class criticism that Appavoo expresses so skillfully with domestic and village metaphors becomes muted, undermining the relationship between caste and class oppression.

Appavoo understood that in order to reach poor rural Dalits with a liberation theology it would need to be in a cultural medium that was familiar, accessible, and flexible enough to be manipulated in order to make the theology useful and transformative. His answer was the medium of folk music. However, he also understood that he had to carefully transmit his songs by teaching the parameters of re-creation and the theory of intersectionality—the interrelationship between caste, gender, and class oppression—to his students. This is why he nurtured those students whose potential and commitment he saw by engaging with them as if they were his own family members, spending time talking about theology, politics, and social change while sharing food at his dinner table, thus creating a deep understanding and commitment to these ideas.

Rajamanikam's study, however, shows Appavoo's influence on someone who was more distant and not engaged in a dialogical relationship with him. Appavoo's influence was transformative in that Appavoo instilled a commitment to folk music in Rajamanikam, who had grown up with middle-class aspirations encoded in the practice of karnatak music. Rajamanikam did not, however, completely absorb the importance and intersection of class, caste, and gender oppression addressed in Appavoo's theology. His own compositions demonstrate that he understood the problem of middle-class materialism, but not the middle-class (Victorian) markers of identity associated with the rejection of village practices like slaughtering animals and the separation of domestic tasks from the culture of public ritual. This led to a class compromise by Rajamanikam in the rewriting of Appavoo's lyrics and thus the failure to understand the intersectionality between class and caste oppression. Rajamanikam can, however, be commended for absorbing and putting into action Appavoo's practice of singing folk songs in a stylistic way that best conveys their message and for trying to compose from the people's perspectives. Another of Appavoo's students, Francis Devadoss, also lived Appavoo's theological praxis from the people's perspectives, while he had an almost opposite childhood experience, that of middle-class comfort.

FRANCIS DEVADOSS

Francis Devadoss is a Paṟaiyar born in 1965 in Pulipurakoil near Madarandagam, Tamil Nadu. His family was middle class, but had to negotiate their outcaste identity to garner middle-class respect. His father worked in the sugar factory as an officer and his mother studied up to eighth standard and received teacher training. However, she was primarily a housewife, never working as a teacher. Because of the nature of factory positions, the family moved about every five years. They always lived in villages and their middle-class status allowed them to rent a house in the main part of the village, as opposed to in the *cēri* (outcaste ghetto) where the others of their caste lived. Their class status in the village prevented close ties with their community (and Paṟaiyar culture).[37] Furthermore, because of Francis's father's management position in the factory their closest relationships were with upper-caste people. In the various villages where they lived they rented either a Brahman's house or a Mudiliar's house and the landlords spent a lot of time visiting with them. However, his father consciously chose not to hide his caste behind his middle-class status. "Our father always says . . . [his] caste freely. They also know we are from Dalit background."[38] Whether they wanted to or not, the family could not hide their outcaste status because relatives would come to visit and other upper-caste people in the village who might have had relatives living in the same village from which their relations come would determine their caste. "People simply knew, [or] they will easily find out."[39]

Not only did Francis have little exposure to village folk culture as a child, but as many middle-class Christian children, he studied in a hostel: Carley Higher Secondary School in Tambaram, a diocesan hostel just outside of Chennai. Hostel activities included cultural programs in the evenings and at Christmas, which led to Francis developing skills in drama. While he had no formal training in music, he and the other hostelers learned and primarily sang the Christian classical genre of *kīrttaṉai*. Francis went on to complete his high school at St. Joseph's Higher Secondary School in Chengalpattu and completed a Bachelor of Commerce degree in 1982 from Quaid E. Milleth Arts College near Tambaram.

While Francis had a fairly protected middle-class life growing up, he did, however, experience oppression as an outcaste.

> When we were studying in a village school, if you go to the [main village] houses for water, they will only give like this [makes gesture of pouring from a distance above so as not to touch the person receiving, and the receiver holding his hands up as a cup to avoid touching the vessel.] But I didn't have the idea, the background of what is this [meaning]. Our friends also kept their hands that way. We even enjoyed that.[40]

Francis did not realize that this gesture to avoid having the children touch the vessel for fear of pollution was a form of discrimination or oppression. Further, like many middle-class Christians, he either did not know his caste or did not know that it was of such low status until college.

In college he observed students calling each other by their caste name such as Naiyakar or Reddiyar. "At that time I also wanted to know my caste." When he found out that it was Paṟaiyar, he said, "Automatically that consciousness came. We are Paṟaiyar. [But] they won't call 'Paṟaiyar.'"[41] By the mid-twentieth century in India, to publicly say the name of an outcaste *jāti* or to name someone by such a term had become illegal. "So automatically we came into that conscious that we are low caste. So we can't boldly say our caste. That kind of oppression also came at the time I was a student."[42] This was the beginning of a period of internalized casteism for Francis; even saying his caste name was equivalent to swearing.

LEARNING WITH THE PEOPLE: BUILDING DALIT CONSCIOUSNESS

After college, Francis became a clerk for a diocesan project called the Social Action Center (SAC). Rev. Sathianathan Clarke encouraged him to leave his village and join the project, offering Francis a starting salary of Rs. 500. The project was mainly concerned with rehabilitation work, but under the direction of Clarke and Rev. John Jayaharen it soon became a local social movement organization in the Madarandagam/Chengalpattu area.

> Every evening we went to the villages and taught the children night school classes. After night school we met the women's groups and youth groups. We discussed the village issues. After discussion we [put together] petitions. The next morning we [would] go to the Talak office to give [the] petitions. We had *more* programs . . . I enjoyed so much in my life. We realized God's ministry in that place, only. At that time [1985–86], pastors were organizing the TECCA classes. So John Jayaharan called people from TTS and Paraṭṭai Annan came there every time [to run the TECCA classes]. Rev. Carr also came sometimes.[43]

Unlike most of his other students who first met Paraṭṭai at TTS, Francis was first exposed to him through TECCA (lay theology) classes. It was in these rural theological education and social action contexts that Francis first became Paraṭṭai's disciple. Paraṭṭai's influence on Francis was felt most in relation to people's movements. Further, although he sang some folk songs as a child, his interest in them only developed after working with Paraṭṭai.

PARAṬṬAI'S TEACHING

Francis Devadoss was inspired by the content of Paraṭṭai's social songs as well as the way he taught them. He said Paraṭṭai always chose a song to teach that was related to the social message he was trying to convey. He also taught his students and villagers to think critically, specifically to approach the Bible critically, bringing new understandings to many old lessons. For example,

> We always think Solomon is a wise man. [Paraṭṭai would ask,] "How did Solomon exploit the people?" That kind of teaching is very new for us. Because we always taught [that] the fear [of] the Lord is the beginning of wisdom. [Paraṭṭai would critically ask,] "What is the wisdom that Solomon has?" That kind of teaching is very appealing [and encouraged] us to approach Paraṭṭai Annan more.[44]

Paraṭṭai also taught his students to provide people with the biblical background associated with the ideas of social change that the facilitator wants to communicate. Then the facilitator should connect the social issues and biblical foundations to "feelings" or responses of the people. His best example of biblical contextualization as related to social issues were his songs based on Psalms such as "Āṇḍavanē Nī Emakku, Koṭṭai Kallu Koṭṭai" (You Are Our Fortress, Psalm 94)

(PURL 5.7) and Paraṭṭai's "Āṇṇē Tambi Māppiḷḷē" (Big Brother, Little Brother), which references and reinterprets biblical passages (II Corinthians 8; John 3:5; Leviticus 25:23; Acts 2:44) (PURL 5.8).

Paraṭṭai's work in the villages and with SAC in the mid-1980s was marked by the use of his *Nimunda Naḍa* song collection. Most of these songs were secular "awareness" songs related to the local realities of village people's lives but included examples of protest against early forms of American globalization and its impact at the local level as well as feminist and labor songs. One of these songs in particular "Paḍā Pēsārākīdu" (Intolerable), protests against American drug companies "dumping" or reselling in India medicine banned by the American Federal Drug Administration. Many of these songs carried themes about money's dominating value over people and their labor including the feminist song, "Otta Saḍa, Reṭṭai Saḍa" (One Braid, Two Braids).

Francis particularly liked the song "Yāruṇgaiyā Tāṟnda Jāti" (also known as "Otta Saḍa, Reṭṭai Saḍa"*)*. He claimed that most urban people saw village people as very poor and very low (degraded). In this song Paraṭṭai asks the question, "Who are the degraded people?" Then he declares that these people (so-called outcastes) do not depend on anybody. They have only one set of clothes, which they wash and put on again. They are as conscious about their dignity as anyone else. But some people make money by showing their bodies on the cinema screen. Paraṭṭai declares that these people are the degraded people, not our poor Dalit village people. While this song does not bring a critical feminist perspective to the exploitation of women in the media, it does challenge middle-class media productions as claiming mainstream acceptance and value over folkloric forms. It also expresses an innate sense of agency among the oppressed.

ORU OLAI IN THE VILLAGES

Francis's early impressions of Paraṭṭai were heavily influenced by the practice of *oru olai,* or as Paraṭṭai called it in the mid 1980s, *karaḍipatti. Karaḍipatti* or "Beartown" is an imaginary place which Paraṭṭai named in an odd way using the Tamil word for bear (*karaḍi*) as a means to attract people. Francis knew and transmitted to villagers the *oru olai* myth, which he understood as the practice of an apostolic life as described in the book of Acts.[45] Francis and others involved in the TECCA program had decided to attempt an experiment in *oru olai* in Muli village in Karanguzhi. They wanted to stay in a village and actually experience this idea. Paraṭṭai had decided at one point to leave TTS and come to the village to stay with them, but ultimately was unable to because of health problems.

Paraṭṭai trusted his students and activists to be able to implement these ideas and ultimately depended on them to substitute for him as a teacher and facilitator as he got sicker with heart problems. One of the workshops he offered was on the use of puppet shows as a medium for communication of Dalit theology and ideas for social change. Francis described the trust Paraṭṭai had in him when he asked him to lead a puppet workshop in his place. "At that time he (was) not able to come. Paraṭṭai Annan asked me to go and teach because we are very much involved in this idea. Also he [wanted to] encourage us." He said to Francis, "In the place of Paraṭṭai, you go and do."[46] Although Francis had only been working with Paraṭṭai for about a year (in 1986), and he was a young activist, Paraṭṭai entrusted him as a disciple.

I asked Francis what results and changes SAC saw after using TECCA strategies, and introducing Paraṭṭai's songs. His answer focused on the extensive involvement of people in the social issues that affected them, particularly the strategy of taking power into their own hands to accomplish things for the good of the community (PURL 5.9). He believes that they created a powerful social movement independent of influential project money and accomplished a great deal. For example, in Muli village the people went on procession to demand a separate road. Instead of waiting for the government to act and give permission to build the road the people worked together and dug a separate road to link to the main one. The government did not want to allow it because the land was privately owned, but the people, without fear of reprisal, proceeded anyway. Only recently the government finally paved the road.

Another example of social action that Francis witnessed involved women protesting *arrack* (country alcohol) production. Women from Muli village went to the local police station to complain about the production of *arrack* in the area, its accessibility to their husbands, and resulting negative effect on their lives. The police did not take the issue seriously. So the women took rods and sticks and went to the place where the *arrack* was produced, destroying everything. This was not an action that SAC condoned, but the women had received education, awareness, and empowerment of the means to act against their oppressions and chose to take these extreme measures. Indeed Francis said that after this action some of the men involved in SAC got worried about the empowerment of the women, being afraid that the women might scold them also.

CHRISTIAN MINISTRY AND TTS

Francis did not originally contemplate ministry as a viable career option because no one from his immediate family had been a pastor or catechist. It was not Paraṭṭai, but Sathianathan Clarke who suggested that Francis consider the ministry. Indeed he says that Paraṭṭai never spoke to him about the ministry. They always spoke, "night and day. . . . about the people."[47] After a few attempts to pass the entrance exams at TTS, Francis was admitted in 1991. He took courses in communication from Paraṭṭai and was always impressed by his simple way of teaching. The three most important lessons that he learned from Paraṭṭai in these courses were the concepts of Humanly Produced and Transmitted Media (HPTM), EPSI-PEGS analysis, and purpose analysis. Francis described his understanding of purpose analysis as consistently and vigilantly analyzing someone's discourse and their intentions when they approach him to discuss something. He emphasized how helpful this technique was in his ministry:

> In the ministry, pastoral life, so many people, [with] so many ideas, will come and report other people. In [my] past experience the congregation members always say negative things about the others. But . . . [when I learned about] Paraṭṭai Annan's purpose analysis, [I learned to ask] "Why is he saying that? What is his idea? What is behind that?"[48]

Indeed there could be reasons related to caste, money, personal interest, or politics in someone's intentions. "We [should always] stand (with) some altertness," Francis believed.

Francis described HPTM as a communication method. He used the example of Jesus who advised his disciples not to go to the people to proclaim the "miracles" that had occurred in his ministry. Then Francis retorted that this command would have the opposite effect of encouraging the spread of this news. Paraṭṭai taught that sharing news or ideas with the people was the fastest way to communicate important messages of social change or justice instead of depending on official communication media systems. "HPTM means that Paraṭṭai Annan always wants to share *everything* with the people."[49]

> He always says that the media is always saying the false news. He told a story [about] the ringing bell. [On] the tree, lot of bells are there. If you say any[thing] false [the] bell rings. If you say some more [that is] false, more bells ring. On the TV [when we hear about the] LTTE [Tamil Tigers] or [that in] Sri Lanka the people are [leading a] peaceful life. At that time, all the bells are ringing.[50]

Francis understood EPSI-PEGS as a simplified form of Marxist analysis. In a nutshell he said, "In every problem, the eight elements are involved," and we must examine the issue with this in mind to understand the problem and the best action to take.

While Francis had met Paraṭṭai's family while working for SAC, at TTS he continued to spend a lot of time with them. Francis especially appreciated Paraṭṭai's wife Dorathy because she supported Paraṭṭai's lifestyle. Francis said that Paraṭṭai always declared, "Look how people live so simply. Why should we be any different? We should also sacrifice."[51] He appreciated that Dorathy was as willing to freely give and share with those in need, opened her house and table to others all the time, and did not strive for upper-class mobility as many wives of middle-class professors would. She did not make demands of Paraṭṭai for greater material well-being, and Francis learned important lessons about simplicity from both of them.

Francis described Paraṭṭai as a simple man, exclaiming that one could never find him sitting in a chair at a table in his house; he always sat on the floor. Students would then also sit with him on the floor. Indeed with laughter in his voice Francis recalled, "Sometime you lay down in Paraṭṭai's house to talk about something [with him]. [We had] that kind of relationship. He shared everything with us. Sometime he will give us advice about studies, relationships, or how to behave."[52] As Paraṭṭai's attention was in great demand by other students and Francis already knew Paraṭṭai well, he saved his visits for nighttime when he would often sit with the family, share whatever food there was, and talk about all sorts of things.

Similarly, it was Francis's style *not* to have direct involvement in events like the Christmas Carol Service choir, but instead to sit in the back of rehearsals and observe Paraṭṭai's teaching methods, for he felt he learned more that way. Observing the process by which the Carol Service came together from song rehearsal to final performance with accompanying musicians, he came to understand the importance of all of the elements of a song including the interludes and background music that contribute (he says "give more weight") to communicating a social message.

At TTS Francis became the human rights secretary, bringing to the seminary his extensive experience organizing people. His early exposure with "living *oru olai*" in a village context led him to be actively involved with expanding the practice of *oru olai* at TTS beyond the Sunday Service community meal. He explained that he and his set of classmates were the first to introduce, with Paraṭṭai, in the mid 1990s the practice of *oru olai kañji* once a month. They drew on the village model of this practice; that is, at festival time and periods of hardships, people collected small contributions of raw rice from each house, brought it to a common pot, and cooked it together. The result at TTS, as in the village, was always more than enough simple *kañji* food that was more delicious because of the variety of rice mixed together along with the heightened spiritual experience of sharing simple food, fellowship, and theological dialogue.

Francis's seminary class was also the first to shift the practice of graduates inviting faculty to separate special meals after the Valedictory Service. Instead they introduced a common community meal for which all of the students shared the cost and to which the staff (gardeners, cleaners, etc.) were also special invited guests. Thereby they broke down class barriers within the seminary community, asking why the focus had always been on the students treating only their teachers (those above them in the hierarchy). Instead they decided to also celebrate the staff members of the college who had done so much to support their accomplishments.

BACK TO THE PEOPLE

Francis Devadoss's exposure to Paraṭṭai's *Girāmiya Isai Vaṟipāḍu* (*Village Music Liturgy*) in his last two years at seminary (1994–96) and his various experiences putting *oru olai* into practice helped him bring Paraṭṭai's musico-theology to the congregations with which he worked after his ordination. Indeed his commitment to Paraṭṭai's theology, liturgy, and songs has been steadfast to the point that Christian people know him as the "folk song pastor." Francis declared that Paraṭṭai's music is "very very very related to the people's life, village people's life. We teach about the oneness [unity]; without the oneness we can't celebrate, we can't worship our God. He rooted it to the people's life. He took examples of the people's life."[53] In particular Francis believes that "The Confession" of Paraṭṭai's *Village Music Liturgy* is very powerful. Further, he explained the important connection "The Confession" has with the theology of the communion serving song, "Virundu Parimāṟuṟadu" (Meal Sharing Song—see chapter 2).

> In these songs I am very interested in the confession. [The Christian people,] they always confess their internal problems, [their] sin. But without seeing [addressing] the other person's struggle and problems, it is also a sin. You must respond to this. And then the communion song [sings]—*mantiramāyamilla. . . . tiruvirundu viḍutalai.* . [It is not magic or illusion, not the feast given in remembrance of the dead, or the rituals of *sastirams.* Holy meal, the rare medicine that liberates.] That is very empowering . . . We don't think it is a medicine. It is given for our liberation.[54]

Francis connects a consciousness of sharing resources to alleviate the sins of social inequalities that Appavoo articulates in "The Confession," with the sharing of the communion meal as a living practice that metaphorically is the (medicinal) cure for these sins.

There are many songs of Paraṭṭai's that Francis Devadoss uses regularly and finds a positive reception for in the villages especially for youth and women's fellowship, including "Bumiyil Vāṟuṟa," "Inikkāda Tēnumilla," "Tāyi Tagappanārē," "Āṇḍavanē," and "Sagalajaṉaṅgaḷe" (PURL 5.10). He felt that all of these songs have had an impact, but focuses particularly on "Tāyi Tagappanārē," explaining that this song not only gives villagers a model of critical behavior toward those in power, but reflects their own experience and understanding of the world, especially the intimate knowledge of how political and church leaders are corrupt and divide the people for their own power. "'Tāyi Tagappanārē,' [explains] the problems that are destroying the unity of the people; jāti madam [caste and religion]. They can easily understand the idea, yes! And also, our leaders, they are always against us. In the villages [they] very much understand this, yes yes."

In his work in the city of Chennai, however, Francis, like Rajamanikam, has seen that some middle-class Christians have problems with the use of spoken language in Paraṭṭai's songs and the reference to slaughtering goats found in "Tāyi Tagappanārē." Paraṭṭai refers to the typical village practice of slaughtering goats for festivals, usually done for ritual purposes by Hindus (but also for celebratory reasons by Christians). Francis says middle-class people feel it lacks holiness or is too Hindu. Furthermore, the folk music and spoken language of Paraṭṭai's songs is aurally associated with Hinduism and poor Dalit culture for many middle-class urban Christians. Indeed Francis narrated how a Nadar Christian woman from Chennai referred to these songs as "*cōccai cōccai pasiradu*" (degraded disgusting language), declaring them unfit for use in the church.[55] To fight this mentality, Francis learned from Paraṭṭai that before singing one of his songs to town or middle-caste congregations, Francis must first teach *about* the song.

> Educate the background of the songs . . . how Paraṭṭai wrote these songs, what experiences influenced them. And then, [when you] introduce the song, it will be very powerful. Straight away introducing (even for us) it is very difficult to accept. After that, [you] understand the background and the emotions and the feelings of the song. That kind of teaching we must [first] give to the people. After that we must teach the songs, it will be more powerful. Everybody can accept[56] (PURL 5.11).

Francis has also found that not all the pastors who studied with Paraṭṭai, who know his songs and theology, are able to stand against such criticism in the urban middle-class churches. He finds many caving in to the desires of the congregations when the priest receives negative or passive neutral reactions to preaching about Dalit theology or using Paraṭṭai's songs.

> Zoe: [You say] pastors go with what the people want. But what do the people want?
>
> Francis: In the cities they always want to sing the *pālmālai* [translated hymns].
>
> The peoples also do not want to go back to see their struggles [in general and specifically in the villages].

Francis continues describing how most city Christians are only interested in improving their social status and thus are not interested in theological teaching that engages with the social issues of the poor. Instead they request, "You give some blessings message." Thus when the pastor once or twice receives no response to such teachings they succumb to the will of these congregants.

> Zoe: So how do you deal with that struggle?
>
> Francis: I always say what Paraṭṭai Annan said, boldly. "You who think you can cover the eyes of the Lord by throwing offerings in the box, beware. The Lord of the Hosts has eyes of wisdom not eyes of flesh, and he will not be silent. He will listen to the cry of the poor; get angry with you, and destroy your glamour." [from "Aṇḍavanē Nī Emakku, Koṭṭai Kallu Koṭṭai" (You Are Our Fortress)].[57]

Francis interprets this as, "Don't think that through your offertory you can . . . save your self. You can't have a good relationship with God [that way], because God [is] always hearing the voice of the struggling people. He is always with them. So you must respond to this voice."

Finally, in our 2009 interview, I asked Francis what he thought was the future of Paraṭṭai's theology now that he has died.

> I think Paraṭṭai Annan's theology is not *his* theology. It is the people's theology. It is always *alive* with the people. The only response is we pastors and the [Church] leaders must know the feelings of the people. It is the only response to Paraṭṭai Annan's theology . . . We can't teach [it]. People already have these ideas about God, about the society, and everything. People know [it]. Paraṭṭai Annan [has] only *collected feelings* and given it to us as a medicine or tablet. Dalit people or . . . the suffering peoples, [they] always have this theology with them. If you want to save it, you learn [it] with the people.[58]

In his youth Francis led a comfortable middle-class lifestyle that separated him from other outcaste people. Then, through doing social justice consciousness-raising work with Appavoo (who he always called Paraṭṭai Annan, or big brother with messy hair) after college and seeing the examples of SAC and TECCA members taking decisive action against their oppressions, Francis became a Dalit with a commitment to spreading Paraṭṭai Annan's theology and music. In his ministry as a CSI pastor, he became completely of and with the poor and Dalit people. Through the late 1990s and early 2000s, he used Paraṭṭai's teaching methods to easily spread the praxis of Dalit liberation throughout many villages in northern Tamil Nadu. Yet, as he has begun the difficult work of engaging with city congregations in the last few years, it has been Paraṭṭai's teaching methods of biblical and social contextualization that have not only given him the tools of successful transmission, but the courage to stand up and be persistent, not to back down from the radical message of social change in Dalit theology, even as he meets with resistance from middle- and upper-class Christians (see Fig. 9).

Appavoo's students are the carriers or transmitters of his theology to the people for whom it was intended: poor, lower castes, and outcastes, most of whom live in villages. The case studies above explore the dynamics of musical and theological transmission within TTS and experimentation with Appavoo's music and ideas in the early careers of three of his former students. Below, I turn the focus toward examining the process of reception and use of his songs by villagers.

RECEPTION BY VILLAGERS

To determine if Appavoo's music had carried a consciousness of oppression to villagers, if they had acted on that critical awareness, and if they had felt the need and the ability through the folk transmission system to change his lyrics and music to facilitate their liberation, I focus on the following themes: 1) unity; 2) the use of folk music, spoken language, and constructions of the feminine in Christian theology; and 3) the use of the paṟai drum as a symbol of Dalit identity. I found that in some cases there was an incomplete transmission of Appavoo's goals for a total consciousness of class, caste, and gender oppression primarily because of internal conflicts or power relations among Dalits. Thus, in order to avoid romanticizing Appavoo's music as intrinsically liberating, I focus instead "on the ambiguities and points of internal conflict within [this] subaltern communit[y]," as anthropologist Sherry Ortner theorizes is necessary in resistance studies (Ortner 1995, 177). I determined further that the presence of either Church or secular activists in an area, particularly his students, who could support the emancipatory message of Appavoo's songs, either through dialogue or contextualized use in direct action, more thoroughly facilitated the realization of a new consciousness of oppression for Dalits and an active response.

My primary field assistant in my reception study of Appavoo's music among Dalit villagers was Appavoo's eldest daughter Adri, who was thirty years old at the time. Her presence was an advantage as she could hear the minutest changes in performance of his songs and interpret the subtleties of meanings that particular villagers understood from Appavoo's lyrics. We conducted over forty interviews at twenty-four different villages or towns in both English and Tamil with individuals and groups of villagers. These included intensive interviews with former students of Appavoo's who are now either CSI priests or social activists: Rajamanikam, Benjamin Inbaraj, Jacqolin Jothi, Francis Devadoss, Anandan Selvaraj, and Johnson Jebakumar. We spent approximately three days at each site, hosted by a former seminary student at each. We focused first on observing and videotaping the performance of Appavoo's music by villagers, often in the context of a church service. This was followed by group feedback interviews in which we discussed changes or re-creation of the musical or textual aspects of the songs, the villager's interpretation of the text, and any sense that the songs contributed to a positive transformation in how the villagers understood their identity, valued their cultural material and its use in Christian worship, and had been empowered to stand up against their oppression.

The song "Tāyi Tagappanārē" (Oh, Mother and Father) that Appavoo composed in 1993 was one of the most commonly heard and widely transmitted songs we encountered throughout Tamil Nadu. It engaged villagers in two central issues: 1) Dalit consciousness and unity; and 2) the use of folk music, domestic metaphors, and spoken village dialect in liturgy as a means to reclaim a positive value for the culture of the outcastes (PURL 5.12).

***Tāyi Tagappaṉārē* (Oh, Mother and Father)**
by J. T. Appavoo

CHORUS
Tāyi tagappaṉārē sagalattaiyum pettavarē—eṉga
Oh, Mother and Father,[59] parent who created everything,
Sāmi uṉṉaivaṅki sentamiḻil pāṭṭu paḍiccōm
Our Sami, we'll worship you sing'n songs in pure literary Tamil.
Kāsilla meḻugutiri koṇḍu varala
We have no money so haven't brought candles.
Yeṅga ottumayā ottumaiyā kāṇikkaiyā paḍaiccōm
Our Unity, Our Unity we offer you.

VERSE 1
Nīdi nērmaiya maṟandu
We have forgotten justice and honesty.
Suyanalatta nīdiyiṉum
We say [believe] that selfishness is justice.
Sādi madam pēra solli
In the name of caste (*sādi*) and religion
Saṅḍa pōḍḍu setṟi pōṉōm
We fight and separate into pieces.

Tai māsa sīṉi poṅga
In January (the month of Tai starting January 15th) we have sweet *poṅgal,*
Aiyā nī jīva poṅga
But Sir you are the life *poṅgal* overflowing.[60]
Meyyā atilirundā uyyum vaṟi irukka
If we are true to that we will find the path to life.

Tappu tālam pāṭṭa keḍuttiḍum
A mistake in *tala* will spoil the song.
Sanḍa sassaravu oppuṟavanīkkum
A disagreement will spoil our unity.
Uppu kaṇḍam sāratta koḍukkum
Salt crystals create thirst.
Oṇ uṟavu enga ottuma valakkum
Your fellowship [relationship] will build our unity.

VERSE 2
Āṭṭumandai ākkiyē enkalai
You make us your flock of sheep,
Veṭṭi kaṟiyākki biriyāṉi señci
But they cut us up and make biriyani.
Kūtta sukkā vaṟvalumē señci
They fry us like a side dish and recklessly eat us.
Kūsāma tiṅgiṟa sūṭṭāntāṉtān atikam
Oh Sir, you are the only true shepherd.

Meyyāṇa aṭṭiḍaiyar aiyāvē nīṅgadānē
You offer only good things and won't let shame come to us.
Seyvāyē sīr siṟappu siṟumanukāma kāttu
You lead us near clean water and feed us healthy grasses.
Suttattaṇṇī oḍappakkam oḍḍi sattumikka pullu
If bad tigers and wolves come you will attempt to save us
Tiṇṇattaṟukirāy, tushtappuli onāyanga vandākka kashṭappaḍḍu kāttu pāta naḍatturāy
And lead us on the right path.

"Tāyi Tagappanārē" includes all three major tenets of Appavoo's theology. The first tenet is expressed as sharing food in one family with God as the living *poṅgal* rice. *Poṅgal* is the Tamil harvest festival and the type of sweetened rice cooked for the whole village to share at this event. The second tenet reveals God as the universal parent, mother and father, of this family. The third tenet reverses the devaluation of "untouchables" by reclaiming the value of village Dalit and folk cultural material, particularly vernacular language and music.

The music of "Tāyi Tagappanārē" reflects Appavoo's neo-folk style of composing. Its sound integrates stylistic elements of Tamil folk music, while not drawing on the tune-type of any specific folk genre. Its folk sound is primarily heard in its melodic rhythm and percussion accompaniment, which follows the typical $\frac{6}{8}$ or triple against duple metrical accent layering of Tamil folk music. It also employs a simple melody and performance practice of call and response at the end of the line.

The first verse of this song defines the Christian God as both mother (*tāyi*) and father (*tagappanārē*) using a common Tamil phrase that combines these two words to mean "parents." Most of the villagers I worked with interpreted and accepted this theological construction of God emphasizing that God has the "feminine" qualities of *aṉbu* or affection, nurturing, and care. One Dalit village Christian man named Keba reflected on the universal and bi-gendered qualities of God through interpreting the first verse, with the following statement:

> There is no one other than God. He feeds us as a shepherd. He is the means of *kāranam* [grace]. God the triune God is good to all people. To all the world. To all the people of the earth. Mother and Father means creator of all the universe.[61]

However, in Davandavakam village near Uttakkotai another young man discounted the term *tāyi* and the construction of God as mother. He argued that the form of the noun, *pettavarē* (parent), here included a masculine ending. Adri and I knew that Appavoo's intent was to construct God as equally feminine and masculine. Yet she admitted that Appavoo made a grammatical oversight in this case. An older male villager argued further that Protestant Christianity more strongly rejected the feminine aspect than Catholicism, which embraced Mary the mother of Jesus. This demonstrated that deeply ingrained patriarchal ideologies in both Tamil language and Protestant theology were Appavoo's greatest challenges.

While a feminine, nurturing relationship with God may have seemed unacceptable for some, the majority of poor Dalit villagers spoke of God in this song as completely available. They emphasized their experience of full inclusion as loved children of the Christian God, reflecting a historical consciousness of Dalits being outcasted and marginalized from Brahmanical Hinduism. For example, Dalits were not able to enter Shaivite or Vaishnavite temples until the 1930s. The writer Kancha Illiah (1994) claims that śudras and untouchables are not "Hindus," but worshippers of local village protective goddesses (like Yellamma—goddess of the boundaries) who have a completely different set of practices from Brahmanical Hinduism. Appavoo also argues that Dalits have separate religious practices and purposes for worship such as unification and protest that are distinct from Sanskritic Brahmanical Hinduism (1994a: 114–116).

Appavoo indigenizes Christianity to include essential elements of Dalit village religion. However, some Dalit males were able to reinscribe gender oppression through their interpretation of the song's grammar. By discounting Appavoo's acknowledgment of a protector motherly God, they failed to connect Dalit oppression with gender oppression. While these lyrics promote both a Dalit consciousness and a sense of valued inclusion of the feminine, they may need grammatical revision to prevent readings that constrain a more complete liberation.

VILLAGE CULTURE

Appavoo draws on several aspects of Tamil village culture in his music to create an empowered identification for lower-caste villagers. These include sound elements (genre codes) and folk style, spoken language including concrete and metaphoric images that resonate within the village context, and the function of folk music as a tool of communication and protest.

In the majority of the villages we visited, people described Appavoo's songs as having *girāmiya siyal* (village flavor). For example, in one of his earliest songs, "Iṉikkāda Tēnumilla," that is now printed in the CSI hymnal, he uses the image of crows scavenging for food to communicate unity (PURL 5.13). Village people commonly observe the sharing behavior of crows. A woman in Arangapalayam village described it this way: "If one crow finds food it will not eat it alone, but it will call all its fellow crows and share it with them. So like this, we Christians should unite together and tell God's love to everyone."[62] Rev. Rajamanikam described this cultural identification saying, "They are mingled with the song because the song brings their own tune, their own spirit, their own thoughts, their own feelings, so the song is their song."[63] Rev. Johnson Jebakumar said,

> I was a TECCA student when I was studying eleventh standard. There were many songs at Sriperumpudur. These rustic-smelling songs lead villagers

to seek God in the rural situation. While singing Paraṭṭai's song unconsciously we experience a revival.[64]

In our interview at Sakaravalasu a woman began crying after hearing the "Repentance of Sin" from Appavoo's folk music liturgy sung in Tamil lament or *oppāri* style. When asked why she was crying she said that the lyrics, which referenced people with no food except rice gruel, and the lament style remind her of her impoverished condition.[65]

Appavoo's songs are considered accessible and easy because they use the people's language or village dialect to communicate rural images and metaphors. In "Tāyi Tagappanārē" Appavoo reclaims the village vernacular as worthy of use in Christian ritual with the line "we'll worship you sing'n' songs in pure literary Tamil." The form of the verb "we sing" does not actually employ pure or literary Tamil, but is in spoken Tamil, reversing its usual degraded value to claim it as *the sen* or high literary Tamil. In our reception study, Dalit Christians constantly commented on Appavoo's technique of narrating his songs from the village people's subject position, their everyday language, experiences, and problems.

The area of east central Tamil Nadu near the town of Madurandagam has seen a significant change in the lives of Dalits since Appavoo's songs were first taught there in the early 1980s. Many of these changes were sparked through rural theological training courses (TECCA), in which Appavoo used his songs as a vehicle to transmit Dalit theology, and through consciousness raising and organization by a secular group called the Social Action Center (SAC). SAC helped villagers with problems like acquiring sources of clean water, flood relief, and caste and labor disputes. Gunadayalan, one of the organizers of SAC, explained Paraṭṭai's (Appavoo's) influence:

> If you say songs, we can only talk about Paraṭṭai. . . . It was only Paraṭṭai Annan who gave an empowerment to organize people through these songs . . . Especially in our area, village side. [His] songs have rejuvenated [us] [literally created a renaissance, upsurge, or upheaval,] and through the songs, change has occurred. Village people were invited to many training programs. At that time, Paraṭṭai Annan would come here to give us training . . . These ideas of his, they worked inside of us and a feeling was aroused within us to continue to work in this field for these people's liberation . . . From him we got messages, which we took to the villages and performed through street theater and entertainment programs.[66]

The Dalit villager Keba (referred to earlier), a man in his twenties from Madurandagam, exemplifies the shift toward Dalit consciousness that has occurred over the last ten years in this area through referencing Appavoo's song:

> "Tāyi Tagappanārē" speaks about caste and religion. There are many people who oppress villagers. They oppress us and make biriyani to eat for themselves. There is no one to liberate us except Jesus. He is a liberating God.[67]

Keba named the upper-caste land-owning Reddiyars and Naidus as the greatest source of oppression for the Dalit people in this area, but felt that the situation had improved over the last ten years particularly for the younger generation, because Dalits had gained confidence through education and economic self-sufficiency.

> Because of education, restrictions have gone away to some extent. There is no fear these days. In those days we were not allowed to wear *chappals* [sandals, when walking through the main areas of the village] . . . We had to depend on them [the upper castes] for food. Now we go to the city, work, and earn money. About ten years ago we had to work for the Reddiyars. Now there is economic independence, [Dalits have become] teachers and doctors.[68]

Keba qualified his comments by saying that there are still people in the village who work as coolie day laborers, including his parents, whose fear-driven behavior had not changed significantly. I asked him if singing songs like "Tāyi Tagappanārē" had been helpful in this process of gaining confidence and a Dalit consciousness. He responded by quoting the line "Sādi madam pēra solli / saṅḍa pōḍḍu setṟi pōṉōm" [In the name of caste and religion / We fight and separate into pieces] and said:

> Yes. Before we sang "old songs" [*kīrttaṉai* in classical karnatak style]. Now when we sing these songs . . . it is encouraging. If we clap while singing, it is encouraging. . . . The song "Tāyi Tagappanārē" is definitely about Dalit issues . . . This is how our parents continue to be oppressed. These feelings come. If there is this much oppression now, how much they must have suffered before. Now it is better. Now there is no use in being afraid.[69]

When I asked him how he felt when he sang the line "Sādi madam," he responded by identifying the internalization of caste oppression and fear. Then he said that Appavoo's song was clearly about Dalit Christians being abused (cut into pieces) by upper castes. He asserted that he would boldly proclaim that he was a Dalit even if it meant losing reservation benefits from the government. Indeed he argued against the government's discourse that Christian Dalits received foreign aid as a justification for not giving the same reservation benefits to Christian Dalits as "Hindu" Dalits receive. He stated, "We should fight against the government. The government wants proof that we are *not* getting aid from foreign countries. In the village there is no aid or benefit."[70]

Such an understanding of internalized casteism and fear might be expected from a young man like Keba, who has raised his status from that of his parents by studying hard and working to pay his graduate school fees. However, a ten-year-old village boy responded in a similar fashion. Adri observed him enthusiastically singing "Tāyi Tagappanārē" with his classmates at evening vespers in the Church of South India boarding school at Kanchipuram. When she asked what he liked about this song, he replied, "It says caste is wrong," expressing an understanding of how identities divide people. Rev. Johnson Jebakumar confirmed that Appavoo's songs need little theological explanation. The fact that these boys learned this song in two sessions from one of their older peers also speaks to the accessibility of Appavoo's folk songs.

The next morning of our visit to Kanchipuram, I videotaped approximately fifty of these boys singing Appavoo's songs at their morning vespers dressed in white button-down shirts and blue shorts, hair oiled and faces powdered, sitting on the ground of their hostel veranda. To engage with them using a dialectic method, I first asked them if they knew the song "Tāyi Tagappanārē" (which of course I knew they did, as Adri reported them singing it the evening before). Then I began singing the song alone. Several of them appeared dumbfounded, possibly seeing a white woman sing Tamil for the first time. After the first line, an older boy who had been playing a set of bongos began to accompany me with a typical Tamil folk pattern in triple meter with duple tension. I then gestured to the rest of the boys to join the singing on the word "unity" in the refrain—further reflecting my dialogical and advocacy method in this study. They sang the song from the heart with great gusto, another older boy accompanied, playing the snare drum like a *tavil* with a stick on one end and a hand on the other (PURL 5.14).

Observing these boarding school children sing Appavoo's folk music was what ethnomusicologist Tim Rice calls a "transformative experience during fieldwork that led to new understandings" (Rice 1997, 105). It demonstrated the accessibility and ease of transmission of Appavoo's songs and the enthusiasm with which village people sing them. Further, it exemplified the transformation from elite to Dalit culture of Christian music transmission within the institutional boarding school system. As I have demonstrated in other work, through emphasizing classical song forms like *kīrttaṉai* for the last 150 years, Christian boarding schools have played a significant role in inducting villagers into middle-class values and, in the process, alienating them from the empowering aspects of their village culture (Sherinian 2005a, 2007). Observing and participating in the process of Appavoo's music powerfully entering the mainstream of Christian culture gives me hope that, with time, institutional reform as well as personal transformation is possible.

UNITY

The theme of unity or *ottumaiya* and "one family under a parent God who shares one food," is emphasized throughout the song "Tāyi Tagappanārē." Appavoo criticizes the forces of hierarchy that divide people within and outside the Christian community, particularly strictures regarding inter-caste pollution that prevent people of different castes from sharing food and creating the social bonds (*paṟakkam*) that accompany such relationships. He emphasizes that unity is the means to action in the face of oppression and in the struggle for a just society. Appavoo's central symbol for unity is people living in Eucharistic relationships of sharing, or *oru olai,* not hierarchical relationships of social difference like caste, class, and gender. In a 2002 sermon Appavoo defined his theology of Eucharist in the Indian context.

> The whole creation is one family of God the parent [*pettavarē*] . . . and . . . the Eucharist is the food of [that] one family. Jesus' act of breaking and sharing bread with the disciples denotes the relational aspect of the Eucharist. Eucharist is not just a ritual that forgives our sins. We are united as a family of the only one divine parent. We are born again as the daughters and sons of the divine parent when we partake in this sacrament. Therefore after partaking we cannot be the sons and daughters of a Brahmin, Syrian, Nadar, Paṟaiyar, Pallar, Chakkiliyar. The relations we have in the Eucharist should annihilate the caste system. Eucharist is an act of sharing. As a sacramental ritual it should lead us to sharing, not just the elements, but everything like material goods, power, status, [and physical] space.[71]

Oru olai constructs Christian theology as a vehicle for advocating the redistribution of wealth, status, and power within Tamil society. This action begins by revaluing the village outcaste cultural practices of communal sharing. The chorus of "Tāyi Tagappanārē" emphasizes offering unity over material goods like candles. In the second verse, he uses the image of the Poṅgal harvest festival in which the village shares the sweet *poṅgal* cereal, cooked in one pot as a metaphor for the life-giving Eucharistic hope of God as "*jiva poṅgal*" (life *poṅgal*).

In our interview with a congregation of Chakkiliyar Christians in the village of Sakarvalasu, discussion of whether or not to claim a Dalit identity highlighted the division among outcaste Christians, which is particularly strong in this area of western Tamil Nadu. Many of the Paṟaiyar Christians centered in the towns of Dharapuram and Karur have become middle class as a result of several generations of missionary-supported education. Further, they were able to maintain control of the church institutions and the opportunities for education and jobs within them because very few upper-caste Christians (landowning castes and Nadar merchants) live in this district as compared to most of the other areas of Tamil Nadu. As a result, many Chakkiliyar Christians have experienced discrimination at the hands of middle-class Paṟaiyars, and most have remained impoverished. Thus the skepticism among Chakkiliyars about the possibility of reconciliation with other outcaste Christians is very real, while ironically we found that among the most oppressed, hope and willingness to unite remains.

The Chakkiliyar villagers explained the difficulty of trying to assert the term Dalit for themselves when speaking to members of the upper castes or to government officials who insisted that they know their *jāti* name.[72] When Adri attempted to further engage them about how to address the problem of subcaste divisions among Dalits, they emphasized that there was little unity among the outcastes because there was no "connection" (*toḍarpu*—relation, link), no "relationship" (*uṟavu moṟai*), particularly that which would allow for the possibility of exchange in marriage. At that point, Cruz Dorai, the local Revival of Rural Congregations (RRC) worker who was our primary host in this village, took on a more activist preacher role advocating that they try not to distinguish (literally, "see") the subcaste identities. He also dialoged with them about *oru olai* as a strategy for unification. They knew this as the common village practice at festival time and now as a theological means to liberation to which they had been introduced the day before through Appavoo's *Girāmiya Isai Vaṟipāḍu.* While most remained skeptical, they agreed that great good could come from being united especially through the symbolic and real action of combining raw rice from each household into one cooking pot to make a common meal. We also shared Appavoo's songs with the villagers as they shared their drumming and folk dances (PURL 5.15).

Class divisions among outcastes are one of the most difficult issues that Appavoo struggled against and that we observed created tension among Christians. The tendency for class privilege to accrue to particular castes has reinforced a sense of division among outcaste groups. While hope and determination is present in Appavoo's songs and the hearts of the most oppressed people, it was clear from this study that a dialogical engagement that included elements of advocacy as well as an experiential process such as *oru olai* to prove that people could unite was necessary for real transformative action to occur among the most oppressed. However, those Dalits who have class or gender privilege were usually reluctant to share or forgo their advantages and as a result sometimes resisted engaging with or tried to change the elements of Appavoo's songs that reminded them of village culture.

THE PAṞAI AND DALIT UNITY

In 1998, the Christian Chakkiliyars of Arangapalayam united against upper-caste land-owning Counders in the area who insisted they come to play the paṟai drum to spread the news of a Hindu temple festival. Playing the paṟai is the traditional "Hindu ritual" occupation of this lowest outcaste *jāti,* which they were still required to fulfill even after converting to Christianity several generations earlier. One hundred boys and girls of this village went to the Counders as a group declaring boldly, "We will no longer do this for you. We won't worship Hindu gods."[73] By refusing to fulfill the Hindu ritual function of their caste, the Chakkiliyar's discourse appears to be religious. Yet what fueled their resistance is not anti-Hinduism, but the occupation of funereal performance associated with polluted bodies expected of them by virtue of their caste. Thus, to perform the paṟai, even for a Hindu festival, reinscribes their "outcaste" social identity. In other areas, particularly eastern and northern Tamil Nadu, the paṟai is being reclaimed as positive (non-polluting) through its use in Christian services and festival events.

CONCLUSION

The reception study T. Adri Paul and I carried out in 2002 showed that Appavoo has successfully used folk music to create and transmit Dalit liberation theology. As a reflection of a valued village identity, his songs resonated among the people throughout Tamil Nadu and engaged them in the re-evaluation of their cultural resources as liberating. However, the process of transformation was never unencumbered. We found that claiming a Dalit identity has been an act of personal empowerment especially for the younger generations, but unless there are larger changes in identity formation in the society, as well as education and economic independence to support this new subjectivity, individuals and the Dalit community will continue to struggle for recognition and tangible status change. We also found that while all of the case studies presented here involved a process of negotiation, there was sometimes an incomplete transmission of Appavoo's goals for a total consciousness of oppression, primarily because of gender bias, casteism, and classism among the outcaste *jātis*. We also determined that the presence of either Church or secular activists, as part of such organizations as the Revival of Rural Congregations and the Social Action Center, as well as priests like the Revs. Jacqulin Jothi, Rajamanikam, and Francis Devadoss (former students of Appavoo) who could dialogically support the emancipatory message of Appavoo's songs, more thoroughly facilitated the realization of oppression for Dalits and the means to fight it.

6

PERFORMING GLOBAL DALIT CONSCIOUSNESS

Through Tamil folk music Dalits have been transformed spiritually, psychologically, and socially from centuries of caste discrimination, as well as contemporary class and gender oppression. This study demonstrates that folk music is an effective form of transmission of Dalit Christian theology to villagers and the poor. Yet it is clear from the reception of Dalit theologian Theophilus Appavoo's music by villagers that there is still work to be done to make his theology holistically effective.

My analysis of the song "Tāyi Tagappanārē" in the previous chapter focused on the reception by Dalit villagers of Appavoo's three tenets: universal family, *oru olai,* and the strategy of reversal. In the village context these tenets articulated a Dalit consciousness, connected multiple forms of oppression, and promoted action, which included participation in liturgy, change in lyrics or music to make them more meaningful or precise, and change in society. I observed that the music brought a consciousness of oppression and reinforced the growing self-esteem and subject reformation among village Dalits. Yet this reception study also shows that some of Appavoo's lyrics need to be re-created to communicate the integral relationship among caste, class, and gender oppression. Further, transmission by trained priests and activists has supported the most effective interpretations and use of his songs and thus needs to continue to keep Paraṭṭai's music relevant as a change agent.

In this final chapter, I address if and how Dalit theology in Tamil folk music can be an effective tool beyond the village, beyond Tamil Nadu, beyond India, beyond Christianity, and beyond the simple construction of Dalit as "former outcaste" or anti-caste, to a broader construction of Dalit as a unifying umbrella identity for the oppressed. How can Paraṭṭai's theology have global relevance for a global audience? How can locally contextualized issues of oppression be made universal? To address these questions I use Paraṭṭai's most universal song,

"Nalla Seydi" or "Good News" to show how his musical sound, compositional strategies, and lyrical theology give us direction toward these universal goals and performance strategies. Then I examine how international contexts like the 2001 United Nations World Conference Against Racism at Durban, South Africa, and the 2004 World Social Forum in Mumbai were also places where Dalits have effectively used performance to assert a globalized Dalit consciousness against the will of the Indian state. The universal relevance of Paraṭṭai's theology and message of liberation for Dalits can best be seen through his song "Nalla Seydi" (PURL 6.1).

Nalla Seydi **(Good News)**
By J. T. Appavoo

Angels: We have come to proclaim the good news. *Diyalangadi diyalo.*[1]
We are the mighty angels. *Ayalankadi ayalo.*[2]
The majority[3] of those who wear the cassock[4] tell lies.
Thus we have disrobed and come as innocent[5] Gypsies.
We searched for Mary. *Diyalandadi diyalo.*
Gabriel: A sea of tears has hidden the Madonna. *Ayalo.*
Āraro ārirarō, oh, women why are you weeping?
Women: *Oppāri:* It will take seven ages to tell our woes.
It is always hell here with such yelling, beating, and kicking.
If we even talk to our younger brothers, they will find fault.[6]
Even when we laugh alone,[7] they scold us and call us prostitute.
We are afraid, sir. We are afraid!
If we become pregnant [before marriage] like Mary did,
They will surely humiliate[8] us.
We don't want your blessing. Get out! Get out!
Angels: Don't be afraid, *Ammā.* Only through you can the suffering of Galilee end.
Halla Hallelujah!
The Holy Spirit will come! Only through you can all the people unite.
Halla Hallelujah!
Your patience, love, and compassion will be the fighting sword in this struggle.
You will teach people about *ora olai* and give birth to the people who struggle.
Don't be afraid, *Ammā.* Only through you can the suffering of Galilee end.
Halla Hallelujah!
Gabriel: Where have the shepherds gone?
Dalits: We come singing *ēṟṟap pāṭṭu.*[9] Oh, angels!
We won't go to Bethlehem because we have been
outcaste [kept at a distance] as *cēri* dwellers. Oh angels,
we are afraid to disobey [the caste rules].

The caste devil has offered a big garland [of flowers].
But now, no glory [is given] to God.
That devil is making us dance to its tune.[10]
If our sufferings were measured now, it would fill ten million barrels.
Angels: *Dandananakad*. Kill caste! Beat the drum in the traditional[11] way.
Dance as David did so that the foolish troublemakers may tremble.
Fear not! Fear not! Oh, Dalit people!
Only *you* have the war drum to drive your fear away.
If you play the urumai, uḍukai, paṟai, pambai, tavil, tappu, tarai, and tappattai drums[12] with one heart, hallelujah will resound in Galilee.
Fear Not! Fear Not!
All people come together in Christ to bury the corpse of caste.
Gabriel: Holy to God in the Highest!
Nature: God's angel! Please wait! You have forgotten us.
Oh, angels who pronounce grace, *O valai O valai*[13]
Why have you forgotten the creation? *O valai O valai*
The air, water, sea, and forests, *O valai O valai*
have been polluted. *O valai O valai*
Upon seeing this pollution, will you hurry away? *O valai O valai*
Graciously proclaim the Good News [for us]. *O valai O valai*
Gabriel: If the child born of Mother Mary comes to rule,
If the whole world becomes one family in *ora olai,*
The power of money, caste fanaticism, women's oppression, and violence will cease. All of creation will bear eternal life, eternal life, eternal life.
Angels: All of creation awaits, O Child Jesus.
We are going to Galilee in search of you.
We will walk in your path, O Child Jesus. (repeat)
Come, come with us to help bear any obstacles that may appear. (repeat)
Come with us, come with us . . .

The Good News is the meaning and purpose of the Gospels. It is the story of the coming of Christ and his mission to bring liberation to the oppressed. The Nazareth Manifesto, Luke 4:16–19, signified the beginning of Jesus' ministry and defined his mission. It states, "He has anointed me to preach the Gospel to the poor . . . to set at liberty those who are oppressed." From a perspective of liberation theology, this is the most important message in the New Testament.[14] It is the Gospel of Christ. It is also Good News for all: an inclusive universal message.

In Tamil the word *naccedi* [literally, "good news"] is the word used for "Gospel." The New Testament scholar and Dalit theologian Dr. Rev. Gnanavaram explained that the content of the Gospel (or its interpretation) differs from context to context. In a class society the Good News is provision to the poor. In a caste society it is liberation for untouchables. In a patriarchal society it is liberation for women. "For Dalits, and in a caste context, the content of the Gospel should be liberation from caste oppression and the atrocities of caste, the annihilation of caste, the removal of untouchability. In the name of caste and *varnashrama dharma,*[15] the removal of untouchability is the Gospel for Dalits" (pers. comm., Gnanavaram, December 6, 2008). Many Indian liberation theologians believe Christianity is the reversal of power structures to bring to the center those on the periphery, like Dalits who are only conditionally allowed into the center of the village and in many places are still not allowed into village Hindu temples. Dr. Gnanavaram claims that the universal message of the Good News is the restoration of lost humanity, reclamation of lost identity, and restoration of the image of God in whatever way it has been lost in whichever context.[16] Dalit theology is to bring the lost of humanity to the center of Christian ministry and consciousness.

In Appavoo's song, "Nalla Seydi," the Good News additionally functions to analyze the contemporary situation through looking back to the story of Jesus' birth and providing guidance and hope for the future. The Good News, while historically contextualized, is always forward-looking like mythology or folklore. Appavoo's "Nalla Seydi" is a dialogue between the angels (their leader Gabriel) and Dalit women (Mary mother of Jesus), the Dalit people as shepherds, and the creation.

Appavoo's message is that through their faith in Jesus, their love, patience, compassion and most importantly their unity, the oppressed can alleviate their own and the people's suffering from casteism and poverty. "You will teach people about *ora olai* and give birth to the people who struggle." This is Appavoo's interpretation of the Evangelical call of the Gospels. That is, he advocates the practice of the Good News as shared communal eating and the labor necessary for its production: *oru olai.* His message is also geared toward acknowledging and then breaking the cycle of fear that prevents Dalits from taking the risks necessary to bring about change in their lives.

"Nalla Seydi" is the pinnacle of Appavoo's theology as folk music in the form of a single song. He includes all of his theological tenets, the primary elements of his neo-Marxist theory of social analysis, and an array of folk genres. He brings all of these together under one of the most important Christian theological ideas: Good News for the oppressed. The song's multiple stanzas are broken into proclamations or expressions of personal experience and responses. There are three primary exclamations (by women, Dalits, and nature), two in a style of lament.

In "Nalla Seydi," Appavoo articulates the suffering of Dalit people, especially from the perspective of Dalit women. Yet he places this articulation in the context of Mary's dialogue with the angel Gabriel and a larger dialogue that he understands among God, people, and the earth.[17] While he recognizes the present suffering of the oppressed, as does much liberation theology that focuses on analysis of social problems, he is proscriptive and hopeful for the future. His primary message is patience, love, and compassion leading to unity as a sword in the present struggle. Thus he does not advocate passivity. Music is a weapon in this struggle through the powerful, unified sound of folk drums, which create fear in those who dominate.

Stylistically Appavoo brings together a diversity of Tamil folk music mixing several different genres within this one song. These include *kuravan/kuravanci* (Gypsy song), *talattu* (lullaby), *oppāri* (lament), *ēṟṟap pāṭṭu* (used when drawing water from a well), *kummi* (women's narrative circle dance), *kōḷāṭṭam* (circle dance with sticks), *mēḷam* (folk drum ensemble), and *temmāṅgu* (cart song). At the end of the song he uses *tohaira,* an epitome or summarizing announcement in spoken prose, to make his final theological statement defining the Good News.

THE GOOD NEWS OF FOLK GENRES

In the first stanza of "Nalla Seydi" the angels come from heaven to announce the Good News to the shepherds in fields. In Luke's Gospel, 2:10–11, the angels sing the first Christmas carol announcing the birth of Christ. Similarly to the shepherds in Luke's Gospel, the response of the Dalit people in Appavoo's song is to refuse to listen to the angel's message out of fear. They refuse the Good News because external and internalized oppression prevails.

Appavoo composes the first stanza in *nari kuravan paṭṭa* or "Gypsy" song style, distinguished by the mnemonic syllables "*diayalangadi diyalo*" and the exhilarating tune-type (generic melody) for this genre. In Appavoo's 2004 recording of "Nalla Seydi," drums are the sole accompaniment for the angel's voices lending a simple folk quality to the song. The angels, like many Gypsies in India who are nomadic, travel to proclaim the Good News and to search for Mary, God's chosen mother for Jesus. Appavoo uses his theological strategy of reversal by placing the Good News in the hands and voices of Gypsies, outsiders to the institution of the Church, instead of the powerful clergy (distinguished by their cassocks), whom he bitingly criticizes as "liars." Such a strategy of reversal is core to the Gospels, which in the Beatitudes of the Sermon on the Mount, Matthew 5:2–12 unequivocally states that the poor and oppressed will inherit the Kingdom of God: a stark reversal of the earthly power structure.

The angel Gabriel then enters the scene singing a *talattu* or lullaby genre to describe the Madonna as hidden behind a sea of women's tears. This is a typical metaphor within a Tamil lullaby, which commonly describes the crying child's tears using images of large bodies of water such as the cascade of a waterfall (pers. comm., Gandhi Mary, December 8, 2008). Women also use this genre, similarly to *oppāri*, to lament their own sufferings, experiencing catharsis through the baby's cries and asking it to declare who beat it and made it cry. Through the mask of lullaby, the mother is able to vocalize her problems so that others can hear. Her problems may be that her husband or someone else has beaten her, that her husband is having an affair with another woman, money problems, or that her husband has gone far away for work. The genre is further semiotically marked with the use of the *talattu* melodic tune type sung in a soft airy male voice and use of *talattu* mnemonics of "*ayalo āraro āriraro̅.*"

The voices of Dalit women then respond to Gabriel's lament using the funeral genre of *oppāri*. They boldly lament the pain, violence, shame, and restricted feminine behavior in their lives. At the end of the stanza, out of fear, women forcefully reject the "blessings" of Gabriel and ask him to leave.

The angels then enter for the second time with a hopeful response to the Dalit women's lament of their oppression. In the attempt to alleviate the women's fears, the angels explain that the Dalit women, using their own cultural resources, are the key to ending the suffering of Galilee. That is, their values of love, compassion, and patience along with their Dalit cultural knowledge of sharing, expressed through the practice of *ora olai*, will bring liberation. Appavoo encodes this hopeful, joyful sentiment with the lively dance evoking the sound of *kummi* and *kōḷāṭṭam*. These circle-dance genres performed by women during festivals and other celebratory events involve hand clapping or stick beating respectively and are signified with a quick tune type and the mnemonics of "*ta na na ne, ta na nā ne, ta na na na na na ne.*"

The next two stanzas express another example of the caste oppression experienced by Dalits with an empowering response by the angels that places confidence in and encourages the use of Dalit cultural resources as a means to liberation. Gabriel asks, "Where have the shepherds gone?" The Dalit people respond declaring that they come singing the folk genre of *ēṟṟap pāṭṭu* (water-drawing song) with its typical slow lamenting pace, but that their outcaste status prevents them from going to Bethlehem. In this way Appavoo further contextualizes the story of Jesus' birth in Indian culture with the self-description of the Dalits as those who have been outcaste to the *cēri* (village ghetto) and thus cannot go to a central location such as Bethlehem, the implication being that they are adhering to the village rules which continue to restrict their participation in village deity festivals or their entry in village temples. Dr. Gnanavaram described it this way: "We are not included in the center [the ur, or a holy place like Bethlehem]. We are on the periphery" (pers. comm., December 6, 2008). Indeed the Dalits assert that they are afraid to break these "caste rules." As in many of his songs, Paraṭṭai constructs caste as a devil. Here he emphasizes how some deify the devil as rich, powerful, and controlling through offering it a garland, while the Christian God gets no glory.

The text and the genre of *ēṟṟap pāṭṭu* come together in the last line of the stanza which states that if the Dalit's "sufferings were measured . . . , it would fill ten million barrels." That is, they can measure their suffering as one pours buckets of water drawn from the well into barrels. The slow arcing pattern of the melodic contour of each line of this stanza reflects the song genre and its associated work, which involves a person climbing up and down a ladder to make the water bucket descend down and then ascend up from the well. Appavoo emphasizes key lyrics by placing them at the top of the melodic arc. These include, "we come singing," "Bethlehem," "outcaste," "disobey," "big garland," "to God," "that devil," and "measuring."

The end of the Dalit lament is immediately contrasted with up-tempo unified folk drumming and the assertion by the angels to "kill caste." The song goes on to describe how Dalits should beat their folk drums—paṟai, uṟumi, tavil, uḍukkai—often considered polluting by upper castes, in the traditional way and that they should dance as did David of the Hebrew Bible. In this line, Appavoo brings together the two contextual sources he commonly draws from for his theology: the biblical context of the Holy Land and Tamil village culture.[18] Appavoo asserts that if the Dalit people can unify under the sound of the Dalit war drum [literally, *por paṟai*], the "foolish troublemakers" who propagate caste sentiments will tremble, leading to Dalit liberation: "hallelujah will resound in Galilee." The angels proclaim that the people should not be afraid, but turn to their own music and dance for encouragement and empowerment against their oppression saying, "Only *you* have the war drum to drive *your* fear away." They proclaim that unification in Christ will bury the corpse of caste.

The fast duple beat of this stanza reinforces the duple accent pattern of the beating of sticks found in the folk dance genre of *kōḷāṭṭam*. This is particularly clear on the word "*payapaddad*!" (don't be afraid). Further, the sticks used in this genre are intended to represent the folk genre of *silumbaṭṭam* (stick fighting). Finally, there is a strong musical homology of unity in the monophonic rhythmic texture played by the folk drum ensemble and the monophonic melodic line sung by both male and female voices in this recording.

At this point the song has addressed the needs of women, and the angels have asserted that the Dalits (all the oppressed) should come together to bury the corpse of caste. With this, the angel Gabriel sings "Holy to God in the Highest!" The listener may feel that Appavoo has drawn to a close the song and his Dalit theology of the Good News. Then suddenly, in a spoken female voice, Nature interrupts asking, "Have you forgotten us? Listen to what we have to say too. Include us in the proclamation of the Good News also." By turning to the "forgotten" anguish of nature or the creation, Appavoo constructs Dalit theology as universally inclusive, and asserts that Dalit theology must go beyond caste issues and beyond the needs of humans. This also reflects the more recent inclusion of environmentalism in the scope of Indian liberation theology and its presence in Appavoo's neo-Marxist theory of social analysis.[19]

Appavoo effectively encodes Nature's voice by using the folk song genre of boat song. This is characterized by mnemonics that ebb and flow like the rhythm of waves. He uses the phrase "*O valai*" as a mnemonic sung by the chorus of fisher people, while the phrase also has the literal meaning of "O my net (it can also be interpreted as wave)." Using a light lamentation style, not full *aṟagai* (crying), but *pulambu* (weeping), Nature describes how people have turned their backs on the creation by polluting the earth, air, sea, and forests and further refused to notice or acknowledge their actions. Finally, Nature asks the angels to "proclaim the Good News (for us)," a move of universality by Appavoo, as concern for the environment is an issue that crosses national and social boundaries.

Finally, in the last two stanzas, Appavoo presents a summary of his theology in *tohaira* style. While ancient Tamil poets used *tohaira,* here Appavoo presents it as a spoken announcement by a village paṟai drummer who beats his frame drum in a simple pattern while crying out his announcement in a monotone prose style with a rising lilt at the end of each line. Appavoo proclaims his Dalit theology one more time in a conclusive way:

> If the child born of Mother Mary comes to rule,
> if the whole world becomes one family in *oru olai*
> the power of money, caste fanaticism, women's oppression, and violence
> will cease. All of creation will bear eternal life, eternal life, eternal life.

Jesus Christ shows the way to bring an end to class, caste, and gender oppression, bringing eternal life for all creation (including nature) through people becoming one universal family that equally shares their material and labor resources.

The angels respond to this announcement with great joy bringing the story of the coming of the Good News to a close on a hopeful note with the celebratory, dance-inducing Tamil folk ballad genre of *temmāṅgu*. All of creation waits for the Child. The angels (along with the Dalits and women) will proceed to search for Jesus, not in Bethlehem, but in Galilee—the center of his teaching.[20] They are committed to follow the model of his life (repeated twice in the song), while humbly recognizing the need to ask for his continuing guidance and to be with them along the way as they face challenges and obstacles on the path to liberation.

Appavoo has reclaimed the paṟai drum, the frame drum of the outcaste Paṟaiyar and Chakkiliyar *jātis*, commonly associated by upper castes as the polluting drum essential to funerals. He has brought the paṟai to the center of Protestant liturgy in the performance of his *Girāmiya Isai Vaṟipāḍu* and included it in the sound and text of songs like "Nalla Seydi." Appavoo's positive reclamation of and emphasis on Dalit drumming in "Nalla Seydi" as a significant tool in Dalit liberation struggles is not only drawn from village culture and the biblical context. It is also paralleled in international political forums such as the 2001 United Nations World Conference Against Racism and the 2004 World Social Forum in Bombay. Through percussion performance on the streets of Durban, Dalit groups defined their identity beyond the Indian domestic political and social sphere to claim a more universal understanding of oppression.

In a move of liturgical reform that reclaims a positive village Dalit identity through the use of this "degraded" drum and folk style, thus developing cultural and psychological self-esteem along with empowered consciousness through sensory impact, and social change, Appavoo liberates Indian Christianity. Paṟai drumming troupes have similarly brought empowered Dalit subjectivity through their music to national and international forums of power.

At the 2001 United Nations World Conference Against Racism, Racial Discrimination, Xenophobia, and Related Intolerance (WCAR) in Durban, South Africa, the relationship between race and caste were fiercely debated inside and outside the conference. Caste discrimination is still experienced by 260 million people world wide, and the international movement against it reached a turning point at Durban (Narula 2004). Dalit activist and human rights groups from India lobbied for a discussion of caste to be included on the agenda and in the action statements of the conference. They hoped that the global dimensions of caste as a form of racism would be explicitly recognized. However, Savitri Kunadi, India's representative to the United Nations, put on record India's official position that "the caste system does not fall within the purview of racial discrimination," and further that it is an internal domestic issue, not a global phenomenon to be brought under scrutiny as a problem of international human rights.[21] Basil Fernando of the Asian Human Rights Commission described the Indian Dalit's response:

> The delegation of 200 Dalits, wearing their badges and head straps with the words "Cast away Caste" and telling their histories, won the hearts of everyone. In their demonstrations, they sang, "Down, Down, Castism; Up, Up, Humanism." Of their drums, an observer at a conference session said, "It was the Dalits' drum that helped all victims here at Durban dance together." These long-time sufferers of one of the worst forms of discrimination that humanity has known stole the hearts of everyone and became the humanizing factor at this conference. (Fernando 2001)

Dalit drumming groups from India, including the Tamil women's paṟai group Sakthi Kalai Kural (Female Power Cultural Group) of the Sakthi Folk Arts Centre, were invited to Durban by an Indian NGO. They were not an official part of the U.N. conference, but had a significant impact on raising the participant's consciousness to Dalit issues. Sister Chandra, leader of Sakthi, told me that they were invited and organized along with several other Dalit drumming groups who gathered before the conference in a parallel NGO conference. Three members of Sakthi joined together with Dalit artists from Karnataka, Andhra Pradesh, and Gujarat to form one group. They performed together on the streets to demonstrate how Dalit folk artists are treated in India and how Dalits in India experience oppression[22] (PURL 6.2). They also carried posters while they performed to educate people about the 260 million Dalit people in India. They challenged the Indian government's denial of caste saying,

> See the NGO groups were telling that [the] caste problem is exactly like the race problem in other countries. But our country, our government, was not willing to tell in that way. Our government feels that we don't have caste problem in India. But we know, the people who are experiencing [it] will say, "Yes, we have! Even today we say, we experience that." How can we say that we don't have?[23]

Sister Chandra further described the impact and solidarity she thought Sakthi helped create at Durban through performance.

> I felt there was a global march. Our troupe was invited to lead that. So, [there was] such a big crowd. By beating [the paṟai], we got the way to go inside. And you know we went in front and everyone wanted to come in front

and dance and shout and say the slogans. It was a thrilling experience. There I felt, it is not only in India we have these working class people. It is all over the world.[24]

Indian gender and sexuality activist Pramada Menon reflected on Sakthi's presence and performance at Durban.

> The use of the drumming was an excellent way to forefront the Dalit issue. I am not sure that many people understood who the Dalits were or what they wanted, but once the drumming began and they began their walk through the conference site, one had to reckon with them and deal with their music and the black jackets that they were wearing . . . [It was a] very innovative way of getting one's voice heard—saying nothing that may put them in a position of confrontation, but nevertheless ensuring their presence and making sure that their silence made them heard . . . I followed them around since the music mesmerized me and also saw the exhibitions that they had put up.[25]

After much negotiation, demonstrations with music and dance, and a fast by the Dalit caucus representatives at Durban, a statement was adopted to the WCAR's Draft Programme of Action asking states "to prohibit and redress discrimination on the basis of work and descent." While the Dalits wanted to include the term "caste" as a separate category of discrimination, they compromised, glossing "caste" instead as discrimination based on both work and descent. The Committee on the Elimination of All Forms of Racial discrimination (CERD) concluded that "the term 'descent' contained in Article 1 of the convention does not refer solely to race and encompasses the situation of dalits" (Narula 2004). The Indian government, however, wanted to exclude both "caste" and "work," relegating untouchability to the category of descent. In the end, the Indian government's intensive lobbying resulted in the final document excluding any mention of caste-based discrimination.[26] However, a year later the CERD held a special debate on the issue of descent-based discrimination declaring that, "caste discrimination is one of the many forms, and not the only form, of descent-based discrimination." Furthermore, a parallel NGO conference "affirmed the conclusions of the CERD and the U.N. Subcommission on the Promotion and Protection of Human Rights that untouchability, bonded labor, manual scavenging and other caste-based abuses are repugnant and insidious forms of racial discrimination" (Narula 2004).

The struggle by Indian Dalits to bring awareness of their plight to an international audience raises many questions about identity reconstruction through music and performance. At Durban, the Dalit drummers attempted to unify the entire conference on a platform of common humanity that was determined to resist and overcome all types of oppression based on the circumstances of one's descent and work, not just race. The action statements of the conference, influenced by the powerful lobby of the Indian government, on the other hand, disconnect the categories of difference, race and caste, and attempted to deny the existence of caste as a form of oppression in India.

The women's paṟai group Sakthi returned to India to continue their work of empowering Dalit women through folk performance and to take their message to other countries such as Japan and Korea.[27] However, the resistance that the Dalit drummers and activists felt from the Indian government at Durban also had local ramifications: their loud and clearly effective presence at the conference brought harassment and threats to Sakthi when they came back to India.[28]

CODA

Dalit Christians are active agents, taking the most liberating elements and practices of Christianity such as shared communal eating and living, cultural and ritual elements of the poor and oppressed, social justice and questioning of the status quo to create a Dalit Christianity in liturgy and theology. This work has attempted to "restore the integrity of the voices of resistance," to local as well as international hegemony (Doniger 2002). That is, voices that actively sing resistance to both the local violence of caste, gender, and class oppression as well as the Sanskrit captivity of Tamil Christian culture, the intolerance of Hindu and Christian fundamentalism, and the cultural imperialism inherited from the West.

In this study of the global reach of Dalit resistance through music, my analysis challenges understandings of race and caste as differentiated forms of identity and supports a musicological identity theory of performative critical subject formation. Thus Dalit drumming and singing, as a unifying experience of resistance, is the basis for a theory and practice of critical, phenomenological subject formation.

However, my intent in this final chapter is to retune the dial of identity away from essential difference and the tendency of the Tamil Dalit and Christian Dalit movements to be limited by identity politics, to instead move toward investigating strategies that the oppressed use to constitute a transcultural experiential affinity of subject reformation in their efforts to resist oppression.

In his study of the history of a mutually influential discourse of action and solidarity between African Americans and Dalits in the late nineteenth and early twentieth centuries, Ajay Gandhi outlines how "African-American, nationalist, and dalit intellectuals have continually employed each other's experience as an example for their own mobilization" (2004, 11). Gandhi argues that this correspondence is based not on solidarity of origins or body type, but "rather is located in the universal responses engendered by power's capriciousness" (ibid., 28). If we focus on how oppressive identities have been resisted and reconstructed, we see that Dalits, like African Americans and many others, have used the creative cultural action of music and religion as a means not only to resist, but to perform a critical, oppositional subjectivity: a transformative self-actualization of the oppressed from essentialized objects to critically conscious actors. Bell hooks writes that this "process emerges as one comes to understand how structures of domination work in one's own life, as one develops critical thinking and critical consciousness, as one invents new, alternative habits of being, and resists from that marginal space of difference inwardly defined" (1990, 15).

In the Indian context those formerly called untouchables have practiced a process of *critical consciousness* through folk music to reject the stigma of untouchability and negotiate alternative habits of being, reconstituting themselves through performative action as Dalits. A significant step in this process has been to analyze the hegemonic social processes that value their music and culture as degraded or similarly untouchable. This analysis has led to action for social and psychological change with a focus on unity and sharing in opposition to reification of difference. Through songs like "Nalla Seydi" and the drumming of Dalit groups from various parts of India outside the U.N. conference on race at Durban, many have attempted to reach across oppressed identities within India to define Dalit broadly, forging fluid correspondences among the multiple oppressions: outcastes, the poor, women and by extension those affected by racism. I have argued here that the folk music that expresses this fluid identity politics is also adaptable and flexible. That is, as a musical style, Tamil folk music is re-creative through its transmission; thus it supports continual processes of empowered critical subject reformation.

Participation in critical performance is a strategy of unification that becomes a shared experience of resistance to oppression across essentialized difference and the means to liberating subject formation. In Tamil Nadu, Christian folk music is used to negotiate an alternative Dalit consciousness among oppressed untouchables divided by class and gender. Similarly, the Dalit performance of identity at Durban forces a reconsideration of global experiences of oppression, racism and casteism. It directs us to look at strategies of survival and resistance through cultural technologies—such as folk music—as modes of action that protest, transform identity, and gather others into a movement of participation in shared humanity.

While this strategy produced greater critical consciousness in both contexts, it did not always produce immediate structural change. At Durban, powerful states co-opted the U.N. manifesto, while in Tamil Nadu forces of patriarchy and classism clouded calls for inclusion. As we see in the song "Nalla Seydi," there are challenges on the path of liberation. Yet with commitment, hope, and faith in the knowledge that through action (performance) the message of Dalit liberation can be heard locally and globally, these challenges are being met (see Fig. 10). In this post-postcolonial world in which the construction of colonial subjects as victims is critically turned inward (Doniger 2002), we see government officials of Indian descent showing little affinity with, or concern for, the issues of their Dalit brothers and sisters in Durban, while others beyond the identity of Dalit or "Indian" who have been brought into consciousness through Dalit performance stand in affinity with the plight of Indian Dalits and their experience of oppression. Within the country, decolonizing becomes decasting (pers. comm. Joe Arun, April 12, 2009.)

Dalits in Tamil Nadu and at Durban are able to transform themselves and those around them not just in relation to caste, but also gender, class, and race. Through performing Tamil folk music, they have become active agents challenging internalized low self-esteem and fear, transforming relations of power locally and internationally to create tangible effects.

For some Indians, Christianity has been used to support hegemonic unequal social and economic structures. Tamil Christian Dalits, on the other hand, through the production, transmission, and re-creation of the music of theologians like Rev. J. T. Appavoo, have begun to embrace folk music and village culture as a means to create Christian songs and liturgies that reflect their world view and articulate a theology of liberation against caste, class, and gender oppression. Christianity has been liberated by Dalits through returning to the core mission in the Nazareth Manifesto: liberation for and by the poor and the oppressed. In the Tamil context this has meant reclaiming the transformative elements of Tamil village culture and identity in folk music and spirituality.

Appendix 1. Song Transcriptions

The Lord's Prayer

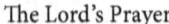

The Lord's Prayer (*continued*)

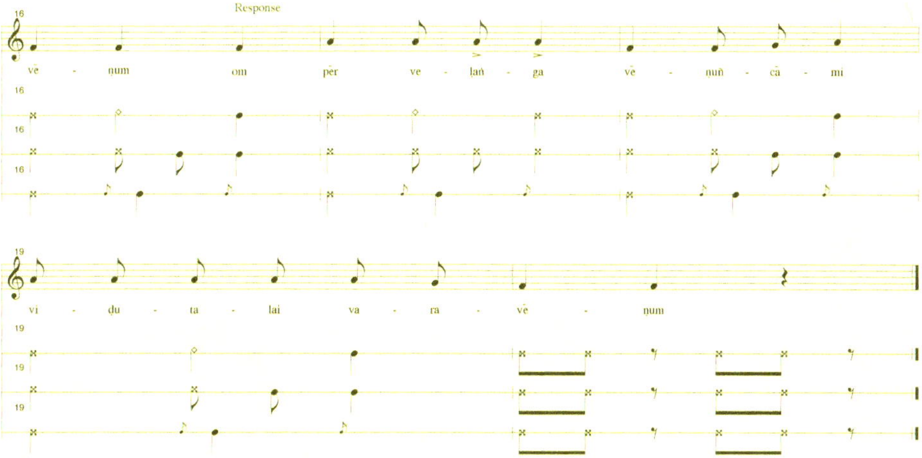

Repentance of Sin

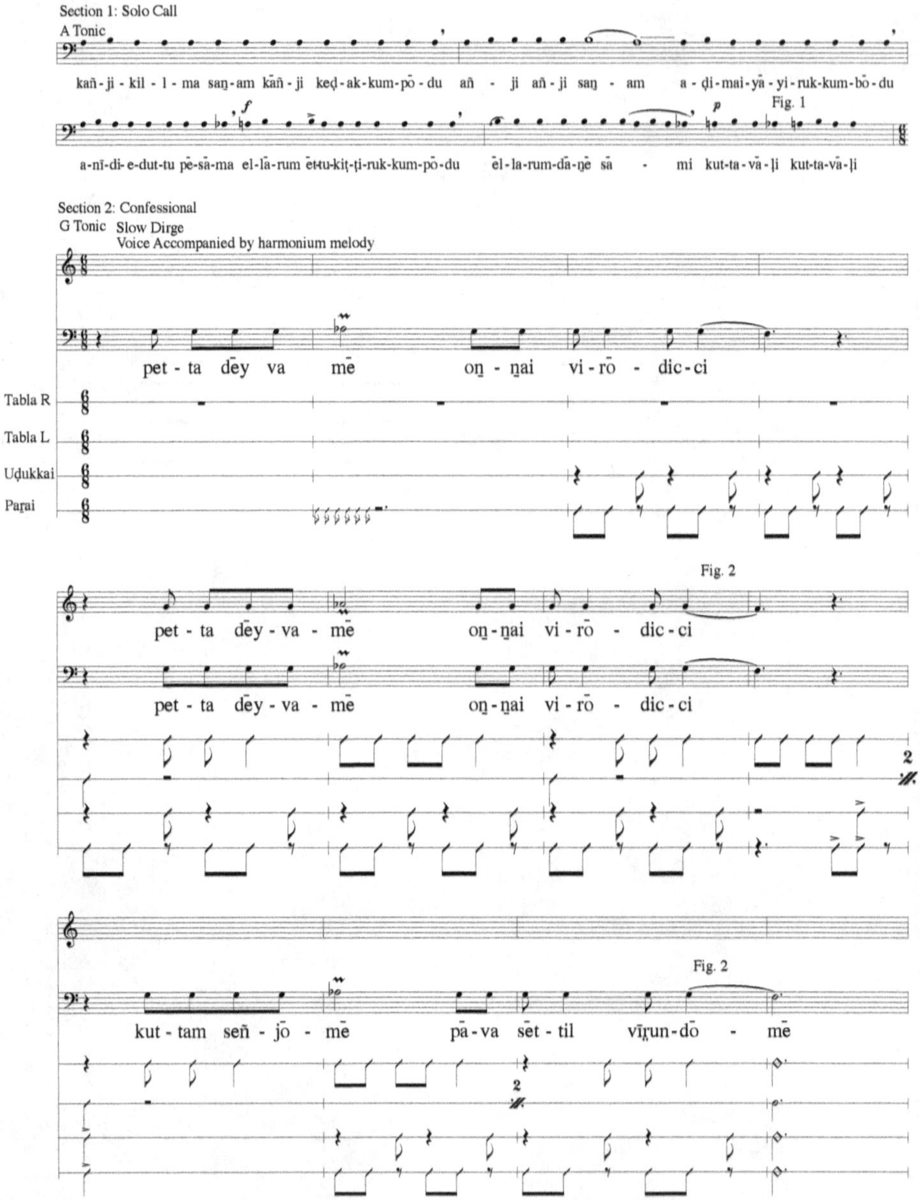

Meal Sharing Song

E tonic, no accidentals

Greetings and Praise of God: Section 1

Greetings and Praise of God: Section 1 (*continued*)

Greetings and Praise of God: Section 1 (*continued*)

Greetings and Praise of God: Section 2

Greetings and Praise of God: Section 2 (*continued*)

Greetings and Praise of God: Section 2 (*continued*)

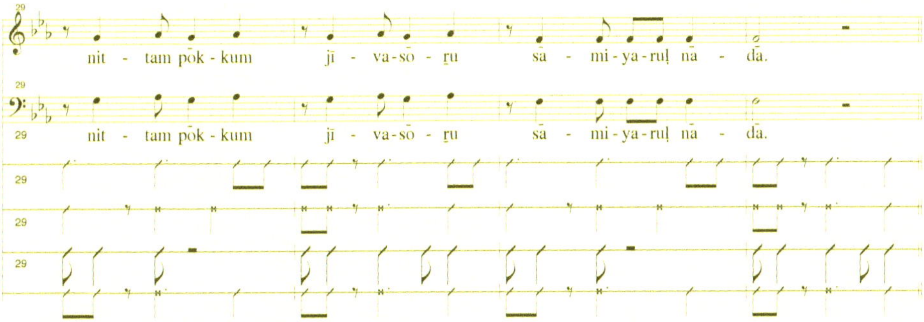

Greetings and Praise of God: Section 3

Greetings and Praise of God: Section 4

Greetings and Praise of God: Section 4 (*continued*)

Greetings and Praise of God: Section 4 (*continued*)

Appendix 2. Song Lyrics by Rev. J. Theophilus Appavoo

Ammāḍi Kuṭṭi Poṇṇē (My Little Girl)

CHORUS
Oh my little girl, you are always crying.
Get up! Rise up! You are the freedom giving *sindhu* song.
(male voice)
Declare who beat you. Kill that arrogance.
You have to become like Mother Mary [bold enough to be a virgin]
That male dominance devil, that demon,
Threaten and drive it away, oh Mother.
VERSE 1
The words which Gabriel spoke, there is no one here to repeat.
The people who teach the Bible are shamelessly getting dowry these days.
The Elizabeths of our city are burning like witches in kerosene oil.
When they come forward to welcome liberty, the stoves will explode.
(Oh, my little girl)
VERSE 2
As salvation came from Mary's belly
You have the inspiration of Virgin Mother Mary.
Don't worry! Salvation will come from your lap.[1]
The powerful people's position will be destroyed.
Trembling they will fall.
The powers that will spoil you in your youth,
Will become powerless, my girl. (Oh, my little girl)

Inikkāda Tēnumilla (Without Sweetness There Is No Honey)

REFRAIN
Without sweetness there is no honey.
Without glitter there is no gold.
If you do not proclaim the gospel,
You are not a Christian.
VERSE 1
Like crows call each other,
Whatever happiness we have, we shall share!
Without salt in fish curry, into the trash box it will go.
If you do not announce Jesus' Gospel,
You are not a Christian.
VERSE 2
Like parents who give birth and bring up ten children,
Honest people talk about it.
If I am shy, the neighbors will laugh at us.
All of the love of ten core parents (100 million)
Won't equal the love of God.
If you forget to speak of this,
He will become only a dead body.

Allēlūyā Allēlūyā (Alleluia)

REFRAIN
Allēlūyā Allēlūyā Allēlūyāvē
Alleluia, Alleluia, oh Alleluia
Āṇḍavaṉuk Kallēlūyā Allēlūyāvē
To God Alleluia, oh Alleluia.
VERSE 1
Parisutta ālayattil tarisitta Āṇḍavaṉa
Let us worship God in the world
Vallamai viḷaṅgum vāṉa viriviṉilē ārātiṅga
Whom we have seen in the church
Nallavarē kākkā kuruvi paṟavaikaḷoḍa
Let's praise him, our community leader
Namba Vallavara vāṟttiḍa vāṅgō murugaṅgaḷōḍa.
along with the birds and animals.

VERSE 2

Uṟumi mēḷam muṭṭittāḷam

Let's praise Him with the [folk drums] uṟumi ensemble,

-periya mōḷam uḍukkai ōlam

the periya (big) drum and the *uḍukkai* (tension) drum;

Pambai mattāḷattōḍa pōḍuṅgaiyya Siṅgitāḷam

the wailing pamba, bells and hand claps.

Kummiyāṭṭam oyilāṭṭam vīrasilambaṭṭam

Let's praise him with folk dances, circle and line dancing, and brave stick fighting.

Ādi kummāḷamā ārāticci -paṇṇuṅga ārpāṭṭam

Come on woman let's dance kummi, worship! Let's make a spectacle.

Pudiya Pudiya Talaimuṟaikku, Pudiya Pudiya Siluva (For Every Generation There Is a New Cross)

REFRAIN

For every new generation there is a new cross

That cross should show the deep loving concern of God

VERSE 1

There are bunches and bunches of grapes on the vine.

This bride's [virtuous woman or the church] only desire is to join her husband [Jesus] there.

When she comes to the Garden he hangs from the cross suffering.

He tells the people to go to the village because there are tears there.

VERSE 2

For every place there is a separate cross.

It is not just beauty to be worn and seen,

but a miraculous act and expression of love and action.

As one flock, they should go carrying the King's cross.

Bumiyil Vāṟuṟa (Living on Earth)

Bumiyil Vāṟuṟa makkaḷē ellārum

All the people living on earth

Kūḍiyē vāruṅga kumbiḍalām

Come together to worship

Āravārattōḍa āṉandamā pāḍa

Sing with enthusiasm and happiness

Āṇḍavar saṉṉiti sērndiḍalām

Let's join God's presence.

Āṇḍavanē Eṅga Āṭṭiḍaiyaṉ (The Lord Is Our Shepherd)

VERSE 1

Elaminnā elēla ela elala elo, elala elo Elaminnā elē la ela elama elo, elama elo

Ela ela elē la ela elala elo, elala elo Elaminnā elē la ela elama elo, elama elo.[2]

Lord! You are the shepherd who supports us.

You find a fountain-like flowing river,

and gather us in the green pasture of *arugam* grasses[3] to protect us.

VERSE 2

When we walk on the dark path, we have no fear because you are with us.

When there is no grass, you split branches with your staff.

When the tiger approaches, you drive it away with your rod.

You will help us find the right path, and grace[4] will follow like a dog follows its master.

VERSE 3

Lord, you are our king and we lack nothing.

You welcome us by beating the drums, offering us betel nut, blowing trumpets, and decorating the entry with banana stalks.

VERSE 4

You lay out a great feast for us, then invite us to sit grandly in your royal court.

Giving us an equal share[5] creates envy[6] in our enemies,

while bliss overflows in our hearts.

Lord! *Eleela ela*[7] you are our shepherd *Eleela ela*[8] and King, King, King!

Āṇḍavanē Nī Eṅga Koṭṭai[9] (Lord, You Are Our Fortress)

CHORUS

Lord, you are our fortress, a stone fortress.

But to the wicked, you are a whip, a thorny whip.

SUB CHORUS

Take revenge, Oh Lord (*Sāmi*),[10] on those who shed the blood of the poor.

Shine your spotlight on them.

He who has destroyed your freedom, *Sāmi,*

Tear his heart and plant your cross.

VERSE 1

He has exploited the poor and little by little has cut their *tāli.*[11]

How can you let the sinners go?

He punches the widow in her mouth and kicks the head of the fatherless child.

He has sold justice and righteousness and amassed it as wealth. This is harmful to the people.

(Take Revenge!)

VERSE 2

You who think you can cover the eyes of the Lord[12] by throwing offerings in the box, Beware!

The Lord of Hosts has eyes of wisdom, not eyes of flesh, and he will not be silent.

He will listen to the cry of the poor; get angry with you, and destroy your glamour.

(Take Revenge!) (sub-chorus, first half and chorus)

VERSE 3

Will the divinity simply let the rulers do more and more evil through the law?

He thrashes the heart of those who demand justice

And brands those who walk righteously as terrorists.

His cart does not run with a wheel pin, but by instigating castism and communalism.

FINAL CHORUS

Take revenge, Oh Lord (*Sāmi*)

On the thugs and bloody fools who run away from the path of love.

Aṇṇaṭa Aṇṇaṭa (Elder Brother)

REFRAIN

O Brother, Brother, Brother.

Angel Gabriel! Our elder brother.

The Gospel news you sang to us on that day still has not happened.

VERSE 1

As you foretold, God is not glorified in our church.

Instead, the glamorous style of movie stars and politicians is stored in the church.

The sin of seeking one's own glory has led to[13] the worship of fostering[14] violence.

VERSE 2

We search for peace on earth every single day.

But, whether Punjab, Sri Lanka, Paramakudi, Andhra, or the wetlands of Tanjore, wherever we look there is war and violence.

The missiles and bomber planes fly overhead.

The poor worry; they have no peace of mind.

Virgin Mary gave birth to a single lion, our precious gold. But the pigs, who are fostering violence, are a litter.[15]

VERSE 3

Love came to humankind. It blossomed in a cowshed on Mary's lap.
But some humans have drunk the poison of violence, becoming Dracula.
They have in turn, threatened others, put them in a jail of fear, and made them into animals.
Now there are only one or two that remain human. They are the only ones who wear the golden silk dress of love.

Āṇṇē Tambi Māppiḷḷē[16] (Elder and Younger Brother, Son-in-Law)

CHORUS

Elder and younger brother, son-in-law, elder and younger sister, sister-in-law, daughter-in-law, what does the Bible say? Why do you look so confused?

VERSE 1

Jesus is our leader.[17] Liberation is his name.
So says the Bible. If we understand[18] that, our worries will fly away.

VERSE 2

Grace means giving, says 2nd Corinthians, chapter 8.
Toiling for equality, this is in verses 13 and 15.

VERSE 3

Read John 3:5! We should become the children of one father.
We must be reborn. We must forget the caste of our previous birth.

VERSE 4

What does Leviticus 25:23 say?
It says that we have no land ownership rights because the land belongs to the divine.

VERSE 5

Read the Acts of the Apostles 2:44.
We have to live together (as a family) and cook common food in only one pot.[19]

Otta Saḍa, Reṭṭai Saḍa (One Braid, Two Braids)

One braid, two braids
Walk upright and roar like a whip.
Our army shall mend the world, even for women.
We shall find for the right solution
They who consider us cheap and
Mock us – they are a mob of trouble-makers.
They will go like cowards with their faces averted downwards–
Our uniqueness will then be understood by all.
This society is torn apart.
Torn everywhere.
It cannot be mended again
We shall stitch a new one, come oh woman!
It is a rotten snack
Throw it away to the gutter!
An egalitarian society – Come woman, let us cook it.
Only we know exactly how to prepare it.
Silk sari, colored sari
We wear them along with ornamental jewels
We are fed up with all the beatings! – To change our people,
Leave the kitchen and come join us– Hey woman
The female lioness is very brave.

Notes

PREFACE

1. Throughout this book I use Appavoo's pen name "Paraṭṭai" and his birth name "Theophilus Appavoo" interchangeably. Yet my tendency will be to use "Paraṭṭai" when referring to his music as he used this pen name on all of his cassettes and CDs to distance himself from its authorship, encouraging villagers to more freely re-create the songs to meet their needs for resistance and identity.

2. Hindu philosophy and law regarding food portrays untouchables as primarily receivers, in that they can only receive cooked food, not give it to anyone of a higher caste. Upper-caste Brahmins, on the other hand, are constructed as primarily givers of cooked food. Further, lower castes are also absorbers of negative ritual substances such as karma, faults, evils, and inauspiciousness transferred through foodstuffs (Mines and Lamb 2002, 270). I will argue that focus on these constructions obscure Dalit people's labor as agricultural workers and cleaners that provide the means to life, every day, for the rest of society.

3. J. T. Appavoo, lecture, University of Oklahoma. September 17, 2005.

4. These are different types of folk drums.

5. http://www.mnsu.edu/emuseum/history/mncultures/crow_dog.htm. Accessed January 11, 2011.

6. The point I am trying to emphasize is that Appavoo was not trying to convert (missionize) anyone. He overwhelmingly worked with village Christians and low castes who had been Christians for at least three generations.

7. Greg Downy (2002: 497) draws on Barthes' concept of "grain of the voice" or the "materiality of the body" in the voice (1997) as source for understanding phenomenological embodiment in Brazilian *capoeira*.

8. Kay Shelemay, who first encountered my work on this topic, moved to Harvard University in the middle of my studies. As a result Mark Slobin advised my dissertation writing process.

9. J. T. Appavoo interview, Madurai, July 1, 1994.

10. Rev. Cannon Carol Hampton, Eulogy for Rev. J. Theophilus Appavoo, Oklahoma City, OK. November 5, 2005.

11. Pers. comm., Rev. Jacqulin Jothi, November 23, 2005. While this idea was obvious to me as a music scholar, it seemed to poignantly strike my non-musician friends while singing Appavoo's songs at his funeral.

INTRODUCTION

1. See Kriya Dictionary of Contemporary Tamil (Ramakrishnan 1992, 932). The Tamil nationalist poet Bharathiyar used *viḍutalai* with a clear secularist interpretation as the title of his song inspired by the French national anthem (composed in the French colony of Pondicherry) (S. Sowmya recording, *Bharathiyar Songs.* 1999, pers. comm. B. Balasubrahmaniyan). *Vīḍutalai* was also the title of the journal for the highly secularist anti-caste Self-Respect Movement (still published today). It is rarely used, and is not at all intended here, as synonymous with the sanskritic *moksha* or liberation from the cycle of death and rebirth.

2. Dr. Rev. M. Gnanavaram, telephone conversation with author, January 11, 2011.

3. A bi-gendered understanding of the qualities of God is common among Indian liberation theologians partly as a result of the influence of feminist theology. However, its use goes back in Tamil Christian hymnody to H. A. Krishna Pillai's nineteenth-century use of the Shaivaite reference to God "*amme appanē*," ("Mother-Father").

4. The first three points were taken from a statement by The Lutheran World Federation (2002), while I have added the fourth point regarding segregation, which the LWF indicates in their statement is a natural consequence of this discrimination: "Caste-based discrimination and similar forms of discrimination." www.lutheranworld.org/ . . . /OIAHR-Statement_on_Caste-based_Discrimination_22-03-2002.pdf. Accessed on August 19, 2009.

5. http,//www.imadr.org/geneva/2002/cerd2002.1.html. Committee on the elimination of racial discrimination. Sixty-first session/ Geneva, 5–23, August 2002. "Discrimination based on caste and similar forms of social hierarchy," Joint Statement. Accessed on June 6, 2006.

6. This precaution is based on the concept that the physical substances which make up the lower caste's basic nature is such that they are able to absorb the waste or impurities (whether bodily waste or air) of the upper castes, where as the lower castes are generally polluting to the upper and thus absorption across physical boundaries should be avoided.

7. Anupama Roa in *Representing Dalit Selfhood,* http://www.india-seminar.com/2006/558/558%20anupama%20rao.htm, found that Ambedkar first used the term "Dalit" in his newspaper *Bahishkrit Bharat.* S. Anand, publisher for Navayana Press, says that there is little unanimity as to its origins, but that it "derives from 'pad-dalit,' which means to 'grind down'/ 'crush down' and was used in relation to grains . . . So it conveys the meaning of totally ground down, and it was in this sense that Ambedkar is supposed to have used it" (e-mail to author, June 2, 2006).

8. The name "Dalit Panthers" was inspired by the American civil rights group, the Black Panthers. See V. T. Rajshekar (1987), *Dalit: The Black Untouchables of India,* for a contemporary comparison of the Dalit and African American struggles.

9. See Ambedkar's (1945) writing on the Pune Pact for a thorough critique of Gandhi in relation to caste issues.

10. In the rest of this book, I have attempted to use and explain the historical term within each period I discuss. However, generally I use the specific caste name, such as Paraiyar, or the term Dalit, which has been chosen by activists reflecting their present self-definition and their perspective on their present and historical place in Indian society. Those Christians I found who would most likely shy away from using the term Dalit to describe themselves are the middle- and lower-class outcastes with conservative middle-class aspirations.

11. Christians from outcaste jātis such as Paraiyar, Pallar, or Chakkiliyar tended to "be in the closet" about their caste identity, especially if they were middle-class urbanites. They would avoid all discussion of their identity unless they trusted me greatly or were a Dalit activist, in which case they proudly used the term Dalit to refer to themselves. Some said they were Christian, and had no caste.

12. See also Pullapilly (1976) for a case that describes the hegemony of caste hierarchy in Kerala but that shows that caste structure is not all pervasive. It also shows the interrelation of caste with religion, economics, political ideology, and activism and the possibility of changing the nature of caste through these variables.

13. See the description of the practice of "love feasts" or inter-caste dining among members of the American Madurai Mission in Chapter Three. Hudson (2000, 92–93) discusses both practical and theological justifications for caste separation developed among Christians. The non-Christians with whom the upper-caste converts wished to maintain their social status and familial relationships carefully observed the relationship between Vellalars (upper-caste non-Brahmin Tamils) and lower caste Christians in church ritual. Hudson (1997, 157) describes how Muslims and Hindus literally gazed at the Christian converts through the church windows. The result was separate seating within the church and communion order based on caste hierarchy. Upper castes also feared criticism if they ate with outcaste converts in community fellowship. Hudson further describes how non-Christian Indians understood Christianity as creating unclean and disorderly people because of the similarities between European Christian practices of eating meat and drinking alcohol and similar practices of outcastes that had long been seen as unclean.

14. Anglo-Indians, a very few Brahmins, Naidus, Vaniyars, Tevars, Servais, Kallars, Pallars, and Chakkiliyars make up the minor groups.

15. Appavoo (1993, 30), citing a study by Demel (in Raj 1990, 37), notes that seventy-two percent of the total female agricultural labor in Tamil Nadu is Dalit and eighty percent of Christian Dalits are landless. Furthermore eighty percent of Dalits live below the poverty line.

16. Elder's model was similar to, but earlier than, Louis Dumont's 1970 model. It is common in Tamil Nadu to only think of three *varna* categories, Brahmin, Śudra, and Avarna or outcaste. However, this puts all of the middle castes (Vellalars to Nadars) in one larger category, when the practice among them is to make great distinctions between "good" (non-polluting) Śudras and "polluting" Śudras. Thus I attempt to determine and reference the hierarchy used in each locale. Throughout Tamil Nadu the land-owning agricultural castes such as Vellalars, Counders, or Vaniyars may be considered Śudra, but are generally Brahmanical in practice. Some are vegetarian or

semi-vegetarian and generally hold great socio-economic power and status, particularly in the villages.

17. The high percentage of Nadars during this period is likely because of their concentration in urban areas as grocery wholesalers and store owners as well as their increasing dominance in Christian institutions like schools and the YMCA. In Northern districts of Tamil Nadu, such as North Arcot, the percentage of Dalit Christians is closer to ninety percent of the Christian population particularly in rural areas.

18. See Kent (2004, 17) in which she cites a 1938 study by J. S. Ponniah indicating that within the churches of the Madurai Church Council associated with the American Congregationalist Mission (ABCFM) sixty-six percent of the members were outcastes or Dalits, nineteen percent Nadars, and 1.8 percent Vellalars.

19. The largest Christian group under Elder's category of "Proprietors needing capital," were Nadars, who comprised 7.9 percent of this population, reflecting their domination of the grocery and many manufacturing industries. In contrast, 6.1 percent of Vellalars and 4.6 percent of Nadars were professionals. Only 1.7 percent of Paṟaiyars fell in that professional category.

20. Oddie indicates this increasing consciousness resulted from gradual changes over a lengthy period. Factors that significantly affected this consciousness were travel to other parts of the world as indentured workers (for example to Burma and Malaysia) and legal equality under British law as well as long term acquaintance with mission societies and the opportunity to get an education (1991, 159).

21. Ebe Sunder Raj in "Why the Dalit Seek Christ" (2003) finds that "the *Padial* system of untouchable slaves of Madras Presidency was fought valiantly by the workers of the Church Missionary Society in 1891, and it was through their efforts that the Padial Protection Law was enacted." http://eficor.org/publications/dristi_dec-mar03/dalitchrist.htm. Accessed July 18, 2006. Eliza Kent writes that through their association with foreign missionaries, "Christian converts also gained the right of access to public roads, exemption from extracted unpaid labor (*ūḻiyam*), and a regular day off from work to observe the Christian Sabbath" (Kent 2004, 3).

22. See chapter 2 for more detail on the effect of these movements on Tamil Christian priests and theologians.

23. Referencing the blues as a protest medium particularly for African American women in the 1920s and 1930s, Angela Davis argues that the blues may not have represented the expression of formal political dissent, yet "critical aesthetic representation of social problems must be understood as constituting powerful social and political acts" (1998, 101 and 113).

24. The Pulaya "lyric" (or *kīrttaṉai*), "Our slave work is done, our slave bonds are gone," is quoted in Samuel Mateer, *Native Life in Travancore* (London, 1883), 317–318. In *India Awakening* (New York, 1911, 89–90), Sherwood Eddy (American Madura Mission) referred to this as an old slave song heard in the Pulaya congregation in Nagarcoil. Webster (1992, 189n23) compiled this information.

25. We do, however, have ethnographic and oral historical evidence of early twentieth-century use of Christian folk music (generally outside of the village church building) among both Paṟaiyars near Aruppucottai and Nadars in Tirunelveli (interview with Rev. Dr. M. Thomas Thangaraj, March 12, 1997.).

26. The primary argument against ordination is that if a woman is menstruating she will pollute the altar. The rejection of women's ordination is particularly salient in the churches that have organized themselves denominationally around conservative caste identities, such as the Anglican Nadars. In most of the dioceses of the Church of South India since the mid 1990s women's ordination has been allowed.

27. See James Freeman, *Untouchable: An Indian Life History* (1979), for salient examples of blatant caste transgressions by upper castes when they deemed it convenient.

28. Through an analysis of gendered performance spaces (women inside and men outside) at a middle-class housewarming, I argue that the use of "classical Indian" style in domestic rituals, conservative dress, and reserved behavior, represent a morally conservative sensibility, and protect a newly middle class status within the interior domestic space (Sherinian 2007, 273).

29. C. S. Karunakaran interview, Karur, August 11, 1994.

30. The Dravidians of South India consciously distinguish themselves from the Northern Aryans and South Indian Brahmins. This difference is most acutely felt in language, Tamil, Malayalam, Telugu, and Kannada are languages of the Dravidian language family, separate from the Indo-Aryan Sanskrit, Hindi, and other North Indian languages.

31. Appavoo (1993, 330) quoting Antony Raj (1992).

1. HOW CAN THE SUBALTERN SPEAK?

1. I borrow the term "identifying culture" from ethnomusicologist Margaret Kartomi's important discussion of culture contact terminology (1981, 229).

2. Scruggs considers the reconceptualization of Christian practice through musical elements that were previously considered prohibited from use in the sacred context of Christianity. He studies the well known South American liberation theology mass, *La Misa Campesina Nicaragüense.*

3. Here I am not as concerned with individual style or the influence of individuals in performance or composition. While such culture brokers play a significant historical role in the production of performance procedures and style, I am more concerned with the propagation of meaning by larger cultural units. For a more thorough understanding of the strategic use of style by individual participants in Indian music, see Richard Wolf (1991).

4. I thank music theorist Sarah Reichardt for sharing with me her understanding of musical semiotics.

5. See Sherinian (2007) for an analysis of the way in which musical style is associated with the identities of Christian caste and class as an index of change among Tamil Christians. In particular I show how the transformations in performance practice of the *kīrttaṉai* by lower-caste Protestants reveals their aspirations for upward mobility and civil rights.

6. Untouchable Paṟaiyars, Pallars, and Chakkiliyars experienced a similar process of inculcation through the American Congregational missionaries. But in their case, they were inculcated to the musical values of the local elites transmitted to them through karnatak classical Christian music.

7. See T. M. Scruggs (2005, 91–92) for a similar construction of the idea of re-indigenization over time through continual engagement with local cultural elements.

8. The exception to this is the editing undertaken by the Christian Literature Society editorial committee (made up of progressive theologians) in the late 1980s to make some of the text less sexist and less anti-Hindu (Francis 1988). Some sanskritized Tamil words were replaced with more contemporary, accessible, de-sanskritized Tamil vocabulary.

9. See Amanda Weidman (2006) especially 180–191 for a discussion of the wider Tamil Isai movement and caste politics.

10. Appavoo, interview, Madurai, July 1, 1994.

11. One manifestation of this that I observed in Vedal village near Kanchipuram in 1999 was the (self-imposed) pressure placed upon male youth in a poor village congregation (where there was no organ) to spend money on an electronic keyboard in order to replicate Christian light music they had heard through cassettes.

12. Tamil Christian light music songs are often highly westernized in their use of simple functional harmony, guitar and keyboard instrumentation, and rhythm (using "waltz timing"—$\frac{3}{4}$ meter), while their vocal style remains indigenous and similar to film music. However, these songs are less influenced by local Tamil folk aesthetics than many Tamil film songs produced after the 1970s when the film music producer Ilaiyaraaja's folk style became popular. Their western pop sound makes them very attractive to urban middle-class Christians.

13. *Nāṭṭupuṟa isai* was used by Dr. K. A. Gunasakaran as the title of his book, *Nāṭṭupu Nikāṟkalaikal.* Joseph Palackal (pers. comm., Boston, July 3, 1997) asserts that the terms for folk music in Malayalam are very similar and are translated the same, *nātōtīppāttu* or *nātanpāttu* and *grāmīṇa gānangal.* They are translated respectively as "that which runs through the land," "song of the land," and "village song."

14. See Paul Green (1997) for a discussion of the negative association of folk music with untouchables, widows and women. Green also discusses the folk music genre of *oppāri* as a form of protest. For examples of ongoing prejudice against untouchables who play the *paṟai* drum and sing funereal laments, see Isabelle Clark-Deces (2005, 4).

15. The use of folk genres like the lullaby may be waning among the middle and upper classes, however (pers. comm. with Dilip Menon, May 29, 2004). In a speech given in Middletown, Connecticut on May 7, 2004, about propagating Tamil music abroad, the famous film composer Ilaiyaraaja asked the middle- and upper-middle-class immigrant Tamil community in attendance if they sang Tamil lullabies to their children as he had learned from his mother. The answer was no.

16. See Appavoo (1986) and Green (1997).

17. Nostalgia for rural landscape and village culture is aimed toward middle-class urban Dalits who have fled the village, and all its negative associations, physically and psychologically.

18. The *paṟai* is a frame drum played with the hands or played with two sticks, one of which is flat on one side.

19. In the process of funeral performance Paṟaiyar drummers inherently "re-pollute" themselves through being associated with the pollution of the dead body, and having to touch the body in order to pick up coins or rice placed on it as their payment.

20. For example Richard Wolf studied and wrote about style and karnatak *vina* and vocal music before studying tribal music of Nilgiris (2005); Carol Babiracki studied classical flute before focusing on tribal music in Jharkhand (2000–2001); Peter Manuel studied the semi-classical genre of *thumri* (1983 and 1989), before turning to the analysis of popular music and cassette culture; and Amy Catlin wrote about the karnatak *kriti* genre (1980) before studying an array of folk practices throughout India as well as the practices of African migrants to India called Sidis (2008).

21. It would be beneficial to the field for a scholar to pursue this subject further.

22. The "great" and "little" dichotomy is further reified in the classic anthropological literature of Redfield 1955, Marriott 1960, and Singer 1959.

23. Interview Appavoo, Madurai, July 1, 1994.

24. Appavoo's student Evangeline Anderson-Rajkumar has also applied his concepts of structural sin in her paper "Politicizing the Body, A Feminist Christology." The Asia Journal of Theology, April 2004.

25. Benjamin Inbaraj, interview, Madurandgam, July 16, 2002.

26. Gunadayalan, interview, Madarandagam, July 17, 2002.

2. SHARING THE MEAL

1. Rev. Benjamin Inbaraj, e-mail to author, March 5, 2005.

2. Benjamin Inbaraj, interview, Madarandagam, July 16, 2002.

3. See *Saraswativijayam* (1892) by the nineteenth-century outcaste writer from Kerala, Potheri Kunhambu, translated by Dilip Menon, for a tropic vision of redemption of both oppressing Syrian Christian landlord and untouchable Pulaya slave.

4. Johnson Jebakumar, interview, Andrewpuram, July 11, 2002.

5. Appavoo's degrees were many. He earned an Education Diploma from the Government Teacher's Training College in Vadalore (1959), a B.A. in History and Geography from the University of Madras (1963), an M.A. in Religion and Philosophy from Madurai Kamaraj University (TTS) (1975), a Bachelor of Divinity from Serampore University (1978), a Master of Theology from Edinburgh University in Scotland (1993), and an honorary doctorate from Gurukul Theological College (2004).

6. J. T. Appavoo, interview, Madurai, March 10, 1994.

7. In a letter written in 1829, Vedanayagam Sastriar differentiated Protestant music practices from the loud outdoor parade music used by Roman Catholics in their festivals. This included use of the long double reed *nāgasvaram*. See below for a full text of the letter (Hudson 2000, 149, 152). While this letter was written almost two hundred years after the Paravar conversions, it is likely that at this early point the Catholics used similar indigenous instruments to that which were used in Hindu *tēr* festivals. See Waghorne (2002) for a contemporary description of a Catholic *tēr* festival and a detailed comparison of the similarities and conscious differences from a Hindu *tēr* festival.

8. Letter of Fr. Laerzio to the Jesuit general on December 30, 1608. Quoted by D. Ferroli, *The Jesuits in Malabar,* I, 340, in Thekkedath (1982, 213).

9. The missionary John de Britto, for example, was martyred in 1693 after disregarding the warning of a local *setupati* (noble) not to convert people in Marava territory.

10. In 1762, Schwartz shifted his career and loyalties from the Danish mission to work as a diplomatic envoy for the British.

11. Ziegenbalg used a Tamil printing press beginning in 1713 sent from the Pietist center at Halle (Hudson 2000, 41). Hudson indicates further that the first printed books produced outside of Europe were Catholic Tamil writings and that there had been four Catholic printing presses in India since 1548 (2000, 41).

12. For an extensive discussion of this diverse milieu and Vedanayakam Sastriar's use of Tamil poetics, especially with the kuravañci genre, see Peterson (2002).

13. I believe that Devasagayam used these songs to evangelize, to communicate the Bible stories and attract listeners in the eighteenth century.

14. The second document, *Sadiausara Sambaveney* (Dialogue on the Difference of Caste), written in 1824, was combined with *Saditeratoo* to form a larger document sent in protest to the missionaries.

15. Timbrel is a small frame drum, possibly *kañjīra. Taboret* is a large frame drum, possibly the paṟai, the *tampannai,* or the double-headed *tavil.* Tumtum may be the paṟai, but more likely the *tasa* or *tunumpu,* a shallow dish/kettle drum played vertically with leather straps by Paṟaiyars along with the paṟai.

16. According to Sastriar, the CMS missionary J. C. Kohlhoff referred to the use of any instrument as heathenism, although Sastriar could easily support their "simple and classical" use with biblical references such as the 150th Psalm. Kohlhoff also judged as an act of "pride and blasphemy" Sastriar's use of the traditional practice of Tamil poets "signing" their lyrics by registering their names in the final stanzas (Hudson 2000, 153).

17. See Waghorne (2002) and Bayly (1989).

18. *Nāgasvaram* and *tavil* are associated with the karnatak music in their performance by members of the Isai Vellalar community in Brahmanical temple contexts, and their use of raga and tala. However, lower caste musicians also use *nāgasvaram* and *tavil* in folk contexts. See Yoshitaka Terada (1997).

19. Gurupatham (1993) studied seventy-three *kīrttaṉai* or lyrics from the thirteenth edition of the *Tamil Hymnal* (1980). Of these, thirty *kīrttaṉai* use ten different ragas that fall under the twenty-eighth *melakarta, harikambodji;* thirteen *kīrttaṉai* use five different ragas under the twenty-second *melakarta, kharahara-priya;* and ten *kīrttaṉai* use three different ragas under the twenty-ninth *melakarta, sankarabharanam.* Five of these are in the *melakarta sankarabharanam,* which has a scale equivalent to the western major. Nine *kīrttaṉai* use four different ragas under the twentieth *melakarta, natabhairavi.* Four *kīrttaṉai* use the eighth *melakarta, todi,* and one uses the sixty-fifth, *mechakalyani.* Walter Kaufman (1976, xxxiii), in his extensive study of South Indian ragas, states that the six basic scales or *mela*-ragas (29, 28, 22, 20, 15, and 8) and their *janya* ragas, or subordinate forms, "are particularly favored by South Indian [Hindu] performers and their audiences." That these have the most *janya* ragas, he adds, indicates their importance and popularity.

20. Translation by Samuel Timothy.

21. Gurupatham conducted his study of 350 people in the five district councils of the CSI Trichy/Tanjavur diocese. It is not clear if the study was conducted in both rural and urban areas.

22. Ziegenbalg claimed that hundreds of Muslims and Hindus observed Tranquebar church services through the windows and doors of the church. Thus seating within the church and communion order held great significance to the wider milieu including those non-Christians with whom the Vellalars wished to maintain their social status (Hudson 2000, 51).

23. Eating together is a very intimate act in Tamil culture. Thus to associate with one of a different nature, that is one who gets food from a different source (the Paṟaiyars eat beef and most Vellalars are vegetarian) might lead one to become attached to them as *paṟakkam*. Getting too close to someone of a lower caste would make one become of that caste, thereby threatening one's relationship with family and caste, which is essential to Tamil personhood. See Trawick (1990, 99) who argues that habituation is hard to overcome and develops from exposure to and absorption of certain things so deeply that they become one's own personality.

24. See Sherinian (2005a, 146–147) for an analysis of Sastriar's *kīrttaṉai* on sin.

25. Emmanuel Jebarajan, interview, Madurai, August 30, 1994.

26. M. Thomas Thangaraj, telephone interview, Boston to Atlanta, March 17, 1997.

27. Emmanuel Jebarajan, interview, Madurai, August 30, 1994.

28. See Hardgrave (1969) for an extensive study of the Sanar caste and its shift in caste status from lower Śudra to upper-caste Kshatriya over the nineteenth century. See William Pinch (1996) for other cases in North India involving upward mobility and caste name/status change.

29. In the old Tranquebar Mission (1706 to 1825), fourteen Malabarians [Tamils] were ordained, all of whom were Vellalars (Hudson 2000, 29). The exception is the presence of outcaste catechists, especially when they were used to convert and serve all-outcaste villages or congregations.

30. The only exception I have found to this was Rev. Emmons White and his wife Ruth who in the early twentieth century promoted both karnatak music, especially among young people in their boarding schools, and the use of folk dances like *oyilāṭṭam* and *kummi* in villages, to transmit the Bible stories and the *kīrttaṉai*.

31. Page seven of a letter written by Edward Webb, December 31, 1852, from Dindigul to Rufus Anderson, secretary of the ABCFM in Boston. From Letters and Papers of ABCFM, Vol. 226, Madura Mission, vol. 2. Letter begins on page 440 of the collection.

32. Furthermore, Shem Vedanayakam recounts that 300 of Vedanayakam Sastriar's songs were published, whereas Webb writes that there were only 150 compositions in Tamil meter.

33. From the minutes of the October 3, 1849, meeting of the American Madura Mission at Tirumangalam, #286 and #381. Archives of the American Board of Commissioners of Foreign Missions (ABCFM), Lamont Library, Harvard University, Cambridge, MA.

34. Interview with C. J. Karunakaran, September 11, 1994.

35. Likewise, in 1850 American Congregationalist missionaries consciously shifted policy to the primary use of Tamil in seminary education. However, one of the motivating factors was to limit the knowledge of English and non-theological Christian

matters of their native clergy in order to keep them dependent on the mission for jobs and to maintain a class system between the natives and missionaries. Harris argues that while the ABCFM missionaries wanted to Christianize the Indians, they wanted to limit their material and "worldly" aspirations, particularly through limiting their access to English. See Cox (2002) for further examples of this patronizing attitude by missionaries.

36. This movement toward indigenization is articulated in an 1852 letter from Rev. Edward Webb to Rufus Anderson in his attempt to gain ABCFM administrative support for the publication of the first Tamil Hymnal.

37. Called Mrs. Echard's Day School, it was a free school and the first in the district besides those for girls of the Devadasi caste, classical temple dancers (Nautch dancers) who were normally educated (Chandler 1912, 56). In 1836 there were sixty-five girls of a total of 1,214 students. By 1842 they had two hundred girls enrolled (1912, 56). They also eventually started a girls' boarding school partly to educate girls to become pious wives of the future male pastors and catechists. Many of the girls also became teachers. The caste breakdown at one early point in this school showed that fifty-six of ninety-four students were Paṟaiyars, Pallars, or untouchables.

38. Dennis Hudson, pers. comm., November 5, 1997. The CMS and the Congregationalists were both Calvinist, which accounts for their common anti-caste policies; however, the CMS still embraced the strict Episcopal order in liturgy whereas the Congregationalists (and LMS) had "free" orders. In the Tamil context the freer the order of worship the more likely the congregation or mission was to use *kīrttaṉai* and Tamil music.

39. This is conjecture, shared by Dennis Hudson (pers. comm., April 17, 1997), as we have no historical records of these opinions from Paṟaiyars. We do have American missionary observations that the villagers responded very positively when the *kīrttaṉai* were introduced after 1853.

40. This edition (Francis, 1988) lists 112 individual contributors. Vedanayakam Sastriar composed fifty-eight of the 448 pieces.

41. Ruth White writes of hiring a skilled karnatak music teacher (likely Srinivasan Iyengar) in her November 1, 1929, letter to the American Board in Boston (ABCFM Archive, Cambridge).

42. In the Tamil tradition of naming a child after a grandparent, Theophilus Appavoo got his name from Edward Appavoo.

43. See David (1986, 28) for details on these doctrinal standards.

44. David (1986, 100). Edward may also have been a Catholic in that as many as fifty percent of the converts in 1880 were former Roman Catholics (1986, 106) and Theophilus Appavoo considered this possibility as several of his relatives were Catholic.

45. This story was told again by Theophilus Appavoo's father James David to Theophilus's daughter Adri at her grandmother's funeral in 1994.

46. Appavoo, interview, September 22, 1994.

47. Ibid.

48. Edward's individual "rational" conversion may also fit the profile of the typical convert of the Arcot Mission of the Reformed Church in America during this period in the Vellore area. Grafe (1990, 52) emphasizes the mission's concern with personal conversion.

49. This also points to the cultural affinity between these groups as missionaries were considered by many upper castes to be untouchables because they "ate flesh and moved with untouchables" (David 1986, 113). Also see Moon (2001, 11) who details how Mahars worked as cooks for European Military officials and missionaries.

50. Other societies only required participation in love feasts by their mission employees.

51. There is evidence of at least one middle-class Paṟaiyar community who were very successful goldsmiths in the town of Mayiladuthurai (a central east coast town) near Nagapattinam. C. Ayyathurai Patthar (a Paṟaiyar) accumulated so much wealth that he was made a trustee of an orthodox Brahmin temple, Sri Parimala Renganathar Koil at Thiruvizhanthur. This case reinforces the need for fluidity in the understanding of caste and class status (Gajendran Ayyathurai, pers. comm., July 31, 2006).

52. Report of the Third Decennial Missionary Conference held in Bombay, December 1892 and January 1893, Webster (1992, 183).

53. John Webster, lecture, Overseas Mission Center (OSMC), New Haven, January 29, 1993. Webster points out that these Dalit converts were not "outcasted" by their kin for converting, unlike many upper-caste Tamils. They continued to marry Hindu cousins and participate in kinship responsibilities.

54. The Telugu *kīrttaṉai* hymn book was compiled by Jacob Chamberlain, a well known AMRCA missionary active during the 1880s in the Vellore area when Edward converted. Chamberlain was also a distant ancestor of mine on my mother's side. We both trace our ancestries back to William Chamberlain (c. 1630 in America). Jacob Chamberlain Letter Book, box 271, p. 249, Yale Divinity School archives.

55. In the "Virundu Parimāruṟadu" (Meal Sharing Song) of his *Village Music Liturgy,* Appavoo uses the metaphor of Jesus as a *nattuvaitiyam* preparing a medicine of liberation (the Eucharist) in the upper room where Jesus and the disciples had their last supper. For Appavoo, a *nattuvaitiyam* is a respectable traditional occupation for a Dalit that should be reclaimed against the forces of modernity.

56. Likely Simon had another non-Christian name for the first twenty years of his life before conversion, but this is not known.

57. Outcastes did whatever they could to educate their children, even if it meant going hungry (Khare 1984).

58. Samuel was eighty when he died in 1966. J. T. Appavoo, interview, Madurai. Sept 22, 1994.

59. See Freeman (1979, 67) for an image of being forced to sit on the veranda of the school building to listen separated from children of higher castes. Dilip Menon (pers. comm.) also confirmed this common practice. Also see Khare (1984, 71) *The Untouchable as Himself* for a discussion of the importance and value of various levels of education for Chamars in Lucknow, especially education beyond high school as a means to social mobility. A Chamar clerk who became a progressive songwriter sang, "Education—unlimited—is that democratic right of the deprived." He proclaimed further that, "The caste Hindus also cannot deny anymore. Equality in educational opportunity is now the root of all other equalities" (1984, 71).

60. At this time, there was no frequent transportation from Cuddalore to Pondicherry. Appavoo believes Samuel had at least six carts. He hired workers who would take the carts in the morning and deliver the day's earnings in the evening.

61. The Dalit author Bama's father also served in the army, an opportunity that helped many Dalits out of severe poverty (2000). See Constable (1997) for the history of Dalits, including many Christian Dalits serving in the military, and the development of a sense of martial Kshatriya identity. Also see Moon (2001, 46) who says that a Mahar (Maharashtan Dalit) from every household of Kamathi went to work for the army as cooks, butlers, washermen, or drivers.

62. Many Dalits had migrated to the hill stations to work on the tea plantations in the late nineteenth and early twentieth centuries. Through Christian contacts, many found cash-wage work in the tea plantations of the western Ghats, earning enough money to return to the plains, pay off their debts, buy land for themselves, and invest in their children's education (Manickam 1982, 82). C. J. Ponnaiya, a Paṟaiyar convert from the first mass conversion village called Perunkarunaipalayam (the "village of great grace"), said the tea plantations hired European management that treated the workers well, giving fair wages and good medical care (interview, Dharapuram, June 15, 1994).

63. The production of Tamil talkies began in Madras studios in 1934. A few Brahmin women or women from the Devadasi community who had married Brahmins and others of "respectable families" had begun to star in screen roles lending an aura of respectability to the field that led to several of the most famous classical singers of the day—including M. S. Subbalakshmi—to act. Singing ability played a greater role in their success than did acting (Baskaran 1981, 170). Backup singers became more common in the 1940s. Also see Amanda Weidman (2006).

64. Many untouchables did, however, perform in both the Madras and Bombay film studios as instrumentalists or studio musicians for they had learned to play Western instruments, and had studied music theory and Western notation in Christian institutions. They remained, however, anonymous to the public. See Booth (2008).

65. Appavoo, interview, Madurai, July 1, 1994.

66. Ibid.

67. Ibid. This is Appavoo's perception of Naina Pillai with which others may not agree. See Yoshitaka Terada (2000) for the history of the Isai Vellalar caste, who are hereditary temple musicians, and their struggles for equal status as karnatak musicians with Brahmins.

68. The Self-Respect Movement rested on five pillars: 1) No god; 2) No religion; 3) No Gandhi; 4) No Congress; and 5) No Brahmins (Ryerson 1988, 87). E. V. Ramaswamy's anti-religious stance began after the Vaikom incident of 1924 when some members of lower castes had changed religion to be able to walk on upper-caste streets but had still been attacked and killed. In other words, becoming a Christian or Muslim did not eradicate untouchability and its oppression.

69. C. R. W. David, interview, Madurai, April 25, 1994. Many of the older theologians at TTS (such as Dyanandan Francis and Lawrence Adigular) were atheists for some time during this period but came back to the church, bringing with them their values of indigenization and equality.

70. Mariyanandam received a conservatory degree from the Annamalai University Music College. He studied with the famous T. N. Swaminathan Pillai. Pillai also taught members of the Devadasi community such as my teacher T. Viswanathan who became nationally and internationally recognized for his skill.

71. Among the theologian/Tamil scholar/composers of this generation are V. P. K. Sundaram, Sathiya Sathchi, Poon Dinakrin, D. A. Danapandian, and Dyanandan Francis.

72. For example, V. P. K. Sundaram emphasized the roots of Tamil Isai and the contribution of Tamils to karnatak music in his Tamil treatise on the *Silapadikaram*. Lawrence Adigular, a Tamil professor at TTS, taught that in the ancient Tamil grammar book *Tolkappiyum*, music is a category of language.

73. Letter from Emmons White, written July 18, 1922, to the American Board in Boston, confirms the fear of Anglican domination. ABCFM Archives, Cambridge.

74. See Rajaiah and Kumaresan (1970) for the history of the negotiations.

75. My evidence is the recent trend in the late 1990s and early 2000s toward local parishes splitting apart, often along caste lines. Moreover, in several larger cities a handful of traditional Anglican congregations remained separate from the CSI although their priests are ordained as CSI ministers.

76. Appavoo, interview, Madurai, September 21, 1994.

77. Ibid.

78. Ibid.

79. Appavoo also sometimes attended and participated in music making at the local Arcot Lutheran Church in Cuddalore, which had traditionally taken a stronger stance against caste prejudice (pers. comm., David Rajendaren, Madurai, December 8, 2011.

80. *Visuvāsigal* is literally a loyal person of faith; the people in the congregation who had come for the program.

81. Appavoo, interview, Madurai, March 10, 1994.

82. Ibid.

83. Ibid.

84. Ibid. See Menon (1994) for a discussion of the history of how the Indian Marxist movement led by upper castes in India conflated caste with class therefore avoiding any need to transform the caste system. Menon argues that capitalism has helped the upper castes consolidate their strength.

85. Appavoo declared this was "great for a small town like Cuddalore." J. T. Appavoo, interview, Madurai, March 10, 1994.

86. While Chinniah discontinued this practice of fusion, many others continued to accompany the raga (modal) based *kīrttaṉai* with harmony to the point that it has become the dominant practice in urban churches.

87. J. T. Appavoo, interview, Madurai, March 10, 1994.

88. Ibid.

89. Ibid.

90. Ibid.

91. J. T. Appavoo, interview, Madurai, September 21, 1994. The lyrics in the 1978 TTS Carol Service program song number 8 read, "*ammā mariyammā koñjam sollammā*" (Mother Mary, say a little bit), "*ayyā mēypparayyā koñjam keḷumayyā*" (he is the liberator).

92. Appavoo, interview, Madurai, March 10, 1994.

93. Ibid.

94. Appavoo, interview, Madurai, September 21 1994.

95. Ibid.

96. The song "Āṇḍavanē Eṅga Āṭṭiḍaiyan" also called "Ēla Ēla Ēlēla Āṇḍavanē" is #39 in the 1993 TTS song book *Puttuyir Pādalhal* (David 1993).

97. Appavoo, interview, Madurai, September 21, 1994.

98. Ibid. All three of these castes are lower castes, but not Dalits.

99. Ibid. This reflects his song-writing experience of needing to have deep feelings about something in order to gain the inspiration to compose lyrics and a song.

100. Appavoo, interview, Madurai, March 10, 1994. Appavoo believes the term "Dalit" was not introduced at TTS until about 1987 when the principal Gnana Robinson helped Danny Gnanasakaran start the Dalit Liberation Movement.

101. Ibid.

102. Ibid.

103. Mohan Larbeer, interview, Madurai, February 1, 1994.

3. PARAṬṬAI'S THEOLOGY

1. Appavoo's painting of an indigenous image of the second coming of Christ, which hangs in the library of TTS, is illustrative. His Christ is a Dalit woman playing the paṟai drum. She leads her united community as they follow playing other folk instruments. Christ the liberator is portrayed as "pariah" and female—those most oppressed in Indian society.

2. Since the early 2000s TTS has been holding ten-day workshops at the Rural Theological Institute for second-year students in which they study their choice of folk performing arts, including paṟai drumming. A significant number of non-Dalit students choose not to study paṟai because they cannot escape the mental attitude that the drum is polluted. John Jayaharan challenges such students that they should not engage with it until they are prepared for an internal caste transformation by saying, "Don't touch it, it will liberate you." Pers. comm. John Jayaharan, Madurai, December 12, 2011.

3. Pers. comm., S. Jebarajan, October 2005.

4. The phrase *ammaiyappā* has been used in indigenized Christian lyrics since at least the nineteenth century when, in the most famous example, H. A. Krishna Pillai borrowed it from Vaishnavite traditions for use in Christian *kīrttaṉai,* particularly number 132 (*jenmamār karuvilē*). Francis (1988).

5. The Holy Spirit here is also described as *sūriyan* or sun, a common metaphor from Indian religion and philosophy. The rising sun is also an identifying symbol of hope on the flag (*koḍi*) of the Dravida Munnettra Kazhagam (D. M. K.), one of the original Tamil non-Brahmin Dravidian political organizations. Appavoo uses *ottumaya,* or unity, extensively in his songs to emphasize this essential value among the oppressed.

6. Appavoo, lecture, Nagercoil, September 20, 1994.

7. In our interview, Appavoo said people differentiate themselves from Jesus saying that he can go where other people cannot. Appavoo did not clarify this, but he may have meant that many Tamil Christians believe "Jesus can go to heaven whereas I, as just a human full of sin, cannot," an idea that reinforces karmic concepts of the inherent sinfulness of untouchablity.

8. Appavoo, interview, Madurai, July 18, 2004.

9. Through Brahmanical mythological constructions of the deity hierarchies, the implication of lower status has been associated with some popular Tamil gods like Murugan, who married a lower-caste woman and was constructed as the less clever son of Shiva, compared to his brother Ganesh (Appavoo 1986, 71). Although Murugan was the stronger of the two brothers, when put to a test to determine who could go around the universe faster than the other, Ganesh won the competition. Murugan jumped on his peacock and road around the universe. His pot-bellied brother Ganesh instead cleverly encircled his parents, Shiva and Parvati, who are considered the embodiment of the universe. Appavoo believes this story is used to degrade Murugan, making him look foolish in the eyes of the Tamil folk who see the god as challenging the caste system. Counter myths have been constructed among the people, however, to protest the dharmic degredation of Tamil culture proscribed by the Hindu lawgiver Manu (Appavoo 1986, 72).

10. See also Borg (1994, 53–56) and Joachim (1969).

11. The word for sin in this passage is *ūttai,* which literally means foul-smelling (body) waste (Ramakrishnan, Kriya Dictionary 1992, 164). Thus the metaphor of cleaning away sin is appropriate here. C. J. Fuller's (1992) discussion of the identification of the Tamil goddess with rivers and their support of both human and agricultural fertility grounds the source of this metaphor in rural religious symbolism.

12. My conservative Brahmin music guru reprimanded me for not speaking "good" or clean Tamil when, out of habit, I used the word *sōṟu* for rice. I first learned to call rice *sōṟu* from Mary, my lower-class Dalit Christian cook.

13. Appavoo, interview, Madurai, August 18, 1994.

14. Ibid.

15. Paper given by Radhika Iyer, Conference on Religion in South India, Toronto, June 14, 1997.

16. Appavoo, interview, Madurai, August 18, 1994.

17. Temperature is an important aspect of Hindu rituals. Foods are classified as hot and cold (Brenda Beck 1969), and the village goddesses, particularly unmarried ones, are considered hot, needing animal sacrifices to cool and placate them. In Hindu mythology heat is ambiguous. It can be destructive, yet creative.

18. Appavoo also described that he used a husky voice as a rural code and onomatopoetic device when he sang about the breeze of the coconut grove. Appavoo, interview, Madurai, August 18, 1994.

19. Other important publications include *Towards a Dalit Theology,* by M. E. Prabhakar (1988), *Emerging Dalit Theology,* by Xavier Irundayaraj (1990), *Reader in Dalit Theology,* by Arvind Nirmal (1991), *Indigenous People, Dalits,* by James Massey (1994), *Christianity and Dalits,* by Sathianathan Clarke (1998), and the recent anthology that includes chapters by Dalit faculty from TTS and the Chennai Diocese, *Frontiers of Dalit Theology,* edited by V. Devasahayam (1997). *Frontiers of Dalit Theology* includes two articles by J. T. Appavoo.

20. Many lower-caste and Dalit activists, such as the author Kancha Ilaiah who wrote *Why I Am Not a Hindu: A Sudra Critique of Hindutva Philosophy, Culture, and Political Economy* (1994), reject being called Hindu and having been appropriated into the Hindu fold. They argue that their religious practice, deities, and origins are com-

pletely different from Brahminical Hinduism. Most unpoliticized lower-caste people, on the other hand, simply accept the term as applied to them by the social and political system.

21. While faculty members at English language ecumenical seminaries like the United Theological College in Bangalore teach Dalit theology, their emphasis on direct praxis (action and reflection) and the production of mediums of expression for Dalit theology that can reach the populations most in need of emancipation becomes limited by issues of linguistic and social distance (class) between the majority of these students and their vernacular-speaking congregations. In these contexts Dalit theology is more theoretical than contextual practice.

22. Most of the TTS faculty, including Appavoo, read Paulo Freire's *Pedagogy of the Oppressed* in the late 1970s and early 1980s. Frieire's method of engaging the oppresed had a significant impact on the TECCA program. Pers. comm. John Jayaharan, December 12, 2011.

23. From the TTS Dalit Resource Centre membership pamphlet published in the early 2000s.

24. Beginning in the late 1990s, Appavoo published in the newsletter of the Dalit Resource Centre at TTS a series of short stories he called *Paraṭṭaiyin Davū* or *Paraṭṭai's Lies.* The title reflects his strategy of reversing the degraded value of folklore. That is, on the surface we believe that only lies can come from a Paraṭṭai (disheveled fellow). But like the Tamil folk saying, "In the eyes of a poor man, I saw God," Paraṭṭai intends his audience to believe the truth actually comes from those with the least authority or "knowledge."

25. Paraṭṭai comments in this recitation of the myth that he is "just shifting my myth from the ancient times to the modern times."

26. Paraṭṭai laughs and says, "*using the values that people have, you know.*" I then asked, "Do we *want* to eat 5 star chocolate?" to which he replied, "No, it is, my purpose, that's very important, my purpose and my audience. I calculate my audience, my audience has these values that 5 *star* is a great food. If I say *kañji* [rice gruel] then they won't give any value to that" (interview, July 1, 1994).

27. This appears to reference the story of the women who discovered Jesus' body gone from the grave, and then believed it was the risen Christ when he appeared to them. They did not need direct confirmation from God, as might be expected from God speaking directly to an individual.

28. Appavoo, interview, July 1, 1994, Madurai.

29. Appavoo defined it more specifically as a vessel with water kept on a stove in order to cook rice. July 1, 1994.

30. In the *oru olai* myth, food literally dropped from the heavens.

31. See Appavoo's *Village Music Liturgy,* "Sāmiya Vaṇaṅguṛadu" (Invocation).

32. Appavoo, interview, Madurai, July 1, 1994.

33. Ibid.

34. Ibid.

35. Ibid.

36. Ibid.

37. Ibid.

38. See the explanation of Appavoo's holistic neo-Marxian social analysis system of EPSI-PEGS in the Introduction.

39. Appavoo, interview, Madurai, July 1, 1994.

40. Ibid.

41. Ibid.

42. Ibid.

43. Ibid.

44. Ibid.

45. Ibid.

46. Appavoo, interview, Madurai, July 1, 1994.

47. Appavoo, lecture given to Basic Christian Communities at Nagercoil, September 20, 1994.

48. See Sherinian (2005a) and Hudson (2000) for a discussion of the concept of *paṟakkam* or attachment in Tamil culture.

49. Appavoo, lecture given to Basic Christian Communities at Nagercoil, September 20, 1994.

50. Appavoo, sermon given at TTS, Madurai, July 24, 1994.

51. Appavoo, interview, Madurai, March 10, 1994.

52. See Appavoo's *Village Music Liturgy,* "Lord's Prayer."

53. Appavoo, interview, Madurai, July 1, 1994.

54. Appavoo, interview, Madurai, March 10, 1994.

55. Appavoo, sermon delivered to students in the TTS summer music camp, Madurai, May 5, 1994.

56. Appavoo, interview, Madurai, August 18, 1994.

57. Although Appavoo's main point here is class analysis, it is interesting to note the importance of the deity's vehicle as a common theme borrowed from Hinduism.

58. Appavoo, lecture given to Basic Christian Communities at Nagercoil, September 20, 1994.

59. I witnessed such a scene at a Christian wedding in Erode in 1993. Poor people and beggars were sifting through the leftovers on banana leaves piled as garbage outside the wedding hall. They were collecting rice and meat and packaging it up to take with them.

60. Appavoo, lecture given to Basic Christian Communities at Nagercoil, September 20, 1994.

61. Aaron was a wealthy member of the Vellalar caste baptized by Ziegenbalg in 1718. He served as a catechist in the city and villages in the Tanjore area before his ordination. Interview with Sundar Clarke, Madras, August 8, 1994.

62. Muslims made up approximately thirty percent of the electorate before partition in 1947 and thus if combined with an untouchable and tribal electorate (twenty-four percent of the population) could have formed a majority over the middle- and upper-caste Hindus.

63. Clarke argues further that the agenda for Indian Christian theology was heavily influenced by the ideology of the Brahmo Samaj movement and reflected a dialogue between Christianity and Brahmanism (1998, 37). Sugirtharajah (1993, 1) refers to this as the "Sanskrit captivity" of the national church that replaced the former Western colonial hegemony. See Sherinian 1998 for an extensive discussion of the canonization

of classical Tamil Music and literature as a symbol of indigenous identity in the late nineteenth and early twentieth centuries.

64. I refer theoretically to Appavoo's book *Folklore for Change* (1986). My reception study revealed that Appavoo's songs were in use by Tamil Christians and secular social activists at Clarke's field sites in the Karunguzhi area in the early 1980s. Clarke's greater focus on non-Christian Dalit practices in his fieldwork may have prevented him from recognizing or investigating the impact of Appavoo's songs, while Clarke did become fully aware of them after I took a class with him at Harvard Divinity School in 1995. This was three years before his book *Dalits and Christianity: Subaltern Religion and Liberation Theology in India* was published in 1998.

65. Webster (1992, 189) found the Punjabi hymn in J. F. W. Yongson, *Forty Years of the Punjab Mission of the Church of Scotland* (269–270), and the Pulaya lyric in Samuel Mateer, *Native Life in Travancore* (London, 1883, 317–318). In *India Awakening* (1911, 89–90).

66. See Appavoo's communication theories on alternative media for the oppressed in *Folklore for Change* (1986, 2–25).

67. The practice of whipping is also discussed by Clarke (1998, 103). He references a Dalit song that describes the goddess as present in the *neem* leaves used for driving out women's afflictions.

68. This song was recorded in 1993 on cassette and distributed nationally in India by members of the Student Christian Movement.

69. Clarke (1998,119) says that the paṟai drum is referred to as the big or *periya* drum as a means to reconstruct its identity as positive. This indirect strategy of positive inversion was Appavoo's intention during the 1980s when "Allēlūyā" was composed, an early stage of his theological career. By the early 2000s he had become even more direct.

70. Clarke indicates that the *uḍukkai* (or *uḍukku*) and *bambai* (or *pamba*) drums are made of goat skin (not as polluting as cow) and are used by priests and their immediate ritual assistants (1998, 110).

71. Clarke does not discuss the rise in economic status and change of subjectivity by many Dalits and Nadar Christians who were given access to education and left the villages (many rejecting its culture in the process) and their changing subjectivity. Thus an uniformed reader of his work may assume all Dalit Christians are poor villagers.

72. Appavoo has been highly influenced by Dalit feminism and the global feminist theological discourse as taught and discussed at TTS. However, he rarely cites any such sources in his written work. This may be because he places his writing in the context of communications theory. Therefore the connections made in this chapter, and any misrepresentations therein, are mine.

73. Townes (1995, 105) says, "By 1870, color increasingly divided the Black community. Lighter skinned worshipers split from the African Methodist Episcopal Church to form their own denomination—Colored Methodist Episcopal (later changed to Christian Methodist Episcopal). Fair skinned bishops were the rule in the CME church."

74. Normative Church is the ideal Church or the way the Church "should be."

75. Gayle Murchison and Eileen Hayes, pers. comm., July 5, 2005.

76. Jeff Titon, pers. comm., July 5, 2005.

77. Also see Appavoo's interpretation of the wedding at Canaan at which Jesus waits to turn the water into wine so that it can go to the poor people after all the wealthy people have had their fill or "eaten high on the hog." Oscar J. Jordan describes the chitlin circuit as "a string of music venues in the South that sold chitlins' and other soul food dishes." http://www.soul-patrol.com/funk/jh_chitlin.htm. Accessed July 4, 2005.

78. bell hooks preaches that "we need to call attention to those black artists who successfully attract diverse audiences without pandering to a white supremacist consumer market while simultaneously creating a value system where acquisition of wealth and fame are not the only measures of success" (hooks 1990, 39).

4. ETHNOGRAPHY AS TRANSFORMATIVE MUSICAL DIALOGUE

1. Literally, "noise problem" (*pōṭaratal*).

2. Another meaning for the word *pālā* translated here as child, is protector. Both meanings apply to this context.

3. The TTS Centre for Social Analysis actively involves student interns in direct action to empower women. This includes union organizing of women construction, sanitary, and domestic workers, organizing slum dwellers, scavengers, rural women, and women affected by male alcoholism and violence.

4. Since 2009 feminist theology as a separate course was taken out of the B. D. curriculum to be replaced by a more holistic integration of feminist perspectives in each seminary subdiscipline (i.e., New Testament, church history, missiology, etc.). However, the application of these feminist perspectives is now left up to the individual instructor who may or may not have the ideological will or training to apply these. The Master of Theology curriculum still includes courses in feminist theology, the women's movement in India, caste, class, and patriarchy as well as social analysis.

5. *Eḍuppu* is the place in the tala, or rhythmic cycle, where the lyrics begin. The entrance is commonly either on the beat or $\frac{1}{4}$, $\frac{1}{2}$, or $\frac{3}{4}$ after the first beat of the cycle.

6. TTS founders used the term "contextualization" as a primary part of their ethos (Amirtham 1990, 60–64), although Christian theologians often use the terms "indigenization" or "inculturation" today (Deitrich 2002).

7. The majority of TTS students did not grow up in urban slums. While a small percentage may have grown up in villages, they are likely the children of schoolteachers and thus are lower class, but not poor.

8. Kambar Manickam, interview, Madurai, August 3, 1994.

9. See Larbeer and Alexandar 2000, on Dalit art.

10. Kambar Manickam, interview, Madurai, August 3, 1994.

11. My interpretation of the use of white clothing in this context as representing angels and a sense of purity is that it is a Western idea commonly held by Tamil Christians. In the Tamil Hindu context white is usually an inauspicious color worn, for example, by widows.

12. The keyboard solo after the *anupallavi* used a buzzing synthesizer timbre and a dotted quarter-note pattern that imitates a mosquito flying back and forth.

13. I observed and videotaped an example of such discrimination at a tea stall in a village near Madurai in 1994. Further, a Dalit drumming teacher and I experienced this differentiation between us in a village near Paramagudi in 2008. I was also told that TTS faculty members observed such discrimination about fifteen years earlier in the Kanyakumari district. Other informants have told me that in many Brahmin households they keep a separate set of dishes and tumblers for non-Brahmin guests and especially for servants or occasional workers.

14. Nabokov also discusses male ritual musicians called *pampaikkarar* who sing and play percussion instruments to induce the possessed into trance. The trance, which takes the form of a dance, is intended to allow for direct communication between the musicians and the possessing demon (1997, 303).

15. Former TTS principal, Kambar Manickam emphasized that Appavoo's theology draws and centers upon the essential symbol and role of women in all aspects of village/Dalit culture and religion. Kambar Manickam, interview, Madurai, August 3, 1994.

16. I was away for several weeks before the service and no one else among the organizers knew music well enough or had the time to follow through on the idea. Within a few years after my research a female student instrumentalist did play often at TTS.

17. Translation by Britto Vincent.

18. Some people believe that a pan-regional form of spoken Tamil does not exist. However, Appavoo claimed that he used a common spoken Tamil understandable to all. Gandhi Mary, a Tamil scholar, analyzed his songs concluding that he did use a common spoken poetic Tamil that draws on the hegemonic spoken form that is drawn from the Madurai area dialect (pers. comm. Dr. Gandhi Mary, December 18, 2011). In this traditionally Methodist area from which Rajaiah comes there had been a long-standing practice of freedom in liturgical creation. Rajaiah told me that not everyone would welcome these songs, but many villagers would because they are illiterate. Rajaiah only knew a little harmonium, but said he would teach the melodies using the cassette recording of these songs. He also plans to use the karnatak TIVP, but to include a number of the folk songs from the TTS songbook *Puttuyir Pāḍalhal* (1993, #8 "Bumiyil Vāṟuṟa," #10 "Vaṟipaḍuvōm Varir," #11 "Allēlūyā Allēlūyā," and #13 "Āṅḍvar Iyēsuva," by Mohanraj Peter). Rajaiah, interview, April 12, 1994.

19. Rajaiah believed that Appavoo's service was too difficult because, although the words are in spoken Tamil, they are still not words used in daily language. I have also heard this criticism from others and found that villagers did not always pick up his songs upon first hearing, while they usually did on second hearing (see chapter 5).

20. Although Rajaiah believed music is essential and powerful he was not completely comfortable with the format of a fully sung liturgy because he believed it does not leave enough room for meditation.

21. Rajaiah, interview, Madurai, April 12, 1994.

22. These vocables are one of several types associated with agricultural field songs (Gunasekaran 2006, 2).

23. Translation by Victor Prem Kumar.

24. I traveled with Rajaiah during the summer holiday to a village parish outside of the town of Karur (a former Methodist Dalit mass movement area) where he had been

assigned as pastor. He successfully used this same service with the small CSI congregation there.

25. Similarly Prem Kumar adapted Appavoo's song "Tāyi Tagappanārē" re-creating the style by adding harmony and a "waltz feel" to fit the context of a girl's TELC (Lutheran) boarding school choir at Usilampatti where he taught music.

26. When I first met Prem I said that my last name, Sherinian, sounded like the common (Brahmin) name Subramaniam. He then added the *yānai,* which means elephant, and *kutti,* which means small or my small one. Thus he used the name to tease me about my physical size.

27. Later in the year I financially helped Prem Kumar produce a cassette recording of half a dozen of his songs. We used the TTS recording studio employing the recording engineer and several professional musicians along with the best seminary vocalists.

28. One design also included flowerpots. The decorated pot sat in the middle of the *kōlam.* As one woman moved to step into the *kōlam* and take the pot after a prayer had been said, she quickly slipped out of her sandals signifying that the space and ground of the *kōlam* women's art was sacred.

29. Fast loud rolls are played on the *tavil* at significant ritual moments both in folk *nāyaṉam/tavil* ensembles and the temple *periya melam* ensemble traditions to rid the locale of any other inauspicious noise or presence (see Terada 2000, 140).

30. The 15th of January was called Cow Poṅgal because of the focus on these animals.

31. Most middle-class Christian women have given up the tradition of drawing *kōlam* as they consider it a Hindu ritual. However, lower-caste Christians like Mary who live in mixed neighborhoods were likely to at least create Christianized or secular designs in order to fit in with their women neighbors who routinely practice this art every morning in the process of sweeping and watering down the dirt area in front of their door.

32. Christy had left the college by that point.

5. RECEPTION AND TRANSFORMATION FROM SEMINARY TO VILLAGE

1. Rajamanikam, interview, Chinnadharapuram, June 26, 2002.

2. Johnson Jebakumar, interview, Andrewpuram, July 13, 2002.

3. http://www.dmk.in/histmain.html. Accessed June 22nd 2008.

4. In the Trichy area the DMK built a bridge that helped poor people travel to work, and collected money for poor women to get married. John David saw these actions as very Jesus-like. He asserted that ninety percent of the Tamil Evangelical Lutheran Church members are also DMK members.

5. They sing about early leaders like Periyar and Annandurai.

6. John David believed Karunanidhi was able to communicate with the poor who are his greatest supporters because he makes literary Tamil easy; he makes it attractive and sweet. John David asserted that poor Christians support Karunanidhi, while oth-

ers support communists, the ADMK party, and the Congress party. He also believes Karunanidhi treats the people equally, as Jesus did.

7. Jacqulin Jothi, interview, Madurai, January 7, 2008.

8. Ibid.

9. One has to get the Bishop's permission and usually diocesan financial support to enter the seminary.

10. Jacqulin Jothi, interview, Madurai, January 7, 2008.

11. The Catholic hierarchy seemed to have little problem with the use of folk and village cultural material in these ways. The Protestant churches, on the other hand, were much more conscious of the class symbolism that these folk practices carried, often rejecting them for use in town- or city-based programming.

12. Jacqulin Jothi, interview, June 11, 2002.

13. Ibid.

14. Ibid.

15. Ibid.

16. Jacqulin Jothi, interview, Madurai, January 7, 2008.

17. Ibid.

18. Ibid.

19. Ibid.

20. Ibid.

21. A man named Abraham was the first convert in the first mass movement village of Perunkarunaipalayam near Dharapuram (Manickam 1988, 164). He had found a Christian tract and, after becoming convinced of the need to convert, he petitioned the LMS mission organization (run by Rev. Popley in Erode) that sent the Wesleyan Methodist J. J. Ellis to work with the people of Perunkarunaipalayam.

22. We also visited the villages of Orathapalayam and Sakaravalasu near Mulanur, where the vast majority of the CSI congregation members were Chakkiliyars.

23. As the title indicates, this song answers the question "Who is the Blessed Man?" The answer is based on Psalm 1. Paraṭṭai employs a folk tune, which is used by farmers during traditional irrigation work called *ēṟṟam*. The mnemonic syllables that are sung to accompany this song are "*elelambadi elam*."

24. Rajamanikam, interview by Zoe Sherinian and T. Adri Paul, Chinnadharapuram, June 26, 2002.

25. Kent (2004, 4) argues that a change in women's behavior toward a more "respectable" model marked the successful conversion to Christianity as well as the general interior and exterior transformations of Christian groups in the nineteenth and early twentieth centuries.

26. Rajamanikam, interview by Zoe Sherinian and T. Adri Paul, Chinnadharapuram, June 26, 2002.

27. Ibid.

28. Translation by T. Adri Paul.

29. M. Rajamanikam, interview by Zoe Sherinian and T. Adri Paul, Chinnadharapuram, June 26, 2002.

30. Ibid.

31. Ibid.

32. Ibid.

33. Discussion with T. Adri and M. Rajamanikam, Chinnadharapuram, June 26, 2002.

34. Biriyani is a dish of rice and lamb cooked together in spices.

35. M. Rajamanikam, interview by Zoe Sherinian and T. Adri, Chinnadharapuram, June 26, 2002.

36. Ibid.

37. For example, Francis did not learn to play the paṟai drum.

38. Francis Devadoss, interview, Chennai, April 13, 2009.

39. Ibid.

40. Ibid.

41. Ibid.

42. Ibid.

43. Ibid.

44. Ibid.

45. "The angel Gabriel came and destroyed all of the *aḍuppu* or stoves and instead gave food from above in heaven. They all came and shared their food out of one pot. They would go to [work in] the fields and [return to] everyone having common food. If you go and fire the stove separately, they won't burn, because one *olai*, only one . . . He developed that kind of idea, having common food." Francis Devadoss, interview, Chennai, April 13, 2009.

46. Ibid.

47. Ibid.

48. Ibid.

49. Ibid.

50. Ibid.

51. Ibid.

52. Ibid.

53. Ibid.

54. Ibid.

55. Ibid.

56. Ibid.

57. Ibid. The implication here is the attempt to bribe God with offerings.

58. Ibid.

59. A bi-gendered understanding of the qualities of God is common among Indian liberation theologians partly as a result of the influence of feminist theology.

60. This is a Tamilization of the Eucharist. The rhyme pattern here is a good example of the mnemonic rhyming device of alliteration called *mōnai.*

61. M. Keba, interview, Karunkuzhi, July 14, 2002.

62. Kanimariyal and congregation, interview, June 28, 2002. Arangapalayam, Tamil Nadu.

63. Rajamanikam, interview with Zoe Sherinian and T. Adri, Chinnadharapuram, June 26, 2002.

64. Johnson Jebakumar, interview, Andrewpuram, July 13, 2002.

65. Sakaravalasu, interview, June 27, 2002.

66. Gunadayalan, interview, Madurandagam, Tamil Nadu, July 15, 2002.

67. Keba, interview, Karunkuzhi, Tamil Nadu, July, 14, 2002.

68. Ibid. Greater economic independence was also indicated as important in Arangapalayam village where the Chakkiliyars said that even having a small business like being a mason or having a cycle shop had led to a degree of economic independence that helped create a much greater of sense of self-worth and a lack of fear as opposed to a slave mentality. Arangapalayam community interview, June 28, 2002. This ability to acquire economic independence was reinforced by evidence I found in fieldwork conducted in 2008–09 with a drummer who was also mason.

69. Keba, interview, Karunkuzhi, Tamil Nadu, July, 14, 2002.

70. Ibid.

71. Appavoo, sermon notes, TTS, June 19, 2002.

72. Arangapalayam community interview, June 28, 2002.

73. Arangapalayam community interview, June 28, 2002.

6. PERFORMING GLOBAL DALIT CONSCIOUSNESS

1. Mnemonic rhythmic and melodic syllables used by the Tamil Gypsies.

2. Mnemonic rhythmic and melodic syllables used by the Tamil Gypsies.

3. Literally means "three quarters majority."

4. The reference here is to Christian priests or pastors.

5. Synonyms include "spotless" or "faultless."

6. This is a reference to the still common restriction of young women from having social contact with the male sex.

7. The implication here is a female enjoying her independence.

8. Synonyms include "chastise."

9. A folk genre associated with drawing water from a well.

10. Literally means "jerking movements" or "unrestrained behavior."

11. To beat in the "proper" way is also implied here.

12. These are different types of folk drums.

13. *O valai, o valai* are mnemonic syllables used in fishermen's folk genres, but also literally means "O net, o net."

14. In his last public lecture that was given at the University of Oklahoma several weeks before he died in 2005, Paraṭṭai focused on Luke 4,16–21 as the defining text of Christianity, the Christian mission, and the purpose behind the composition of Christian music.

15. Gnanavaram emphasized that the phrase *varnashrama dharma* in this context does not mean justice as some may argue, but *adharma* or that which is not in accord with the law, or evil and wickedness.

16. I am thankful to Rev. Dr. Gnanavaram, a close friend of Paraṭṭai's, who shared these ideas with me in a personal communication, December 6, 2008.

17. Appavoo symbolized this in the image of the cross with God as the upper vertical section of the cross and the people and the earth on opposite sides of the horizontal piece.

18. This biblical reference to David playing instruments and dancing has historically been used by Tamil Christians to legitimate the use of local instruments, which had

often been disparaged by puritanical, Calvinist, and Victorian Christianity brought by the nineteenth-century missionaries to India.

19. The "E" in "PEGS" of EPSI-PEGS stands for "environment."

20. Appavoo may have been communicating that Dalit musico-theology needs to be practiced primarily in the Dalit villages and *cēris*. That is, where the Dalits come from as Jesus came from Galilee.

21. http,//www.ambedkar.org/News/Durbanconference.htm. Accessed Sept. 11 2004.

22. Sr. Chandra, interview, Dindigul, February 11, 2009.

23. Ibid.

24. Ibid.

25. Pramada Menon, pers. comm. December 5, 2008

26. *Journal of Asia-Pacific Human Rights Network* 5 (October 2002).

27. Chandra, interview, Dindigul, February 11, 2009.

28. I am unable to give any more details of the content of the harassment nor the source of this information to protect the members of Sakthi.

APPENDIX 2

1. The implication is that the baby in your womb will help his/her people like Jesus.

2. Mnemonic, rhythmic, melodic syllables.

3. The best Indian grass for fodder.

4. Literally, in Tamil, the phrase means "material benefit" and "overall blessings."

5. *Puṅgu* is a very important word in Tamil folk vocabulary. It can mean one's opportunity or rights to participate in a community event, especially in a festival. It can also mean those with whom you share or divide your inheritance (property).

6. "Burns the stomach" in Tamil implies jealousy here.

7. Mnemonic, rhythmic, melodic syllables.

8. Mnemonic, rhythmic, melodic syllables.

9. This song is based on Psalm 94.

10. Bi-gendered term for deity in Tamil village religions.

11. Cutting a *tāli* means "killing or slowly torturing."

12. The implication here is the attempt to bribe God with offerings.

13. Literally, "put incense to or to worship."

14. Literally, "growing or raising violence."

15. Literally, "many."

16. This song is also known as "Yeṉṉa Sollutu Tirumarai" (What Does the Bible Say?)

17. Literally, "head man."

18. Literally, "listen to."

19. *Olai* literally means "stove." Appavoo uses this to denote his theological tenet of a collective "Eucharistic" lifestyle of sharing food and the labor necessary for its production. He advocates *oru olai* as a means to unify poor and Dalit communities to fight against their oppressions.

References

Allen, Matthew H. 1998. Tales Tunes Tell Tales Tunes Tell: Deepening the Dialogue Between "Classical" and "Non-Classical" in the Music of India. *Yearbook for Traditional Music,* 30:22–52.

Allen, Matthew, and T. Sankaran. 2000. The Social Organization of Music and Musicians: Southern Area. In *Garland Encyclopedia of World Music.* Vol. 5, South Asia, ed. Alison Arnold, 383–396. Levittown, PA: Garland Publishing.

Ambedkar, B. R. 1945. *What Congress and Gandhi Have Done to the Untouchables.* Lahore: Classic.

Ambedkar.org. "Durban conference must discuss Caste issue." http://www.ambedkar.org/News/Durbanconference.htm. Accessed Sept. 11, 2004.

American Madurai Mission at Tirumangalam. 1849. Minutes of the meeting of October 3, 1849. #286 and #381. *Archives of the American Board of Commissioners of Foreign Missions.* Houghton Library. Harvard University. Cambridge, MA.

Amirtham, Samuel, C. R. W. David. 1990. *Venturing Into Life: The Story of the Tamil Nadu Theological Seminary.* Madurai: Tamil Nadu Theological Seminary.

Anderson-Rajkumar, Evangeline. 2004. Politicizing the Body: A Feminist Christology. *The Asia Journal of Theology* 18 (1): 82–109.

Appadurai, Arjun. 1986. Is Homo Hierarchicus? *American Ethnologist.* 13 (4): 745–761.

Appasamy, A. J. 1930. *Christianity as Bhakti Marga: A Study of the Johannine Doctrine of Love.* Madras: Christian Literature Society.

Appavoo, J. T. 1986. *Folklore for Change.* Madurai: Tamil Nadu Theological Seminary.

———. 1992. Oru Olai: The Vision and Its Potential for Dalit Liberation. Unpublished paper. University of Edinburgh, Edinburgh.

———. 1993. Communication for Dalit Liberation: A Search for an Appropriate Communication Model. Master of Theology Thesis. Edinburgh: University of Edinburgh.

———. 1994a. Dalit Religion. In *Indigenous People: Dalits. Dalit Issues in Today's Theological Debate,* ed. J. Massey, 111–121. Delhi: ISPCK. no. 5.

———. 1994b [1999]. *Girāmiya Isai Vaṟipāḍu.* In *Pudiya Pudduyir Pāḍalhaḷ,* 154–161. Tamil Nadu Theological Seminary. Madurai, India.

———. 1997. Dalit Way of Theological Expression. In *Frontiers of Dalit Theology,* ed. V. Devasahayam, 283–289. Madras/Delhi: GLTCRI & ISPCK.

———. 1997. Communication for Dalit Liberation. In *Frontiers of Dalit Theology,* ed. V. Devasahayam, 363–372. Madras/Delhi: GLTCRI & ISPCK.

——. 2002. Sermon Notes. Tamil Nadu Theological Seminary. Madurai, India. June 19.

Araújo, Samuel et al. 2006. Conflict and Violence as Theoretical Tools in Present-Day Ethnomusicology. Notes on a Dialogic Ethnography of Sound Practices in Rio de Janeiro. *Ethnomusicology* 50 (2): 287–313.

Arcot Mission of the Reformed Church of America. 1903. *Jubilee Commemoration* 1853–1903. Madras: SPCK Press.

Babiracki, Carol. 1991. Tribal Music in the Study of Great and Little Traditions of Indian Music. In *Comparative Musicology and the Anthropology of Music: Essays in the History of Ethnomusicology*, ed. Bruno Nettl and Philip Bohlman. Chicago: University of Chicago Press.

——. 2000/2001. Saved by Dance: The Movement for Autonomy in Jharkhand. *Asian Music* 32 (1): 35–58.

Bakhtin, Mikhail. 1981. Discourse in the Novel. In *The Dialogic Imagination: Four Essays*. Austin: University of Texas Press. [259–422. 1934/35]. 276–277.

Bama. 2000. *Karukku*. Trans. Lakshmi Holmstrom. Chennai: MacMillan India Limited.

Barthes, Roland. 1977. The Grain of the Voice. In *Image-Music-Text*. Trans. Stephen Heath, 179–189. New York: Noonday Press.

Barz, Gregory, and Tim Cooley, ed. 1997. *Shadows in the Field: New Perspectives for Fieldwork in Ethnomusicology*. New York: Oxford University Press.

Barz, Gregory. 2005. Soundscapes of Disaffection and Spirituality in Tanzanian *Kwaya* Music. *The World of Music* 47 (1):5–30.

Baskaran, Theodore. 1981. *The Message Bearers: The Nationalist Politics and the Entertainment Media in South India, 1880–1945*. Madras: Cre-A.

Bate, Bernard. 2009. *Tamil Oratory and Dravidian Aesthetic: Democratic Practice in South India*. New York: Columbia University Press.

Bayly, Susan. 1989. *Saints, Goddesses and Kings: Muslims and Christians in South Indian Society, 1700–1900*. New York: Cambridge University Press.

Beck, Brenda. 1969. Color and Heat in a South Indian Ritual. *Man* 4 (4):553–572.

Bhabha, Homi. 1994. *The Location of Culture*. New York: Routledge.

Blackburn, Stuart, and David Arnold. 2004. *Telling Lives in India: Biography, Autobiography, and Life Histories*. Bloomington: Indiana University Press.

Bohlman, Philip. 1988. *The Study of Folk Music in the Modern World*. Bloomington: Indiana University Press.

Booth, Gregory. 2008. *Behind the Curtain: Making Music in Mumbai's Film Studios*. Oxford: Oxford University Press.

Borg, M. 1994. *Meeting Jesus Again for the First Time: The Historical Jesus and the Heart of Contemporary Faith*. New York: Harper Collins.

Brown, Michael J. 2000. Panem Nostrum: The Problem of Petition and the Lord's Prayer. *Journal of Religion* 80 (4):595–614.

Bugge, Henriette. 1994. *Mission and Tamil Society: Social and Religious Change in South India (1840–1900)*. Richmond, VA: Curzon Press.

Burnad, Fatima. The Tsunami Exacerbates Dalit Women's Sufferings from Caste Discrimination. *India: Asia Pacific Forum on Women, Law and Development*. http://www.apwld.org/tsunami_dalitwomen.htm. Accessed June 20, 2008.

Burnim, Mellonee, and Portia Maultsby, eds. 2006. *African American Music: An Introduction.* New York: Routledge.

Campbell, Patricia Shehan. 2004. *Teaching Music Globally: Experiencing Music Expressing Culture.* New York: Oxford University Press.

Carman, John, and P. Y. Luke. 1968. *Village Christians and Hindu Culture: Study of a Rural Church in Andhra Pradesh, South India.* London: Lutterworth.

Catlin, Amy. 1980. *Variability and Change in Three Karnataka Kriti-s: A Study of the South Indian Classical Music.* Ph.D. Dissertation. Brown University.

Catlin-Jairazbhoy, Amy, and Edward A. Alpers, ed. 2008. *Sidis and Scholars Essays on African Indians.* Trenton, NJ: Red Sea Press.

Center for Social Concerns, University of Notre Dame. An Introduction to the Principals of Catholic Social Thought: The Preferential Option for the Poor and Vulnerable. http://centerforsocialconcerns.nd.edu/mission/cst/cst4.shtml. Accessed August 17, 2009.

Chamberlain, Jacob. "Letter Book," box 271, p. 249, Yale Divinity School Archives. New Haven. Yale University.

Chandler, John S. 1912. *Seventy-Five Years in the Madurai Mission.* Madurai: American Madurai Mission Press.

Chatterjee, Partha. 1993. *The Nation and Its Fragments: Colonial and Postcolonial Histories.* Princeton: Princeton Univeristy Press.

Clark-Deces, Isabelle. 2005. *No One Cries For The Dead: Tamil Dirges, Rowdy Songs, and Graveyard Petitions.* Berkeley: University of California Press.

Clarke, Sathianathan. 1998. *Dalits and Christianity: Subaltern Religion and Liberation Theology in India.* Delhi: Oxford University Press.

Clifford, James. 1988. *The Predicament of Culture: Twentieth-Century Ethnography, Literature, and Art.* Cambridge: Harvard University Press

Cone, James. 1997. *God of the Oppressed.* Maryknoll, NY: Orbis Books.

Constable, Philip. 1997. Early Dalit Literature and Culture in Late Nineteenth- and Early Twentieth-Century Western India. *Modern Asian Studies* 31, (2): 317–338.

Cox, Jeffery. 2002. *Imperial Fault Lines: Christianity and Colonial Power in India, 1818–1940.* Stanford: Stanford University Press.

Danielson, Virginia. 1997. *The Voice of Egypt: Umm Kulthum, Arabic Song, and Egyptian Society in the Twentieth Century.* Chicago: University of Chicago Press.

Davis, Angela. 1998. *Blues Legacies and Black Feminism.* New York: Pantheon.

David, C. R. W. ed. 1993. *Pudduyir Pāḍalhaḷ.* Madurai: Tamil Nadu Theological Seminary.

David, Immanuel. 1986. *Reformed Church in America Missionaries in South India, 1839–1938: An Analytical Study.* Bangalore: Asian Trading Corporation.

David, Sharmila 2007. *Biennium Report for the Year 2005 –2007: Tsunami Relief, Rehabilitation and Reconstruction Programme.* Board for Socio-Economic Concerns, C. S. I. Diocese of Madras, Chennai, India.

Dayanandan, P. 2002. Dalit Christians of Chengalpattu Area and the Church of Scotland. In *Local Dalit Christian History,* ed. George Ommen and John C. B. Webster. ISPCK Contextual Theological Education Series 25. Delhi: ISPCK.

Devasahayam, V. 1997. Introduction. *Frontiers of Dalit Theology,* ed. V. Devasahayam, xi–xv. Chennai: ISPCK/Gurukul.

Deitrich, Gabriele. 1993. *Reflections on the Women's Movement in India: Religion, Ecology, Development.* New Delhi: Horizon India Books.
——. 2002. Inculturation versus Globalisation. Unpublished paper given at the Silver Jubilee Celebration of Ishvani Kendra, India.
Dickey, Sara. 1993. *Cinema and the Urban Poor in South India.* Cambridge: Cambridge University Press.
Dravida Munetra Karagam (DMK) Official Homepage. Anna Arivalayam, Chennai, Tamilnadu, India. http://www.dmk.in/histmain.html. Accessed June 22nd 2008.
Doniger, Wendy, and Brian K. Smith. 1991. *The Laws of Manu: With an Introduction and Notes.* New York: Penguin Books.
——. 2002. Foreword: The View From the Other Side: Postpostcolonialism, Religious Syncretism, and Class Conflict. In *Popular Christianity in India: Riting Between the Lines,* ed. Corinne Dempsey and Selva Raj, xi–xix. New York: SUNY Press.
Dumont, Louis. 1970. *Homo Hierarchicus.* Chicago and London: University of Chicago Press.
Dutt, Ashok K., and Allen G. Nobel. 2003. Urban Development in South Asia. In *Challenges to Asian Urbanization in the 21st Century,* ed. Ashok K. Dutt, Allen G. Nobel, G. Venugopal, and S. Subbiah, 1–19. Dordrecht: Kluwer Academic Publishers.
Elder, Joseph Walter. 1954. "Caste in the Churches of South India in Madura." Master of Arts Thesis, Dept. of Sociology and Anthropology, Oberlin College, Oberlin, OH.
Faustina. 1997. From Exile to Exodus: Christian Dalit Women and the Role of Religion. In *Frontiers of Dalit Theology,* ed. V. Devasahayam, 92–99. Madras/Delhi: GLTCRI & ISPCK.
Fernando, Basil. 2001. Dalit Drum Sounded Proud at Durban. Asian Human Rights Commission. http://wcar.alrc.net/mainfile2.php/Comment/53/?print=yes. Accessed Dec. 4, 2008.
Firth, Cyril Bruce. 1983. *An Introduction to Indian Church History.* Madras: Christian Literature Society.
Forrester, D. B. 1980. *Caste and Christianity: Attitudes and Policies on Caste of Anglo-Saxon Protestant Missionaries in India.* London: Curzon Press.
Foss, Karen, Sonja Foss and Cindy Griffin. 1999. *Feminist Rhetorical Theories.* Thousand Oaks, CA: SAGE.
Fox Strangways, A. H. 1914. *The Music of Hindustan.* Oxford: Clarendon Press.
Francis, T. D. 1978. *Christian Poets and Tamil Culture.* Madras: University of Madras.
——. 1988. *Tamil Kīrttaṉai and Songs of New Life.* Madras: Christian Literature Society.
Freeman, James. 1979. *Untouchable: An Indian Life History.* Stanford: Stanford University Press.
Freire, Paulo. 1970 [1984]. *Pedagogy of the Oppressed.* New York: The Continuum Publishing Corporation.
Fuller, C. J. 1992. *The Camphor Flame: Popular Hinduism and Society in India.* Princeton: Princeton University Press.
Gnanavaram, M. 2001. "Dalit Theology" and the Parable of the Good Samaritan. *Journal for the Study of the New Testament* 50 (1):59–83.

Grafe, Hugald. 1990. *The History of Christianity in Tamilnadu from 1800 to 1975*. Vol. 4, pt. 2 of *History of Christianity in India*. Bangalore: Church History Association of India.

Green, Paul. 1997. Professional Weeping: Music, Affect, and Hierarchy in a South Indian Folk Performance Art. *Ethnomusicology Online* 5. ISSN 1092-7336. www.research.umbc.edu/eol/5/greene/

Gunasekaran, K. A. 2006. Tamil Folk Music Varieties in Decolonization. Paper given at the Society For Ethnomusicology annual conference, Honolulu, Hawaii, 2006.

Gurupatham, Rev. M. Thomas. 1993. *The Role of Vedanayagam Sastriyar's Lyrics in Tamil Christian Worship*. Master of Theology Thesis, Madurai, Tamil Nadu Theological Seminary.

Gutierrez, Gustaveo. 1983. *The Power of the Poor in History*. New York: Orbis Books.

Hanson, Thomas Bloom. 1999. *The Saffron Wave: Democracy and Hindu Nationalism in Modern India*. Princeton NJ: Princeton University Press.

Hardgrave, Robert L. 1969. *The Nadars of Tamilnadu: The Political Culture of a Community in Change*. Berkeley: University of California Press.

Hardgrave, Robert L., and Stephen M. Slawek. 1989. Instruments and Music Culture in Eighteenth Century India: The Solvyns Portraits. *Asian Music* 20 (1):1–92.

Harris, Paul William. 1999. *Nothing But Christ: Rufus Anderson and the Ideology of Protestant Foreign Missions*. New York: Oxford University Press.

hooks, bell. 1984. *Feminist Theory from Margin to Center*. Boston: South End Press.

———. 1990. *Yearnings: race, gender and cultural politics*. Boston: South End Press.

———. 1994. *Teaching to Transgress: Education as the Practice of Freedom*. New York: Routledge.

Hudson, Dennis. 2000. *Protestant Origins In India: Tamil Evangelical Christians, 1706–1835*. Grand Rapids, MI: William B. Eerdmans Publishing Company.

Human Rights Watch. 1999. *Broken People: Caste Violence Against India's "Untouchables."* New York. http://www.hrw.org/legacy/reports/1999/india/. Accessed June 8, 2008.

Ilaiah, Kancha. 1994. *Why I am Not a Hindu: A Sudra Critique of Hindutva Philosophy, Culture and Political Economy*. Bombay: Samya.

Innasi, S. 1994. *Dimensions of Tamil Christian Literature*. Madras: Mariyakam.

Irundayaraj, Xavier. 1990. *Emerging Dalit Theology*. Madurai: Tamil Nadu Theological Seminary.

Iyer, Radhika. 1997. Conference Paper. Conference on Religion in South India, Toronto, June 14, 1997.

Joachim, J. 1969. *Jerusalem in the Time of Jesus*. London, S. C. M. Press.

Jones, Serene. 2000. *Feminist Theory and Christian Theology: Cartographies of Grace*. Minneapolis, MN: Fortress Press.

Jones, Sir William. *1784 (1792)*. "On the Musical Modes of the Hindus" *Asiatic Researches*, 3; rpt. London. 55–87.

Jordan, Oscar. http://www.soul-patrol.com/funk/jh_chitlin.htm. Accessed July 4, 2005.

Journal of Asia-Pacific Human Rights Network 5 (Oct. 2002).

Junghare, Indira. 1983. Songs of the Mahars: An untouchable caste in Maharashtra, India. *Ethnomusicology* 27 (2):271–295.

Kaplan, Caren. 1992. Resisting autobiography: out-law genres and transnational feminist subjects. In *De/colonizing the subject: the politics of gender in women's autobiography*, ed. Smith, Sidonie, and Julia Watson, 115–138. Minneapolis: University of Minnesota Press.

Kaplan, Steven, ed. 1995. *Indigenous Responses to Western Christianity.* New York: New York University Press.

Kartomi, Margaret. 1981. The Process and Results of Musical Culture Contact: A Discussion of Terminology and Concepts. *Ethnomusicology* 25: 227–249.

Kaufman, Walter. 1976. *The Ragas of South India: A Catalogue of Scalar Material.* Bloomington: Indiana University Press.

Kent, Eliza. 1999. *Respectability: Gender and Conversion to Christianity in Colonial South India.* Ph.D. Dissertation. University of Chicago. Chicago, Illinois.

———. 2004. *Converting Women: Gender and Protestant Christianity in Colonial South India.* Oxford: Oxford University Press.

Khare, R. S. 1984. *The Untouchable as Himself: Ideology, Identity, and Pragmatism among the Lucknow Chamars.* Cambridge: Cambridge University Press.

Kinsler, Ross. Leadership in an Age of Globaliztion. http://www.pcusa.org/globaled/kinsler.htm. Accessed June 4, 2006.

Kooiman, Dick. 1989. *Conversion and Social Equality in India: the London Missionary Society in South Travancore in the 19th century.* New Delhi Manohar Publishers.

Kunhambu, Potheri. 1892. *Saraswativijayam.* Trans. Dilip Menon (2002). New Delhi: The Book Review Literary Trust.

Kuriakose, M. K. 1999. *History of Christianity in India: Source Materials.* Madras: Christian Literature Society.

Larbeer, P. Mohan. 2003. Ambedkar on Religion: A Liberative Perspective. Delhi, ISPCK.

Larbeer, P. Mohan, and V. Alexander eds. 2000. *The Colours of Liberation.* Madurai: Dalit Resource Centre, Tamil Nadu Theological Seminary.

Lehmann, E. Arno. 1956. *It Began at Tranquebar.* Madras: Christian Literature Society.

Lorde, Audre. 1984. *Sister Outsider.* Berkeley: The Crossing Press.

Manickam, S. 1977. *The Social Setting of Christian Conversion in South India: The Impact of the Wesleyan Methodist Missionaries on the Trichy—Tanjore Diocese with Special Reference to the Harijan Communities of the Mass Movement Area 1820–1947.* Wiesbaden: Franz Steiner Verlag.

———. 1988. *Studies in Missionary History: Reflections on a Culture-Contact.* Madras: Christian Literature Society.

———. 1993. *Slavery in the Tamil Country.* 2nd ed. Madras: Christian Literature Society.

Manuel, Peter. 1989. *Thumrī in Historical and Stylistic Perspectives.* Delhi: Motilal Banarsidass.

Marshall, Paule. 1983. *Praise Song for the Widow.* New York: Plume.

Massey, James, ed. 1994. *Indigenous People: Dalits. Dalit Issues in Today's Theological Debate.* ISPCK Contextual Theological Education Series 5. Delhi: ISPCK.

Menon, Dilip. 1994. *Caste, Nationalism and Communism in South India: Malabar 1900–1948.* Cambridge: Cambridge University Press.

———. 2004. A Place Elsewhere: Lower-caste Malayalam Novels of the Nineteenth Century. In *India's Literary History,* ed. Stuart Blackburn and Vasudha Dalmia, 483–515. Permanent Black: Delhi Permanent Black.

———. 2006. *The Blindness of Insight: Why Communalism is about Caste & Other Essays.* Pondicherry: Navayana Press.

Mines, Diane and Sarah Lamb ed. 2002. *Everyday Life in South Asia.* Bloomington: Indiana University Press.

Moffatt, Michael. 1979 *An Untouchable Community in South India: Structure and Consensus.* Princeton, NJ: Princeton University Press.

Moon, Vasant. 2001. *Growing Up Untouchable in India: A Dalit Autobiography.* Lanham, MD: Rowman and Littlefield Publishers.

Mosse, David. 2005. Dalit Christians, Catholic Priests and Dalit Activism in Contemporary Tamil Nadu. Unpublished Conference Paper. Activism and Civil Society in South Asia, June 26-28, 2005. Oxford University. Oxford, England.

Mundadan, A Mathias. 1984. *History of Christianity in India, Vol. 1 From the Beginning up to the Middle of the Sixteenth Century (up to 1542).* Bangalore: Theological Publications in India.

Nabokov, Isabelle. 1997. Expel the Lover, Recover the Wife: Symbolic Analysis of a South Indian Exorcism. *Journal of the Royal Anthropological Institute* 3 (2):297–316.

———. 2000. *Religion Against the Self: An Ethnography of Tamil Rituals.* New York: Oxford University Press.

Nadar, Raam Kumar. 2004. Nadars—Nadar Community's Bussiness Activities. What They Do? http://nadar.kuttyjapan.com/nadar-what-they-do.asp. Accessed March 5, 2010.

Narula, Smita. 2004. Caste Discrimination. In *Caste, Race and Discrimination. Discourses in International Context,* ed. S. Thorat and Umakant, 283–291. New Delhi: Rawat.

Neill, Stephen. 1985. *A History of Christianity in India, 1707–1858.* Cambridge: Cambridge University Press.

Nirmal, Arvind. 1991. *A Reader in Dalit Theology.* Madras: Gurukul.

Oddie, Geoffrey. 1991. *Hindu and Christian in South-East India.* London: Curzon Press.

Ortner, Sherry. 1995. Resistance and the Problem of Ethnographic Refusal. *Comparative Studies in Society and History* 37 (1):173–193.

———. 1996. *Making Gender: The Politics and Erotics of Culture.* Boston: Beacon Press.

Overland, Martha Ann. Indian Scholars Protest Conference Restrictions. *Chronicle of Higher Education,* June 29, 2001.

Pandithar, Abraham M. 1984 [1917]. *Karunamirtha Sagaram.* New Delhi: Asian Educational Services.

Paul, Rajaiah. 1967. *Triumphs of His Grace: Lives of Eight Indian Christian Layman of the Early Days of Protestant Christianity in India, Every One of Whom Was a Triumph of His Grace.* Madras: Christian Literature Society.

Peterson, Indira Viswanathan. 1998. The Evolution of the Kurvanci Dance Drama; Negotiating the 'Folk' and the 'Classical' in the Bharata Natyam Canon. Special Issue on the Performing Arts of South India. *South Asia Research* 18:39–72.

——. 2002. "Bethlehem Kuravañci of Vedanayaka Sastri of Tanjore: The Cultural Discourses of a 19th century Tamil Christian Poem." In *Christians, Cultural Interactions, and the Religious Traditions of India*, ed. Judith Brown and Robert E. Frykenberg, 9–36. Grand Rapids, MI: W. Eerdmans.

Peterson, Indira Viswanathan, and Davesh Soneji, eds. 2008. *Performing Pasts: Reinventing the Arts in South India*. Delhi: Oxford University Press India.

Pinch, William. 1996. *Peasants and Monks in British India*. Berkeley: University of California Press.

Popley, H. A. 1920 [1966 3rd ed.] *The Music of India*. New Delhi: YMCA.

Prabhakar, M. E. 1988. *Towards a Dalit Theology*. Delhi: ISPCK.

——. 1997. Caste-Class, Patriarchy and Doing Dalit Theology. In Devasahayam 1997, 117–129.

Price, David. 2004. *Threatening Anthropology: McCarthyism and the FBI's Surveillance of Activist Anthropologists*. Durham: Duke University Press.

Pullapilly, Cyriac K. 1976. The Izhavas of Kerala and their Historical Struggle for Acceptance in the Hindu Society. In *Religion and Social Conflict in South Asia*, ed. Bardwell Smith, 24–46. Leiden: Brill.

Qureshi, Regula Burckhardt. 2007. *Master Musicians of India: Hereditary Sarangi Players Speak*. New York: Routledge.

Racine, Josiane, and Jean-Luc Racine. 2004. Beyond Silence: A Dalit Life History in South India. In *Telling Lives in India: Biography, Autobiography, and Life Histories*, ed. David Arnold and Stuart Blackburn, 252–280. Bloomington: Indiana University Press.

Raj, Antony. 1992. The Dalit Christian Reality in Tamil Nadu. *Jevadara* 22 (128): 78–89.

Rajaratnam, K. 1997. Foreword. In Devasahayam 1997, ix–x.

Raja Selvi, M. Kamal. 1997. The Dalit Women, the fourth class citizen. In Devasahayam 1997.

Rajaiah, David Paul, and J. Kumaresan. 1970. *Church of South India–Lutheran Conversations: A Historical Sketch*. Madras: Christian Literature Society.

Rajshekar, V. T. 1987. *Dalit: The Black Untouchables of India*. Atlanta: Clarity Press.

Ramakrishnan, S. ed. 1992. *Kriya Dictionary of Contemporary Tamil*. Madras: Government of India, Department of Education.

Ramendra, N. Why Dr. Ambedkar Renounced Hinduism. http://ambedkar.org/Babasaheb/Why.htm. Accessed July 4, 2008.

Rayan, Samuel. 1992. Outside the Gate, Sharing the Insult. In *Leave the Temple: Indian Paths to Human Liberation*, ed. F. Wilford, 125–145. Maryknoll, NY: Orbis Books.

Rice, Tim. 1994. *May It Fill Your Soul: Experiencing Bulgarian Music*. Chicago: University of Chicago Press.

——. 1997. Towards a Mediation of Field Methods and Field Experience in Ethnomusicology. In Barz and Cooley 1997, 101–120.

——. 2003. Time, Place, and Metaphor in Musical Experience and Ethnography. *Ethnomusicology* 47 (2):151–179.

Roa, Anupama. 2006. Representing Dalit Selfhood. From *Dalit Perspectives: A Symposium on Changing Contours of Dalit Politics*. http://www.india-seminar.com/2006/558/558%20anupama%20rao.htm.

Rodriguez, Clemencia. 2003. The Bishop and His Star: Citizens' Communication in Southern Chile. In *Contesting Media Power: Alternative Media in a Networked World*, ed. Nick Couldry and James Curran, 177–194. Boulder, CO: Rowman and Littlefield.

Ryerson, Charles. 1988. *Regionalism and Religion: The Tamil Renaissance and Popular Hinduism*. Madras: Christian Literature Society.

Sambamurthy, P. 1984 [1952]. *A Dictionary of South Indian Music and Musicians*. Vol. 2, A-F, 2nd ed. Madras: The Indian Music Publishing House.

Sanneh, Lamin. 1992. *Translating the Message: The Missionary Impact on Culture*. Maryknoll, NY: Orbis Books.

Sastriar, Vedanayagam. 1829. "'Saditeratoo,' by Vedenayaga Sastree, the Evangelical Poet of Tanjore 1829." British Museum: Oriental Printed Books and Manuscripts, Cat: OR. 11,742.

Scott, James C. 1985. *Weapons of the Weak: Everyday Forms of Peasant Resistance*. New Haven: Yale University.

———. 1990. Domination and the Arts of Resistance: Hidden Transcripts. New Haven: Yale University Press.

Scruggs, T. M. 2005. (Re)Indigenization?: Post-Vatican II Catholic Ritual and "Folk Masses" in Nicaragua. *World of Music* 47 (1):91–123.

Sewa Bharati Tamilnadu (Public Charitable Trust). (January 2, 2005). Interim Report on The Tsunami devastation in Tamil Nadu. www.sewainternational.com /download/tsunami/Tsunami_Earthquake_Appeal_Report_Interim.pdf Accessed June 20, 2008.

Shelemay, Kay Kaufman. 1997. The Ethnomusicologist, Ethnographic Method, and the Transmission of Tradition. In Barz and Cooley 1997, 141–156.

Sherinian, Zoe. 1998. *The Indigenization of Tamil Christian Music: Folk Music as a Liberative Transmission System*. Ph.D. Dissertation. Wesleyan University, Middletown, Connecticut.

———. 2002. Dalit Theology in Tamil Christian Folk Music: A Transformative Liturgy by James Theophilus Appavoo. In *Popular Christianity in India: Riting Between the Lines*, ed. Corinne Dempsey and Selva Raj, 233–253. New York: SUNY Press.

———. 2005a. The Indigenization of Tamil Christian Music: Transculturation and Transformation. *World of Music* 47 (1):125–165.

———. 2005b. Re-presenting Dalit Feminist Politics Through Dialogical Musical Ethnography. *Women and Music* 9:1–12.

———. 2007. Musical Style and The Changing Social Identity of Tamil Christians. *Ethnomusicology* 51 (2):238–280.

———. 2008. One *kirttanai*: Three Songs. In *Performing Pasts: Reinventing the Arts in South India*, ed. Indira Viswanathan Peterson and Davesh Soneji, 312–348. Delhi: Oxford University Press India.

Small, Christopher. 1987. *Music of the Common Tongue: Survival and celebration in Afro-American Music*. New York: Riverrun Press.

———. 1998. *Musicking: The Meaning of Performing and Listening*. Hanover, NH: Wesleyan University Press.

Sowmya, S. 2000. *Bharathiyar Songs*. Inreco: The Indian Record Mfg. Co. Ltd., compact disc.

Spivak, Gayatri C. 1988. Can the Subaltern Speak? In *Marxism and the Interpretation of Culture*, ed. Cary Nelson and Lawrence Grossberg. London: Macmillian.
Subramanian, Lakshmi. 2006. *From the Tanjore Court to the Madras Music Academy: A Social History of Music in South India*. New Delhi: Oxford University Press.
Sugirtharajah, Rasiah S. 1993. *Readings in Indian Christian Theology*. Delhi: ISPCK.
Summit, Jeffrey. 2000. *The Lord's Song in a Strange Land: Music and Identity in Contemporary Jewish Worship*. Oxford: Oxford University Press.
Sunder Raj, Ebe. 2003. Why the Dalit Seek Christ. *Evangelical Fellowship of India Commission on Relief*. http://eficor.org/publications/dristi_dec-mar03/dalitchrist.htm. Accessed July 18, 2006.
Tamil Nadu Theological Seminary, ed. 2000. *Putiya Puttuyirppāḍalha*. Madurai: Tamil Nadu Theological Seminary.
Terada, Yoshitaka. 2000. T. N. Rajarattinam Pillai and Caste Rivalry in South Indian Classical Music. *Ethnomusicology* 44 (3):460–490.
Thangaraj, M. 2003. Evaluation of the ten point programme for the development of Dalit Christians in Tamil Nadu. Chennai: Madras Institute of Development Studies.
——. 1990. Toward a Singable Theology. In Amirtham and David 1990, 109–118.
The Lutheran World Federation. 2002. Caste-based discrimination and similar forms of discrimination. www.lutheranworld.org/What_We_Do/OIahr-Statement_on_Caste-based_Discrimination_22-03-2002.pdf. Accessed on August 19, 2009.
The International Movement Against All Forms of Discrimination and Racism. 2002. Discrimination based on caste and similar forms of social hierarchy. http://www.imadr.org/descent/un/. Accessed on June 6, 2006.
Thekkedath, Joseph. 1982. *From the Middle of the Sixteenth to the End of the Seventeenth Century (1542–1700)*. Vol. 2 of *History of Christianity in India*. Bangalore: The Church History Association of India.
Thumma, Anthoniraj. 2000. *Dalit Liberation Theology: Ambedkarian Perspective*. Delhi: ISPCK.
Titon, Jeff. 1997. Knowing Fieldwork. In *Shadows in the Field: New Perspectives for Fieldwork in Ethnomusicology*, ed. Gregory F. Barz and Timothy J. Cooley, 87–100. New York and Oxford: Oxford University Press.
Townes, E. M. 1995. In *A Blaze of Glory: Womanist Spirituality as Social Witness*. Nashville, TN: Abingdon Press.
Trautmann, Thomas. 1997. *Aryans and British India*. Berkeley: University of California Press.
Trawick, Margaret. 1990. *Notes on Love in a Tamil Family*. Berkeley: University of California Press.
United Nations Tsunami Recovery Support. 2007. "Tusnami India—Three years After: A Report of the United Nations." http://www.un.org.in/untrs/content_01.asp?ref=pa_12. Accessed July 8, 2008.
Vedanayagam, Shem, ed. [1899] 1987. *Life of Vedanayaka Sastriyar, the Evangelical Poet of Tanjavur*. Tanjavur: R. J. Printers.
Viramma, Josiane Racine, and Jean-Luc Racine. 1997. *Viramma: Life of an Untouchable*. London, Verso.
Viswanathan, Gauri. 1998. *Outside the Fold: Conversion, Modernity, and Belief*. Princeton, NJ: Princeton University Press.

Viswanathan, S. 2005. *Dalits in Dravidian Land: Frontline Reports on Anti-Dalit Violence in Tamil Nadu (1995–2004).* Pondicherry: Navayana Press.

Waghorne, Joanne. 2002. Chariots of the God/s: Riding the Line Between Hindu and Christian. In *Popular Christianity in India: Riting Between the Lines,* ed. Corinne Dempsey and Selva Raj, 11–37. New York: SUNY Press.

Walker, Alice. 1983. *In Search of Our Mothers' Gardens.* New York: Harcourt Brace Jovanovich.

Webb, Rev. Edward. 1852. Letter to Rufus Anderson, December 31, 1852. Letters and Papers of ABCFM, Vol. 226. Houghton Library, Harvard University. Cambridge, MA.

———. 1854. Letter from Mr. Webb, January 2, 1854. *The Missionary Herald* 50 (5):150–152.

———. 1875. *Christian Lyrics for Public and Social Worship* (5th Ed.) Revised by G. T. Washburn. Nagercoil: Madras Tract and Book Society, London Mission Press.

Webster, J. C. B. 1992. *A History of the Dalit Christians in India.* San Francisco: Mellen Research University Press.

Weidman, Amanda J. 2006. *Singing the Classical, Voicing the Modern: The Postcolonial Politics of Music in South India.* Durham: Duke University Press.

Welsh, Sharon. 1985. *Communities of Resistance and Solidarity: A Feminist Theology of Liberation.* Maryknoll, NY: Orbis Books.

White, Emmons. 1922. Letter from White to the American Board of Commissioners of Foreign Missions, July 18, 1922. ABCFM Archive, Houghton Library, Harvard University: Cambridge, MA.

———. 1957. *Appreciating India's Music: an introduction to the music of India, with suggestions for its use in the churches of India.* Madras: Christian Literature Society.

White, Ruth. 1929. Letter to the American Board of Commissioners of Foreign Missions, November 1, 1929. ABCFM Archive, Houghton Library, Cambridge: MA. Harvard University.

Willard, Augustus. 1834. "Treatise on the Music of Hindostan."

Wilson, Kottapalli. 1982. *The Twice Alienated Culture of Dalit Christians.* Hyderabad: Booklinks.

Wingate, Andrew. 1997. *The Church and Conversion: A Study of Recent Conversions to and from Christianity in the Tamil Area of South India.* Delhi: ISPCK.

Wolf, Richard K. 1991. Style and Tradition in Karaikkudi *Vīṇa* Playing. *Asian Theatre Journal* 8 (2):118–141.

———. 2005. *The Black Cow's Footprint: Time, Space, and Music in the Lives of the Kotas of South India.* Delhi: Permanent Black.

Wolf, Richard K., and Zoe C. Sherinian. 1999. Tamil Nadu. In *The Garland Encyclopedia of World Music, Vol 5. South Asia: The Indian Subcontinent,* ed. Alison Arnold, 903–928. New York: Garland Publishing.

INTERVIEWS

Appavoo, J. T. Ten hours of interviews from March to September of 1994: March 10, July 1, July 18, August 18, September 22. Madurai, Tamil Nadu.

Arangapalayam Congregation, June 28, 2002. Arangapalayam, Tamil Nadu.

Chandra, Sr. Feb. 11, 2009. Dindigul, Tamil Nadu.

Clarke, Bishop Sundar. August 8, 1994. Madras, Tamil Nadu.
David, C. R. W. April 25, 1994. Madurai, Tamil Nadu.
Devadoss, Francis. April 13, 2009. Chennai, Tamil Nadu.
Gnanavaram, M., telephone, January 11, 1011.
Gunadayalan. July 15 and July 17, 2002. Madurandagam, Tamil Nadu.
Inbaraj, Rev. Benjamin. July 16, 2002. Madurandagam, Tamil Nadu.
Jebakumar, Rev. Johnson. July 11 and 13, 2002. Andrewpuram, Tamil Nadu.
Jebarajan, Emmanuel. August 30, 1994. Madurai. Tamil Nadu.
Jothi, Rev. Jacqulin. January 7, 2008. Madurai, Tamil Nadu.
Kanimariyal. June 28, 2002. Arangapalayam, Tamil Nadu.
Karunakaran, C. S. September 11, 1994. Karur, Tamil Nadu.
Keba. M. July 14, 2002. Karunkuzhi, Tamil Nadu.
Larbeer, Mohan. February 1, 1994. Madurai, Tamil Nadu.
Manikam, Kambar. August 3, 1994. Madurai, Tamil Nadu.
Ponnaiya, C. J. June 15, 1994. Dharapuram. Tamil Nadu.
Rajaiah, M. J. April 12, 1994. Madurai, Tamil Nadu.
Rajamanikam, Rev. M. June 26, 2002. Chinnadharapuram, Tamil Nadu.
Rajasekaran, J. February 15, 2009. Madurai, Tamil Nadu
Sakaravalasu Congregation, June 24, 2002. Sakaravalasu, Tamil Nadu.
Thangaraj, Dr. M. Thomas. March 17, 1997. Atlanta to Boston telephone interview.

LECTURES AND SERMONS

J. T. Appavoo, lecture given to Basic Christian Communities Workers. September 20, 1994. Nagercoil, Tamil Nadu
J. T. Appavoo, sermon given at TTS. July 24, 1994. Madurai, Tamil Nadu.
J. T. Appavoo, sermon given at TTS. June 19, 2002. Madurai, Tamil Nadu.
J. T. Appavoo, sermon delivered to students in the TTS summer music camp. May 5, 1994. Madurai, Tamil Nadu.
Webster, John. Overseas Mission Center, Yale University. January 29, 1993. New Haven, CT.
Rev. Cannon Carol Hampton, Eulogy for J. T. Appavoo. St. Paul's Cathedral. Nov. 5, 2005. Oklahoma City, OK.

J. THEOPHILUS APPAVOO'S RECORDINGS REFERENCED

Nimunda Naḍai (Stand Tall), 1985 (rereleased 2008).
Māṭṭukkōttil Reḍiyāccu (*The Cow Barn is Ready*), 2000.
He Gives All Blessings, 2004.

Index

Page numbers in italics refer to illustrations.

abolition movement, xv
accommodation: cultural, 21, 78
action, xix, xx, 2, 156
activist ethnomusicology 48–49
Adi Samayam, 114, 119, 151–152, 169, 177, 178, 246; as source for Dalit theology, 131, 246
Adlin Reginabai, 192–193, 206
advocacy anthropology and ethnomusicology, 34, 49, 50, 249, 251; sound, agents, and ideology, 54, 57–58, 60
African Americans: assimilation, 163–164, 165; blues as protest, 296n23; chitlin circuit, 163, 311n77; community, 160; denominations, 310n73; middle class and Dalit experience, 265–266, 294n8; womanist theology, 128, 158
agency, xii, 38, 117, 265, 267; and the individual, 69; as negotiation between self and community, 69
agricultural metaphors, 114
All India Music Conferences, 103
All India Radio, 103
Allen, Matthew, 53
alternative media, xiv, 47
Ambedkar, Dr. Bhimrao Ramjee, 14, 97; critique of Gandhi, 295n9; Dalit movement, 23; separate electorate, 309n62; and women, 27
American Board of Commissioners for Foreign Missions (ABCFM), xv, xvii, 6, 20, 85–86, 88, 89–90, 95, 221, 295n13, 296n18; anti-caste discrimination policies, 87, 92, 94; boarding schools, 91, 93; indigenization policies, 78, 91, 94, 301n35; language and patronizing attitude, 301–302n35; love feasts, 92; training in karnatak music, 94
American College, Madurai, 20
Anderson-Rajkumar, Evangeline, 27, 56
Anglicization, 78, 80, 85, 91, 103, 107
Annamalai University, 103, 303n70
Anthonyraj, Fr., 21, 31
anthropology, xv
Appadurai, Arjun, 15
Appaswamy, A. J., 152
Appavoo, Edward, 71, 72, 117, 302n42, 302n44
Appavoo, Rev. James Theophilus, *201;* as Anglican, 100; as atheist, 105, 107, 108, 109, 117; challenge to modernity, 100, 301n55; as choir director, 107–108, 109, 110, 175, *198;* and class consciousness, 54; as communication professor and theorist, 112, 237, 310n66; as composer, 108, 111, 112, 113, 245, 304n99; creative accomplishments, 67, 113; critique of Solomon, 234; and CSI reform, 47, 59, 66; in Cuddalore, 67,100, 104; and Dalit identity, 114–115; daughter Adrina (Adri), 116, *197,* 224–225, 228–229, 243, 245, 249, 251, 252, 300n45; daughter Neena, 11, 116, 186; degrees, 110, 299n5; dramatic productions, 174, 175; environmentalism/nature, 261; eucharist as "medicine of liberation," 62, 63, 65; family, 31, 67, 94, 98, 99, 100,

300n42, 301n56; family in Vellore, *196;* father (James David), 100–101, 104, 117, 300n45; feminist songs, 28, 210, 219, 223, 224, 235; feminist theology, 123, 171, 310n72, 315n59; folklore and folk arts, 112; *Folklore for Change* (1986), 67, 310n64, 310n66; folk music defined, 45–46, 117; folk re-creation, 226; folk songs/music, 28, 67, 100, 112, 113, 114, 116, 120, 203, 215, 218, 250, 257, 267; folk style, 42, 116; freedom theology, 109; and gender, 28, 118; *Girāmiya Isai Vaṟipāḍu,* 43, 54, 55, 56, 57, 119, 239; grandfather Samuel, 100, 303n56, 303n58, 303n60; Humanly Produced and Transmitted Media (HPTM), xiv, 237; intersectionality, 28, 118, 157, 231–232; and karnatak music, 67, 94, 101, 104, 108, 117; and light music, 66, 105, 117; meaning of Christianity, 256, 316n14; as middle class, 67, 100, 104–105, 114; music as accessible, 247, 249, 312n19; musical dialogue, 116, 203; musical indigenization, 46, 75, 117, 246; and Nadars, 104, 105, 107–108, 117, 203; neo-Marxism EPSI-PEGS, 30–31, 113, 117, 133, 141, 142, 237, 257; and *oru olai,* 106, 120, 188, 235, 238; as performing musician, 105–106, 111; proscriptive vision for liberation, 166; use of puppet show, 236; reclaiming, 267; recordings, 113, 224; rejection of Evangelicalism, 105; at RTI (Rural Theological Institute), 112; sanskritized Christian identity, 117; secular awareness songs, 235; as seminary student, 110, 111, 118; sharing food/family relationship, 106, 187, 203, 231, 237; students of, 119, 183–186, 193, *198,* 203–204, 205, 211, 218, 220, 234–243, 253, 294n11; at the Tamil Nadu Theological Seminary (TTS), 55, 66, 67, 118, 187, *198,* 202, 237; as teacher, 11, 67, 106, 107–108, 109, 110; teachers of, 17, 42, 69, 111, 119; theology, 28, 31, 55, 116, 118, 119, 120, 121, 132–150, 154, 215, 218, 241, 242–253, 252, 257, 261; transmission, 57, 108, 116, 117, 155, 188, 191, 227, 234, 242; and Western music, 108; wife (Dorathy), 116, 239. See also *oru olai*

Appavoo, J. T., recordings: He Gives All Blessings, 116; *Māṭṭukkoṭṭil Reḍiyācci,* 222–223, 224; *Nimindu Naḍa,* 209

Appavoo, J. T., songs: "Allēlūyā Allēlūyā," 156, 189, 234, 286–287, 312n18; "Ammāḍi Kuṭṭi Poṇṇē," 182, 223, 224–225, 285; "Āṇḍavanē Eṅga Āṭṭiḍaiyaṉ," 113, 226–227, 240, 288; "Āṇḍavanē Nī Emakku Koṭṭai," 228–229, 234, 240, 241; "Aṇṇātte Aṇṇātte," 227, 289–290; "Āṇṇē Tambi Māppiḷḷē," 189, 227, 290; "Bumiyil Vāṟuṟa," 184, 216, 240, 287, 312n18; "Inikkāda Tēnumilla," 216, 226, 227, 240, 246, 286; "Maṉasamātta," 155, 167–171, 176–179; "Māṭṭukkoṭṭil Reḍiyācci," 216, 227; "Nalla Seydi," 255–258; "Olakattula Kuḍuttu Vassavaṅga," 222, 314n23; "Otta Saḍa, Reṭṭai Saḍa," 211, 235, 291; "Paḍā Pēsārākīdu," 235; "Pēccu Tandiramā," 113; "Pudiya Siluva," 112, 287; "Sagalajaṉaṅgaḷe," 240; "Tāyi Tagappanārē," 182, 191, 203, 204, 216, 227–228, 229–230, 240, 243–246, 248, 249, 313n25; "Uruppadiyar Oru Kāriyam," 213; "Villabara Saṇaḍaiyillē,"113, 114. See also *Girāmiya Isai Vaṟipāḍu,* (Village Music Liturgy)

Aruyndhatiyar, 14

āsīrvādam (prosperity or blessing) theology, 42–43, 64, 66, 105, 117

Azariah, Bishop M., 129, 211

Bama (author), 304n61

Basic Christian Communities, 210

beef eating, 95, 115, 303n49

Berchman, Fr. S. J., Tamil Christian evangelical songs, 215

Bhabha, Homi, 25

bhakti, 80, 81, 83, 84, 185
Bharatiya Janta Party, 53. *See also* Hindu Fundamentalism
Bible, 97, 186, 188, 209, 235, 258, 308n27; Appavoo's teachings, 234; beatitudes (Matthew), 258; Hebrew, 260; Isaiah, 184–185; Nazareth Manifesto (Luke), 256, 267, 316n14; parables, 149; playing music in, 316n18; Psalms, 234–235, 314n23, 317n9; study, 215–216; translation, 76, 103
Blackburn, Stuart, 68–69
blessings, 226, 241, 317n4
Bollywood music, 43; singers, 100, 101, 304n63; untouchables in, 304n64
"born again" transformation, 137, 138, 145, 250
Brahminical Christianity, xvii, 173; and theology, 64, 111, 132
Brahminical Hinduism, 52, 63, 64, 66; culture, 125; mythology, 124
Brahmins: Aryans, 138; as demonic gang, 176; with nothing to eat, 139–140; as weak and lazy, 136
British Society for Promoting Christian Knowledge (SPCK), 78
Burnim, Mellonee, 59

call and response, 57
Calvinism, 78, 84, 300n38, 316–317n18
capitalism, 177
cassettes, 298n11
caste, 294n4; annihilation, 250, 256, 257; anti-caste, xii, 111, 116; and capitalism, 108; and Christian denomination, 85, 103–104; communalism, 87; and conviction of Christian equality, 85; Counders, 138, 252, 295n16; dependency, 64; as the devil, 167, 177, 230–231, 256, 260; discrimination among Christians, 19–22, 77, 79, 80, 90, 104, 110, 240, 248, 295n13, 300n14, 305n75; discrimination by upper castes, 208–209; distinction in context, 113; and excommunication, 79, 84; hierarchy, xii, 13, 75, 295n12; inter-caste dining, 92; inter-caste relationships, 108, 120; Madras Missionary Conference (1850), 92; and marriage, 109; miscegenation, 15, 79; and musical aesthetics, 39; negotiation, 16; origin myth, 135; pervasiveness, 16, 293n12; protest, 87; and race, 262–266; raising status, 87, 101, 116; and region, 115; replication by music scholars, 49; scheduled, 115, 116; segregation and separation 21, 75, 76, 77, 79, 82, 83, 84, 87, 99, 125, 145, 244, 260, 303n59; Tamil, 295n16; Tamil Christian, 16, 17, 75, 117, 205, 293n14, 295n14; transformation, 120; two-tumbler system, 177; violence, 14–15, 75
castism, internalized, 208–209, 233, 248–249, 258
catechists, 88, 92; as composers, 74, 76; *kīrttaṉai* transmission, 92; outcaste, 97, 301n29; preaching with song, 91, 99
Catholics/Catholicism, 73, 74, 79–80, 299n7, 302n44, 314n11
census, 18
cēri (village ghetto), 13, 57, 75, 255, 259, 317n20
Chakkiliyar, 14, 183, 204, 221–222, 227, 229, 251, 252, 262, 295n11, 297n6
Chandra, Sr. Angelina, 263–264. *See also* Sakthi Kalai Kural
Chennai, 25
Chennai Sangamam, 53
Chinniah, Rev. Honest, xvii, 17, 105, 106, 107, 108, 109, 110, 117–118; harmonizing kīrttaṉai, 305n86
choirs, 104; karnatak, 107
Christian caste culture, 72; missionary rejection of, 92
Christian liturgy, 46
Christian songs and music, 52, 80, 88, 113, 120, 171, 233, 241, 266, 296n25, 302n38; history, 68, 117; identity, 31, 47, 68, 82, 91; transmission, 249; at TTS, 173
Christians: anti-union, 212; assumed as outcaste, 101; castes, 295n14; concern

and work for poor, 215; denominations, 85, 103, 305n75; duty, 228; failed unification, 103–104, 303n75; first century, 137; history, 68; identity, 86, 92, 98, 101, 112, 117; literacy, 99; literature, 70; lower-caste, 89, 91, 94; middle class, 43, 118, 168, 205, 214, 229, 240; percentage in India, 21, 98; percentage of outcaste, 21, 87, 98, 99, 128, 296n19; percentage in Tamil Nadu, 21, 98; rural, 18, 23, 24, 46, 47, 58, 67, 86, 91, 98; South India United Church, 101, 103; upper caste, 40, 69, 79, 82, 88, 97, 251; upper class, 56, 92; urban/city, 241
Christmas, 80, 233; carol service, 111, 168–171, 174–180, *198*, 216, 305n91; carols, 258; and white clothing, 311n11
Church Mission Society (CMS), 78, 79, 80
Church of South India (CSI), xvii, 4, 90, 110, 131, 172, 211, 219, 298n21; Anglican separation from, 108; department for Dalit Concerns, 130, 204; Diocese of Madras, 217; domination by Nadars, 106, 107, 108; formation, 23, 103; hymnal, 246; liturgical and musical reform/change, 47, 69, 179, 250, 262; liturgy, 148,183; Trichy-Tanjore Diocese, 183, 221, 301n21; women's ordination, 297n26
Clarke, Sathianathan, 23, 131, 150–157, 307n19, 310n64; Hindu symbolic world, 23; on mass conversion, 22; oral theology, 24, 153; and SAC, 233–234; theo-phonia, 153, 154
Clarke, Bishop Sundar, 150
class, 18, 20, 104, 110, 303n84; and aesthetics, 25, 39; differences between missionaries and converts, 91; mobility, 39–40, 68, 87, 108; private property, 134–135, 138–139, 167, 177
classical Indian music and culture, 44, 53, 76, 80, 82, 108, 111, 116; as national art, 53. *See* also "great traditions"
colonial domination, 38
colonialism, 51; and modernity, 68
Communism, 23
community, 121, 139, 158, 159, 161–162, 174, 188; as radically relational, 159; transformative power of, 164
Cone, James H., 59
consciousness, xiv; critical, 266
conversion, xvi, 18, 293n6, 296n21; as change of values, 132; as civilizing, 86, 91; of Dalits or outcastes, 21, 23, 25, 74, 85, 95, 97, 117, 303n53, 304n68; through Dalit theology, 109; denominations, 85; and equality, 97; to escape upper-caste tyranny, 70, 86, 97, 98; and gender, 29; of higher- or upper-castes, 74, 76, 83, 84, 97; isolation of converts, 72; mass, 85, 97–98, 304n62; with music, 70, 91; negotiation with missionaries, 77; rice Christians, 98, 221; self-initiated 25, 221, 314n21; and translation, 71; trickle down theory, 73; and violence, 304n68;
Crow Dog, Leonard, xvi
Cuddalore, 99, 100, 106, 107, 114, 305n85; Arcot Lutheran Church, 305n79
cultural relativity, 90
cultural rights, 128–129
culture contact, 35

Dalit Christians, 16, 56, 119, 265, 295n10, 296n17; as children of God, 245; conversion, 67, 70, 96; government quota (reservation) discrimination, 129, 248–249; and Hindu relatives, 303n53; middle class, 25, 31, 310n71; in the military, 100, 304n61; and missions, 24; rural, 23; subcaste division between, 251, 253; as teachers, catechists, and priests, 23, 100, 229; urban lower-class, 192; urbanite, 2, 97; villagers, 113, 114, 119, 235, 249, 316n68
Dalit festivals, 122, 137; Arts festivals, 44–45, 130, 131, 140
Dalit folk songs, 28, 222; as humanizing, 263
Dalit history, 35, 96, 99
Dalit identity, 42, 114, 116, 156, 203, 251, 252, 266, 293n11; affinity with African American, 265–266; class divisions

among Dalits, 251–252; cultural identity, 67, 68, 120, 249; as farmers, 126, 128; internal power relations, 242; internalized shame, 25, 31, 42, 120, 295n11; middle class, 165, 230, 231, 298n17; through music/performance, 262, 264, 266; and parai drum, 242; positive, 63, 119, 128; reinvention, 114; self-naming, 148; transmission, 191; as universal, 262, 265; use of term, 115, 306n100
Dalit liberation: and cultural equality, 29; through economic self-sufficiency, 316n68; through education, 248; through musical sound, 260; and women, 27, 206
Dalit Liberation Movement, 306n100; internationalization of, 33, 262–265; politics, 176, 186; roots, 23, 96; in Tamil Nadu, 128; and unions, 212
Dalit liberation theology, 14, 35, 63, 96, 119, 120, 121, 128, 131, 236, 257, 265; and academic departments, 129; and Adi Samayam, 138, 150; as Christian, 128, 262; in dialogue with upper castes, 157; feminist, 29–30, 169, 205, 206, 315n59; and folk culture/music, 40, 44, 45, 54, 57, 117, 118, 119, 130, 173, 174, 262, 267; as holistic liberative living, 119; musico-theology, 317n20; as oral, 151–154; roots, 96; transmission, 31, 174, 191, 231, 242, 252; as worship, 119
Dalit Panthers, 14
Dalit religion. *See* Adi Samayam
Dalit Resource Centre, 130. *See also* Tamil Nadu Theological Seminary (TTS)
Dalitization, 71, 225
Dalits, 3, 14, 57, 120, 128, 257, 294n7; Christ as Dalit, 306n11; comparison with shepherds, 259; consciousness, 243, 248, 254, 255; folk artists, 263; as global oppressed, 254; survival knowledge, 139, 177; unity, 243; women, 258, 259, 295n15. *See also* Dalit identity
Daniel, Rev. C. J., 25, 91, *195*
Danielson, Virginia, 69
de Britto, John, 300n9
de Nobili, Robert, 73, 75, 87; and caste equality, 74; as a Roman Brahmin, 74
denomination, Protestant, 39
dependency, caste and gender, 134, 139
Devadasis, 302n37, 304n70
Devadoss, Rev. Francis, *201*, 203, 232–243, 253, 315n37; and Appavoo, 234–242; in Chennai, 240; as folk song pastor, 239; future of Appavoo's theology, 241 oppression in village school, 233; and the Social Action Centre (SAC), 233–236, 242; transmission strategies, 240; at TTS, 237–239
dharma, 316n15
diachronic scales, 41
dialogical processes, 2, 31, 56, 58, 63, 69, 120, 253; field processes, 54, 133, 249; field relationships, 49, 59–60, 170, 186–187, 205; teaching 170; theology, 131, 133, 154; transmission, 170, 231, 243
Dietrich, Dr. Gabrielle, 28, 130
Dinakaran, Paul, 105
discipular ethnography, xviii
Doniger, Wendy, 97, 265, 267
Dower, John, 50–51
Downey, Greg, xvi
dowry, 223, 224; as bride price, 29
Dravida Munnettra Kazhagam (DMK), 23, 102, 207, 306n5, 313n4; Karunanidhi, 207, 313n6; and women's rights, 207
Dravidian language, 297n30; oration, 205, 206
Dravidian movement, 30, 41, 42, 101, 102, 105, 304n68; influence on Tamil Christian scholars, 103

Elder, Joseph, 18, 295n16
English language: education, 86, 91; hymns, 38, 40, 100
environmentalism, 261, 317n19; ecology, 126
EPSI-PEGS, 30–31, 113, 117, 133, 141, 142, 237
ethnography, 167, 170
ethnomusicology, xii, 2, 34; and biography, 63, 68; and Brahmin teachers'

influence, 53; and classical South Asian music, 34, 53, 299n20; and orientalism, 49, 51, 53; and replication of local hierarchies of musical value, 48–49, 50; structuralism, 59. *See also* advocacy anthropology and ethnomusicology
Eucharist, 2, 63, 124–125, 126, 163, 182, 193, 237; to annihilate caste, 250; secularization of, 144; Tamilization of, 315n60; theology of, 250; transubstantiation, 143
Evangelical Christianity, xv, xvi, 42, 63, 64, 66, 141, 145, 185, 230–231; and classism, 105, 117
Evangelism, 90, 94, 300n13

Fabricius, Philip, 76
feminism, xix, 111, 166, 169, 311n4; Dalit, 224; male dominance, 223; shared values of, 206; and theology, 28, 29–30, 32, 121, 123, 158–166, 169
folk music, xix, 39, 42, 44, 52, 54, 59, 113, 116, 119, 156, 179, 224, 242; as *cōccai* (degraded), 44, 119, 120; community skills, 133; estrangement from liberating aspects, 91, 97; genres, 223, 224, 225, 226, 255–256, 257, 258–262, 316n9, 316n13; idioms, 128, 185, 245, 246; idioms in *kīrttaṉai*, 41, 80, 84, 204, 266; indigenous terms, 298n13; instruments, 46, 80, 116, 119, 224, 252, 316n12; in liturgy, 243, 267; mnemonics, 259, 261; nasal timbre quality, 116; participation, 150; as protest and resistance, 45, 57, 60, 91, 147, 246, 264, 265, 298n14; purpose, 45; reclaiming, 46, 91, 117, 119, 120, 176, 179, 243, 252, 267; recomposition/re-creation, 133, 202–203, 266; rejection of, 25, 31, 40, 48, 87, 113, 314n11; sound and performance, 133, 225; as training for empowerment, 210–211, 250, 260; as transformative, 31, 48, 91, 117, 119–120, 128, 147, 185, 264; transmission system, 57, 114, 123, 170, 191, 202, 242, 254; at TTS, 173; and value, 25, 34, 40, 44; village flavor, 246
folklore, 235; counter myths, 307n9; degraded value of, 308n24
food, 180, 182, 186–188, 214, 244, 247, 293n2, 307n17, 308n 30; production, 139; sharing 191, 192, 193, 205, 315n45
forgiveness, conditional, 140
free will, 138
Freire, Paulo, xxi, 129, 170; *Pedagogy of the Oppressed,* 4, 163, 308n22

gamaka, 41
gender, 29, 137; neutrality, 126; separation, 175, 181, 297n28, 316n6
gharānā, xviii
Girāmiya Isai Vaṟipāḍu, (Village Music Liturgy) 2, 43, 128, 146, 180, 183, 193, 214, 215, 237, 251; "Adoration," 1; "Confession of Sin," 183, 239; "Greetings and Praise of God," 120, 122, 274–283; "The Lord's Prayer," 2, 63, 159, 270–271; "Repentance of Sin," 54–55, 56–57, 247, 272; "Sāmiya Vaṇaṅguṟadu" (Invocation), 308n31; "Virundu Parimāṟuṟadu" (Meal Sharing Song), 63, 65, 66, 99, 239, 273, 303n55
girāmiya pāṭṭu, 44
global/local, 254; music mix, 179
Gnanasekaran, Danny, 131, 191, 306n100
Gnanavaram, Rev. M., 2, 3, 22, 257, 260, 294n2, 316n15
Goa, 72
God: as bi-gendered, 315n59; as Dalit, 127–128; as farmer (Vevasāyi), 126, 127, 148, 155; as Father and Mother, 4, 10, 28, 123, 144, 167, 169, 170, 176, 184, 243, 245, 294n3, 306n4; feminine qualities, 245; as liberator, 248, 305n91; as parent, 137, 155, 159, 245, 250; as *sāmi,* 288, 317n10; as working class, 148;
Goddess (Amman): sonic power, 156; village, 29, 151, 155–156
Good News, 184, 185, 255–258, 266, 267; as forward looking, 257
grace of God, 63, 64, 65, 125, 126, 245; potential, 126
"great traditions," 52–53

Gunadayalan, 58, 151
Gunasakaran, K. A.
Gurukul Lutheran Theological College and Research Institute, 129
Gutierrez, 4
Gypsy, 255, 258

Hampton, Rev. Cannon Carol, xx
Hanson, Thomas Bloom, 52–53
harmonium, 220
harmony, 39, 41, 52, 53, 86, 106, 108, 295n6, 296n12
hereditary caste musicians, 13, 102
hermeneutic, 2
Hindu fundamentalism, 52–53, 54, 166, 265
Hindu nationalism, 23, 53
Hinduism, Brahmanical, 16, 97, 245–246
Hinduism, village, 46, 307–308n20
history of religions, 35
hooks, bell, 158, 164, 311n78; collective self-recovery, 164, 165; racial solidarity, 163; *Yearnings: Race, Gender, and Cultural Politics*, 163–165
hope, 127, 142
Hudson, Dennis, 76, 83, 293n13, 295n13, 302n39
Humanly Produced and Transmitted Media (HPTM), xiv, 237
hymns, 75, 79; German, 40, 76; Tamil, 76, 88

identity politics, 121, 166, 265; musical, 162
identity reformation, xvi, 55; subject, 266
Ilaiah, Kancha, 29, 246, 307–307n20
Ilaiyaraaja, 57, 113, 298n12, 298n15
imperialism, 89–90, 91, 97, 112, 176, 265
Inbaraj, Rev. Benjamin, 56–57, 64, *198*
inculcation, 39, 41, 86, 87, 93
indigenization, xii, xvii, 68, 86, 87–88, 311n6; as accommodation 21, 34, 78, 87, 89; as acculturation, 43, 47, 88; of art (*kōlam*) 189–190, 192; as assimilation, 41; Christian, 35, 114, 117, 265; as Christianization, 42, 43, 73, 74, 78, 91, 105, 267; as cultural resistance, 48; as elite Hinduization, 91; as an elite model, 75, 84, 88, 91, 94; enculturation, 120, 128, 131; of the Eucharist, 182; as inculcation, 41 73; limits of folk music, 25; as reclaiming, 126, 185 (*see also* Appavoo); re-indigenization, 35, 38, 47, 75, 152, 170, 298n7; resistance to, 87, 107; as reversal, 146; taxonomy, 38; as translation, 41
Indophobia, 78
instruments, 79–80, 116, 298n15, 300n16
intersectionality: of caste and class, 231, 305n84; of caste, class, and gender, 27, 33, 157, 203, 204, 220, 231–232, 242, 253, 254, 256, 261, 265; lived experience of, 206; and race, 266, 267; and Tamil language value, 30
inversion. *See* reversal strategy
irony, 177
Isai Vellalar, 101, 300n18, 304n67
Islam, 53, 152

Jayaharan, Rev. John, 234, 306n2
Jesus, 207, 262, 306n7, 311n77; as child of Mary, 123–124, 223, 224, 256, 317n1; coming to serve, 137; as elder brother (mūttavar), 123–124; and intersectionality, 261; as liberator, 156, 248; as redemption for Dalits, 147; riding donkey of working people, 178; the risen Christ, 143; theology of sharing, 219
Jewish society, 223; social levels, 124
joint family, 137, 161
Jones, Serene, 158, 161–162
Jones, Sir William, 51
Jothi, Rev. Jacqulin, 192–193, *198*, *199*, 204, 205–219, 253, 294n11; and Appavoo, 209–210; on Appavoo's theology, 218–219; Basic Christian Communities, 210; caste and class discrimination; 208–209; Catholic School, 207; and DMK oration, 207, 208; daughter (Eucharista), 199, 213; father (John David), 206, 207, 208; grace, 192, 193, 198, 199; Nagarcoil fisher women's internship, 206, 210; in Pondicherry 214–219;

Seethalakshmi Ramaswamy College, 207–209; Tsunami relief, 217–218; at TTS, 192–193, 219; unionizing, 212–213; in Vedal village, 212–214; work with Nadars, 214–216, 218

kaḍamai, 13
kālākshēpam, 94, 100
Kaplan, Steven, 38, 42, 43
karma, 43, 56, 185
karnatak music, xvii, 25, 77, 100, 110, 112; Christian, 23, 38, 39, 40, 41, 42, 66, 75, 79, 88, 101, 107, 168, 173, 175, 180, 211, 301n30; Christian *gītam,* 174; Christian *slōka,* 174; as ideal style, 94, 103, 220; medium of transmission of theology, 117; as noise pollution, 176; Tamil contribution to, 303n72; training for Christians, 94, 110, 168, 302n41; training for outcastes, 100, 117
Kartomi, Margaret: and identifying culture, 295n1; and musical transculturation, 35
Kavinesan. *See* Solomon, Kavinesan
Kent, Eliza, 28–29, 86, 93, 223, 314n25
Kingdom of God, 142, 147, 148, 183, 258; and values, 133
kīrttaṉai, xvii, xvii, 19, 38, 41, 42, 52, 60, 77, 79, 81, 82, 84, 87, 88, 94, 99, 100, 103, 104, 112, 302n38, 302n39, 304n4; at Christian boarding schools, 91, *195*, 233, 249–250; as class mobility, 175, 250, 297n5; contemporary relevance, 82; domination by pāmālai, 106; edited, 298n8; and Evangelism, 78, 90, 91; lower caste composers, 94; as "lyrics," xvii, xviii, 81, 88, 180–181, 296n24, 300n19; *manipravalam* Tamil, 30, 184; modernization of, 86; with organ accompaniment, 106, 108, 305n86; publication of, 88–89, 307n19, 308n24, 152; Pulaya, 24; C. T. E. Rhenius and elimination of kīrttaṉai, 78–79; Telugu hymn book, 303n54; theology, 82; among village Christians, 91, 94, 192, 248, 302n39
kōlam, 189–190, 192, 313n28, 313n31

Krishna Pillai, H. A., 77, 304n4
Kuppusamy, Pushpavanam, 44

Lady Doak College, xvii, 19
language, 30–31, 41, 71; as educational medium, 87
Larbeer, Mohan, 115
Last Supper, the, 137
liberation, 2, 56, 75, 111, 120, 239; of cultural resources, 128; as viḍutalai, 48, 57, 294n1
liberation theology, 113, 120, 267; Black, 59; challenges to, 267; Latin/South American, 297n2; psychological 137–138; and shame, 138; womanist, 121
light music, 38, 39, 42, 116, 117; Christian music, 43, 66, 105, 111, 185, 227, 298n11, 298n12
literacy, and music, 92
liturgy, 86, 87, 120, 146, 171, 180, 312n20; and cultural identity, 121; freer order, 302n38
Lord's Prayer, the, 2, 63, 159, 270–271
love feasts (agape meal), 92, 95, 295n13, 303n50
Lutheran Church: Arcot, 305n79; Tamil Evangelical, 192, 211, 313n4

Madras Christian College, 211
Madurai, xvii, 5, 18, 19, 72, 74, 75, 106, 112, 113, 114; and American Congregational mission, 86, 87, 89; Christian community, 168, 171, 174, 179, 180, 181, 191
Madurandagam, 130, 150
Magimaidoss, Rev. Enose, 193, *199*, 211–212, 214
mangalam, 82
Mangeshkar, Lata, 223
Manickam, Rev. Kambar, 172
Manickam, Dr. S., 98
Manu, 97, 305n9; and rape, 27
marginal music, 54
Mariyanandam, T., 103, 304n70
Marshall, Paule, Praise Song for the Widow, 164
Marxism, 111, 113, 142; Appavoo's neo-Marxism, xiv, 4, 30, 31, 54

Mary. *See* Jesus: as child of Mary
Mary, Kamala, 19, 193, 307n12
Menon, Dilip, 14, 16, 298n15, 305n84, *Sarasativijayam*, 70
Menon, Pramada, 264
middle class, 114, 117, 148, 180, 298n12; corruption, 126; embrace of Appavoo's theology, 203
milk and honey, 135
mimesis, 71
missions/missionaries, 16, 87; American Congregationalists, 78, 85, 87, 88–89, 89–90, 93, 221, 296n18, 297n6, 301n31, 301n33, 301n35 (*see also* American Board of Commissioners for Foreign Missions [ABCFM]); American Missouri Evangelical Lutheran India Mission; 86; Anglican, 78, 85, 86, 87, 93; Arcot Mission of the Reformed Church of America, 94, 95, 96, 99, 302n48, 303n54; as beef eaters, 95, 303n49; boarding schools, 25, 91, 92–93, 251; British, 26, 39; British Baptist and William Carey, 85; British Society for Promoting Christian Knowledge (SPCK), 78, 85, 86; caste/cultural accommodation, 77, 84, 90; caste rejection, 92, 96; Calvinist Anglican, 78; Catholic, 17, 25, 72; Chamberlain, Jacob, 303n54; critique of low castes as heathen, 177, 179; J. S. Chandler, 81; Church Mission Society (CMS), 78, 103, 296n21, 302n38; conversion, 12, 16, 21, 23, 74, 75, 77, 78, 84, 85, 91, 95, 96, 98, 117; and education/schools, 86, 87, 97; Ellis, J. J., 98, 314n21; endogamy, 87; and folk music, 46, 88; German Lutherans (Danish-Halle also called Tranquebar), 41, 51, 75, 76, 78, 84, 85; and hymns, 40, 76; Jesuits, 72, 74, 75; jobs for outcastes, 97; Leipzig Lutherans, 85; London Mission Society (LMS), 86, 96, 302n38, 314n21; love feasts, 92, 95; (non)cultural interference policies, 76; persecution of, 75; Protestant, 17, 75, 90; rejection of instruments, 316–317n18; C. T. E. Rhenius, 78–79; Salvation Army, 86; scholars of music and early ethnomusicologists, 52; and social justice, 96; Society for the Propagation of the Gospel (SPG), 78, 85, 100, 103; and Tamil language and literature, 30, 90, 102; translation by, 75, 76; as transmitters of religion and/or culture, 90; trickle down theory, 73; Wesleyan Methodists, 85, 93, 221; St. Francis Xavier, 72, 87. *See also* Schwarz, C. F.; Ziegenbalg, Bartholomew
mnemonic devices, 123, 317n2, 317n7, 317n8; vocables, 312n22, 314n23, 316n1, 316n2, 316n13
modernization, 39; theory of value free scholarship, 51
mood, 126, 127
Mosse, David, 21, 23
mrdangam, xvii
Mukkuvar caste, 72, 87
Murugan, 124, 307n9
music: as action and liberation, 146, 193, 266; departments, and eurocentrism, 51; early scholarship by Westerners, 52; as resistance, 24, 258; as theology, 49, 120, 130, 193, 254
musical change, 61
musical production, 31
musical style, 38, 39, 48, 71, 84, 103, 113, 297n3; and cultural context, 90; hierarchy, 80
musical value, 31, 34, 38, 42, 46, 101, 117; and ethnomusicology, 48, 50; inversion, 54, 55, 57, 101, 114, 120; and Tamil Christians, 50, 80, 84, 88, 117, 297n5; and Western and elite inculcation, 44, 84, 111
musical virtuosity, 48–49; in the Western cannon, 51
Muslims, 301n22, 309n62

Nadars, xviii, 16, 17, 20, 25, 39, 86, 100, 103, 104, 106, 108, 117–118, 205, 214, 240, 296n17; and ABCFM, 86, 296n19; and CMS, 78, 85; high dowry, 223; as Indian "Britishers," 86; Kanyakumari,

115; as Kshatriya, 87 (*see also* Panditar, Abraham); and LMS, 85; merchants, 251; migration, 106, 179, 310n71; as Shanar, 17, 74, 86, 301n28; social work in Pondicherry, 215; support of Western hymns, 104, 107
nāgasvaram, 72, 79, 300n18
ñanappāṭṭu, 38, 40, 76, 88, 90, 99
nationalism, 101
Native Americans, xvi, xx
nāṭṭupāṭṭu, 44
Navaneethakrishnan, Vijayalakshmi, 44
Nirmal, A. P., 129

Oberlin College, xvii
Oberlin Shansi Memorial Fellowship, xvii, 19
oppāri (lament) 55, 56, 57, 63, 247, 255, 258, 298n14; as lullaby, 259
oral medium, 71, 131, 151; oral history, 95
organ, xviii, 39, 79, 86, 106
orientalism, 51, 52, 87
Ortner, Sherry, 47, 67, 157; resistance studies, 242
oru olai, 32–33, 55, 63, 64, 65, 92, 120, 133, 137, 158, 257, 259, 261, 317n19; church as one body, 144; as Eucharistic life style, 250, 317n19; as karaḍipatti, 235; myth, 133–140, 157, 315n45; *poṅgal* as, 124; as one's share or *puṅgu*, 317n5; in practice, 140–141, 162, 163, 171, 173, 177, 180, 186, 193, 205, 211, 219; strategy for subcaste unification, 251; as table fellowship, 126, 145, 206, 214, 216, 257; theological issues, 143–144, 251; at TTS 187–188, 206, 237
outcaste, 34, 86, 93, 97; abuse by teachers, 99; American, 162; contribution to music and liturgy, 87; conversion, 18, 22, 23, 25; education, 87, 92, 93, 97, 99, 303n57, 303n59; financial patronage from missions, 95, 97, 98; identification with upper-castes, 93; as middle class, 95, 97, 114, 232–233, 303n51; migration for jobs, 232, 302n62; on plantations, 301n62; as teachers, 100, 232; as without identity, 147
Pallar, 14, 85, 115, 116, 293n11, 300n37
pāmālai, 38, 40, 76, 88, 90, 99, 103, 106
Panditar, Abraham, 103
paṟai (frame drum), xix, 13, 46, 55, 57, 113, 125, 252, 260, 263–264, 298n14, 298n18, 300n15; and Dalit theology, 119–120, 128, 156, 242, 261, 304n2, 310n69; and non-Dalits, 306n2; in Protestant liturgy, 262; as war drum, 256, 260
Paṟaiyar, xviii, 13, 14, 87, 88, 91, 17, 115, 116, 179, 211, 232, 233, 295n11; and conversion, 25; as cooks, 95, 304n61; deities, 155–156; at girl's school, 302n37; and instruments, 80, 119, 155, 298n15; and *kīrttaṉai*, 104, 107, 297n6; literate, 99; Lutheran, 205; middle class, 251, 303n51; musicians, 94, 100, 109, 119, 304n64; ordination of priests, 77; as *paṟai* drummers, 262, 298n19; percentage of population in South Arcot, 67; *Saṅguḍi*, 29, 301n23, 302n37, 302n39, 302n62, 303n51; tea plantation workers, 220, 221, 304n62; as teachers or professionals, 296n19; working for factories, 232
paṟakkam, 83, 84, 301n23
Paraṭṭai, 59, 60, 69, 293n1, 308n24; as bi-gendered, 135, 157; as trickster, *194*
Paraṭṭai Kural, xix
Paravar fishing caste, 72, 73, 87
Pariah, 74, 75; boarding school cooks, 92
pastors/preachers (clergy), 18, 258, 316n4; early Tamil, 301n29
Pasumalai, 20
phenomenology, 265, 293n7
pietism, 76, 80, 83
Pillai, Kanchipuram Naina, 101, 304n67
Pillai, T. N. Swaminathan, 304n70
Plutschau, Henry, 76
politics of sound; 49
pollution, 13, 46, 57, 252, 262, 293n2, 294n6; and blood, 27; and purity, 27–28, 233, 250
Poṅgal, 74, 180, 244, 250, 313n30; Christianized, 189, 190; as living rice, 124, 245; at TTS 188–191
Popley, H. A., 52, 80

Portuguese, 72, 73, 87
possession, 57
postcolonial subject, 14
poverty, 125
Prabhakar, M. E., and intersectionality, 27
praxis, xvi, 2, 31, 58, 121, 131, 150, 205, 214, 242; versus theory, 308n21
prayer, 206, 211
Price, David, 51
Protestants, 31, 41, 314n11
purpose analysis, 149, 237, 308n26

raga, xvii, 25, 41, 52, 53, 57, 76, 80, 81, 82, 84, 88, 100, 101, 109, 305n86; in *kīrttaṉai,* 91, 108, 300n19; simple, 89
Raja Selvan, Dr. J. Arun, 191–192, 193
Rajamanikam, Rev. M., *200,* 204, 216, 220–232, 246, 253; use of Appavoo's folk songs, 227; and class compromise, 220, 231, 232; concern for elderly, 226; folk music, 222, 231; and karnatak music, 220–221; and reaction to *Māṭṭukkoṭṭil Reḍiyācci* cassette, 224; at RTI, 222; at TTS 220
Rajasekaran, Jesudasan, 50
Ramaswamy, Periyar E. V., 102, 304n68, 313n5
rasa, 81–82
Rayan, Samuel, 147–148
reception, xiv, 5, 33, 121, 131, 150, 202, 254; of Appavoo's theology by villagers, 242–253; of music by urban congregations, 240
reconciliation, 157, 160
recreation, xii, xiv, 2, 31, 57, 114, 120, 252; as recomposition, 43, 169, 170, 225, 226, 230–231, 242, 254, 266
redemption and forgiveness, 299n3
reflection, xx
relationship, 33, 59, 226, 251; radical relationality, 143–144, 166
reversal strategy, 119, 120, 133, 146–149, 163, 245, 257, 258, 310n69
rhythm, 125
rice, living: *kañji* as body of Christ, 163, 180, 182–183; *sōru,* 125
Rice, Tim, 59
Rural Theological Institute (RTI), 112, 113, 114–115, 222
ruralism: identity, 129; metaphors for, 124, 125, 126, 127; nostalgia/purity, 124; raspy vocal timbre code, 127, 307n18

Śaiva *bhakti,* 77, 91, 101
Sakthi Kalai Kural, 263–265
salvation, xvi, 43, 96, 97, 123, 179;
Sambamurthy, Professor P., 44, 52, 57
Sanskrit, 73, 84; canticles for wedding and funerals, 74
Sanskritization, 23, 41, 117, 309n63; Christianization as, 93
schools: Brahmin girls college, 207–209; Catholic, 207; Christian Boarding, 179, *195,* 209, 229, 232–233, 249–250, 301n30, 302n37; Panchayat, 206; teacher training, 179, 232; village oppression of outcastes, 233
Schwartz, C. F., 52, 76, 79, 300n10; and Vedanayakam Sastriar, 78
Scott, James, xiv
Scruggs, T. M., 38, 131–132, 295n7
self-reflexivity, 54, 171
Self-Respect Movement. *See* Dravidian movement
self-sufficiency, 139
Senate of Serampore College, 130
sharing, 64, 117; food, 19–20, 65, 250, 259; medicinal cure for sin, 239
sin: corporate, 56, 132, 229; cure for, 239; and living water, 124; personal, 56, 64, 83; and private property, 125; in song texts, 126, 127, 299n24, 307n11; as an untouchable, 228
Sindhu Bhairavi (film), 44
Small, Christopher, xvi, 58
Social Action Centre (SAC), 58, 130, 151, 233–236, 247, 253
social analysis, 129, 130
social gospel: nineteenth-century movement, 22, 128; sustainability, 23
Solomon, Kavinesan, 168, 175, 179
sound as theology, 49
spirituals, xv, 59
Student Christian Movement, 20

subaltern, 34, 42, 71, 151, 153; practice theory, 47; praxis, 34
Sundaram, V. P. K., 111, 118, 305n71, 305n72

table fellowship. See *oru olai*
tala, xvii, 25, 53, 76, 81, 88, 100, 101, 107, 244, 311n5
Tamil, 30, 73, 89, 172; Bible translation, 76; Christian liturgical, 74, 76, 90; as *cōccai* or degraded, 44, 240, 307n12; Coimbatore dialect, 183; *koḍuntamiṟ*, 30; literary, 77, 94, 103; *manipravalam*, 30, 40–41, 74, 83; oration, 205, 206; *pēccu* (spoken), 30, 42, 44, 46, 79, 113, 144, 173, 183, 242, 243, 246, 247; preaching, 94, 206; regional spoken, 312n18; Sanskritized Tamil, xvii, 41, 82, 111; *sen*, 30, 42, 103, 111, 172, 207, 247
Tamil Christians, 35, 90; and ordination, 84, 94; and persecution, 75; and social identity, 35, 102; as theologian/composers, 305n71
Tamil Dalit, 120
Tamil Hymnal, 41, 81, 88–89, 298n19, 302n36; *Christian Lyrics for Public and Social Worship*, 94, 99; hymns, 74, 76, 84
Tamil Isai Movement, 102, 103; influence on Tamil Christian scholars, 103
Tamil literature, 102, 103, 208
Tamil Nadu Theological Seminary (TTS), xv, xvii, xviii, 5, 31–32, 66, 82, 110, 112, 115, 118, 129, 173, 193, 205, 236–237, 304n69, 306n100; Centre for Social Analysis, 211, 219, 311n3; choir, 168, 174; Christmas carol service, 111, 168–171, 174–180, *198*, 238, 305n91; community meals/*oru olai*, 180, 187, 238; Dalit Arts Festival, 45, 130, 131; Dalit Resource Centre, 130–131, 308n23, 308n24; feminism, 169, 311n4; liturgies, 180–188; music practice at, 110, 114, 116; political vocabulary, 186; Poṅgal, 188–191; as producer of indigenized music, 171–174; recording studio, 175; street theater group, 218; student's identity, 311n7; summer music camp, 145; theology, 210; transmission of values and arts to children, 191, 193; vernacular-language, 172
Tamiṟ Icai/Isai, 42, 102, 305n72
Tamiṟ Isai Vaṟipāḍu, 111, 172, 180
Tanjavore/Tanjore, 25, 41, 74, 75, 85, 88, 89; Maratha kings 77
tavil, 72, 90, 175, 179, 189, 190, 249, 300n18, 313n29
teachers, 10, 13, 18, 25, 26, 84, 92, 93, 97, 99, 100, 104
TECCA (Theological Education for Christian Commitment and Action), xviii, 129–130, 188, 202, 236; Honest Chinniah, 130; rural, 54, 130, 137, 154, 234, 235, 247, 308n22
temperature, 307n17
tension and release, 63; melodic tension, 65
Thangaraj, Rev. M. Thomas, xii, 86, 111, 118, 296n25; liturgical experimentation, 111, 118; singable theology, 130
theologians, as atheists, 102, 302n69
theology, xiii; use of feminine in, 242; through folk music, 114, 171; Indian Christian Theology, 16, 76, 83, 101, 153, 309n63; of the oppressed, 132; oral, 120; of pluralism, 76, 77, 82–83; prescriptive, 143; proscriptive, 258; Protestant, 245; as sound, 47, 168, 180; in Tamil, 93; upper-caste, 23, 83
Tirunelveli, 85, 86, 103, 106
Titon, Jeff, xv
Townes, Emily, 140, 158–166; *In a Blaze of Glory: Womanist Spirituality as Social Witness*, 159
Tranquebar/Tarangambadi, 41, 76, 78, 301n22, 301n29; seminary, 78
transformation xiv, xv, 164, 171, 178, 252; bodily pain as, 178; music as means of, 71, 109, 114, 117, 120, 121, 159, 162, 243, 249, 266
transmission, xii, xviii, 42, 123, 158, 191; Christianity, 93; human 71; incomplete, 252–253; oral, 41, 88, 155, 227;

songs through publication, 90; of theology, 117, 120, 155
transubstantiation, 143
Trautmann, Thomas, 51, 52, 78
Trinity (Christian), 120, 123
tsunami (December, 2004), 215, 216,
Tutu, Bishop Desmond, xv
two-tumbler system, 177, 312n13
Tyagaraja, 88

ululation, 191
Umm Kulthum, 69
unions, 130
United Nations World Conference Against Racism, 129, 255, 262–265, 266; statement on caste as work and descent, 264
United Theological College, Dalit theology department, 308n21
unity, 58, 63, 120, 121, 123, 156, 173, 242, 246, 249, 258; as an offering, 228, 243; as *ottumayā*, 123, 228, 244, 250, 306n5; threats to, 203; as a weapon, 258
universal family, 65, 120, 123, 133, 144–146, 244, 261
untouchability, 13, 97, 257, 266, 304n68; Christianity as, 75; as form of racial discrimination, 264; unhearability and unseeability, 50, 56
untouchables, 73, 115, 117, 120; association with folk music, 298n14; biographies, 69, 99, 297n27; conversion, 85, 117; as cooks, 303n49; missionaries as, 303n49; transformation to Dalit, 203, 245
upper castes, 38, 41, 57, 87; domination of the Church, 101; kings, 178; upper-caste Christians, 16, 17, 111
utopian vision, 142

values, changes in, 176, 178
varna, 13, 18
Vedanayakam Sastriar, xvii, 41, 75, 77, 80–82, 84, 88, 89, 300n16; *Bethlehem Kuravañci*, 83; compositions/publications, 80, 83, 88–89, 94, 152, 301n32, 302n40; family history, 77–78; and King Serfoji II, 78; Protestants vs. Catholics, 299n7; *Saditeratoo* (Explaining Caste), 79, 84; and theology, 82
Vellalar, 17, 41, 74, 75, 76, 77, 79, 82–83, 84, 85, 86, 91, 104, 106, 150, 301n22, 301n23, 309n61; cultural and political hegemony, 94; *Isai Vellalar*, 101, 304n67; and Tamil Evangelical Lutheran Church, 107; tastes and values, 93
Vellore, 94, 99, 303n54
vernacular, 14, 87
vevasāyi [farmer], 126, 127
Victorian propriety, 25, 28
village culture, 246; metaphors, 246
Village Music Liturgy. See *Girāmiya Isai Vaṟipāḍu*
Virgin festival: Catholic, 72; Tuticorin, 72
Virgin Mary (*Kannimari*), 123
Viswanathan, T., 304n70

"We Shall Overcome," xv
Webb, Rev. Edward, *kīrttaṉai* collection, 41, 88, 89, 90, 92, 93, 99, 301n31, 301n32, 302n36
Webster, Rev. John C. B., 96, 97, 98, 153, 296n24, 303n52, 303n53
wedding at Canaan, 148, 149, 309n59, 310n77
Welsh, Sharon, 132
Western style music, 43; keyboard, 221; training for Christians, 108, 221, 302n64
Western Tamil Nadu, 314n22
Westernization, 39, 177; of tuning systems or temperament, 41,
White, Rev. Emmons, 52, 94, 301n30; Mrs. Ruth White, 302n41, 305n73
Wielenga, Rev. Bas, 130
Wilson, Kottapalli, 129
womanist theology, 128, 158
women: and Christian history, 28; circle dances, 259; conversion of, 28; girls schools and education, 93, 99, 302n37; International Women's Day, 181;

laborers, 212–213, 311n3; lamenting oppression, 255, 257, 259; and liberation, 27, 169; liturgy, 181, 312n16; and male alcohol abuse, 210–211, 236, 311n3; and ordination/as pastors, 192, 211, 219, 297n26; and sin, 27; teachers, 116, 302n37; at TTS, 169; wives of pastors 302n37; women's fellowship, 216, 234
women's movement: history of, 219; Madurai (*Peṇṇurimai Iyakkam*), 182, *197*
women's studies, 129, 130
work, as source of power, 137, 139
World Social Forum, 255, 262

Xavier, St. Francis, 72

YMCA, 296n17

Ziegenbalg, Bartholomew, 51–52, 76, 300n11, 301n22

DR. ZOE C. SHERINIAN is Associate Professor and Chair of Ethnomusicology at the University of Oklahoma. A percussionist and filmmaker, her first ethnographic film on the changing status of Dalit drummers is titled *This Is a Music: Reclaiming an Untouchable Drum.*

www.ingramcontent.com/pod-product-compliance
Lightning Source LLC
Chambersburg PA
CBHW021759220426
43662CB00006B/122
* 9 7 8 0 2 5 3 0 5 6 7 7 1 *